Lieutenant General

Jubal Anderson Early

C.S.A.

Lieutenant General
Jubal Anderson Early
C.S.A.

AUTOBIOGRAPHICAL SKETCH AND NARRATIVE OF THE WAR BETWEEN THE STATES

With Notes by

R. H. Early

SMITHMARK

This edition published in 1994 by SMITHMARK Publishers Inc.,
16 East 32nd Street, New York, NY 10016

SMITHMARK books are available for bulk purchase for sales
promotion and premium use. For details write or call the
manager of special sales, SMITHMARK Publishers Inc.,
16 East 32nd Street, New York, NY 10016; (212) 532-6600.

This edition published by special arrangement with
W.S. Konecky Associates, Inc., 156 5th Avenue, NY, NY 10010.

ISBN: 0-8317-1173-6

Printed in the United States of America

10 9 8 7 6 5 4 3 2 1

CONTENTS

CONTENTS

AUTOBIOGRAPHICAL SKETCH

According to the record in the family Bible, I was born on the third day of November, 1816, in the County of Franklin, in the State of Virginia. My father, Joab Early,[1] who is still living, is a native of the same county, and while resident there, he enjoyed the esteem of his fellow-citizens and held several prominent public positions, but in the year 1847, he removed to the Kanawha Valley in Western Virginia. My mother's maiden name was Ruth Hairston, and she was likewise a native of the County of Franklin, her family being among the most respected citizens. She died in the year 1832, leaving ten children surviving her, I being the third child and second son. She was a most estimable lady, and her death was not only the source of the deepest grief to her immediate family, but caused universal regret in the whole circle of her acquaintances.

Until I was sixteen I enjoyed the benefit of the best schools in my region of country and received the usual instruction in the dead languages and elementary mathematics. In the spring of 1833, while General Jackson was President, I received, through the agency of our member of Congress, the Hon. N. H. Claiborne, an appointment as cadet in the United States Military Academy at West Point.

I repaired to the Academy at the end of May and was admitted about the first of June in the same year. I went through the usual course and graduated in the usual time, in June, 1837. There was nothing worthy of particular note in my career at West Point. I was never a very good student, and was sometimes quite remiss, but I managed to attain a respectable stand in all

---

[1] Died at the home of his son, Robert H. Early, in Lexington, Mo., 1870.

my studies. My highest stand in any branch was in military and civil engineering and that was sixth. In the general standing on graduation my position was eighteenth in a class of fifty.

I was not a very exemplary soldier and went through the Academy without receiving any appointment as a commissioned or non-commissioned officer in the corps of cadets. I had very little taste for scrubbing brass, and cared very little for the advancement to be obtained by the exercise of that most useful art.

Among those graduating in my class were General Braxton Bragg, Lieutenant General John C. Pemberton, Major Generals Arnold Elzey and Wm. H. T. Walker, and a few others of the Confederate Army; and Major Generals John Sedgwick, Joseph Hooker, and Wm. H. French and several Brigadier Generals of minor note in the Federal Army. Among my contemporaries at West Point were General Beauregard, Lieutenant General Ewell, Major General Edward Johnson and some others of distinction in the Confederate Army; Major Generals McDowell and Meade and several others in the Federal Army.

The whole of my class received appointments in the United States Army shortly after graduation. By reason of the Indian War in Florida, there had been a number of resignations and deaths in the army and very few of the class had to go through the probation of brevet lieutenants. I was appointed Second Lieutenant in the Third Regiment of Artillery, and was assigned to Company " E," which afterward became celebrated as Sherman's battery. We did not enjoy the usual leave of absence, but in August, 1837, a number of my class, myself included, were ordered to Fortress Monroe to drill a considerable body of recruits which were in rendezvous at that place, preparatory to being sent to Florida, where the Seminole War was still in progress. From Fortress Monroe, with several other officers, I accompanied a body of recruits which sailed for Florida, and we landed at Tampa Bay in October, 1837. From Tampa Bay I went to Gary's Ferry, on Black Creek, and there joined my company, which was comprised almost entirely of recruits recently joined. My Captain (Lyon) was an invalid from age and infirmity, and both the First Lieutenants were absent on special duty, so that being the senior Second Lieutenant, I was assigned to the command of the company. In that capacity I went through the campaign of 1837-8 under General Jessup, from the St. John's River south into the Everglades, and was present at a skirmish with the Indians on the Lockee Hatchee, near Jupiter Inlet, in January, 1838. This was my first " battle," and though I heard some bullets whistling among the trees, none came near me, and I did not see an Indian.

The party of Seminoles with which we had the skirmish was subsequently pursued into the Everglades and induced to come in and camp near us at Fort Jupiter, under some stipulations between General Jessup and the chiefs, about which there was afterwards some misunderstanding which resulted in the whole party being surrounded and captured; and my company was employed with the rest of the troops in this work. This was my last "warlike exploit" for many years. After this we remained near the sea-coast, inactive for the most of the time, until late in the spring, when, as all active hostilities had ceased, we were marched across to Tampa Bay, from whence my company, with some other troops, was shipped to New Orleans, and then sent up the Mississippi, Ohio and Tennessee Rivers to Ross' Landing (now Chattanooga) to report to General Scott, who had charge of the removal of the Cherokees, with whom some difficulty was apprehended. My company was stationed near Ross' Landing, and it was soon discovered that there would be no trouble with the Indians.

It had not been my purpose to remain permanently in the army, and, as there was to be no difficulty with the Cherokees, and the Seminole War was thought to be at an end, I determined to resign for the purpose of going into civil life. I tendered my resignation and received a leave of absence until it could be acted on. Under this leave I started from Ross' Landing, on July 4, 1838, for my home, by the way of Nashville and Louisville. Upon arriving at Louisville, I found from the papers that the army had been increased, and that I was made a first lieutenant in my regiment. Had this news reached me before the tendering of my resignation, that resignation might have been withheld, but it was now too late to alter my plans.

In the fall of 1838, I commenced the study of law in the office of N. M. Taliaferro, Esq., an eminent lawyer residing at the county seat of my native county, who some years afterward became a judge of the General Court of Virginia. I obtained license to practise law in the early part of the year 1840, and at once entered the profession. In the spring of the year 1841, I was elected by a small majority, as one of the delegates from the County of Franklin, to the Virginia Legislature, and served in the session of 1841 and 1842, being the youngest member of the body.

In the following spring, I was badly beaten by my former preceptor in the law, who was a member of the Democratic Party, while I was a supporter of the principles of the Whig Party, of which Mr. Clay was the principal leader.

My political opponent, though a personal friend, Mr. Taliaferro, held the position of prosecuting attorney in the circuit courts of several counties, and as these offices were rendered vacant by his election to the Legislature, I received the appointments for the Counties of Franklin and Floyd, having previously been appointed prosecuting attorney in the county court of Franklin. These appointments I held until the reorganization of the State government under the new constitution of 1851.

In the meantime, I continued the practice of law in

my own and the adjoining counties, with very fair success until the breaking out of the war between the United States and Mexico, consequent upon the annexation of Texas. Though I had voted, in the presidential election of 1844, for Mr. Clay, who opposed the annexation of Texas, yet, when war ensued, I felt it to be my duty to sustain the government in that war and to enter the military service if a fitting opportunity offered. When the regiment of volunteers from Virginia was called for by the President, I received from the Governor and Council of State the appointment as Major in that regiment, and was mustered into service on the 7th of January, 1847. Colonel John F. Hamtramck, of the County of Jefferson, and Lieutenant Colonel Thomas B. Randolph, of the County of Warren, were the other field officers. The regiment was ordered to rendezvous at Fortress Monroe and the superintendence of the drilling there and the embarkation for Mexico were entrusted to me. Two extra companies were allowed to the regiment, and, on account of some delay in the organization of them, I did not sail from Fortress Monroe with the last detachment of these companies until March 1st, arriving at Brazos Santiago on the 17th, to learn, for the first time, the news of General Taylor's victory at Buena Vista. We proceeded up the Rio Grande at once and the whole regiment was assembled at Camargo, under the command of the Colonel, the day after my arrival there.

About the first of April the regiment moved from Camargo for Monterey, by the way of a little town called China, as an escort for a provision train. One-half of the regiment was left temporarily at China under Lieutenant Colonel Randolph, and the other half moved to Monterey under my command—Colonel Hamtramck having become too sick to remain on duty. We were encamped at the Walnut Spring near General Taylor's headquarters, and there I met, for the first time, Colonel Jefferson Davis, of the First Mississippi Regiment, who has become illustrious as the President of the Confederrate States. I was struck with his soldierly bearing, and he did me the honor of complimenting the order and regularity of my camp. After being here a short time, the battalion under my command relieved an Ohio regiment, which had been garrisoning Monterey, but was going home, and for two months I acted as miltary governor of the city. It was generally conceded by officers of the army and Mexicans that better order reigned in the city during the time I commanded there, than had ever before existed, and the good conduct of my men won for them universal praise. Some time in the month of June, the whole regiment, under the command of the Colonel, moved to Buena Vista, a few miles from Saltillo, and joined the forces of General Wool, at that point. It remained near that locality for the balance of the war, for the most part inactive, as all fighting on that line, except an occasional affair with guerillas, ceased after the battle of Buena Vista. I had, therefore, no opportunity of seeing active service. For a short time I was attached, as acting Inspector General, to the staff of Brigadier General Caleb Cushing, who commanded the brigade to which my regiment was attached, until he was ordered to the other line. During this period I contracted, in the early part of the fall of 1847, a cold and fever, which eventuated in chronic rheumatism, with which I have ever since been afflicted. My condition became such that I received a leave of absence in the month of November, and returned to the States, on a visit to my friends in the Kanawha Valley.

After improving a little I started back to Mexico, and on my way I had the luck to meet with that fate, which is very common to Americans who travel much, that is, I was on a steamboat which was blown up, the 8th of January, 1848, on the Ohio River, a few miles below the mouth of the Kanawha. I had a very narrow escape, as half of my state-room was carried off and some pieces of the boiler protruded through the floor, cutting and burning my feet when I jumped out of the berth. The explosion took place about 1.00 o'clock at night, when it was very dark and extremely cold, and before the passengers, who were not killed, could get ashore and obtain shelter, they were very much exposed; but, after getting over the first effects of the slight injury received, I experienced a decided improvement in my rheumatism, though I would not advise blowing up in a western steamboat as an infallible remedy.

I rejoined the regiment about the first of February, and commanded the greater part of it during the rest of the war—three or four companies having been detached to the town of Parras—as Colonel Hamtramck had returned to Virginia on recruiting service. At the close of the war, I carried the regiment to the mouth of the Rio Grande, and had it embarked at Brazos for Fortress Monroe, going on one of the vessels myself. I was mustered out of the service with the rest of the regiment in the first part of April, 1848, being the only field officer on duty with it. It had no opportunity of reaping laurels during the war, but I can say that it had not sullied the flag of the State, which constituted the regimental colors, by disorderly conduct or acts of depredation on private property, and non-combatants. It had been my fortune to have the disagreeable duty of breaking in the regiment at the beginning and I had commanded it for a much longer time than any other field officer. Being rather a strict disciplinarian and, in consequence thereof, naturally regarded by inexperienced troops as harsh in my treatment of them, I was by no means popular with the mass of the regiment prior to the commencement of the return march from Saltillo, but I can safely say that, on the day they were mustered out of service at Fortress Monroe, I was the most popular officer in the regiment, and I had the satisfaction of receiving from a great many of the men the assurance that they had misjudged me in the beginning and were now convinced that I had been their best friend all the time.

I returned to the practice of law and continued it until the commencement of the late struggle between the Southern and Northern States.

After my return from Mexico, I was the only one of my name left in my county, as all the rest of my father's family had removed to the Kanawha Valley.

In the year 1850 I was a candidate for the convention called to revise the constitution of Virginia, but I was defeated by an overwhelming majority, receiving only about two hundred votes in a district polling several thousand. I opposed firmly and unflinchingly all the radical changes, miscalled reforms, which were proposed, and as the people seemed to run wild in favor of them, not only was I beaten, but so were all other candidates professing similar sentiments.

In the year 1853, I was again a candidate for the Legislature, but was badly beaten, as the county had become strongly wedded to the opposite party.

My practice had become very considerable, and at the close of my professional career, I believe I was regarded as among the best lawyers in my section of the State. My most important contest at the bar and my greatest triumph was in a contested will case in Lowndes County, Mississippi, in the autumn of 1852, in which a very large amount of property was involved. I went to Mississippi to attend to this case specially, and I contended single-handed and successfully with three of the ablest lawyers of that State.

I had in a very limited degree the capacity for popular speaking as generally practised in the States, and it was regarded that my forte at the law was not before a jury as an advocate, but on questions of law before the court, especially in cases of appeal.

I was never blessed with popular or captivating manners, and the consequence was that I was often misjudged and thought to be haughty and disdainful in my temperament. When earnestly engaged about my business, in passing through a crowd I would frequently

pass an acquaintance without noticing him, because of
the preoccupation of my mind, and this often gave of-
fence. From all of which it resulted that I was never
what is called a popular man. I can say, however, that
those who knew me best, liked me best, and the preju-
dices against me were gradually wearing off as the people became better acquainted with me.

My labors in my profession were rather spasmodic,
and by procrastination, I would often have to compass
a vast deal of work in a very short time, on the eve of
or during the session of a court. I was careless in securing and collecting my fees, very often relying on
memory as the only evidence of them, and the consequence was that my practice was never very lucrative.

I have now given a sketch of my life up to the time
of the beginning of the great struggle in the South for
independence, and like most men, I had done many things
which I ought not to have done, and left undone many
things which I ought to have done, but I had done some
good, and had not committed any very serious wrong,
considering it in a mere worldly point of view. I would,
however, by no means, commend my life as a pattern
for the young, unless it be in the sincerity and integrity
of purpose by which I claim to have ever been actuated.

As there have been some descriptions of my person
attempted, in which I have failed to recognize the slightest resemblance, I will state that, up to the time of my
service in Mexico, I was quite erect and trim in stature.
My average weight for many years was from 154 to
164 pounds—during the war it was about 170 pounds.
The stoop with which I am now afflicted is the result of
rheumatism contracted in Mexico, and when casual ob-
servers have seen me bent up, it has been very often
the result of actual pain to which I have been very much
subjected for the last nineteen years. One writer, who
was actuated by the most friendly motives and ought
to have known better, has described me as having a
rough, curly head and shaggy eye-brows, whereas the

fact is that my hair always has been, and what is left still is, as straight as an Indian's, and my eyebrows are very moderate and smooth. Some writer, who certainly never put himself in a position to see me during the war, has described my dress as being habitually like that of a stage-driver. All tailors who have ever worked for me up to the present time will testify to the fact that I have always been one of the most particular men about the cut and fit of my clothes among their customers.

During the war I was almost constantly in the camp or field, except when wounded, and I had no time to get new clothes if I had been able. My tastes would always have induced me to dress neatly and genteelly if I could have indulged them.

So much for my life previous to the war. Henceforth it will be developed in my narrative.

THE WAR BETWEEN THE STATES

CHAPTER I.

THE INVASION OF VIRGINIA.

AFTER the fall of Fort Sumter, the Government at Washington commenced concentrating a large force at that city under the superintendence of Lieutenant General Scott of the United States Army, and it was very apparent that Virginia would be invaded.

When the ordinance of secession had been passed by the Virginia convention, and the authority had been given to the Governor to call out troops for the defence of the State, Governor Letcher called for volunteers. The Navy Yard at Gosport, near Norfolk, and the arsenal and armory at Harper's Ferry were taken possession of by militia forces hastily assembled, but not until the United States officers had partially destroyed both.

As soon as General Lee reached Richmond, which was very shortly after his appointment to the command of the Virginia forces, he entered actively on the work of reorganization.

The day the convention took recess to await the result of the popular vote, I tendered my services to the Governor, and received from him the commission of Colonel in the volunteer service of the State. On reporting to General Lee, I was ordered to repair to Lynchburg, and take command of all the Virginia volunteers who should be mustered into service at that place, and organize them into regiments, as they were received by companies. I took command at Lynchburg on the 16th of May, and proceeded to organize the volunteers, which were being mustered into the Virginia service at that point, by Lieutenant Colonel Daniel A. Langhorne.

While there, I organized and armed three regiments, to-wit: The 28th Virginia Regiment (Colonel R. T. Preston) and the 24th Virginia Regiment (my own), both as infantry, and the 30th Virginia Regiment (Colonel R. C. W. Radford), as cavalry. This latter regiment was subsequently designated the 2d Virginia Cavalry.

On the 24th of May, the day after the election in Virginia ratifying the ordinance of secession, the Federal troops, under the command of Brigadier General McDowell, crossed over from Washington into Virginia, the bands playing and the soldiers singing "John Brown's soul goes marching on"; and John Brown's mission was, subsequently, but too well carried out in Virginia and all the Southern States under the inspiration of that anthem.

The Confederate Government had sent some troops to Virginia, and a portion of them along with some of the Virginia troops were concentrated at and near Manassas Junction on the Orange & Alexandria Railroad, about thirty miles from Washington. Brigadier General Beauregard was sent to take command of the troops at Manassas, and other troops had been sent to Harper's Ferry, to the command of which General Joseph E. Johnston was assigned. As soon as it was ascertained that the Federal troops had crossed over and occupied Alexandria, I commenced sending the regiments organized by me, as they were ready, to Manassas. The infantry was armed with smooth-bore percussion muskets, but there were no belts or bayonet scabbards or cartridge boxes for them, and they had to be supplied with cloth pouches for their ammunition. The cavalry regiment, consisting of nine companies, was armed principally with double-barrelled shot guns, and sabres of an old pattern which had been collected in the country from old volunteer companies. The State had very few arms of any kind, and those furnished the infantry had been borrowed from North Carolina. There were no cavalry arms of any value.

I also armed and sent off a number of companies to be attached to regiments already in the field.

Having attended the convention when it re-assembled in June, as soon as the ordinance of secession was signed, I received orders to turn over the command at Lynchburg to Colonel Langhorne and join my regiment in the field. The Confederate Government had now reached Richmond, and that city became the capital of the Confederacy.

I reached Manassas and reported to General Beauregard on the 19th of June. I found my regiment (the 24th Virginia) under Lieutenant Colonel Peter Hairston, located about four miles east of the Junction, for the purpose of watching the fords of Bull Run immediately above its junction with the Occoquon, and those on the latter stream above the same point. At this time no brigades had been formed, but in a few days the regiments under General Beauregard's command were organized into six brigades, as follows: a brigade of South Carolina troops under Brigadier General Bonham, a brigade of Alabama and Louisiana troops under Brigadier General Ewell, a brigade of South Carolina and Mississippi troops under Brigadier General D. R. Jones, a brigade of Virginia troops under Colonel George H. Jerrett, who was subsequently replaced by Brigadier General Longstreet, a brigade of Virginia troops under Colonel Philip St. George Cocke, and a brigade composed of the 7th and 24th Virginia, and the 4th South Carolina Regiments under my command, but the 4th South Carolina had been sent to Leesburg in Loudoun and did not join, it being subsequently replaced by the 7th Louisiana Regiment.

After this organization the troops were located as follows: the 4th South Carolina Regiment and Wheat's Louisiana Battalion were at Leesburg under Colonel

Evans; Bonham's brigade was at Fairfax Court-House, Cocke's at Centreville, and Ewell's brigade at and near Fairfax Station, all in front of Bull Run; while D. R. Jones' brigade was encamped on the south of the Run near the railroad, at a place called Camp Walker, Longstreet's at the Junction, and the 7th and 24th Virginia Regiments of my brigade, camped separately, northeast and east of the Junction, from three to four miles distant. The cavalry, consisting of Colonel R. C. W. Radford's regiment of nine companies and several unattached companies, was employed mainly on scouting and picketing duty with Evans, Bonham, and Ewell, one company being on my right to watch the lower fords of the Occoquon, and the landings on the Potomac below the mouth of the Occoquon, where it was subsequently joined by another.

It was my duty to watch the right of our line, and the two companies of cavalry on that flank, Eugene Davis' and W. W. Thornton's companies of Virginia cavalry, were placed under my command, and Captain John Scott was assigned to the immediate command of them.

A few days after my arrival, under orders from General Beauregard, I made a reconnaissance to the village of Occoquon, near the mouth of the stream of that name, with the 24th Regiment, and examined the landings of the Potomac as far down as Freestone Point.

Early in July General Beauregard summoned all his brigade commanders to a conference at Fairfax Station, and there disclosed to them, in confidence, his plan of operations in the event of an advance by the enemy, for which he had learned active preparations were being made.

He anticipated that the enemy's main force would move on the road through Fairfax Court-House and Centreville toward Manassas, and his plan was, for all the troops on the north of Bull Run to fall back to the south bank of that stream. Bonham, in the centre on the direct road to Manassas, to Mitchell's Ford; Cocke, on the left, to Stone Bridge on the Warrenton Pike; and Ewell, on the right, to Union Mills; and Evans was to retire from Loudoun and unite with Cocke; while Longstreet was to move up to Blackburn's Ford, about a mile below Mitchell's Ford; D. R. Jones to McLean's Ford, about a mile or two further down; and I was to move up to Union Mills in support of Ewell. His anticipation further was, that the enemy would follow up Bonham and attack him at Mitchell's Ford; in which event the rest of the troops were to cross Bull Run and attack the enemy on both flanks—Longstreet crossing at Blackburn's Ford, and Jones at McLean's Ford, and attacking the enemy's left flank; Ewell at the same time moving up towards Centreville, on the road from Union Mills, and attacking the enemy on his left and rear; while I was to follow Ewell in support and look out for his right flank and rear, and Cocke, supported by Evans, was to come down on the enemy's right flank.

The routes by which all these movements were to be made were pointed out and designated on maps previously prepared, and each brigade commander was instructed to make himself familiar with the ground over which he would have to operate. General Beauregard at the same time informed us that the returns showed an effective force under his command of very little more than 15,000 men.

A few days after this, the 7th Louisiana Regiment, under Colonel Harry T. Hays, arrived, and was assigned to my brigade in lieu of the 4th South Carolina. The 7th Virginia was commanded by Colonel James L. Kemper, and the 24th by Lieutenant Colonel Peter Hairston.

On the 12th of July I made another reconnaissance to Occoquon, with the 7th Virginia Regiment under Lieutenant Colonel Williams, and a section of the Washington Artillery of New Orleans, under Lieutenant Squires, and returned to camp on the 14th.

5

CHAPTER II.

Fight at Blackburn's Ford.

On the night of the 16th information was sent from
General Beauregard's headquarters that the enemy was
advancing, and orders were given for moving early
next morning in accordance with previous instructions.

At daylight on the morning of the 17th, I commenced
the movement of my brigade to its assigned position
in rear of the ford at Union Mills, and on my arrival
there I found General Ewell's force falling back to the
same point. Under previous instructions four companies of the 24th Virginia Regiment had been left under
Major Hambrick to guard the camp of the regiment and
picket on the right of our line, and the two companies
of cavalry under Captain Scott had also been left to
watch our right. Three pieces of artillery, under
Lieutenant Squires of the Washington Artillery, were
attached to my brigade and joined it at the position near
Union Mills. I remained there inactive during the rest
of the day after my arrival, but on the morning of the
18th I was ordered further to the left, to Camp Walker
on the railroad. On falling back, Ewell had burned the
bridges on the railroad between Fairfax Station and
Union Mills, and on this morning the bridge over Bull
Run, at the latter place, was likewise burned.

After remaining for some time at Camp Walker, I
was ordered by General Beauregard to move my brigade
to the gate in rear of McLean's farm on the road from
Blackburn's Ford to the Junction, keeping it in the
woods out of view. The General had now established
his headquarters at McLean's house between my position and those of Generals Longstreet and Jones.
From this last position taken by me, the open fields on
the heights beyond Blackburn's Ford were visible, being
between two and three miles distant. A little before

12 M. we discovered clouds of dust from the direction
of Centreville and bodies of troops moving into the
fields beyond the ford, and while we were speculating
as to whether this was the enemy, we saw the smoke
arise from his first gun, the fire from which was directed
towards Bonham's position at Mitchell's Ford.

After the firing had continued for a short time, I
received an order from General Beauregard to move my
command to the rear of a pine thicket between McLean's
house and Blackburn's Ford, so as to be in supporting
distance of Bonham, Longstreet or Jones. In order to do
this I had to run through open fields in view of the enemy
and this attracted his fire in our direction, but I reached
the cover of the pines without any casualty, and I was
here joined by Lieutenant Richardson, of the Washington Artillery, with two more pieces. The enemy's fire
was continued for some time, and one or two shells
passed through an out-house near General Beauregard's
headquarters.

In the afternoon the General rode towards Mitchell's
Ford, and after he had been gone a short time a very
brisk musketry fire opened at Blackburn's Ford. The
enemy had attacked Longstreet at that point, and after
the firing had continued for some time, I received a message from General Longstreet, through one of his aides,
requesting reinforcements. I immediately put my whole
command in motion towards the ford, but before arriving
there, I received an order from General Beauregard to
carry two regiments and two pieces of artillery to Longstreet's assistance. My command was then moving with
the 7th Louisiana in front, followed immediately by the
7th Virginia, and I ordered the six companies of the 24th
Virginia, which were bringing up the rear under Lieutenant Colonel Hairston, to halt, and directed Lieutenant
Squires to move two pieces of artillery to the front and
halt the rest. I found that General Longstreet's command
had been hotly engaged and had just repulsed an attempt
to force a crossing of the stream.

The position occupied by our troops was a narrow strip of woods on low ground along the bank of the stream, with an open field in rear, while the enemy occupied higher and better ground on the opposite bank. Immediately on its arrival, the 7th Louisiana, Colonel Hays, was put in position in the strip of woods on the left of the ford, relieving the 17th Virginia Regiment and some companies of the 11th Virginia which had been actively engaged; and the 7th Virginia Regiment, Lieutenant Colonel Williams commanding, was formed on the right of the ford, in rear of the strip of woods, and advanced to the bank of the stream, relieving the 1st Virginia Regiment.

These movements were made under fire from the enemy on the opposite bluffs, and while the 7th Virginia was being formed in line, two volleys were fired at it by the enemy, throwing it into some confusion and causing it to begin firing without orders, while there were some of our troops in front of it. It, however, soon recovered from the momentary confusion and advanced with firmness to the front. Lieutenant Squires moved his pieces into the open field in rear of our line and to the right of the road leading to the ford, and opened fire without any guide except the sound of the enemy's musketry, as he was concealed from our view by the woods on the bluffs occupied by him. The six companies of the 24th Virginia Regiment and the remaining pieces of the Washington Artillery, including two pieces under Lieutenant Garnett which were attached to Longstreet's brigade, were sent for, and the companies of the 24th were put in position along the banks of the stream on Hays' left, while the rest of the artillery was brought into action on the same ground with Squires.

Squires had soon silenced the enemy's infantry, which retired precipitately before his fire, but the artillery from the heights beyond the stream had opened on ours, which now responded to that of the enemy. An artillery duel was thus commenced which lasted for a considerable

8

time. The opposing batteries were concealed from each other's view by the intervening woods, and they were therefore compelled to regulate their fire by the sound of the guns. The enemy had the decided advantage of position, as he was on high ground, while our guns were located in a flat nearly on a level with the stream, thus giving them the benefit of a plunging fire. This duel finally ceased and the enemy retired, baffled in his effort to force our position.

In his reports of this affair, the enemy represented our troops as being protected by rifle pits with masked batteries; whereas the fact was that we had nothing in the shape of rifle pits or breastworks, and our guns were in the open field, though concealed from the enemy's view by the intervening woods. These guns had been brought on the field along with my brigade, but were so brought as to elude observation. Before their arrival not an artillery shot had been fired by us from this quarter, and there had been only a few shots earlier in the day from the guns, with Bonham, at Mitchell's Ford above.

As soon as it was ascertained that the enemy had retired, General Longstreet moved to the rear with his two regiments that had borne the brunt of the fight, and I was left to occupy his former position with my brigade and the 11th Virginia Regiment of his brigade. A few were wounded in my command, but I believe none killed. General Longstreet's loss was not heavy, but an examination of the ground on the opposite bank of the Run, next morning, showed that the enemy had suffered severely, quite a number of dead bodies being found abandoned. At one point, where it was apparent a regiment had been in line, over one hundred muskets and hats were found in a row, showing evidently that they had been abandoned in a panic, produced probably by the fire from Squires' guns. Many knapsacks, canteens, blankets and India rubber cloths were found scattered on the ground, proving that the enemy had retired in confusion.

9

LIEUTENANT GENERAL JUBAL A. EARLY

This fight was preliminary to the approaching battle, and its result had a very inspiring effect upon our troops generally. It was subsequently ascertained that the force engaged, on the part of the enemy, was Tyler's division of McDowell's army, which had been sent to the front for the purpose of making a demonstration, while McDowell himself was engaged in reconnoitring on our right, for the purpose of ascertaining whether that flank could be turned by the way of Wolf Run Shoals, just below the junction of Bull Run and the Occoquon. Tyler exceeded his instructions, it appears, and endeavored to gain some glory for himself by forcing our position at Blackburn's Ford, but he paid dearly for the experiment.

During the 19th I continued to occupy the position at Blackburn's Ford, and occasionally small bodies of the enemy could be seen by scouts sent to the opposite side of Bull Run, on the heights where he had taken his position on the 18th, previous to the advance against Longstreet. During the day my troops, with a few rough tools and their bayonets, succeeded in making very tolerable rifle pits on the banks of the stream, and they were not molested by the enemy.

About dark the brigade commanders were summoned to a council at McLean's house by General Beauregard, and he proceeded to inform us of his plans for the next day. He told us that, at his instance, the Government at Richmond had ordered General Johnston to move from the Shenandoah Valley with his whole force to co-operate with ours; and that the General was then on his march directly across the Blue Ridge, and would probably attack the enemy's right flank very early the next morning, while we were to fall upon his left flank. Before he finished the statement of his plans, Brigadier General Thomas J. Jackson, subsequently famous as "Stonewall Jackson," entered the room and reported to General Beauregard that he had just arrived from General Johnston's army, by the way of the Manassas Gap Railroad, with his brigade, about 2500 strong.

10

FIGHT AT BLACKBURN'S FORD

This information took General Beauregard by surprise, and he inquired of General Jackson if General Johnston would not march the rest of his command on the direct road so as to get on the enemy's right flank. General Jackson replied that he thought not, that he thought the purpose was to transport the whole force on the railroad from Piedmont station on the east of the Blue Ridge. After General Jackson had given all the information he possessed, and received instructions as to the disposition of his brigade, he retired, and General Beauregard proceeded to develop his plans fully. The information received from General Jackson was most unexpected, but General Beauregard stated that he thought Jackson was mistaken, and that he was satisfied General Johnston was marching with the rest of his troops and would attack the enemy's right flank as before stated.

Upon this hypothesis, he then decided that, when General Johnston's attack began and he had become fully engaged, of which we were to judge from the character of the musketry fire, we would cross Bull Run from our several positions and move to the attack of the enemy's left flank and rear. He stated that he had no doubt Johnston's attack would be a surprise to the enemy, that the latter would not know what to think of it, and when he turned to meet that attack and found himself assailed on the other side, he would be still more surprised and would not know what to do, that the effect would be a complete rout, a perfect Waterloo, and that we would pursue, cross the Potomac and arouse Maryland.

General Johnston's attack, according to General Beauregard's calculations, was to begin next morning about or very shortly after daybreak. Having received our instructions fully, we retired, and I returned to my position at Blackburn's Ford, where I assembled my colonels, and was proceeding to explain to them the plans for the next day and instruct them to have every-

thing in readiness, when we were startled by a fierce
volley of musketry on our immediate right. This of
course put an end to the conference and every one
rushed to his position in anticipation of a night attack.

The 11th Virginia Regiment, Colonel Samuel Garland,
was moved promptly to the rear of the point where the
firing occurred, which was repeated, and after a good
deal of trouble we succeeded in ascertaining that it
proceeded from two of my companies, which had been
posted in the woods on the bank of the stream to the right
of my position, in order to cover some points where a
crossing might be effected. The officers of one of the
companies declared that a body of the enemy could be
seen, stealthily moving down the opposite bank, and that
the firing had been at that body and had been returned.
The firing by this time had ceased and no movement of
the enemy could be heard. This affair, however, kept
us on the alert all night, but I became satisfied that it
resulted from some mistake, caused perhaps by the movement of some straggling persons of our own command,
in the darkness, in the woods. Such alarms were not
uncommon, subsequently, when two opposing forces were
lying on their arms at night in front of each other. A
very slight circumstance would sometimes produce a
volley at night from the one or the other side, as it
might be.

At light on the morning of the 20th, instead of our
being required to advance to the attack of the enemy
according to the programme of the night before, General
Longstreet came in a great hurry to relieve me, and
with orders for my brigade to move as rapidly as possible to a point on our right on the road leading from
Yates' Ford, below Union Mills, to Manassas Junction.
As soon as relieved, I moved in the direction indicated,
and the head of my column was just emerging into
Camp Walker, from the woods in rear of McLean's farm,
—where I had been on the 18th, at the time the enemy
opened his artillery fire beyond Blackburn's Ford,—when

FIGHT AT BLACKBURN'S FORD

I was met by a courier with orders to halt where I was, as the alarm, upon which the order to me had been founded, had proved false.

As this false alarm was rather singular in its nature, but of such a character that any general might have been deceived by it, I will state how it occurred. A captain of General Ewell's brigade, who had been posted with his company on picket at Yates' Ford not far below Union Mills, retired from his post and reported in the most positive manner that the enemy had appeared in heavy force on the opposite bank of Bull Run and commenced building two bridges. He further stated that he had seen General McDowell on a white horse superintending the construction of the bridges.

As there was no reason to doubt his veracity or courage, General Ewell, of course, sent at once the information to General Beauregard and hence the order for my movement. After the message was dispatched, something suggested a doubt as to the correctness of the report, and the officer making it was sent in charge of another to ascertain the facts. On arriving in sight of the ford he pointed triumphantly to the opposite bank and exclaimed, "There they are. Don't you see the two bridges, don't you see McDowell on his white horse?" when the fact was there was nothing visible but the ford and the unoccupied banks of the stream, which were so obstructed as to render a crossing impracticable until the obstructions were removed.

It was then apparent that it was a clear case of hallucination, produced by a derangement of the nervous system, consequent on a loss of sleep and great anxiety of mind resulting from the nature of the duties in which he had been engaged. Neither his sincerity nor his courage was questioned, and this affair shows how the most careful commander may be misled when he has to rely on information furnished by others. It requires very great experience and a very discriminating judgment to enable a commanding general to sift the truth

13

out of the great mass of exaggerated reports made to him, and hence he has often to rely on his own personal inspection.

I have known important movements to be suspended on the battlefield, on account of reports from very gallant officers that the enemy was on one flank or the other in heavy force, when a calm inspection proved the reported bodies of the enemy to be nothing more than stone or rail fences. Some officers, while exposing their lives with great daring, sometimes fail to preserve that clearness of judgment and calmness of the nerves which is so necessary to enable one to see things as they really are during an engagement; and hence it is that there are so many conflicting reports of the same matters. The capacity of preserving one's presence of mind in action is among the highest attributes of an efficient commander or subordinate officer, and it must be confessed that the excitement of battle, especially when the shells are bursting and the bullets whistling thick around, is wonderfully trying to the nerves of the bravest.

The false alarm out of which the above reflections have sprung, operated as a very great relief to my command, as it enabled my men, who had had very little to eat, and scarcely any rest or sleep for two nights and days, to cook provisions and get a good rest and sleep in the woods where they were halted, and thereby to be prepared to go through the extraordinary fatigues of the next day.

On this day, the 20th, General Johnston arrived at Manassas by the railroad, and an order was issued for his assuming command, as the ranking officer, of all the troops of the united armies. It was now ascertained beyond doubt that all of his troops were coming by the railroad.

CHAPTER III.

EARLY'S BRIGADE AT MANASSAS.

AT this time the largest organizations in our army were brigades, and each brigade commander received his orders directly from headquarters. Since the conference at Fairfax Station, when General Beauregard stated that his effective strength did not exceed 15,000 men, one regiment, the 1st South Carolina, had been sent off by reason of expiration of term of service, and one regiment, the 7th Louisiana, had joined my brigade. Besides this, General Beauregard's troops had been augmented, since the advance of the enemy, by the arrival of six companies of the 8th Louisiana, the 5th North Carolina State Troops, the 11th North Carolina Volunteers, the 13th Mississippi, three companies of the 49th Virginia and Hampton's South Carolina Legion; the latter containing six companies of infantry. His whole effective force, however, did not probably much exceed the estimate made at the time of the conference, as the measles and typhoid fever, which were prevailing, had reduced very much the strength of the regiments, especially among the Virginia troops which were entirely new. To reinforce him, Holmes' brigade of two regiments had arrived from Aquia Creek, and Johnston's troops were arriving by the railroad, after much delay by reason of accidents or mismanagement on the part of the railroad officials.

On the 20th we were not molested by the enemy, and on the morning of the 21st the position of Beauregard's troops was pretty much the same as it had been on the 18th, to wit: Ewell at Union Mills; D. R. Jones at McLean's Ford; Longstreet, reinforced by the 5th North Carolina, at Blackburn's Ford; Bonham, reinforced by six companies of the 8th Louisiana and the 11th North Carolina Volunteers, at Mitchell's Ford;

Cocke, reinforced by some companies of the 8th Virginia Regiment and three companies of the 49th Virginia Regiment, at some fords below Stone Bridge; and Evans at Stone Bridge; while my brigade was in reserve in the woods in rear of McLean's farm. No artillery was attached to my brigade on this day.

The arrival of General Johnston in person and the transportation of his troops on the railroad had, of course, entirely changed the plans of operations as communicated to us on the night of the 19th, but the new plans, which were rendered necessary by the altered condition of things, were not communicated to us, and I had, therefore, to await orders.

Very early on the morning of the 21st the enemy opened fire with artillery from the heights on the north of Bull Run near Blackburn's Ford, and I was ordered to occupy a position in rear of the pine woods north of McLean's house, so as to be ready to support Longstreet or Jones as might be necessary. After being in position some time, I received a request from General Longstreet for one of my regiments to be sent to him, and I sent him the six companies of the 24th Virginia under Lieutenant Colonel Hairston, and two companies of the 7th Louisiana under Major Penn. Not long afterwards I received a request for another regiment, and I carried the remaining eight companies of the 7th Louisiana to Blackburn's Ford, leaving Colonel Kemper with his regiment behind.

On arriving at the ford, I found that the whole of Longstreet's brigade had been crossed over Bull Run, and were lying under cover at the foot of the hills on its northern bank, awaiting a signal to advance against the enemy, who was in considerable force near the point occupied by his artillery at the fight on the 18th. The companies of the 24th were being crossed over to join Longstreet's brigade, and the General ordered the 7th Louisiana to be formed in line in the strip of woods on the southern bank of the stream, covering the ford.

The enemy was keeping up a continuous artillery fire from two batteries, one in front of the ford and the other some distance to the right, which rendered the vicinity of the ford quite uncomfortable, but the troops across the Run were in a great measure under cover.

After Hays' regiment had been put in position, General Longstreet went across the stream to reconnoitre, and in a short time returned and directed me to take Hays' and Kemper's regiments, cross at McLean's Ford, and move around and capture the battery to his right, which he said could be easily taken. I was informed by him that Jones had crossed the Run and was on the hills beyond McLean's Ford, likewise awaiting the signal to advance, and I was directed to move between him and the Run against the enemy's battery. Hays' regiment was moved back to where Kemper's was, and was exposed to the fire from the enemy's batteries which was attracted by the dust arising from its march over the direct road through the pines. A shell exploded in the ranks, killing and wounding four or five men. The two regiments were moved to McLean's Ford, and while they were crossing over and forming, I rode forward to an eminence, where I observed a lookout in a tree, for the purpose of ascertaining the exact position of the battery and the route over which I would have to advance against it. While I was engaged in obtaining this information, Colonel Chisolm, a volunteer aide of General Beauregard, rode up and informed me that General Beauregard's orders were that the whole force should cross Bull Run to the south side.

I think this was about 11.00 A.M. I informed him of the order I had received from General Longstreet, and he stated that Longstreet was crossing, and that the order embraced me as well as the rest. I felt this as a reprieve from almost certain destruction, for I had discovered that the route by which I would be compelled to advance against the battery was along an open valley for some distance and then up a naked hill to the plain on which the battery was located, the greater part of the route being raked by the enemy's guns. The lookout had also informed me that a considerable body of infantry was in the woods near the battery. It turned out afterwards that this battery, which I was ordered to take, was supported by a brigade of infantry, posted behind a formidable abattis of felled timber. An attempt to carry out my orders would very probably have entailed the annihilation or utter rout of my two regiments; and in fact much later in the day, Jones' brigade on moving against this battery sustained a damaging repulse.

After recrossing to the south side, I sent Kemper's regiment to its former position, and moved with Hays' regiment up the Run to Longstreet's position, as I thought he probably desired its return to him. On reaching Blackburn's Ford, I found General Longstreet cautiously withdrawing a part of his troops across the Run, and he informed me that he did not now require Hays' regiment, but would retain the companies of the 24th. Hays was then ordered to move down the Run to McLean's Ford and return in that way to the position at which Kemper was, so as to avoid the artillery fire while passing over the direct route.

I rode directly to Kemper's position, and after being there a short time I discovered clouds of dust arising about McLean's Ford, which I supposed to be produced by Jones' brigade returning to its original position. Fearing that Hays' regiment might be mistaken for the enemy and fired upon, I rode rapidly to Jones' position and found some of his men forming in the rifle pits in rear of the ford, while the General was looking with his field glasses at Hays' regiment, which was advancing from the direction of the enemy's position higher up the Run. I informed him what command it was and requested that his men might be cautioned against firing, for which they were preparing.

As soon as this was done, General Jones asked me

if I had received an order from General Beauregard, directing that I should go to him with my brigade. Upon my stating that I had received no such order, he said that he had received a note from General Beauregard in which he was directed to send me to the General. The note, which was in the hands of one of Jones' staff officers, was sent for and shown to me. It was in pencil, and after giving brief directions for the withdrawal across the Run and stating the general purpose to go to the left where the heavy firing was, there was a direction at the foot in very nearly these words,—"Send Early to me." This information was given to me some time between 12 M. and 1 P.M.*

The note did not state to what point I was to go, but I knew that General Beauregard's position had been near Mitchell's Ford and that he was to be found somewhere to our left. I sent word for Hays to move up as rapidly as possible, directed Kemper to get ready to move, sent a message to General Longstreet requesting the return of the companies of the 24th, and directed my Acting Adjutant General, Captain Gardner, to ride to Mitchell's Ford and ascertain where General Beauregard was, as well as the route I was to pursue.

The messenger sent to General Longstreet returned and informed me that the General said there was a regiment in the pines to my left which had been ordered to report to him, and that I could take that regiment instead of the companies of my own, to save time and prevent the exposure of both to the fire of the enemy's artillery in passing to and from Blackburn's Ford. In this arrangement I readily concurred, and soon found, to my left in the pines, the 13th Mississippi Regiment under Colonel Barksdale, which had very recently arrived. The Colonel consented to accompany me, and as soon as the

---

* In his report General Beauregard states that I did not receive this order until 2.00 P.M. This is a mistake. I could not possibly have reached the battlefield at the time I did, if the reception of the order had been delayed until 2.00 P.M.

command could be got ready, it was started on the road towards Mitchell's Ford.

This movement commenced about or very shortly after 1 o'clock P.M. On the way I met Captain Gardner returning with the information that General Beauregard's headquarters would be at the Lewis house, in the direction of the firing on our extreme left, and that I was to go there. On reaching General Bonham's position in rear of Mitchell's Ford, he informed me that I would have to move through the fields towards the left to find the Lewis house, and he pointed out the direction; but he did not know the exact location of the house. I moved in the direction pointed out, and continued to pass on to our left, through the fields, towards the firing in the distance, endeavoring, as I advanced, to find out where the Lewis house was.

While moving on, Captain Smith, an assistant in the adjutant general's office at General Beauregard's headquarters, passed us in a great hurry, also looking for General Beauregard and the Lewis house. He told me that information had been received at the Junction that 6,000 of the enemy had passed the Manassas Gap railroad, and it was this information (which subsequently proved to be false) that he was going to communicate to the General.

The day was excessively hot and dry. Hays' regiment was a good deal exhausted by the marching and the counter-marching about Blackburn's and McLean's Fords. Barksdale's regiment, an entirely new one, had just arrived from the south over the railroad, and was unused to marching. Our progress was therefore not as rapid as I could have wished, but we passed on with all possible speed in the direction of the firing, which was our only guide. Towards 3 o'clock P.M. we reached the field of battle and began to perceive the scenes usual in rear of an army engaged in action. On entering the road leading from the Lewis house towards Manassas, we met quite a stream of stragglers going to the rear, and were informed by them that everything was over with us. I was riding by the side of Colonel Kemper at the head of the column, and we had the satisfaction of being assured that if we went on the field on horseback, we certainly would be killed, as the enemy shot all the mounted officers. Some of the men said that their regiments had been entirely cut to pieces, and there was no use for them to remain any longer.

It was to the encouraging remarks of this stream of recreants that my command was exposed as it moved on, but not a man fell out of ranks. Only one man who had been engaged offered to return and he belonged to the 4th Alabama Regiment, which he said had been nearly destroyed, but he declared that he would "go back and give them another trial." He fell into the ranks of Kemper's regiment and I believe remained with it to the close of the battle. Captain Gardner had been sent ahead for instructions and had met with Colonel John S. Preston, a volunteer aide to General Beauregard; and on our getting near to the battlefield, Colonel Preston rode to meet us and informed me that the General had gone to the front on the right, to conduct an attack on the enemy, but that General Johnston was on that part of the field near which we were and would give me instructions. He pointed out the direction in which General Johnston was, and I moved on, soon meeting the General himself, who rode towards us when he discovered our approach, and expressed his gratification at our arrival.

I asked him at once to show me my position, to which he replied that he was too much engaged to do that in person, but would give me directions as to what I was to do. He then directed me to move to our own extreme left and attack the enemy on his right, stating that by directing my march along the rear of our line, by the sound of the firing in front, there could be no mistake; and he cautioned me to take especial care to clear our whole line before advancing to the front, and

21

be particular and not fire on any of our own troops, which he was sorry to say had been done in some instances.

Affairs now wore a very gloomy aspect, and from all the indications in the rear the day appeared to be going against us. While General Johnston was speaking to me, quite a squad of men approached us going to the rear, and the General asking them to what regiment they belonged and where going without receiving any satisfactory answer, directed me to make my men charge bayonets and drive them back to the front. I immediately ordered Colonel Kemper to charge them with his regiment, when they commenced making excuses, saying they were sick, or wounded, or had no ammunition. I saw at once there was no fight in them, and I directed Colonel Kemper to move on and not delay battling with such cowards.

Immediately in front of us was a body of woods extending to our left, in which there was a constant rattle of musketry, and I moved along the rear of this woods, crossing the road from Manassas to Sudley, and inclining to the left so as to clear our line entirely. While so moving Colonel Kemper pointed out to me the United States flag floating in the distance on some high point in front of our right, probably the top of a house.

To clear our line entirely on our left, I found that it was necessary to pass beyond the woods in which our troops were, and as I approached the open space beyond, a messenger came to me from Colonel, afterwards General, J. E. B. Stuart, who was on our extreme left with two companies of cavalry and a battery of artillery under Lieutenant Beckham, stating that the Colonel said the enemy was about giving way and if we would hurry up he would soon be in retreat. This was the first word of encouragement I had received after reaching the vicinity of the battlefield. I was then making all the haste the condition of my men, who were much blown, would permit, and I directed my march to a field immediately on the left of the woods, and between Stuart's position and the left of our infantry then engaged.

The messenger from Colonel Stuart soon returned in a gallop and stated that the Colonel said the enemy had only retired his right behind a ridge now in my front, and was moving another flanking column behind said ridge still further to our left, and he cautioned me to be on the lookout for this new column.

Having now cleared the woods, I moved to the front, in order to form line against the flanking column the enemy was reported forming behind the ridge in front of me. I ordered Colonel Kemper, who was in front, to form his regiment, by file, into line in the open field, just on the left of the woods, and sent back directions for the other regiments to move up as rapidly as possible and form to Kemper's left in echelon. Just at this time I observed a body of our troops move from a piece of woods on my immediate right across an open space to another in front of it, and this proved to be the left regiment of Elzey's brigade. I heard a rapid fire open from the woods into which this regiment had moved, and a body of the enemy approached on the crest of the ridge immediately in my front, preceded by a line of skirmishers.

This ridge was the one on which is situated Chinn's house, so often mentioned in the description of this battle, and the subsequent one near the same position. It is a high ridge sloping off towards our right, and the enemy had the decided advantage of the ground, as my troops had to form on the low ground on our side of the ridge, near a small stream which runs along its base. The formation of my troops was in full view of the enemy, and his skirmishers, which were about four hundred yards in front of us, opened on my men, while forming, with long range rifles or minie muskets. Barksdale and Hays came up rapidly and formed as directed, Barksdale in the centre and Hays on the left.

LIEUTENANT GENERAL JUBAL A. EARLY

While their regiments were forming by file into line, under the fire of the enemy's sharpshooters, Kemper's regiment commenced moving obliquely to the right towards the woods into which Elzey's troops had been seen to move, and I rode in front and halted it, informing it that there were no troops in the woods, and pointing out the enemy on the crest of the ridge in front. I then rode to the other regiments to direct their movements, when Colonel Kemper, finding the fire of the enemy, who was beyond the range of our smooth bores, very annoying to his men, moved rapidly to the front, to the cover of a fence at the foot of the ridge. As soon as Hays' regiment was formed, I ordered an advance and Hays moved forward until in a line with Kemper, then their two regiments started up the side of the hill. As we advanced the enemy disappeared behind the crest, and while we were ascending the slope Lieutenant McDonald, acting aide to Colonel Elzey, came riding rapidly towards me and requested me not to let my men fire on the troops in my front, stating that they consisted of the 13th Virginia Regiment of Elzey's brigade. I said to him,—"They have been firing on my men," to which he replied, "I know they have, but it is a mistake, I recognize Colonel Hill of the 13th, and his horse." This was a mistake on the part of Lieutenant McDonald, arising from a fancied resemblance of a mounted officer with the enemy to the Colonel of the 13th. This regiment did not reach the battlefield at all.

This information and the positive assurance of Lieutenant McDonald, however, caused me to halt my troops and ride to the crest of the ridge, where I observed a regiment about two hundred yards to my right drawn up in line in front of the woods where Elzey's left was. The dress of the volunteers on both sides at that time was very similar, and the flag of the regiment I saw was drooping around the staff, so that I could not see whether it was the United States or the Confederate flag. The very confident manner of Lieutenant Mc-

Donald, in his statement in regard to the troops in my front, induced me to believe that this must also be one of our regiments.

Colonel Stuart had also advanced on my left with his two companies of cavalry and Beckham's battery of four guns, and passed around Chinn's house, the battery had been brought into action and opened a flank fire on the regiment I was observing. Thinking it certainly was one of ours, I started a messenger to Colonel Stuart, to give him the information and request him to stop the firing, but a second shell or ball from Beckham's guns caused the regiment to face about and retire rapidly, when I saw the United States flag unfurled and discovered the mistake into which I had been led by Lieutenant McDonald.

I immediately ordered my command forward and it advanced to the crest of the hill. All this occurred in less time than it has taken me to describe it. On reaching the crest we came in view of the Warrenton Pike and the plains beyond, and now saw the enemy's troops in full retreat across and beyond the pike. When Kemper's and Hays' regiments had advanced, Barksdale's, under a misapprehension of my orders, had not at first moved, but it soon followed, and the whole command was formed in line, along the crest of the ridge, on the right of Chinn's house.

We were now on the extreme left of the whole of our infantry, and in advance of the main line. The only troops on our left of any description were the two companies of cavalry and Beckham's battery with Stuart. On my immediate right and a little to the rear was Elzey's brigade, and farther to the right I saw our line extending towards Bull Run, but I discovered no indications of a forward movement.

My troops were now very much exhausted, especially Hays' regiment, which had been marching nearly all the morning before our movement to the left, and it was necessary to give the men a little time to breathe. Beck-

ham's guns had continued firing on the retreating enemy
until beyond their range, and Stuart soon went in
pursuit followed by Beckham. Colonel Cocke now came
up and joined me with the 19th Virginia Regiment.

As soon as my men had rested a little, I directed
the brigade to advance in column of divisions along the
route over which we had seen the enemy retiring, and I
sent information to the troops, on my right, of my purpose to move in their front with the request not to fire
on us. I moved forward followed by Cocke's regiment,
crossing Young's branch and the Warrenton Pike to
the north side. When we got into the valley of Young's
branch we lost sight of the enemy, and on ascending to
the plains north of the pike we could see nothing of
them. Passing to the west and north of the houses
known as the Dogan house, the Stone Tavern, the
Matthews house and the Carter or Pittsylvania house,
and being guided by the abandoned haversacks and muskets, we moved over the ground on which the battle had
begun with Evans in the early morning, and continued
our march until we had cleared our right.

We had now got to a point where Bull Run makes
a considerable bend above Stone Bridge, and I halted
as we had not observed any movement from the main
line. Nothing could be seen of the enemy, and his
troops had scattered so much in the retreat that it was
impossible for me to tell what route he had taken. Moreover the country was entirely unknown to me. Stuart
and Beckham had crossed the run above me, and Cocke's
regiment had also moved towards a ford above where
I was. While I was engaged in making some observations and trying to find out what was going on, Colonel
Chisolm of General Beauregard's volunteer staff passed
me with a detachment of cavalry in pursuit of a body of
the enemy supposed to be across Bull Run above me.

About this time it was reported to me that the enemy
had sent us a flag of truce, but on inquiry I found it
was a messenger with a note from Colonel Jones of the

4th Alabama Regiment, who had been very badly wounded and was at one of the enemy's hospitals in rear of the battlefield, and I sent for him and had him brought in to Matthews' house near where the battle had begun. I also found Lieutenant Colonel Gardner of the 8th Georgia Regiment in the yard of the Carter house, where he had been brought by some of the enemy engaged in collecting the wounded, and suffering from a very painful wound.

Shortly after this President Davis, accompanied by several gentlemen, rode to where my command was. He addressed a few remarks to each regiment and was received with great enthusiasm. I then informed him of the condition of things as far as I knew them, told him of the condition and location of Colonel Gardner, and requested him to have medical assistance sent to him, as no medical officer could be found with my command at that time. I informed him of the fact that I was unacquainted with the situation of the country and without orders to guide me under the circumstances, and asked him what I should do.

He said I had better form my men in line near where I was and let them rest until orders were received. I requested him to inform Generals Beauregard and Johnston of my position and ask them to send me orders. While we were conversing we observed a body of troops across Bull Run, some distance below, moving in good order in the direction of Centreville. I at first supposed it to be Bonham's brigade moving from Mitchell's Ford, but it turned out to be Kershaw's and Cash's regiments of that brigade, which had preceded me to the battlefield and were now moving in pursuit, after having crossed at or below Stone Bridge. Bonham's position at Mitchell's Ford was entirely too far off for his movement to be observed.

As soon as Mr. Davis left me, I moved my command farther into the bend of Bull Run, and put it in line across the bend with the flanks resting on the stream, the right flank being some distance above Stone Bridge. In this position my troops spent the night. They were considerably exhausted by the fatigues of the day, and had had nothing to eat since the early morning. They were now miles away from their baggage and trains. Early in the morning a Virginia company under Captain Gibson, unattached, had been permitted, at the request of the Captain, to join Kemper's regiment and remained with it throughout the day. A South Carolina company belonging to Kershaw's or Cash's regiment, which was on picket at the time their regiments moved from Mitchell's Ford, not being able to find its proper command, had joined me just as we were advancing against the enemy near Chinn's house, and had been attached to Hays' regiment, with which it went into action. Lieutenant Murat Willis had volunteered his services early in the day as aide and been with me through all my movements, rendering valuable service.

The conduct of my troops during the whole day had been admirable, and the coolness with which they formed in open ground under the fire of the enemy's sharpshooters was deserving of all praise. They were in a condition to have taken up the pursuit the next day, but it would have been with empty haversacks, or rather without any except those picked up on the battlefield and along the line of the enemy's retreat.

My loss was in killed and wounded, seventy-six, the greater part being in Kemper's regiment.

The troops which were immediately in my front near Chinn's house constituted the enemy's extreme right, and were, I think, composed in part of the regulars attached to McDowell's army. Their long range muskets or rifles enabled them to inflict the loss on my command, but I am satisfied that the latter inflicted little or no loss on the enemy, as he retired before we got within range with our arms, which were smooth-bore muskets.

As soon as my troops were disposed for the night

and steps taken to guard the front, I rode with my staff officers in search of either General Beauregard or General Johnston, in order to give information of my position and get instructions for the next morning. Not knowing the roads, I had to take the circuitous route over which I had advanced, but I finally reached the Lewis house to find it a hospital for the wounded, and the headquarters removed. Not being able to get here any information of either of the generals, I rode in the direction of Manassas until I met an officer who said he was on the staff of General Johnston and was looking for him. He stated that he was just from Manassas and did not think either of the generals was there.

Taking this to be true and not knowing where to look further, I rode back along the Sudley Mills road to the Stone Tavern, passing over the main battlefield, and rejoined my command after twelve o'clock at night, when I lay down to rest, my bed being a bundle of wheat. While trying to find the generals, I discovered that there was very great confusion among our troops that had been engaged in the battle. They were scattered in every direction, regiments being separated from their brigades, companies from their regiments, while many squads and individuals were seeking their commands. That part of the army was certainly in no condition to make pursuit next morning.

Very early on the morning of the 22nd, I sent Captain Fleming Gardner to Manassas for instruction, and he returned with directions to me from General Beauregard to remain where I was until further orders, and to have my men made as comfortable as possible. A heavy rain had now set in, which continued through the day and night. When it was ascertained that there was to be no movement, I rode over the battlefield and to the hospitals in the vicinity to see about having my wounded brought in who had not been taken care of. The country in rear of the enemy's line of battle of the day before, and along his routes of retreat was strewn with knapsacks, haversacks, canteens, blankets, overcoats, india-rubber cloths, muskets, equipments, and all the débris of a routed army.

A report subsequently made by a Committee of the Federal Congress, of which Senator Wade was chairman, gave a most preposterous account of "Rebel atrocities" committed upon the dead and wounded of the Federal army after the battle. I am able to say, from my personal knowledge, that its statements are false, and the Federal surgeons, left with the wounded, could bear testimony to their falsehood.

CHAPTER IV.

DETAILS OF THE BATTLE OF MANASSAS.

I HAVE now told what I saw and did during the first battle of Manassas, and as many very erroneous accounts of that battle, both in its general features and its details, were given by newspaper correspondents, from both sections, which have furnished the basis for most of the descriptions of it, contained errors—even in works professing to be authentic histories,—I will here give a succinct account of the battle from the authentic official reports, and my own knowledge as far as it extends.

On the morning of the 21st we held the line of Bull Run, with our right at Union Mills and our left at Stone Bridge. Ewell's brigade was at Union Mills, Jones' at McLean's Ford, Longstreet's at Blackburn's Ford, Bonham's at Mitchell's Ford, Cocke at the fords below Stone Bridge, and Evans with Sloan's regiment and Wheat's battalion was at the Stone Bridge. Holmes' brigade, which had arrived from Aquia Creek, was some three miles in rear of Ewell's position. My brigade was in reserve to support Longstreet or Jones, as might be required, and Jackson's and parts of Bee's and Bartow's brigades of Johnston's army—which had arrived by the Manassas Gap Railroad—were held as a general reserve to be used as occasion might require. The Warrenton Pike from Centreville to Warrenton crosses Bull Run at Stone Bridge, and its general direction from Centreville is a little south of west.

McDowell's force had reached Centreville on the 18th, and that day the 19th and 20th had been employed by him in reconnoitring. Contrary to General Beauregard's anticipations, McDowell, instead of advancing against our centre on the morning of the 21st, left one division (Miles') and a brigade of another (Tyler's) to hold Centreville and amuse our right and centre, while

31

he moved two divisions (Hunter's and Heintzelman's) and three brigades of another (Tyler's) against our left, with the view of turning that flank and forcing us from the line of Bull Run. The three brigades of Tyler's division moved directly against Stone Bridge, over the Warrenton Pike, and opened an artillery fire at six o'clock A.M. About the same time fire was opened from two batteries established by the enemy north of Bull Run, near Blackburn's Ford, which was kept up steadily until late in the afternoon. Hunter's division, diverging from the Warrenton Pike, moved across Bull Run at or near Sudley Mills, about three miles above Stone Bridge, and then towards Manassas on the direct road, so as to get in rear of Stone Bridge, while Heintzelman followed Hunter to support him.

When this movement was developed, Colonel Evans, leaving a very small force at Stone Bridge, where the road had been blocked up by felled timber, moved to the left to meet Hunter and encountered his advance north of the Warrenton Pike, sustaining his attack for some time, until overwhelming numbers were accumulated against him. Evans was being forced back when Bee, with the parts of his own and Bartow's brigades which had arrived, came to his assistance, and the advance of the enemy was stopped for some time until Heintzelman's division united with Hunter's and two of Tyler's brigades crossed over above Stone Bridge.

Bee and Evans, though fighting with great obstinacy, were forced back across the Warrenton Pike to a ridge south of it, and nearly at right angles with Bull Run. Here they were reinforced first by Hampton's six companies and then by Jackson's brigade, when a new line was formed and the fight renewed with great obstinacy. Subsequently two of Cocke's regiments were brought up, as also the seven companies of the 8th Virginia, under Colonel Hunter; the three companies of the 49th Virginia Regiment, under Colonel Smith; the 6th North Carolina Regiment, under Colonel Fisher; and two of

Bonham's regiments, under Colonel Kershaw; and engaged in the battle.

The fighting was very stubborn on the part of our troops, who were opposed to immense odds, and the fortunes of the day fluctuated for some time. From the beginning, artillery had been employed on both sides, and a number of our batteries did most excellent service. Colonel Stuart made a charge at one time with two companies of cavalry on the right of the enemy's line. At a most critical period three regiments of Elzey's brigade—which had arrived at the junction by the railroad and been promptly moved to the battlefield under the direction of Brigadier General E. Kirby Smith —came upon the field in rear of our line, and after General Smith had been wounded were moved to our left, under command of Colonel Elzey, just in time to meet and repulse a body of the enemy which had overlapped that flank. A short time afterwards, while the enemy was preparing for a last effort, my brigade arrived on the field, and operated on the left of Elzey's brigade just as the enemy began his attack.

He had been repulsed, not routed. When, however, the retreat began, it soon degenerated into a rout from the panic-stricken fears of the enemy's troops, who imagined that legions of cavalry were thundering at their heels, when really there were only a few companies acting without concert. Kershaw's two regiments with a battery of artillery moved in pursuit along the Warrenton Pike, and made some captures, but the mass of our troops on this part of the field were not in a condition to pursue at once. Ewell's and Holmes' brigades had been sent for from the right, when the day appeared doubtful, but the battle was won before they arrived, and they were ordered to return to their former positions.

D. R. Jones, in the afternoon, made an advance against the battery which I had been ordered to take in the morning, but was compelled to retire with loss. Bonham and Longstreet moved across the Run in the direction of Centreville just before night, but retired to their former positions on the approach of darkness. The enemy retreated in great disorder to Centreville, where he attempted to re-form his troops on the unbroken division and brigade that remained at that place, but shortly after dark he retreated with great precipitation, and by light next morning the greater part of his troops were either in the streets of Washington, or on the southern banks of the Potomac.

Twenty-seven pieces of artillery fell into our hands, some of which were captured on the field, but the greater part were abandoned on the road between the battlefield and Centreville. Besides the artillery, a considerable quantity of small arms, a number of wagons, ambulances, and some stores fell into our hands; and we captured about 1,500 prisoners. Our loss in killed and wounded was 1,852. The enemy's loss was much heavier, and is reported by McDowell.

I have thus given an outline of the battle as it took place, but I have not attempted to give the details of what the several commands did, for which reference must be had to the official reports.

There are several popular errors in regard to this battle, which have been widely circulated by the writings of those who have undertaken to describe it, and about which very few people indeed seem to be correctly informed.

Foremost among them is the opinion that General Johnston yielded the command to General Beauregard, and that the latter controlled the operations of our troops during the battle. This erroneous statement was so often and confidently made without contradiction, that I must confess for a long time I gave it some credence, though when I saw General Johnston on the field he appeared to be acting the part and performing the duties of a commanding general. Each of these generals is entitled to sufficient glory for the part taken in this battle in the performance of his appropriate duties, to render a contest among their friends for the chief glory idle as well as mischievous.

I cannot better explain the truth of the matter than by giving the following extract of a letter from General Johnston himself to me, which is in entire accordance with the facts coming within my knowledge on the field as far as they go, and will not be doubted by any one who knows General Johnston. He says: "General Beauregard's influence on that occasion was simply that due to my estimate of his military merit and knowledge of the situation. As soon as we met I expressed to him my determination to attack next morning, because it was not improbable that Patterson might come up Sunday night. He proposed a plan of attack which I accepted. It was defeated, however, by the appearance of Tyler's troops near the Stone Bridge soon after sunrise. He then proposed to stand on the defensive there and continue the offensive with the troops on the right of the road from Manassas to Centreville. This was frustrated by the movement which turned Cocke and Evans, and the battle fought was improvised on a field with which General Beauregard and myself were equally unacquainted. Early in the day I placed myself on the high bare hill you may remember a few hundred yards in rear of Mitchell's Ford, and General Beauregard soon joined me there. When convinced that the battle had begun on our left, I told him so, and that I was about to hasten to it. He followed. When we reached the field and he found that I was about to take immediate control of the two brigades engaged, he represented that it would be incompatible with the command of the army to do so, and urged that he should have the command in question. I accepted the argument. This, however, left him under me, and was the command of a small fraction of troops."

This places the matter in its true light and does not detract at all from the very great credit to which General Beauregard is entitled for thwarting the enemy's plans until the arrival of General Johnston, and for his able coöperation afterwards. But it is nevertheless true that General Johnston is entitled to the credit attached to the chief command in this, the first great battle of the war.

Another error in regard to the battle is the belief, almost universal, that Kirby Smith, hearing the roar of musketry and artillery while passing over the Manassas Gap Railroad, stopped the cars before reaching the Junction and moved directly for the battlefield, coming upon the rear of the enemy's right flank. This is entirely unfounded in fact. Smith's command consisted of Elzey's brigade, three regiments of which were in the battle, and they moved up from the Junction to the rear of our centre, under orders which General Smith found there on his arrival, and were subsequently moved by Elzey to meet the enemy's right after Smith was wounded. My brigade went to the left of Elzey, and I am able to say that none of our troops got to the enemy's rear, unless it may have been when Stuart made his charge. The reports of Generals Johnston and Beauregard as well as that of Colonel, afterwards Major General, Elzey, show the truth of the matter, and it is a little singular that those writers who have undertaken to describe this battle have taken the newspaper accounts as authentic without thinking of having recourse to the official reports.

Another erroneous statement in reference to the battle which has gone current, is that Holmes' brigade came up at a critical time and helped to save the day, when the fact is that that brigade was further from the field than any of our troops, and, though sent for in the afternoon, did not reach the battlefield at all, but its march was arrested by the close of the fight.

The concentration of Johnston's and Beauregard's forces against McDowell was a master stroke of strategy well executed, and our generals displayed great ability and energy in meeting and defeating the unexpected movement against our left. Claims were put forward in behalf of several commands for the credit of having saved the day and secured the victory.

It is rather surprising to observe that erroneous views often prevail in regard to the relative merits of different commands, engaged in bearing respectively very necessary parts in an action. If a small force has been fighting obstinately for hours against great odds, until it has become exhausted and is beginning to give way, and then fresh troops come up and turn the tide of battle, the latter are said to have gained the day and often reap all the glory. It is not likely to be considered, that, but for the troops whose obstinate fighting enabled the fresh ones to come up in time, the day would have been irretrievably lost before the appearance of the latter. It is an old saying that "It is the last feather that breaks the camel's back," yet the last feather would do no harm but for the weight which precedes it. The *first* feather contributes as much as the last to the catastrophe.

At this battle, but for the cavalry which watched the enemy's movements and gave timely notice to Evans so that he could move to the left and check the advance of Hunter, the day would probably have been lost at the outset. But for the prompt movement of Evans to the left and the obstinate fighting of his men, the enemy would have reached the range of hills on which our final line of battle was formed, thus turning our left completely and necessitating a rapid falling back from the line of Bull Run, which would most assuredly have resulted in defeat. This would likewise have been the case had not Bee arrived to the assistance of Evans when he did and stayed the progress of the enemy by his stubborn resistance.

When Bee and Evans were forced back across the Warrenton Pike, the day would have been lost had not Jackson arrived most opportunely and furnished them a barrier behind which to re-form. From the beginning our batteries rendered most essential service, and the infantry would probably have been overpowered but for their well directed fire. The arrivals of Cocke's two regiments, Hampton's Legion, the ten companies of the 7th and 49th Virginia Regiments, the 6th North Carolina and Bonham's two regiments all served to stem the tide of battle and stay defeat, but still in all probability the day would have been lost but for the timely appearance of Smith with Elzey's command and the subsequent movement of Elzey to our left.

I do not claim to have won or saved the day with my command, but I think it will be conceded by all who read the reports of Generals Johnston and Beauregard, that the arrival of that command and the cool and deliberate manner in which my men formed in line, under fire and in full view of the enemy, and their advance had a material effect in thwarting the last effort of the enemy to flank our line and in precipitating his retreat. I can bear testimony to the very efficient service rendered by Stuart with his two companies of cavalry, and Beckham's battery.

The fact is that all the troops engaged in the battle were necessary to prevent defeat and secure victory, and each command in its proper sphere may be said to have saved the day. It is very unjust to give all the credit or the greater part of it to any one command; and I would not exempt from the general commendation those troops on the right who held that part of the line, under fire, and prevented the enemy from getting to our rear and cutting off our communications.

It is not easy to account for McDowell's delay in making his attack, thereby permitting the concentration against him. So far as he is personally concerned, a ready excuse is to be found for him in the fact that he was inexperienced in command, having before that served in the field only in the capacity of a staff officer; but General Scott, an old and distinguished soldier, was in fact controlling the operations and was in constant communication by telegraph with McDowell, who had been his aide and was selected to carry out his plans. General Scott was in fact the commander and McDowell was merely his executive officer in the field. The former was the responsible man and to his name must be attached the discredit for the failure at Bull Run. Had McDowell's whole force been thrown against our centre on the day Tyler advanced on Blackburn's Ford, our line must have been broken and a defeat to us must have ensued, for at that time our troops were too few and too much scattered to have furnished sufficient resistance to the enemy's overwhelming force, or to have permitted an effective attack on his flanks. By delay this opportunity was lost and the two armies were concentrated against McDowell.

McDowell seems to have made an honest effort to conduct the campaign on the principles of civilized warfare, and expressed a very just indignation at the excesses committed by his troops. In a dispatch from Fairfax Court-House, dated the 18th of July, he said: "I am distressed to have to report excesses by our troops. The excitement of the men found vent in burning and pillaging, which, however, was soon checked. It distressed us all greatly." On the same day he issued an order from which I make the following extract:

"Any persons found committing the slightest depredation, killing pigs or poultry or trespassing on the property of the inhabitants, will be reported to the then headquarters, and the least that will be done to them will be to send them to the Alexandria jail. It is again ordered that no one shall arrest or attempt to arrest any citizen not in arms at the time, or search or attempt to search any house, or even enter the same without permission. The troops must behave themselves with as much forbearance and propriety as if they were at their own homes. They are here to fight the enemies of the country, not to judge and punish the unarmed and helpless, however guilty they may be. When necessary, that will be done by the proper person.

"By command of General McDowell.

"Jas. B. Fry, Assistant Adjutant General."

This order deserves to be exhumed from the oblivion into which it seems to have fallen, and is in strong contrast with the subsequent practice under Butler, Pope, Milroy, Hunter, Sheridan, Sherman, etc. This war order of McDowell's might well have been commended to the consideration of military satraps set to rule over the people of the South in a time of "peace." It did not prevent the burning of the entire village of Germantown, a few miles from Fairfax Court-House, but the citizens agreed that McDowell had made an honest effort to prevent depredations by his troops; and it gives me pleasure to make the statement, as it is the last time I will have occasion to make a similar one in regard to any of the Federal commanders who followed him.

Pursuit of the enemy was not made after the battle in order to capture Washington or cross the Potomac, and as this omission has been the subject of much comment and criticism, I will make some observations on that head.

In the first place, it must be borne in mind that our generals were inexperienced in command.

In the next place, it must be conceded that a commanding general knows more about the condition of his troops and the obstacles in his way than any other can know; and for very obvious reasons he is debarred from making public at the time the reasons and conditions which govern his course.

It must also be considered that he cannot know beforehand as much as the critics who form their judgment from the light of after events. Those, therefore, who ascertained some days after the battle what was the actual condition of McDowell's army on the retreat, must recollect that this was not known to General Johnston until that army was safe from pursuit, even if it had been practicable to accomplish any more than was done with our army in its then condition.

Without having been in General Johnston's confidence, or professing to know more about the motives actuating him at the time than he has thought proper to make public, I will undertake to show that it was utterly impossible for any army to have captured Washington by immediate pursuit, even if it had been in condition to make such pursuit, and that it would have been very difficult to cross the Potomac at all.

In the first place, I will say that the army was not in condition to make pursuit on the afternoon of the 21st after the battle, or that night. All the troops engaged, except Cocke's regiment, the 19th Virginia, the two regiments with Kershaw, and my command, were so much exhausted and shattered by the desperate conflict in which they had participated, that they made no attempt at pursuit and were incapable of any.

Our cavalry consisted of one organized regiment of nine companies, and a number of unattached companies. This cavalry was armed principally with shot guns and very inferior sabres, and was without the discipline and drill necessary to make that arm effective in a charge. Moreover it had been necessarily scattered on the flanks and along the line, to watch the enemy and give information of his movements. It could not readily be concentrated for the purpose of an efficient pursuit, and the attempts made in that direction were desultory.

By light on the morning of the 22nd, the greater part of the enemy's troops were either in the streets of Washington or under the protection of the guns at Arlington Heights.

The question then arises whether, by pursuit on the morning of the 22nd, Washington could have been captured. And I will here call attention to some facts which seem entirely to have escaped the attention of the critics. The Potomac is at least a mile wide at Washington and navigable to that place for the largest vessels. The only means of crossing the river, except in vessels, are by the Long Bridge, the aqueduct on the Chesapeake & Ohio Canal at Georgetown, and the chain bridge above Georgetown.

The Long Bridge is an old wooden structure with at least one draw and perhaps two in it, and could have been easily destroyed by fire, besides being susceptible of being commanded through its entire length by vessels of war lying near Washington, where there were some out of range of any guns we would have brought to bear.

The aqueduct is long and narrow with a channel for the water, which we could not have turned off as it runs from the northern side of the Potomac, and a narrow towpath on the side. One piece of artillery at its northern end could have effectually prevented the passing of troops over it, and besides it could have been easily ruined and some of the spans blown up, so as to render it impassable.

The chain bridge is a wooden structure and could have been easily burned. If therefore the entire Federal Army had fled across the river on our approach, we could not have crossed it near Washington. The largest pieces of artillery we had, capable of being transported, were small field pieces of which the heaviest for solid shot were six pounders, and we had no Howitzer larger than a twenty-four pounder if we had any of that size. None of our guns were of sufficient range to reach across the river into the city. If, therefore, we had advanced at once upon Washington and the Federal Army had fled across the river on our approach, abandoning the city itself, still we could not have entered it, unless the bridges had been left intact; and it is not to be supposed that McDowell, General Scott, and all the officers of the regular army, were so badly frightened and demoralized that they would have fled on our approach, and omitted to destroy the approaches to the city, even if such had been the case with the volunteers, the civil authorities, and the Congress.

All the bridges above, to and beyond Harper's Ferry, had been burned, and the nearest ford to Washington, over which at low water it is possible for infantry to pass, is White's Ford, several miles above Leesburg, and forty miles from Washington. This was then an obscure ford, where, in 1862, General Jackson had to have the banks dug down before our wagons and artillery could cross, and then the canal on the northern bank had to be bridged. We had nothing in the shape of pontoons, and it would have been impossible to have obtained them in any reasonable time.

I had occasion, in 1864, to make myself acquainted with the character of the Potomac and its crossing at and above Washington, and what I state here is not mere speculation. General Johnston had resided in Washington for several years, and must be supposed to have been acquainted with the difficulties.

I have heard some wiseacres remark that if we had gone on, we could have entered *pell-mell* with the enemy into Washington. To have done that, if possible, we would have had to keep up with the enemy, and I don't think any one supposes that a solitary soldier in our army could have reached the banks of the Potomac by daylight the morning after the battle. It is possible to cross a bridge of a few yards in length, or enter through the gates of a city pell-mell with an army, but no one ever heard of that thing being done on a bridge more than a mile in length and with a draw raised in the middle.

The truth is that, while the enemy's retreat was very disorderly and disgraceful, some of his troops retained their organization and the condition of things at Washington was not quite as bad as represented. Spectators in the city, seeing the condition of the fugitives thronging the streets, and the panic of the civilians, may have well supposed that the whole army was disorganized, and so utterly demoralized that it would have fled on the very first cry that the "rebels are coming," but if General McDowell and his officers are to be believed, there still remained on the southern bank of the Potomac a considerable force in fighting condition. Miles' division had not been engaged and Runyon's had not reached Centreville when the battle took place. Besides a considerable force had been retained in Washington under Mansfield.

McClellan states in his report, that, when he assumed command on the 27th of July, the infantry in and around Washington numbered 50,000, and this was much larger than our whole force was after the reinforcements had reached us subsequent to the battle. The strength of our army at this time, as well as on all other occasions, has been greatly exaggerated even by Southern writers; its organization was very imperfect, many of the troops not being brigaded.

If we had advanced, Alexandria would probably have fallen into our hands without a struggle, and we might have forced the enemy to evacuate his works south of the Potomac, but very likely not until after a fight in which our loss would have been greater than the object to be accomplished would have justified. We might have transferred our line to the banks of the Potomac, but we could not have held it, and would eventually have been compelled to abandon it with greater damage to us than the evacuation of the line of Bull Run caused.

So much for the question as between the commanding general and the cavillers. But there is another phase of it, in which a staff officer of General Beauregard, writing for a Northern journal, has endeavored to raise an issue between that general and the Government at Richmond. I have before shown that General Johnston, as commander of the army, was the responsible person, and I believe he has never attempted to evade the responsibility. General Beauregard's agency in the matter could only be as an adviser and lieutenant of the commanding general.

DETAILS OF THE BATTLE OF MANASSAS

The point made against the Government is that Washington could and would have been taken, if the President, Secretary of War, and the heads of the Quarter-master and Commissary Departments had furnished sufficient transportation and supplies, though it is admitted that Mr. Davis left the question of an advance entirely to his generals.

Now in regard to transportation, we had an abundance of wagons to carry all the ammunition needed, and for gathering in provisions, and if the bridges on the railroad had not been burned, we might have moved our depot to Alexandria as we moved, provided we could have advanced to that point, as the enemy had repaired the railroad to Fairfax Station, and had not interfered with it on his retreat. The burning of the bridges on the railroad did not impede the progress of the enemy before the battle, as he did not march on it and Bull Run was fordable anywhere. That burning could only have served the purpose of obstructing the use of the railroad by the enemy in the event of our defeat, which with his means of reconstruction would have been but a very few days, and it did not obstruct our movements for a much longer time. At the time of the battle, the county of Loudoun on the Virginia side of the Potomac, and the whole State of Maryland, were teeming with supplies, and we could have readily procured all the transportation needed from the citizens, if we had not taken it from the enemy, which would probably have been the case if an advance had been practicable otherwise.

Certain it is, that in 1862, after the second battle of Manassas, when the enemy's army had been defeated, not routed, and was still vastly superior in number and equipment to our own, we did not hesitate a moment about supplies, though our army was without rations and Fairfax and Loudoun had been nearly exhausted of their grain and cattle; but taking only transportation for the ammunition and the cooking utensils, and sending the rest of our trains to the valley, except wagons to gather up flour, we marched across the Potomac into Maryland, our men and officers living principally on green corn and beef without salt or bread. Neither was our army prevented from making the movement into Pennsylvania, in 1863, for fear of not getting provisions. We depended upon taking them from the enemy and the country through which we marched, and did thus procure them. The alleged difficulties in 1861 would have been no difficulties in 1862, 1863, or 1864. These were not the real difficulties which prevented the capture of Washington after the battle of the 21st of July, and the issue which is attempted to be made with the Government at Richmond is therefore an idle one.

These remarks are not made with the slightest purpose of disparaging in any way General Beauregard, for whom I have great regard and admiration. When he ordered the burning of the bridge over Bull Run, he had reason to apprehend that his comparatively small force would have to encounter McDowell's whole army before any reinforcements arrived to his assistance, and he had therefore good grounds to regard this as a precaution which the circumstances warranted and demanded.

The foregoing reflections and comments are such as my subsequent experience and observation have enabled me to make, and I do not pretend that a tittle of them occurred to me at the time.

Both of our generals, notwithstanding their inexperience in command, displayed extraordinary energy and capacity in thwarting the plans of a veteran commander, whom the country at that time regarded as one of the ablest military chieftains of the age. If they did not accomplish all that might have been accomplished by an experienced and skilful commander, with an army of veterans, they are not therefore to be condemned; but it is equally unjust to attempt to shift the responsibility to the shoulders of the Government at Richmond.

CHAPTER V.

Operations along Bull Run.

Immediately after the battle of the 21st a portion of our troops were moved across Bull Run and the former line north of that stream was re-occupied. The army at that time was known as the "Army of the Potomac," and General Beauregard's command was reorganized as the 1st corps of that army, with the same brigade commanders as before. I was promoted to the rank of brigadier general to date from the 21st of July, and was assigned to the command of a brigade composed of the 24th Virginia Regiment, the 5th North Carolina State Troops, Colonel Duncan K. McRae, and the 13th North Carolina Volunteers (subsequently designated the 23rd North Carolina Regiment), Colonel John Hoke. The greater part of the army was moved to the north of Bull Run, but I resumed my position on the right of the Junction at my former camps, and remained there until the latter part of August, when I moved to the north of the Occoquon, in front of Wolf Run Shoals, below the mouth of Bull Run. Our line was extended from this point by Langster's cross-roads and Fairfax Station through Fairfax Court-House. Hampton's Legion was composed of a battalion of infantry, a battalion of cavalry, and a battery of artillery, and remained south of the Occoquon on the right, and watched the lower fords of that stream and the landings on the Potomac immediately below Occoquon. Evans had occupied Leesburg.

Captain W. W. Thornton's company of cavalry had been again attached to my command and subsequently, in the month of September, a battery of Virginia artillery under Captain Holman reported to me. In the latter part of August, General Longstreet, who had command of the advanced forces at Fairfax Court-House, threw forward a small force of infantry and cavalry and established strong pickets at Mason's and Munson's Hills, in close proximity to the enemy's main line on the south of the Potomac.

McClellan had succeeded McDowell, in command of the Federal Army opposed to us, and that army was being greatly augmented by new levies.

A few days after I reached my camp in front of Wolf Run Shoals, my brigade was ordered to Fairfax Station, for the purpose of supporting Longstreet, if necessary. After being there a day, I was ordered by General Longstreet to move with two of my regiments to Mason's Hill, to relieve one of his on duty at that place. I took with me the 24th Virginia and 5th North Carolina Regiments, and my movement was so timed as to reach Mason's Hill in the night. I arrived there before light on the morning of the 31st of August, and relieved the 17th Regiment, Colonel Corse. About light on that morning, one of Colonel Corse's companies, which was on picket one mile from the main force in the direction of Alexandria, was attacked by a detachment from a New Jersey regiment, under its colonel, and after a very sharp fight, repulsed the enemy and inflicted a severe punishment on him.

This advanced line at Mason's and Munson's Hills was about twelve or fifteen miles in front of Fairfax Court-House, and was a mere picket line held ordinarily by two infantry regiments with a few pieces of artillery, while a small force of cavalry watched the flanks. From it there were in full view the dome of the Capitol at Washington and a part of the enemy's line on the heights south and west of Alexandria. The two main positions were in sight of each other and about a mile apart. From them smaller pickets were thrown out in front and up to within a very short distance of large bodies of the enemy, those from Mason's Hill being in some cases more than a mile from the main body. The pickets were constantly skirmishing with those of the enemy, and it was very evident that he was much alarmed at this demonstration in his immediate front, as Professor Lowe, who now made his appearance with his balloons, kept one of them up almost constantly, and large parties were seen working very energetically at the line of fortifications in our front. Contemporaneous accounts given by the enemy represent this movement on our part as a very serious one, and he was evidently impressed with the idea that the greater part of our army was immediately confronting him, whereas, if it had not been for his excessive caution and want of enterprise, he might have moved out and captured the whole of our advance force without the possibility of its escape.

After my pickets had relieved those of Corse, it was reported to me that a flag of truce had appeared at the outside picket, where the fight had taken place in the early morning, and I rode to a house in the vicinity of that point and had the person bearing the flag brought to me blindfolded. He proved to be a Dr. Coxe, surgeon of the New Jersey regiment, a detachment of which had been engaged in the above named affair. He stated that he came on the part of Colonel Tyler of the 3rd New Jersey to get the bodies of several men who were missing, and that he was informed that General Kearney, who commanded on that part of the line, had directed Colonel Tyler to send the party with the flag.

I informed him of the irregularity of the proceeding, but after some conversation in which I endeavored to leave him under the impression that we had a large force in the vicinity, I gave him permission to carry off the dead bodies, two of which he had picked up outside of my picket, and two others having been brought in to the picket before his arrival. We remained at Mason's Hill three or four days, and I was then relieved by Colonel Smith in command of the 20th Georgia Regiment. My pickets had been constantly skirmishing with small parties of the enemy, and there had been one or two false alarms of an approach against us, but the enemy made no serious demonstration. This advanced line of pickets was subsequently abandoned, after having been maintained for several weeks, but I did not again return to it.

After leaving Mason's Hill, I moved back to my camp in front of Wolf Run Shoals, again occupying the right of our line. I remained on this flank until the fore part of October, and my regiments picketed at Springfield on the line of the railroad, alternating with those of Ewell's brigade at Langster's cross-roads. On the 4th of October Major General Earl Van Dorn joined our army and was assigned to the command of a division composed of Ewell's brigade and mine. This was the first division organized in the "Army of the Potomac" (Confederate) and I think in the entire Confederate army. In a day or two afterwards my brigade was moved to a position between Fairfax Station and Fairfax Court-House, and remained there until the army was moved back to the line which it occupied for the winter, my regiment picketing at Burke's Station on the railroad in the meantime.

Soon after the organization of the division, Captain Green's company of cavalry, for which Thornton's had been exchanged, was relieved from duty with me and attached to General Van Dorn's headquarters. On the 7th of October, the 20th Georgia Regiment, Colonel W. D. Smith, was attached to my brigade, and joined me in a day or two thereafter. On the 15th of October the whole of our army moved back from the line passing through Fairfax Court-House to me, extending from Union Mills on the right, through Centreville, to Stone Bridge on the left. At the new position Van Dorn's division was on the right, with Ewell's brigade at Union Mills and mine on its left above that point. We proceeded at once to fortify the whole line from right to left.

McClellan's report shows that the troops under his

command in and about Washington, including those on the Maryland shore of the Potomac above and below Washington and the troops with Dix at Baltimore, on the 15th day of October, the day before our retrograde movement, amounted to 133,201 present for duty, and an aggregate present of 143,647. The mass of this force was south of the Potomac, and nearly the whole of it available for an advance. The whole force under General Johnston's command did not exceed one-third of McClellan's, though the latter has estimated our force "on the Potomac" in the month of October at not less than 150,000.

After the occupation of the line at Centreville, the infantry of our army at and near that place was organized into four divisions of three brigades each and two corps. Bonham's brigade was attached to Van Dorn's division, and the command of the other divisions was given to Major Generals G. W. Smith, Longstreet, and E. Kirby Smith, respectively. Van Dorn's and Longstreet's divisions constituted the first corps under General Beauregard, and the other two divisions constituted the second corps under the temporary command of Major General G. W. Smith.

About the same time, General Jackson, with the rank of Major General, was sent to the valley with his old brigade, and the 22nd of October an order was issued from the Adjutant General's office at Richmond, establishing the Department of Northern Virginia, composed of the Valley district, the Potomac district, and the Aquia district, under the command of General Johnston; the districts being assigned to the command of Major General Jackson, General Beauregard, and Major General Holmes, in the order in which they are named. Colonel Robert E. Rodes of the 5th Alabama Regiment had been made brigadier general and assigned to the command of Ewell's brigade, Ewell being temporarily assigned to a brigade in Longstreet's division, and subsequently made major general and transferred to the command of E. K. Smith's division, when the latter officer was sent to Tennessee.

The affair of Evans' command with the enemy at Ball's Bluff occurred on the 21st of October, and Stuart's affair with the enemy at Drainesville occurred on the 20th of December. These are the only conflicts of the "Army of the Potomac" with the enemy of any consequence, during the fall and winter, after the occupation of the line of Centreville. Our front was covered by a line of pickets some distance in front, extending from left to right, and all under command of Brigadier General J. E. B. Stuart of the cavalry, who was especially assigned to that duty, details by regiments being made from the infantry to report to him.

Rodes' brigade was moved to the south of Bull Run to go into winter quarters, leaving my brigade on the right of our line, which was now contracted so as to merely cover McLean's Ford on that flank. About the middle of January, 1862, Major General Van Dorn was relieved from duty with the "Army of the Potomac" and ordered to the Trans-Mississippi Department, General Bonham succeeding to the command of the division as senior brigadier general. On the 30th of January, General Beauregard took leave of the "Army of the Potomac," he having been ordered to Kentucky; and after this time there was no distinction of corps in the "Army of the Potomac," but all division commanders reported directly to General Johnston.

After the 1st of February General Bonham relinquished the command of the division, having resigned his commission to take his seat in Congress, and I succeeded to the command of the division as next in rank —Colonel Kershaw, who was appointed brigadier general, succeeding Bonham in the command of his brigade. My brigade had gone into temporary winter quarters at the point to which it had moved, when we fell back from the line of Fairfax Court-House for the purpose of continuing the construction of the works on our right, which were rendered necessary by the change in the line before mentioned; and it was engaged in building new winter quarters south of Bull Run, and completing the earthworks covering McLean's Ford when the line of Bull Run was abandoned.

About two weeks before the evacuation took place, division commanders were confidentially informed of the probability of that event, and ordered to prepare their commands for it in a quiet way. Up to that time there had been no apparent preparation for such a movement, but an immense amount of stores of all kinds and private baggage of officers and men had been permitted to accumulate. Preparations, however, were commenced at once for sending the stores and baggage to the rear. Owing to the fact that our army had remained stationary so long, and the inexperience in campaigning of our troops, there had been a vast accumulation of private baggage by both officers and men; and when it became necessary to change a camp it was the work of two or three days. I had endeavored to inculcate proper ideas on this subject into the minds of the officers of my own immediate command, but with very indifferent success, and it was very provoking to see with what tenacity young lieutenants held on to baggage enough to answer all their purposes at a fashionable watering place in time of peace.

After the confidential instructions for the evacuation were given, I tried to persuade all my officers to send all their baggage not capable of being easily transported and for which they did not have immediate necessary use, on the railroad to some place in the rear out of all danger, but the most that I could accomplish was to get them to send it to Manassas Junction. This was generally the case with the whole army, and the consequence was that a vast amount of trunks and other private baggage was accumulated at the Junction at the last moment, for which it was impossible to find any transportation. This evil, however, was finally and completely remedied by the burning which took place when the Junction itself was evacuated, and we never had any great reason subsequently to complain of a plethoric condition of the baggage.

Besides this trouble in regard to private baggage, there was another which incommoded us to some extent, and that resulted from the presence of the wives of a number of officers in and near camp. These would listen to no mild appeals or gentle remonstrances, but held on with a pertinacity worthy of a better cause, and I was myself compelled, as a final resort, to issue a peremptory order for some of them to leave my camp.

The order was finally given for the movement to the rear on the 8th of March and early on that morning I broke up my camps and moved with my brigade and that of Kershaw towards the Junction. We were delayed, however, waiting for the movement of the other troops, and did not arrive at the Junction until in the afternoon. A portion of Ewell's division was to move in front of us along the railroad, while the remainder of it, with Rodes' brigade, was to move on a road east of the railroad. Our wagon trains had been previously sent forward on the roads west of the railroad. We waited at the Junction until the troops that were to precede us had passed on, and the last of the trains of cars could be gotten off. Finally at a late hour of the night after the last available train of cars had left, we moved along the railroad past Bristow Station, and bivouacked for the night, my brigade bringing up the rear of our infantry on that route.

A very large amount of stores and provisions had been abandoned for want of transportation, and among the stores was a quantity of clothing, blankets, etc., which had been provided by the States south of Virginia for their own troops. The pile of trunks along the railroad was appalling to behold. All these stores, clothing, trunks, etc., were consigned to the flames by a portion of our cavalry left to carry out the work of their destruction.

OPERATIONS ALONG BULL RUN

The loss of stores at this point, and at White Plains, on the Manassas Gap Railroad, where a large amount of meat had been salted and stored, was a very serious one to us, and embarrassed us for the remainder of the war, as it put us at once on a running stock.

The movement back from the line of Bull Run was in itself a very wise one in a strategic point of view, if it was not one of absolute necessity, but the loss of stores was very much to be regretted. I do not pretend to attach censure to any one of our officials for this loss, especially not to General Johnston. I know that he was exceedingly anxious to get off all the stores, and made extraordinary exertions to accomplish that object. My own opinion was that the failure to carry them off was mainly owing to inefficient management by the railroad officials, as I always found their movements slow and little to be depended on, beginning with the transportation of the troops sent by me from Lynchburg in May and June, 1861.

McClellan in his report assumes that the evacuation of the line of Bull Run, was in consequence of his projected movement to the Peninsula having become known to the Confederate commander, but such was not the fact. Our withdrawal from that line was owing to the fact that our force was too small to enable us to hold so long a line against the immense force which it was known had been concentrated at and near Washington. McClellan's statement of his own force shows that his troops, including those in Maryland and Delaware, numbered on the 1st of January, 1862, 191,840 for duty; on the 1st of February, 190,806 for duty; and on the 1st of March, 193,142 for duty. Of this force he carried into the field in his campaign in the Peninsula considerably over 100,000 men, after having left over 40,000 men to protect Washington. He could have thrown against General Johnston's army, at and near Manassas, a force of more than four times the strength of that army. I have before stated that Johnston's army was composed of four divisions of infantry besides the cavalry and artillery.

The division commanded by me was fully an average one, and that division, including three batteries of artillery and a company of cavalry attached to it, as shown by my field returns now before me, numbered on the 1st of February, 1862, 6,965 effective total present, and an aggregate present of 8,703; and on the 1st of March, 5,775 effective total present, and an aggregate present of 7,154. At both periods a very large number present were on the sick list. The aggregate present and absent on the 1st of March amounted to 10,008, there being at that time twenty-four officers and 962 enlisted men absent sick and 61 officers and 1,442 enlisted men absent on furlough—the rest of the absentees being on detached service and without leave. This will give a very good idea of General Johnston's entire strength, and will show the immense superiority of the enemy's force to his.

The evacuation of Manassas and the line of Bull Run was therefore a movement rendered absolutely necessary by the inability of our army to cope with the enemy's so near to his base, and had been delayed fully as long as it was prudent to do so.

Moving back over the routes designated, Ewell's division and mine crossed the Rappahannock on the 10th of March and took position on the south bank. We remained there several days, when my division was moved to the Rapidan and crossed over to the south bank, Ewell being left to guard the crossing of the Rappahannock. G. W. Smith's and Longstreet's divisions had moved by the roads west of the railroad, and were concentrated near Orange Court-House.

I remained near the Rapidan until the 4th of April, when I received orders to move up to Orange Court-House to take the cars for Richmond and report to General Lee, who was then entrusted with the general direction of military operations, under the President. I

marched to the court-house next day, but found difficulty in getting cars enough to transport my division.
Rodes was first sent off, then Kershaw, and my own
brigade was finally put on board on the 7th. Going
with the rear of this last brigade, I reached Richmond
on the morning of the 8th of April, after much delay
on the road, and found that Rodes and Kershaw had
been sent to General Magruder on the Peninsula, to
which point I was also ordered with my own brigade,
part going by the way of York River, and the rest by
the way of James River in vessels towed by tugs. My
trains and artillery moved by land from Orange Court-
House.

CHAPTER VI.

Manœuvring on the Peninsula.

I LANDED and reported to General Magruder on the morning of the 9th of April.

After the abandonment of the line of Bull Run by our troops, McClellan had moved the greater part of his army to the Peninsula, and by the 4th of April had landed about 100,000 men at or near Fortress Monroe. Magruder at that time occupied the lower Peninsula with a force which did not exceed in effective men 7,000 or 8,000. Upon this force McClellan advanced with his immense army, when Magruder fell back to the line of Warwick River, extending from Yorktown on York River across James River, and checked the enemy's advance. McClellan then sat down before the fortifications at Yorktown and along Warwick River and began a siege by regular approaches.

When I arrived at Magruder's headquarters, I was informed by him that his force, before the arrival of mine, amounted to 12,000, he having been reinforced since the enemy's advance, by troops from the south side of James River and Wilcox's brigade of G. W. Smith's (now D. R. Jones') division, the said brigade having been detached from the army under Johnston. The division carried by me now numbered about 8,000 men and officers for duty, it having been increased to that amount by the return of those on furlough and some recruits; so that Magruder's force now amounted to 20,000 men and officers for duty. McClellan, in a telegram to President Lincoln, dated the 7th of April, says: "Your telegram of yesterday received. In reply I have to state that my entire force for duty amounts to only about eighty-five thousand men." At that time, except Wilcox's brigade, not a soldier from General Johnston's army had arrived, and my division constituted the next reinforcement received from that army by Magruder.

Yorktown had been previously strongly fortified, and some preparations had been made to strengthen the other part of the line, which, however, had not been completed. Warwick River runs diagonally across the Peninsula from the vicinity of Yorktown, and its course for the greater part of the way is through low, marshy country. Though at its head it is quite a small stream, it had been dammed up to within about a mile of the works at Yorktown by dams thrown across at several points, so as to be impassable without bridging at any other points than where the dams were, which later we defended with earthworks.

Between Warwick River and Yorktown were two redoubts, called respectively Redoubt No. 4 and Redoubt No. 5, which were connected by a curtain, with wings or lateral breastworks extending to Warwick River on the one side, and the head of a deep ravine between Redoubt No. 4 and Yorktown on the other. Redoubt No. 4, which was the one nearest Yorktown, was sometimes called Fort Magruder. Gloucester Point, across York River from Yorktown, was occupied by a small infantry force with some heavy batteries. The whole line was nearly fifteen miles in length. The assuming and maintaining the line by Magruder, with his small force in the face of such overwhelming odds, was one of the boldest exploits ever performed by a military commander, and he had so manœuvred his troops, by displaying them rapidly at different points, as to produce the impression on his opponent that he had a large army. His men and a considerable body of negro laborers had been and were still engaged in strengthening the works by working night and day, so that their energies were taxed to the utmost limit.

Before my arrival, Kershaw's brigade had been ordered to the right of the line and assigned to that part of it under the command of Brigadier General

McLaws, and Rodes' brigade had been posted at the works between the defences of Yorktown and the head of the obstructions on Warwick River. On my arrival I was ordered to move my own brigade near the point occupied by Rodes, and I was assigned to the command of that part of the line extending from the ravine south of Yorktown to the right of Wynn's Mill as far as the mouth of the branch leading into the pond made by Dam No. 1, which was the first dam below that at Wynn's Mill. There were two dams on the line thus assigned me, the dam at Wynn's Mill, etc. The troops defending the part of the line thus assigned me consisted of Rodes' brigade; my own, now under the command of Colonel D. K. McRae, of the 5th North Carolina Regiment; the 2nd Florida Regiment, Colonel Ward; the 2nd Mississippi Battalion, Lieutenant Colonel Taylor; Brigadier General Wilcox's brigade; and two regiments temporarily attached to his command under Colonel Winston of Alabama; and the 19th Mississippi Regiment, Colonel Mott. The latter regiment was, however, transferred to another part of the line in a few days.

The only portions of my line exposed to the view of the enemy were Redoubts Nos. 4 and 5 and the works attached to them, the works at Wynn's Mill and part of a small work at the upper dam of Wynn's Mill— the works at Wynn's Mill and the upper dam with the intervening space being occupied by Wilcox's command. Between the works designated, including Dam No. 1, the swamps on both sides of Warwick River were thickly wooded, and it would have been impossible to cross without cutting away the dams, which could not have been done without first driving away our troops. This was also the case below Dam No. 1 to a greater or less extent. Redoubts Nos. 4 and 5 with the curtain and lateral works had been from necessity constructed on ground sloping towards the enemy, and the interior and rear of them were therefore much exposed to his fire. This was also the case at Wynn's Mill, and at both points it had been necessary to cut zig-zag trenches, or bayous, to enable the men to pass into and from the works with as little exposure as possible.

Our side of the Warwick River, between the exposed points, was occupied by thin picket lines. Besides the infantry mentioned, there were several batteries of field artillery in the works, and in Redoubt No. 4 there were two heavy guns and a large Howitzer. Brigadier General Raines had charge of the immediate defences of Yorktown and Gloucester Point.

When I took command I found the enemy busily engaged in constructing trenches and earthworks in front of Redoubts 4 and 5 and of Wynn's Mill. In front of Redoubt No. 5 was a dwelling house, with several out-houses and a large peach orchard extending to within a few hundred yards of our works, under cover of which the enemy pushed forward some sharp-shooters, with long-range rifles, and established a line of rifle pits within range of our works, which annoyed us very much for several days, as nearly our whole armament for the infantry consisted of smooth-bore muskets, and our artillery ammunition was too scarce to permit its use in a contest with sharp-shooters. On the 11th of April General Magruder ordered sorties to be made by small parties from all the main parts of the line for the purpose of fooling the enemy. Wilcox sent out a party from Wynn's Mill which encountered the skirmishers the enemy had thrown up towards his front, and drove them back to the main line.

Later in the day Colonel Ward, with his own regiment and the 2nd Mississippi Battalion, was thrown to the front on the right and left of Redoubt No. 5, driving the enemy's sharp-shooters from their rifle pits, advancing through the peach orchard to the main road beyond, from Warwick Court-House and Fortress Monroe, so as to compel a battery, which the enemy had posted at an earthwork on our left of said road, to retire precipitately. Colonel Ward, however, returned to our

61

works on the approach of a large force of the enemy's infantry, after having set fire to the house above mentioned and performed the duty assigned him in a very gallant and dashing manner without loss to his command. These affairs developed the fact that the enemy was in strong force both in front of Wynn's Mill and Redoubts 4 and 5.

On the night following Ward's sortie, the 24th Virginia Regiment, under Colonel Terry, moved to the front, and cut down the peach orchard and burned the rest of the houses which had afforded the enemy shelter; and on the next night Colonel McRae, with the 5th North Carolina Regiment, moved further to the front and cut down some cedars along the main road above mentioned, which partially screened the enemy's movements from our observation, both of which feats were accomplished without difficulty or loss; and after this we were not annoyed again by the enemy's sharpshooters. About this time Major General D. H. Hill arrived at Yorktown with two brigades from General Johnston's army, and was assigned to the command of the left wing, embracing Raines' command and mine. No change, however, was made in the extent of my command, but I was merely made subordinate to General Hill.

The enemy continued to work very busily on his approaches, and each day some new work was developed. He occasionally fired with artillery on our works, and the working parties engaged in strengthening them and making traverses and epaulments in the rear, but we very rarely replied to him, as our supply of ammunition was very limited.

During the month of April there was much cold, rainy weather, and our troops suffered greatly, as they were without tents or other shelter. Their duties were very severe and exhausting, as when they were not on the front line in the trenches they were employed in constructing heavy traverses and epaulments in the rear of the main line, so as to conceal and protect the approaches to it. In addition to all this, their rations were very limited and consisted of the plainest and roughest food. Coffee was out of the question, as were vegetables and fresh meat. All this told terribly on the health of the men, and there were little or no hospital accommodations in the rear.

In a day or two after General Hill's arrival, Colston's brigade reported to me and occupied a position between the upper dam of Wynn's Mill and Redoubt No. 5. On the 16th the enemy made a dash at Dam No. 1 on my right and succeeded in crossing the dam and entering the work covering it, but was soon repulsed and driven across the river with some loss. This was not within the limits of my command, but a portion of my troops were moved in the direction of the point attacked without, however, being needed. By the 18th, the residue of General Johnston's troops east of the Blue Ridge, except Ewell's division and a portion of the cavalry which had been left on the Rappahannock and a small force left at Fredericksburg, had reached the vicinity of Yorktown, and on that day General Johnston, having assumed the command, issued an order assigning Magruder to the command of the right wing, beginning at Dam No. 1 and extending to James River; D. H. Hill to the command of the left wing, including Yorktown, and Redoubts 4 and 5, and their appertinent defences; Longstreet to the command of the centre, which extended from Dam No. 1 to the right of the lateral defences of Redoubt No. 5; and G. W. Smith to the command of the reserve.

This order, as a necessary consequence, curtailed my command, which was now confined to Redoubts Nos. 4 and 5 and the works adjacent thereto, and they were defended by Rodes' and my brigades, and the 2nd Florida Regiment, 2nd Mississippi Battalion, and 49th Virginia Regiment, the latter regiment having been lately assigned to me for the defence of the head of the ravine south of Yorktown. Shortly afterwards General Hill made a new arrangement of the command, by which Rodes' brigade was separated from mine and General Rodes was assigned to the charge of Redoubt No. 5 and the defences on its right, while I was assigned to the charge of Redoubt No. 4 and the defences on the right and left of it, including the curtain connecting the two redoubts.

The enemy continued to advance his works, and it was while we were thus confronting him and in constant expectation of an assault, that the reorganization of the greater part of the regiments of our army, under the Conscript Act recently passed by Congress, took place. Congress had been tampering for some time with the question of reorganizing the army and supplying the place of the twelve months' volunteers, which composed much the greater part of our army; and several schemes had been started and adopted with little or no success and much damage to the army itself, until finally it was found necessary to adopt a general conscription. If this scheme had been adopted in the beginning, it would have readily been acquiesced in, but when it was adopted much dissatisfaction was created by the fact that it necessarily violated promises and engagements made with those who had re-enlisted under some of the former schemes. The reorganization which took place resulted in a very great change in the officers, especially among the field-officers, all of whom were appointed by election, and as may well be supposed this state of things added nothing to the efficiency of the army or its morals.

In the meantime the enemy's army had been greatly augmented by reinforcements, and by the last of April his approaches in our front had assumed very formidable appearances. McClellan, in his report, states the strength of his army as follows: present for duty, April 30, 1862, 4,725 officers, and 104,610 men, making 109,335 aggregate present for duty, and 115,350 aggregate present. This was exclusive of Wool's troops at Fortress

Monroe. General Johnston's whole force, including Magruder's force in it, could not have exceeded 50,000 men and officers for duty, if it reached that number, and my own impression, from data within my knowledge, is that it was considerably below that figure.

After dark on the night of Thursday the 1st of May, General Hill informed his subordinate commanders that the line of Warwick River and Yorktown was to be abandoned, according to a determination that day made, upon a consultation of the principal officers at General Johnston's headquarters; and we were ordered to get ready to evacuate immediately after dark on the following night, after having previously sent off all the trains. This measure was one of absolute necessity, and the only wonder to me was that it had not been previously resorted to.

The line occupied by us was so long and our troops had to be so much scattered to occupy the whole of it, that no point could be sufficiently defended against a regular siege or a vigorous assault. The obstacles that had been interposed to obstruct the enemy, likewise rendered it impossible for us to move out and attack him after he had established his works in front of ours; and we would have to await the result of a regular siege, with the danger, imminent at any time, of the enemy's gunboats and monitors running by our works on York and James Rivers, and thus destroying our communication by water. About twelve miles in rear of Yorktown, near Williamsburg, the Peninsula is only about three or four miles wide, and there are creeks and marshes intersecting it on both sides at this point, in such way that the routes for the escape of our army would have been confined to a very narrow slip, if our line had been broken. The most assailable point on our whole line was that occupied by Rodes and myself, and when the enemy could have got his heavy batteries ready, our works on this part of the line would have soon been rendered wholly untenable.

Owing to the fact that the ground on which these works were located sloped towards the enemy's position, so as to expose to a direct fire their interior and rear, it would have been easy for him to have shelled us out of them; and when this part of the line had been carried, the enemy could have pushed to our rear on the direct road to Williamsburg and secured all the routes over which it would have been possible for us to retreat, thus rendering the capture or dispersion of our entire army certain. Nothing but the extreme boldness of Magruder and the excessive caution of McClellan had arrested the march of the latter across this part of the line in the first place, as it was then greatly weaker than we subsequently made it.

During the night of the 1st of May, after orders had been given for the evacuation, we commenced a cannonade upon the enemy, with all of our heavy guns, in the works at Yorktown and in Redoubt No. 4. The object of this was to dispose of as much of the fixed ammunition as possible and produce the impression that we were preparing for an attack on the enemy's trenches. This cannonading was continued during the next day, and, on one part of the line, we were ready to have commenced the evacuation at the time designated, but a little before night on that day (Friday the 2nd) the order was countermanded until the next night, because some of Longstreet's troops were not ready to move. We therefore continued to cannonade on Friday night and during Saturday. Fortunately, after dark on the latter day the evacuation began and was conducted successfully—Stuart's cavalry having been dismounted to occupy our picket line in front, and then men attached to the heavy artillery remaining behind to continue the cannonade until near daylight next morning, so as to keep the enemy in ignorance of our movements. There was a loss of some stores and considerable public property which had been recently brought down, for which there was no transportation, as the steamboats expected for that purpose did not arrive, and the whole of our heavy artillery including some guns that had not been mounted had to be abandoned.

Hill's command, to which I was attached, moved on the direct road from Yorktown to Williamsburg, but our progress was very slow, as the roads were in a terrible condition by reason of heavy rains which had recently fallen. My command passed through Williamsburg after sunrise on the morning of Sunday, the 4th, and bivouacked about two miles west of that place. The day before the evacuation took place the 20th Georgia Regiment had been transferred from my brigade, and its place had been supplied by the 38th Virginia Regiment under Lieutenant Colonel Whittle. The 2nd Florida Regiment and the 2nd Mississippi Battalion continued to be attached to my command. No supplies of provisions had been accumulated at Williamsburg, and the rations brought from Yorktown were now nearly exhausted, owing to the delay of a day in the evacuation and the fact that our transportation was very limited.

We rested on Sunday, but received orders to be ready to resume the march at 3 o'clock A.M. on next day, the 5th. My command was under arms promptly at the time designated, but it had been raining during the night, and it was very difficult for our trains and artillery to make any headway. My command, therefore, had to remain under arms until about noon, before the time arrived for it to take its place in the column to follow the troops and trains which were to precede it, and was just about to move off when I received an order from General Hill to halt for a time. I soon received another order to move back to Williamsburg and report to General Longstreet, who had been entrusted with the duty of protecting our rear.

CHAPTER VII.

BATTLE OF WILLIAMSBURG.

ON reporting to General Longstreet at Williamsburg, I ascertained that there was fighting, by a portion of our troops, with the enemy's advance, at a line of redoubts previously constructed a short distance east of Williamsburg, the principal one of which redoubts, covering the main road, was known as Fort Magruder. I was directed to move my command into the college grounds and await orders. There was now a cold, drizzling rain and the wind and the mud in the roads, and everywhere else, was very deep. After remaining for some time near the college, I received an order from General Longstreet to move to Fort Magruder and support Brigadier General Anderson, who had command of the troops engaged with the enemy.

My command was immediately put into motion, and I sent my aide, Lieutenant S. H. Early, forward, to inform General Anderson of my approach, and ascertain where my troops were needed. Lieutenant Early soon returned with the information that General Anderson was not at Fort Magruder, having gone to the right, where his troops were engaged, but that General Stuart, who was in charge at the fort, requested that four of my regiments be moved into position on the right of it and two on the left. As I was moving on to comply with his request and had neared Fort Magruder, General Longstreet himself rode up and ordered me to move the whole of my command to a position which he pointed out, on a ridge in a field to the left and rear of the Fort, so as to prevent the enemy from turning the position in that direction, and to await further orders. General Longstreet then rode towards the right, and I was proceeding to the position assigned me, when one of the General's staff officers came to me with an order to send him two regiments, which I complied with by sending the 2nd Florida Regiment and the 2nd Mississippi Battalion, under Colonel Ward.

With my brigade proper I moved to the point designated before this last order, and took position on the crest of a ridge in a wheat field and facing towards a piece of woods from behind which some of the enemy's guns were firing on Fort Magruder. Shortly after I had placed my command in position, General Hill came up and I suggested to him the propriety of moving through the woods to attack one of the enemy's batteries which seemed to have a flank fire on our main position. He was willing for the attack to be made, but replied that he must see General Longstreet before authorizing it. He then rode to see General Longstreet and I commenced making preparations for the projected attack. While I was so engaged, Brigadier General Rains, also of Hill's command, came up with his brigade and formed immediately in my rear so as to take my place when I moved. General Hill soon returned with the information that the attack was to be made, and he proceeded to post some field-pieces which had come up, in position to cover my retreat if I should be repulsed.

As soon as this was done, my brigade moved forward through the wheat field into the woods, and then through that in the direction of the firing, by the sound of which we were guided, as the battery itself and the troops supporting it were entirely concealed from our view. General Hill accompanied the brigade, going with the right of it. It moved with the 5th North Carolina on the right, then with the 23rd North Carolina, then the 38th Virginia, and then the 24th Virginia on the left. I moved forward with the 24th Virginia, as I expected, from the sound of the enemy's guns and the direction in which we were moving, it would come upon the battery. After moving through the woods a quarter of a mile or more, the 24th came to a rail fence with an open field beyond, in which were posted several guns, under the support of infantry, near some farm houses. In this field were two redoubts, one of which, being the extreme left redoubt of the line of which Fort Magruder was the main work, was occupied by the enemy, and this redoubt was, from the quarter from which we approached, beyond the farm house where the guns mentioned were posted. The 24th, without hesitation, sprang over the fence and made a dash at the guns which were but a short distance from us, but they retired very precipitately, as did the infantry support, to the cover of the redoubt in their rear and the fence and piece of woods nearby.

My line as it moved forward was at right angle to that of the enemy, so that my left regiment alone came upon him and as it moved into the field was exposed to a flank fire. This regiment, inclining to the left, moved gallantly to the attack, and continued to press forward towards the main position at the redoubt under a heavy fire of both infantry and artillery; but the other regiments had not emerged from the woods, and I sent orders for them to move up to the support of the 24th. In the meantime I had received a very severe wound in the shoulder from a minie ball and my horse had been very badly shot, having one of his eyes knocked out. I then rode towards the right for the purpose of looking after the other regiments and ordering them into action, and met the 5th North Carolina, under Colonel McRae, advancing in gallant style towards the enemy. Upon emerging from the woods and finding no enemy in his immediate front, Colonel McRae had promptly formed line to the left and moved to the support of the regiment which was engaged, traversing the whole front which should have been occupied by the two other regiments. He advanced through an open field under a heavy fire from the enemy's artillery and infantry, and soon became hotly engaged by the side of the 24th.

BATTLE OF WILLIAMSBURG

Having by this time become very weak from loss of blood, and suffering greatly from pain, I rode to the second redoubt nearby, in full view of the fight going on and but a few hundred yards from it, for the purpose of dismounting and directing the operations from that point. When I attempted to dismount I found myself so weak, and my pain was so excruciating, that I would not have been able to remount my horse, nor, from these causes, was I then able to direct the movements of my troops. I therefore rode from the field, to the hospital at Williamsburg, passing by Fort Magruder, and informing General Longstreet, whom I found on the right of it, of what was going on with my command.

The 24th Virginia and 5th North Carolina Regiments continued to confront the enemy at close quarters for some time without any support, until Colonel McRae, who had succeeded to the command of the brigade, in reply to a request sent for reinforcements, received an order from General Hill to retire. The 23rd North Carolina Regiment, as reported by Colonel Hoke, had received an order from General Hill to change its front in the woods, doubtless for the purpose of advancing to the support of the regiment first engaged, but it did not emerge from the woods at all, as it moved too far to the left and rear of the 24th Virginia, where it encountered a detachment of the enemy on his right flank. The 38th Virginia Regiment, after some difficulty, succeeded in getting into the field, and was moving under fire to the support of the two regiments engaged, when the order was received to retire.

At the time this order was received, the 24th Virginia and 5th North Carolina were comparatively safe from the enemy's fire, which had slackened, as they had advanced to a point where they were in a great measure sheltered, but the moment they commenced to retire the enemy opened a heavy fire upon them, and, as they had to retire over a bare field, they suffered severely. In going back through the woods, some of the men lost their way and were captured by running into a regiment of the enemy, which was on his right in the woods.

From these causes the loss in those two regiments was quite severe. Colonel Wm. R. Terry and Lieutenant Colonel P. Hairston, of the 24th Virginia, were severely wounded, and Lieutenant Colonel J. C. Badham of the 5th North Carolina was killed, while a number of company officers of both regiments were among the killed and wounded. The loss in the 23rd North Carolina and 38th Virginia was slight, but Lieutenant Colonel Whittle of the latter regiment received a wound in the arm. The brigade fell back to the position from which it advanced, without having been pursued by the enemy, and was there re-formed. The troops of the enemy encountered by my brigade in this action consisted of Hancock's brigade and some eight or ten pieces of artillery.

The charge made by the 24th Virginia and the 5th North Carolina Regiments on this force was one of the most brilliant of the war, and its character was such as to elicit applause even from the newspaper correspondents from the enemy's camps. Had one of the brigades which had come up to the position from which mine advanced been ordered up to the support of Colonel McRae, the probability is that a very different result would have taken place, and perhaps Hancock's whole force would have been captured, as its route for retreat was over a narrow mill-dam.

McClellan, in a telegraphic dispatch at the time, reported that my command had been repulsed by "a real bayonet charge," and he reiterates the statement in his report, that Hancock repulsed the troops opposed to him by a bayonet charge, saying: "Feigning to retreat slowly, he awaited their onset, and then turned upon them: after some terrific volleys of musketry he charged them with the bayonet, routing and dispersing their whole force." This statement is entirely devoid of truth. My regiments were not repulsed, but retired under order as I have stated, and there was *no* charge by the enemy with or without bayonets. This charging with bayonets was one of the myths of this as well as all other wars. Military commanders sometimes saw the charges, after the fighting was over, but the surgeons never saw the wounds made by the bayonets, except in a few instances of mere individual conflict, or where some wounded men had been bayoneted in the field.

Colonel Ward of Florida had led his command into action on the right of Fort Magruder, and he was killed soon after getting under fire. He was a most accomplished, gallant, and deserving officer, and would have risen to distinction in the army had he lived.

This battle at Williamsburg was participated in by only a small part of our army, and its object was to give time to our trains to move off on the almost impassable roads. It accomplished that purpose. The enemy's superior force was repulsed at all points save that at which I had been engaged, or at least his advance was checked. A number of guns were captured from him and his loss was severe, though we had to abandon some of the captured guns for the want of horses to move them.

During the night, the rear of our army resumed its retreat, and the whole of it succeeded in reaching the vicinity of Richmond and interposing for the defence of that city, after some minor affairs with portions of the enemy's troops. A portion of our wounded had to be left at Williamsburg for want of transportation, and surgeons were left in charge of them. I succeeded in getting transportation to the rear, and, starting from Williamsburg after 12 o'clock on the night of the 5th, and deviating next day from the route pursued by our army, I reached James River, near Charles City Court-House, and there obtained transportation on a steamer to Richmond, where I arrived at night on the 8th. From Richmond I went to Lynchburg, and, as soon as I was able to travel on horseback, I went to my own county, where I remained until I was able to resume duty in the field.

CHAPTER VIII.

BATTLES AROUND RICHMOND.

DURING my absence from the army, the battle of Seven Pines, or Fair Oaks, as the enemy called it, was fought on the 31st of May and the 1st of June, and General Johnston had been wounded. General R. E. Lee had succeeded to the command of the army of General Johnston, and it was now designated "The Army of Northern Virginia."

General Lee's army had received some reinforcements from the South; and General Jackson (after his brilliant campaign in the valley of the Shenandoah, by which he had baffled and rendered useless large bodies of the enemy's troops, and prevented McDowell from being sent to the support of McClellan with his force of 40,000 men) had been ordered to move rapidly toward Richmond for the purpose of uniting in an attack on McClellan's lines.*

---

* The following correspondence shows how much the Federal authorities, civil and military, were befogged by Jackson's movements.

"HEADQUARTERS, ARMY OF THE POTOMAC, June 24, 12 P.M., 1862.

"A very peculiar case of desertion has just occurred from the army. The party states he left Jackson, Whiting, and Ewell, fifteen brigades (a) at Gordonsville, on the 21st; that they were moving to Frederick's Hall, and that it was intended to attack my rear on the 28th. I would be glad to learn, at your earliest convenience, the most exact information you have as to the position and movements of Jackson, as well as the sources from which your information is derived, that I may the better compare it with what I have."

"G. B. MCCLELLAN, Major General.
"HON. E. M. STANTON, Secretary of War."

"WASHINGTON, June 25, 2.35.
"MAJOR GENERAL MCCLELLAN:

"We have no definite information as to the numbers or position of Jackson's force. General King yesterday reported a deserter's

BATTLES AROUND RICHMOND

This movement had been made with such dispatch and secrecy, that the approach of Jackson towards Washington was looked for by the authorities at that city, until he was in position to fall on McClellan's rear and left.

Having started on my return to the army, without having any knowledge of the contemplated movement, on my arrival at Lynchburg I found that the fighting had already begun with brilliant results. I hastened on to Richmond and arrived there late in the afternoon of the 28th of June. Though hardly able to take the field

---

statement that Jackson's force was, nine days ago, forty thousand men. Some reports place ten thousand rebels under Jackson at Gordonsville; others that his force is at Port Republic, Harrisonburg and Luray. Fremont yesterday reported rumors that Western Virginia was threatened, and General Kelly that Ewell was advancing to New Creek, where Fremont has his depots. The last telegram from Fremont contradicted this rumor. The last telegram from Banks says the enemy's pickets are strong in advance at Luray. The people decline to give any information of his whereabouts. Within the last two days the evidence is strong that for some purpose the enemy is circulating rumors of Jackson's advance in various directions, with a view to conceal the real point of attack. Neither McDowell, who is at Manassas, nor Banks and Fremont, who are at Middletown, appear to have any accurate knowledge of the subject. A letter transmitted to the Department yesterday, purporting to be dated Gordonsville, on the fourteenth (14th) instant, stated that the actual attack was designed for Washington and Baltimore, as soon as you attacked Richmond; but that the report was to be circulated that Jackson had gone to Richmond in order to mislead. This letter looked very much like a blind, and induces me to suspect that Jackson's real movement now is towards Richmond. It came from Alexandria, and is certainly designed, like the numerous rumors put afloat, to mislead. I think, therefore, that while the warning of the deserter to you may also be a blind, that it could not safely be disregarded. I will transmit to you any further information on this subject that may be received here.

" EDWIN M. STANTON, Secretary of War."

(a) Jackson's command consisted of nine brigades at this time. Whiting with two brigades and Lawton with one had joined him after the engagements at Cross Keys and Port Republic, at which time he had only six brigades, three in Ewell's division, and three in his own.

and advised by the surgeon not to do so, immediately on my arrival in Richmond I mounted my horse, and with my personal staff rode to General Lee's headquarters at Gaines' house, north of the Chickahominy, for the purpose of seeking a command and participating in the approaching battles which seemed inevitable. I arrived at General Lee's headquarters about 11 o'clock on the night of the 28th, and found him in bed. I did not disturb him that night but waited until next morning before reporting to him. The battles of Mechanicsville and Chickahominy * had been fought on the 26th and 27th respectively, and that part of the enemy's army which was north of the Chickahominy had been driven across that stream to the south side.

The troops which had been engaged in this work consisted of Longstreet's, D. H. Hill's, and A. P. Hill's divisions, with a brigade of cavalry under Stuart, from the army around Richmond, and Jackson's command, consisting of his own, Ewell's, and Whiting's divisions. All of these commands were still north of the Chicka-hominy, and Magruder's, Huger's, McLaw's, and D. R. Jones' divisions had been left on the south side to defend Richmond, there being about a division at Drewry's and Chaffin's Bluffs under Generals Holmes and Wise. Magruder's, McLaw's and Jones' divisions consisted of two brigades each, and were all under the command of General Magruder.

A reorganization of the divisions and brigades of the army had been previously made, and my brigade, composed of troops from two different States, had been broken up, and my regiments had been assigned to other brigadier generals. On reporting to General Lee on the morning of the 29th (Sunday), I was informed by him that all the commands were then disposed of, and no

---

* So called by General Lee, though designated by subordinate commanders as the battle of Cold Harbor or Gaines' Mill, according to the part of the ground on which their commands fought.

new arrangement could take place in the presence of the enemy; but he advised me to return to Richmond and wait until a vacancy occurred, which he said would doubtless be the case in a day or two.

I rode back to Richmond that day, and on the next day, the 30th, called on the Secretary of War, General Randolph, who gave me a letter to General Lee, suggesting that I be assigned to the temporary command of Elzey's brigade of Ewell's division, as General Elzey had been severely wounded, and would not be able to return to duty for some time. On the day before, our troops on the north of Chickahominy had crossed to the south side in pursuit of the enemy, and were marching towards James River, and Magruder had had an engagement with the rear of the retreating column at Savage Station on the York River Railroad. On the afternoon of the 30th, I rode to find General Lee again, and, being guided by reports of the movement of our troops and, as I got nearer, by the sound of artillery, I reached the vicinity of the battlefield at Frazier's farm, just about the close of the battle near dark. This battle had taken place between Longstreet's and A. P. Hill's divisions and a large body of the enemy's retreating forces. There had been a failure of other portions of the army to come up as General Lee expected them to do, but the enemy had been driven from the field with a loss of some artillery and a considerable number in killed, wounded and prisoners on his part.

I gave General Lee the letter of the Secretary of War, and next morning he gave me an order to report to General Jackson for the purpose of being assigned temporarily to Elzey's brigade. This was the 1st of July, and I rode past the battlefield of the day before with our advancing troops, until we reached the road leading from across White Oak Swamp past Malvern Hill to James River, where I found the head of General Jackson's column. I rode forward and found the General on the road towards Malvern Hill with a cavalry escort, awaiting a report from some scouts who had been sent forward to ascertain the enemy's position.

On reporting to General Jackson, he directed his adjutant general to write the order for me at once, but while Major Dabney, the then adjutant general, was preparing to do this, the enemy opened with some of his guns from Malvern Hill, and several shells fell near us. This rendered an immediate change of quarters necessary, and the whole party mounted at once and retired to the rear, followed by the enemy's shells in great profusion, as the cloud of dust arising from the movement of the cavalry enabled him to direct his fire with tolerable precision. As soon as we got out of immediate danger, Major Dabney wrote me the necessary order, on his knee, in a hurried manner, and I thus became attached to the command of the famous "Stonewall" Jackson. I found General Ewell's division in the rear of Jackson's column, and upon reporting to him the command of Elzey's brigade was at once given me, it being then about ten o'clock P.M.

The brigade was composed of the remnants of seven regiments, to-wit: the 13th Virginia, the 25th Virginia, the 31st Virginia, the 44th Virginia, the 52nd Virginia, the 58th Virginia, and the 12th Georgia Regiments. The whole force present numbered 1,052 officers and men, and there was but one colonel present (Colonel J. A. Walker of the 13th Virginia Regiment), and two lieutenant colonels (of the 25th and 52nd Virginia Regiments respectively), the rest of the regiments being commanded by captains. General Jackson's command at this time was composed of his own division, and those of Ewell, D. H. Hill, and W. H. Whiting, besides a number of batteries of artillery. Ewell's division was composed of Trimble's brigade, Taylor's Louisiana brigade, the brigade to which I had been assigned, and a small body of Maryland troops under Colonel Bradley T. Johnson.

After remaining for some time in the rear, we finally

moved forward past Willis' Church, to where a line of
battle had been formed confronting the enemy's position
at Malvern Hill. D. H. Hill's division had been formed
on the right of the road leading towards the enemy, and
Whiting's on the left, with an interval between his
right and the road into which the Louisiana brigade
of Ewell's division was moved. My brigade was posted
in the woods in rear of the Louisiana brigade, and
Trimble's brigade was formed in rear of Whiting's left,
which constituted the extreme left of our line. Jackson's division was held in reserve in rear of the whole.
The enemy soon commenced a heavy cannonade upon
the positions where our troops were posted, and kept it
up continuously during the rest of the day. From the
position which I occupied, the enemy could not be seen,
as a considerable body of woods intervened, but many
shells and solid shot passed over us, and one shell
passed through my line, killing two or three persons.

We remained in this position until about sunset, and,
in the meantime, D. H. Hill on our immediate right and
Magruder on his right had attacked the enemy and become very hotly engaged. Just about sunset I was
ordered to move my brigade rapidly towards the right
to support General D. H. Hill. General Ewell accompanied me, and we had to move through the woods in a
circle in rear of the position Hill had first assumed, as
the terrific fire of the enemy's artillery prevented our
moving in any other route. As we moved on through
intricate woods, which very much impeded our progress,
we were still within range of the shells from the enemy's
numerous batteries, and they were constantly bursting
in the tops of the trees over our heads, literally strewing
the ground with leaves.

After moving through the woods for some distance
we came to a small blind road leading into an open flat,
where there had once been a mill on a creek which ran
through swampy ground between our left and the enemy.
On reaching the edge of the open flat I was ordered to

halt the head of my brigade, until General Ewell rode forward with a guide, who had been sent to show us the way, to ascertain the manner in which we were to cross the creek. The musketry fire was now terrific, and reverberated along the valley of the creek awfully. General Ewell soon returned in a great hurry and directed me to move as rapidly as possible. As soon as the head of the brigade, led by Lieut. Colonel Skinner of the 52nd Virginia Regiment, emerged into the open ground, General Ewell turned to him and directed him to go directly across the flat in the direction he pointed, cross the creek, and then turn to the left through the woods into the road beyond, ordering him at the same time to move at a double quick. Before I could say anything General Ewell turned to me and said, "We will have to go this way," and he dashed off in a gallop on a road leading to our right along the old dam across the creek into another road leading in the direction of the battlefield.

I had no option but to follow him, which I did as rapidly as possible, but this required me to make a considerable circuit to get to the point where I expected to meet the head of my brigade. There were now streams of our men pouring back from the battlefield, and on getting into the road leading towards it I lost sight of my brigade, as a woods intervened. I did not find it coming into the road at the point where I expected, and after some fruitless efforts to find it, in which I was often deceived by seeing squads from the battlefield come out of the woods in such manner as to cause me to mistake them for the head of my brigade, I rode back to find if it was crossing the flat.

I saw nothing of it then, and the fact was, as afterwards ascertained, that, after crossing the creek, Colonel Skinner had turned to the left too far, and moved towards the battlefield in a different direction than that indicated. His regiment had been followed by three others, the 13th, 44th, and 58th Virginia Regiments, but the 12th Georgia and 25th and 31st Virginia Regiments, being in the rear in the woods when the head of the brigade moved at a double quick, were left behind, and when they reached the flat, seeing nothing of the rest of the brigade, they crossed the creek at the dam and took the wrong end of the road. In the meantime, while I was trying to find my brigade, General Ewell had rallied a small part of Kershaw's brigade and carried it back to the field. I saw now a large body of men, which proved to be of Toombs' brigade, coming from the field and I endeavored to rally them, but with little success.

While I was so engaged, the 12th Georgia of my own brigade came up, after having found that it had taken the wrong direction, and with that regiment under the command of Captain J. G. Rogers, I moved on, followed by Colonel Benning of Toombs' brigade with about thirty men of his own regiment. Lieutenant Early, my aide, soon came up with the 25th and 31st Virginia Regiments, which he had been sent to find. On reaching the field, I found General Hill and General Ewell endeavoring to form a line with that part of Kershaw's brigade which had been rallied, while Ransom's brigade, or a part of it, was moving to the front.

I was ordered to form my men in line with Kershaw's men, and this was done in a clover field in view of the flashes from the enemy's guns, the guns themselves and his troops being concealed from our view by the darkness which had supervened. General Hill's troops had been compelled to retire from the field as had been the greater part of Magruder's, after a very desperate struggle against immense odds, and a vast amount of heavy siege guns and field artillery. I was ordered to hold the position where I was and not attempt an advance.

The enemy still continued a tremendous fire of artillery from his numerous guns, and his fire was in a circle diverging from the main position at Malvern Hill so as to include our entire line from right to left. This fire was kept up until after nine o'clock, and shells were constantly bursting in front and over us, and crashing into the woods in our rear. It was a magnificent display of fireworks, but not very pleasant to those exposed to it. After being gone some time the part of Ransom's brigade which had advanced in front of us, retired to the rear. Trimble's brigade had arrived from the extreme left, and was posted in my rear. Generals Hill and Ewell remained with us until after the firing had ceased, and then retired after giving me orders to remain where I was until morning and await further orders. During the night General Trimble moved his brigade back towards its former position, and General Kershaw and Colonel Benning retired with their men for the purpose of looking after the rest of their commands.

My three small regiments, numbering a little over three hundred in all, were left the sole occupants of that part of the field, save the dead and wounded in our immediate front. My men lay on their arms in the open field, but they had no sleep that night. The cries and groans of the wounded in our front were truly heartrending, but we could afford them no relief. We observed lights moving about the enemy's position during the whole night, as if looking for the killed and wounded, and the rumbling of wheels was distinctly heard as of artillery moving to the rear, from which I inferred that the enemy was retreating.

At light next morning I discovered a portion of the enemy's troops still at his position of the day before, but it was evidently only a small portion and it turned out to be a heavy rear guard of infantry and cavalry left to protect the retreating army. The position which he had occupied and which our troops had attacked was a strong and commanding one, while the whole country around, over which our troops had been compelled to advance, was entirely open several hundred yards and swept by his artillery massed on the crest of Malvern Hill.

In my view were nearly the whole of our dead and wounded that had not been able to leave the field, as well as a great part of the enemy's dead, and the sight was truly appalling. While watching the enemy's movements I observed to our right of his position and close up to it a small body of troops lying down with their faces to the enemy, who looked to me very much like Confederates. I moved a little further to my right for the purpose of seeing better and discovered a cluster of Confederates, not more than ten or twelve in number, one of whom was also looking with field glasses at the body which I took to be a part of our troops. On riding up to this party, I found it to consist of General Armistead of Huger's division with a few men of his brigade. In answer to my question as to where his brigade was, General Armistead replied, "Here are all that I know anything about except those lying out there in front." He had spent the night in a small cluster of trees around some old graves about two hundred yards from my right.

After viewing them with the glasses, we were satisfied that the troops lying so close up to the position of the enemy were Confederates, and it turned out that they consisted of Generals Mahone and Wright of Huger's division with parts of their brigades. The whole force with them only amounted to a few hundred, and this body constituted the whole of our troops making the assault who had not been compelled to retire. They maintained the ground they had won, after mingling their dead with those of the enemy at the very mouths of his guns, and when the enemy finally retired this small body under Mahone and Wright remained the actual masters of the fight. Before the enemy did retire, a messenger came from Generals Mahone and Wright, with a request for the commander of the troops on the part of the field where I was to advance, stating that the enemy was retreating and that but a rear guard occupied the position. I was, however, too weak to comply with the request, especially as I was informed that their ammunition was exhausted.

Shortly after light, General Ewell came in a great hurry to withdraw my command from the critical position in which he supposed it to be, but I informed him that the enemy had been retreating all night, and he sent information of that fact to General Jackson.

Early in the morning a captain of Huger's division reported to me that he had collected nearby about one hundred and fifty men of that division, and he asked me what he should do with them. I directed him to hold them where they were and report to General Armistead, who was on the field. About this time a considerable body of the enemy's cavalry advanced towards us on the road from his main position of the day before, as I supposed for a charge upon us, and I requested General Armistead to take command of the detachment from Huger's division and aid me in repulsing the charge, but, while I was making the necessary preparations, a few shots from a small party of infantry on the left of the road sent the cavalry back again. By this time our ambulance details had commenced to pass freely to the front for our dead and wounded, and they began to mingle freely with those of the enemy engaged in a similar work. For some time a sort of tacit truce seemed to prevail while details from both armies were engaged in this sad task, but the enemy's rear guard finally retired slowly from our view altogether, on the road toward Harrison's Landing.

It was not until this movement that I discovered what had become of the rest of my brigade, and I then ascertained that when the missing regiments had arrived on the battlefield at a different point from that intended, Colonel Walker had taken charge of them. It was dark by that time, and they got in amongst some of the enemy's regiments, when Colonel Walker quietly withdrew them, as the force into which they had got was entirely too strong for him to attack. My brigade did not draw trigger at all, but it sustained a loss of thirty-three in killed and wounded from the artillery fire of the enemy. During the 2nd it commenced raining, and before night the rain was very heavy, continuing all night. After being employed for some time in picking up small arms from the battlefield, my command was moved to a position near where we had been in line, the day before, and there bivouacked with the rest of the brigade, which had returned to that point the night before.

At the battle of Malvern Hill, the whole army of McClellan was concentrated at a very strong position, with a limited front and both flanks effectively protected. General Lee's entire army was likewise present, and it was the first time during the seven days' fighting around Richmond that these two armies had thus confronted each other.

McClellan's army, however, was so situated that each portion of it was in ready communication with, and in easy supporting distance of, every other part, so that the whole was available for defence or attack, while such was the nature of the ground over which General Lee's army had to move to get into position, and in which it was drawn up after it got in position, that communication between the several commands was very difficult, and movements to the support of each other still more difficult.

General Lee made the attack, and it was his purpose to hurl the greater part of his army against the enemy, but there had been much delay in getting some of the commands into position, owing to the difficulties of the ground and an unfortunate mistake as to roads. When the attack was made, it was very late in the afternoon, and then, from the want of concert produced by the want of proper communication, only a portion of our troops advanced to the attack of the enemy. The troops which did so advance consisted alone of D. H.

Hill's division of Jackson's command, Magruder's command of three small divisions of two brigades each, and three brigades of Huger's division, in all fourteen brigades.

From some mistake in regard to the signal for the advance, D. H. Hill, hearing what he supposed to be that signal, and was probably intended as such, advanced to the attack on the enemy's front with his five brigades alone, and for some time confronted the whole force at Malvern Hill, but after a desperate conflict and a display of useless valor, was compelled to retire with heavy loss. Magruder's command, including Huger's three brigades, was then hurled upon the enemy by brigades, one after the other, but those brigades were likewise compelled to retire after making in vain the most heroic efforts to force the enemy from his position.

In the meantime, Holmes' division of three brigades, Jackson's division of four brigades, Ewell's division of three brigades, and Whiting's division of two brigades, were inactive, while Longstreet's and A. P. Hill's divisions, of six brigades each, were held in reserve some distance in the rear. It is true two brigades of Ewell's division, and Jackson's whole division, were ordered to the support of D. H. Hill after his command had been compelled to retire, but it was only to be thrown into confusion by the difficulties of the way and the approaching darkness, and to be exposed to a murderous fire of artillery, for it was then too late to remedy the mischief that had been done.

In addition to all this, our troops had to advance over open ground to the attack of the enemy's front, while exposed to a most crushing fire of canister and shrapnel from his numerous batteries of heavy guns and field pieces massed on a commanding position, as well as to a flank fire from his gunboats in James River, as it was impossible from the nature of the ground and the position of the flanks to turn and attack either of them.

Moreover, such was the character of the ground occupied by us that it was impossible to employ our artillery, as in attempting to bring the guns into action on the only ground where it was possible to use them, they could be knocked to pieces before they could be used with effect, and such was the result of the few experiments made. Longstreet's and Hill's divisions were held in reserve because they had been heavily engaged at Frazier's farm the day before, but why the rest of Jackson's command was not thrown into action I cannot say, unless it be that the difficulty of communicating, and the impossibility of seeing what was going on on our right, prevented the advance from that quarter from being known in time. Certain it is that I was not aware of the fact that it was any other than an affair of artillery, until ordered to General Hill's support, as the roar of the artillery drowned the sound of the small arms.

General Hill states that his division numbered ten thousand men at the commencement of the fighting north of the Chickahominy, and he had sustained considerable loss in that fighting. General Magruder says his force of three divisions (six brigades) numbered about thirteen thousand men when the movement to the north of the Chickahominy began, and he had been severely engaged at Savage Station. Huger's three brigades numbered perhaps seven or eight thousand, certainly not more. Our troops engaged could not, therefore, have numbered over thirty thousand, and was probably something under that figure, while McClellan was able to bring into action, to meet their assault on his strong position, his whole force, or very nearly the whole of it.

The loss in the two armies was very probably about equal, and we were left in possession of the battlefield, and all the abandoned muskets and rifles of both armies, besides those pieces of artillery abandoned on the retreat, and some wagons and ambulances, but all this did not compensate us for the loss of valuable lives sustained, which were worth more to us than the material of war gained or any actual results of the battle that accrued to our benefit.

Both sides claimed the victory, but I do not think any advantage was gained by either army from the battle, though McClellan made good the retreat of his shattered army to the very strong position at Harrison's Landing. If General Lee's plans for the battle had been carried out, I have no doubt that it would have resulted in a crushing defeat to the enemy.

On the 3rd of July the army was put in motion again, and Jackson's, Ewell's, and Whiting's divisions moved around to the left and approached McClellan's new position by the road leading from Long Bridge to Westover, Ewell's division being in front. On the 4th we arrived in front of the enemy, and advanced, with Ewell's division in line of battle, and skirmished in front, until we encountered the enemy's skirmishers, when our progress was arrested by an order from General Longstreet, who had come up. We remained in line skirmishing heavily with the enemy for a day, when we were relieved by Whiting's division. It was now judged prudent not to attack the enemy in this position, as it was a strong one with very difficult approaches, and on the 8th our army retired, the greater part of it returning to the vicinity of Richmond, thus leaving McClellan to enjoy the consolation of having, after near twelve months of preparation on the most gigantic scale and over three months of arduous campaigning, accomplished the wonderful feat of "a change of base."

McClellan in his report (Sheldon & Co.'s edition of 1864) shows that there was an aggregate present in his army on the 20th of June, 1862, of 107,226, of which there were present for duty 4,665 officers and 101,160 men, making the aggregate present for duty 105,825. See page 53. On page 239, he says: "The report of the Chief of the 'Secret Service Corps,' herewith forwarded, and dated 26th of June, shows the estimated strength of the enemy, at the time of the evacuation of York-town, to have been from 100,000 to 120,000. The same report puts his numbers on the 26th of June at about 180,000, and the specific information obtained regarding their organization warrants the belief that this estimate did not exceed his actual strength.''

He seems to have been troubled all the time with the spectre of ''overwhelming numbers'' opposed to him, and that he should have believed so when he had ''Pro-fessor Lowe'' with his balloons to make reports from the clouds, and his ''Chief of the Secret Service'' and ''intelligent contrabands,'' to fool him with their in-ventions, may be perhaps conceded by some charitable persons, but that he should have written such nonsense as the above in 1863, and published it in 1864, is per-fectly ridiculous. If the United States Government with its gigantic resources and its population of 21,000,000 of whites could bring into the field for the advance on Richmond only 105,000 men, and some fifty or sixty thou-sand men for the defence of Washington, how was the Confederate Government, with its limited means, its blockaded ports, and its population of less than 6,000,000 of whites, to bring into the field, to oppose this one of several large armies of invasion, 180,000 men, and if it could get the men where were the arms to come from?

When I was at General Lee's headquarters, on the night of the 28th of June, at Gaines' house, General Longstreet, who occupied a part of the same house and had accompanied General Lee from the commencement of the operations on McClellan's flank and rear, in-formed me that, when the movement commenced, we had about 90,000 men in all, including Jackson's command, 60,000 being employed in the movement north of the Chickahominy, and 30,000 being left on the south side for the protection of Richmond. This latter number in-cluded the troops at Drewry's Bluff and Chaffin's Bluff. This statement was elicited in reply to a question by me, in which I expressed some surprise at the boldness of the movement, and asked how it was possible for General Lee to undertake it with his force. General Longstreet had no reason to underestimate the force to me, and his estimate was a sanguine one, and, I think, perhaps rather too large, as it was based on the idea that General Jackson's force was stronger than it really was.

The very active campaign and rapid marching of that part of Jackson's command which had been employed in the valley, had very much reduced its strength, and the brigades and regiments were very weak. The whole force was probably somewhere between eighty and ninety thousand, and certainly did not exceed the latter number. A very large portion of the army was armed with smooth-bore muskets, and it was not until after the battles around Richmond, and of second Manassas, that we were able to exchange them for rifles and minie muskets captured from the enemy.

The movement of General Lee against McClellan was a strategic enterprise of the most brilliant character, and at once demonstrated that he was a general of the highest order of genius. Its results, independent of the capture of artillery, small arms, and stores, were of the most momentous consequences, as it relieved the capital of the Confederacy of the dangers and inconveniences of a regular siege for a long while, though it had not resulted in the destruction of McClellan's army as General Lee had desired, and the army and country fondly hoped; but in a thickly wooded country, where armies can move only along the regular roads, and move in line of battle or compact columns along those roads, there are facilities for the escape of a beaten army which one accustomed to reading of European wars cannot well understand. This was peculiarly the case in the country through which McClellan retreated, where the impracticable character of the swamps and woods enabled him to conceal his movements and to protect his trains, rear, and flanks by blocking up the roads and destroying bridges.

BATTLES AROUND RICHMOND

General McClellan, it must be confessed, displayed considerable ability in conducting the retreat of his army after it was out-manœuvred and beaten, notwithstanding the excessive caution he had shown on the Potomac and at Yorktown, and I think there can be no doubt he was the ablest commander the United States had in Virginia during the war, by long odds. During the seven days' operations around Richmond, the two armies were more nearly equal in strength than they ever were afterwards.

CHAPTER IX.

Battle of Cedar Run.

After McClellan had been safely housed at his new base on James River, Major General John Pope, of the United States Army, made his appearance in Northern Virginia, between the Rappahannock and Rapidan Rivers, at the head of an army called the "Army of Virginia," and composed of the corps of McDowell, Banks, and Fremont, the latter being then under Sigel. General Pope issued a vain-glorious address to his troops, in which he declared that he had never seen anything of the "rebels" but their backs; and he talked largely about making his "headquarters in the saddle," and looking out for the means of advancing, without giving thought to the "lines of retreat," which were to be left to take care of themselves. He certainly was producing great commotion in the poultry yards of the worthy matrons, whose sons and husbands were absent in the service of their country, when General Lee sent "Stonewall" Jackson to look after the redoubtable warrior.

After remaining in camp several days near Richmond, Ewell's and Jackson's divisions were ordered to Gordonsville under General Jackson, and, taking the lead, Ewell's division arrived about the 15th of July. On the next day after our arrival, a body of the enemy's cavalry, having crossed the Rapidan, advanced through Orange Court-House towards Gordonsville, and my brigade and the Louisiana brigade were moved out with a regiment of cavalry for the purpose of intercepting the retreat of this body, but it made its escape across the Rapidan by swimming that river, as the water was high. Ewell's division went into camp near Liberty Mills on the Rapidan, on the road from Gordonsville to Madison Court-House, and I remained there, with occasional movements when approaches of the enemy's cavalry were reported, until the 7th of August. In the mean time, Jackson's force had been reinforced by the division of A. P. Hill, and there had been skirmishing and fighting between our cavalry and that of the enemy in Madison County and at Orange Court-House.

General Jackson ordered a forward movement to be made on the 7th of August, and on that day Ewell's division crossed into Madison at Liberty Mills, and moved down the Rapidan toward Barnett's Ford, bivouacking for the night near that point. Early next morning, we moved past Barnett's Ford, driving a small detachment of the enemy's cavalry from the Ford, and took the road for Culpeper Court-House. General Beverly Robertson's cavalry now passed to the front and had a skirmish and some artillery firing with the enemy's cavalry at Robinson's River, where the latter retired. We crossed Robinson's River and bivouacked north of it at the mouth of Crooked Creek, Robertson's cavalry going to the front some two or three miles.

On the morning of the 9th, I was ordered by General Ewell to move forward in advance to the point occupied by our cavalry some three or four miles ahead of us, and to put out strong pickets on the road coming in from the right and left. My brigade had now increased in strength to something over 1,500 officers and men for duty, by the return of absentees. As we moved forward, the 44th Virginia Regiment under Colonel Scott, and six companies of the 52nd Virginia were detached to picket the side roads. Robertson's cavalry was found at a position about eight or nine miles from Culpeper Court-House, not far from Cedar Run, and in his front, in some open fields, bodies of the enemy's cavalry were in view, watching his movements. On our right was Cedar Run or Slaughter's Mountain, and between it and Culpeper road were the large open fields of several adjacent farms in the valley of Cedar Run, while the country on the left of the road was mostly wooded.

After General Ewell came up, my brigade was moved

to the right towards the mountain, for the purpose of reconnoitring, and a section of the battery attached to it was advanced to the front under Lieutenant Terry and opened on the cavalry in our view. This elicited a reply from some of the enemy's guns concealed from our view in rear of his cavalry, but no infantry was visible. My brigade was then moved back to the Culpeper road and along it about a mile, to its intersection with a road coming in from Madison Court-House, where it remained for some hours.

Shortly after noon, Captain Pendleton, of General Jackson's staff, came with an order from the General, for me to advance on the road towards Culpeper Court-House, stating that General Ewell would advance on the right, over ,the northern end of Slaughter's Mountain, with the rest of the division, and that I would be supported by Brigadier General Winder with three brigades of Jackson's division, which would soon be up; but I was ordered not to begin the movement until I received information from General Winder that he was ready to follow me.

While waiting for the message from General Winder, General Robertson and myself reconnoitred the position of the enemy's cavalry, and the country immediately in my front, for the purpose of ascertaining how I would advance so as to surprise the force immediately in front of us. Just ahead of me, the Culpeper road crossed a small branch, a tributary of Cedar Run, and then passed for some distance through a thick woods, leaving a narrow belt on the right of it. Between this belt and the mountain the country was an undulating valley, consisting of several adjoining fields.

All of the enemy's cavalry visible was in the field in this valley, and the position where my command was posted was hidden from its view by an intervening ridge, which crossed the road diagonally from the woods into the fields and fell off into the low grounds on the small branch mentioned. No infantry had yet been discovered, and we were in doubt whether the enemy had any in the vicinity. On the left of the road was a long, narrow meadow on the branch, and as my brigade could not march along the road except by flank, nor without great difficulty through the woods if deployed in line, I determined to form it in the meadow out of view of the enemy, and then advance obliquely across the road, against his cavalry, following it through the fields on a route parallel to the road.

About 2 o'clock in the afternoon, a messenger came from General Winder saying that he was ready to follow me, and I commenced my movement. The brigade was formed in line in the meadow, on the north of the branch, with the 13th Virginia, under Colonel Walker, thrown out as skirmishers to cover the front and flank of the left of the brigade, which had to pass obliquely through the corner of the woods. It then advanced to the ridge behind which the enemy's cavalry was posted, the right regiment (12th Georgia) moving by flank so as to avoid observation, and forming in line as it reached the ridge, when the whole moved over the crest and came in view of the cavalry, which scampered off in a great hurry, receiving as it went a slight volley at long range, by which one or two saddles were emptied.

The brigade then swung around to the left and moved forward in line for about three-fourths of a mile, until we reached a farm road leading from Mrs. Crittenden's house on our right across the Culpeper road, Colonel Walker still continuing to cover the left, by moving with his regiment extended as skirmishers into the woods across the road, until we came to the farm road. At this latter point the Culpeper road emerged from the woods and ran along the left of a field in our front, by the side of the woods to its termination, where it passed between a cornfield on the right and a wheatfield on the left. Colonel Walker immediately re-formed his regiment on the left of the brigade and we advanced across the farm road into the field beyond, to the crest of a ridge, where we discovered a considerable body of cavalry on the opposite side of the wheatfield, on a high ridge over which the Culpeper road ran, and three batteries of artillery opened on us, from over the crest of the ridge in front.

No infantry had yet been seen, but the boldness with which the cavalry confronted us and the opening of the batteries, satisfied me that we had come upon a heavy force, concealed behind the ridge on which the cavalry was drawn up, as the ground beyond was depressed. I therefore halted the brigade, causing the men to cover themselves as well as they could by moving back a little and lying down, and then sent word for General Winder to come up. The position which I now occupied was in an open field on Mrs. Crittenden's farm. Immediately to my right and a little advanced, was a clump of cedars, and from that point the ground sloped off to our right to a bottom on a prong of Cedar Run, the whole country between us and Slaughter's Mountain consisting of open fields. The northern end of the mountain was opposite my right and about a mile distant. On my left was the woods mentioned, which was very dense and extended for a considerable distance to the left.

In front of this woods, about a hundred yards from my left, was the wheat field, in a hollow, or small valley, and immediately in my front was the cornfield, and a small branch ran from the wheatfield through the corn-field, to which the ground sloped. On the farther side of the wheatfield was the high ridge on which the enemy's cavalry was formed, and beyond which his batteries were posted; and it extended across the road into the fields on the right, but was wooded on the left of the road. It was on and behind this ridge the enemy's batteries were posted, and it was in the low ground beyond that I supposed, and it subsequently turned out, his infantry was masked.

Immediately after sending for General Winder, I sent back for some artillery, but this request had been anticipated, and Captain Brown, with one piece, and Captain Dement, with three pieces of their respective batteries of Maryland artillery, soon came dashing up, and were posted at the clump of cedars on my right. They immediately opened on the enemy's cavalry and his batteries, causing the former speedily to retire through the woods over the ridge. Those guns continued to be served with great efficiency during the action and rendered most effectual service.

As there was a long interval between my right and the northern end of Slaughter's Mountain, where General Ewell was, I posted the 12th Georgia Regiment, under Captain Wm. F. Brown, on that flank, to protect the guns which were operated there. During all this time the enemy poured an incessant fire of shells upon us, and we were looking anxiously for the opening of Ewell's guns from the mountain, and the arrival of Winder. General Winder came up as rapidly as possible, and, when he arrived, he took position on my left, and at once had several pieces of artillery brought into action with good effect. Ewell's guns had by this time opened and a brisk cannonading ensued.

From the position I occupied, I had an excellent view of the whole ground—except that beyond the ridge where the enemy's infantry was kept concealed,—and seeing that a force could be moved from our left around the wheatfield, under cover, so as to take the enemy's batteries in flank, I sent information of the fact to General Winder; but, in a very short time afterwards, the glistening bayonets of infantry were discovered moving stealthily to our left, through the woods on the ridge beyond the wheatfield, and I sent my aide, Lieutenant Early, to warn General Winder of this fact, and caution him to look out for his flank. Lieutenant Early arrived to find General Winder just mortally wounded by a shell, while superintending the posting of some batteries at an advanced position, and the information was given to General Jackson who had now arrived on the field.

After the artillery fire had continued some two hours from the time it was first opened on me, the enemy's infantry was seen advancing through the cornfield in my front, but it halted before getting within musket range and lay down. His line overlapped my right and I sent a request to General Jackson for a brigade to put on that flank, which was promised.

Before it arrived, however, several pieces of the artillery battalion attached to A. P. Hill's division, which was just coming up, dashed in front of my brigade down the slope to within musket range of the enemy in the cornfield, and commenced unlimbering, when the enemy's whole force rose up and moved forward. I saw at once that these pieces would be captured or disabled unless relieved immediately, and my brigade was ordered forward at a double quick. On reaching the guns, the brigade halted and opened fire on the enemy, checking his advance and enabling the artillery to open on him with canister. At the same time a heavy force of infantry had moved through the wheatfield, and fire was opened on it from the brigades of Jackson's division on my left, which were posted in the edge of the woods adjoining the field, and the fight became general, raging with great fury. Brown's and Dement's guns opened with canister, and the 12th Georgia was brought from the right and posted on the crest of a small ridge, leading out from the main one around in front of the clump of cedars on my right, so as to have a flank fire on the enemy immediately in front of the brigade.

Just as I had made this arrangement, Thomas' brigade of Hill's division came up to my support as promised, and I posted it on the right of the 12th Georgia, behind the crest of the same ridge, which was so shaped that Thomas' line had the general direction of the main line, but was in advance of it. The arrival of this brigade was very timely, as the enemy was advancing with a line overlapping my right considerably. Thomas confronted this part of the opposing force, and effectually checked its progress, strewing the ground with the killed. While posting this brigade, the left of my own brigade was concealed from my view, and as soon as I had given Colonel Thomas his instructions, I rode to see what was the condition of things on that part of the line. On getting to where I could see, I discovered that it had given way, and the men of several regiments were retiring rapidly to the rear, while a portion of the enemy had crossed the little stream in front of where my left had been. The only thing now standing, as far as I could see, was Thomas' brigade on my right, the 12th Georgia, four companies of the 52nd Virginia, and part of the 58th Virginia.

It was a most critical state of things, and I saw that the day would probably be lost, unless I could hold the position I still occupied. I could not, therefore, go to rally my retreating men, but sent my Assistant Adjutant General, Major Samuel Hale, to rally them and bring them back, while I rode to the rest of my troops and directed their commanders to hold on to their positions at all hazards. On my giving the directions to Captain Brown of the 12th Georgia, he replied: ''General, my ammunition is nearly out, don't you think we had better charge them?'' I could not admit the prudence of the proposition at that time, but I fully appreciated its gallantry. This brave old man was then 65 years old, and had a son, an officer, in his company. The position was held until other troops were brought up and the greater part of the retreating men rallied, and the day was thus prevented from being lost.

The enemy had penetrated into the woods on my left, and the brigades of Jackson's division there posted had been driven back, after a desperate conflict. The left of the line had thus given way, and the enemy had got possession of the woods, from which he had poured a galling fire into the rear of my regiments on the flank, which had been thrown into confusion, and compelled to retire in some disorder. Colonel Walker of the 13th Virginia had withdrawn his own regiment and part of the 31st Virginia in good order, after they had been almost surrounded by the enemy. Only my own brigade, Thomas' brigade, and the three brigades of Jackson's division had been engaged up to this time, but some of the other brigades of Hill's division were now coming on the field, and being at once ordered into action, the temporary advantage gained by the enemy was soon wrested from him, and he was forced back into the wheat-field, and then across it over the ridge beyond.

Colonel Walker with the 13th Virginia, and part of the 31st, and Captain Robert D. Lilley with part of the 25th Virginia, returned to the attack while the woods on our left was being cleared of the enemy, and participated in his final repulse. Finding himself being driven from the field, after sunset, the enemy made a desperate effort to retrieve the fortunes of the day by a charge with cavalry. We had no regular line formed at this time, and our men were much scattered in advancing, when a considerable body of cavalry came charging along the road from over the ridge, towards the position where the left of my brigade and the right of Jackson's division had rested during the action. Without being at all dis-concerted or attempting to make any formation against cavalry, small regiments nearby, among which was the 13th Virginia, poured a volley into the head of the ap-proaching cavalry, when it had got within a few yards, causing it to turn suddenly to its right up through the wheatfield, followed by the whole body, which made its escape after encountering a raking fire from our troops further to the left, by which many saddles were emptied. The attack on the enemy was thus resumed and he was driven entirely from the field.

We were ordered to pursue on the road towards Cul-peper Court-House, and the division of General A. P. Hill was placed in front, my brigade following it. Pur-suit was made for two miles, when the enemy's reinforce-ments, coming to the aid of the beaten troops, were en-countered, and there was some skirmishing after dark between Hill's leading brigade and the enemy, and an affair between one of our batteries and some of the enemy's artillery, but night put an end to any further operations. During the night, General Jackson ascertained that Pope's whole army had concentrated in his front, and he therefore determined not to attack him. In moving forward in pursuit of the enemy from the field, my brigade rejoined the rest of the division under General Ewell, and, after operations for the night were suspended, we bivouacked about where the enemy's infantry had been masked when I first encountered his batteries. The two brigades with General Ewell had not been engaged, but his artillery had done good service, and prevented any attempt to flank us on the right.

On the morning of the 10th (Sunday), after some manœuvring on our part, and a little shelling from the enemy, we moved back and covered the battlefield with our troops, while the wounded were being carried off, and the small arms abandoned by the enemy were being gathered. Later in the day we moved farther back and took position in rear of the battlefield, Ewell's division being posted on the end and side of Slaughter's Mountain, and the other divisions crossing the Culpeper road on our left. We remained in this position all night and next day, but there was no fighting, as each army awaited the advance of the other.

On Monday, the 11th, the enemy requested a truce for the purpose of burying his dead, which was granted, until 2 o'clock in the afternoon, and subsequently extended, at his request, to give him time to complete the burial—the arrangements on our side being under the superintendence of General Stuart, and on the side of the enemy under that of Brigadier General Milroy.*

---

* Milroy, in his report, states that the truce was requested by us, but General Jackson says it was applied for by the enemy, and no one will doubt his word. I know that the extension was applied for by Milroy or his staff officer, for I was on the ground in communication with General Stuart at the time. This same Milroy was himself prevented by me from riding to the rear of the ground on which the enemy's dead lay, and he witnessed the taking from the field, under my directions, of very large quantities of small arms, which had been abandoned by Banks' men on the day of the battle.

LIEUTENANT GENERAL JUBAL A. EARLY

I went on the field under General Ewell's orders, to superintend the burial of a portion of our dead, who had not been buried by their proper commanders. I found on the field, stacked up, a very large quantity of excellent rifles, which the division, detailed to gather them up, omitted to carry off. Some of the enemy's men were taking these rifles, but I made them desist, and demanded that a part already carried off, under direction of a staff officer of General Sigel, should be brought back, which was complied with. I then sent for a detail from my brigade and had these arms carried off in wagons sent to me from the rear, there being six full wagon loads. While this work was going on, I heard a Federal soldier say: "It is hard to see our nice rifles going that way," to which another replied: "Yes, but they are theirs, they won them fairly."

The enemy had very large details on the field, and several general officers rode on it, while the burial was going on. This work was finally concluded a little before dark, when the truce was concluded. The enemy buried on this day over six hundred dead, a very large proportion of which were taken from the cornfield in front of the positions occupied by Thomas' and my brigade on the day of the battle. My detail buried the bodies of 98 of our men, nearly the whole of which were taken from the woods in which the brigades of Jackson's division had been engaged. From the want of sufficient tools on our part and the hardness of the ground where we buried our men, our work was not completed until about the same time the enemy completed his.

On returning to my brigade, I found our troops preparing to move back to our former position south of the Rapidan, as the army of Pope concentrated in our front was entirely too large for us to fight. Our movement to the rear commenced immediately after dark, Hill's division bringing up the rear of the infantry and our cavalry that of the whole army. On the next day, the 12th, Ewell's division recrossed at Liberty Mills and returned to its old camps in that vicinity, the withdrawal of our entire force having been effected without serious molestation from the enemy. In this action, Banks commanded the Federal troops immediately on the field, but Pope came up at its close with a portion of McDowell's Corps and the whole of Sigel's.

The loss in my brigade was 16 killed and 145 wounded, and the loss in General Jackson's whole command was 223 killed, 1,060 wounded and 31 missing, making a total loss of 1,314. The enemy's loss in killed and wounded very greatly exceeded ours, and we captured 400 prisoners, including one Brigadier General (Prince), besides securing one piece of artillery and more than 5,000 small arms.

Pope, or at least his soldiers, had now seen something more of the "rebels" than their backs, and he was soon to see other sights.

Shortly after our return from the battle, Lawton's brigade was transferred from Jackson's division to Ewell's, and Starke's Louisiana Brigade, newly created out of regiments which had been attached to other brigades during the battles around Richmond, and had accompanied Hill's division, was attached to Jackson's division. General Jackson's command, as now constituted, was composed of fourteen brigades, to-wit: four in his own and Ewell's divisions each; and six in Hill's division, besides the artillery attached to the divisions (about four batteries to each); and Robertson's cavalry which was co-operating with us.

CHAPTER X.

OPERATIONS ON THE RAPPAHANNOCK.

THE presence of General Jackson in the vicinity of Gordonsville, again bewildered the minds and excited anew the fears of the Washington authorities. The spectre of "overwhelming numbers" at Richmond and of a speedy advance on the Federal Capital now assumed a fearful shape, and McClellan was ordered to remove his army from Harrison's Landing to Aquia Creek as rapidly as possible, for the purpose of uniting with Pope, and interposing for the defence of Washington—Burnside, with 13,000 men from the North Carolina coast on his way to join McClellan on James River, having been previously diverted from that point to Fredericksburg on the Rappahannock.*

---

* The following correspondence taken from McClellan's report is interesting, as it exhibits the bewilderment of the Federal authorities and the hallucination under which McClellan himself continued to labor in regard to the strength of General Lee's forces:

"WASHINGTON, July 30, 1862, 8 P.M.

" MAJOR GENERAL G. B. McCLELLAN :

" A dispatch just received from General Pope, says that deserters report that the enemy is moving south of James River, and that the force in Richmond is very small. I suggest that he be pressed in that direction, so as to ascertain the facts of the case.

" H. W. HALLECK, Major General."

"WASHINGTON, July 31, 1862, 10 A.M.

" MAJOR GENERAL G. B. McCLELLAN :

" General Pope again telegraphs that the enemy is reported to be evacuating Richmond, and falling back on Danville and Lynchburg.

" H. W. HALLECK, Major General."

OPERATIONS ON THE RAPPAHANNOCK

The execution of the order given to McClellan on the 3rd of August for the evacuation of his base on James River, was not completed until the 16th. In the meantime, General Lee had ordered the divisions of Longstreet, Hood (formerly Whiting's), D. R. Jones, and Anderson (formerly Huger's), to Gordonsville for the purpose of advancing against Pope, and the three first named arrived about the 15th of August, Anderson's following later. The greater part of Stuart's cavalry was also ordered to the same vicinity.

On the 15th Jackson's command moved from its camps and concentrated near Pisgah Church on the road

---

"WASHINGTON, August 6, 1862.

" MAJOR GENERAL G. B. McCLELLAN :

" You will immediately send a regiment of cavalry and small batteries of artillery to Burnside's command at Aquia Creek. It is reported that Jackson is moving north with a very large force.

"H. W. HALLECK, Major General."

The following is an extract of letter from Halleck to McClellan, dated the 6th of August, 1862, explaining the reason for the order for the removal of the troops from Harrison's Landing to Aquia Creek.

"Allow me to allude to a few of the facts in the case. You and your officers, at our interview, estimated the enemy's force around Richmond at 200,000 men. Since then you and others report that they have and are receiving large reinforcements from the South. General Pope's army, now covering Washington, is only about 40,000. Your effective force is only about ninety thousand. You are about thirty miles from Richmond, and General Pope eighty or ninety, with the enemy directly between you, ready to fall with his superior numbers upon one or the other, as he may elect."

" HEADQUARTERS, ARMY OF THE POTOMAC, BERKLEY,
August 14, 1862, 11 P.M.

" Movement has commenced by land and water. All sick will be away to-morrow night. Everything done to carry out your orders. I don't like Jackson's movements, he will suddenly appear where least expected. Will telegraph fully and understandingly in the morning.

" G. B. McCLELLAN, Major General."

" MAJOR GENERAL HALLECK, Washington, D. C."

from Orange Court-House to Somerville Ford on the Rapidan, preparatory to the movement forward. While here the 49th Virginia Regiment, Colonel William Smith, joined my brigade. Pope's army, then reinforced by the greater part of Burnside's Corps under Reno, was in the County of Culpeper, north of the Rapidan; but before we were ready to move it commenced to fall back to the northern bank of the Rappahannock.

On the 20th, our whole army, now consisting of two wings under Longstreet and Jackson respectively, and Stuart's cavalry, crossed the Rapidan—Longstreet at Raccoon Ford, and Jackson at Somerville Ford,—the cavalry having preceded them early in the morning. Jackson's wing, comprising the same force he had at Cedar Run, camped at Stevensburg on the night of the 20th. On the 21st he moved past Brandy Station on the Orange and Alexandria Railroad in the direction of Beverly's Ford on the Rappahannock. Jackson's division under Brigadier General Taliaferro was in front and moved to the ford, where there ensued some cannonading, and a fight between a portion of our cavalry and the enemy on the northern bank. Ewell's division bivouacked in the rear of Taliaferro near St. James' Church.

On the morning of the 22nd the division moved up to the vicinity of the ford, where the cannonading still continued. It was then moved to the left, across Hazel River at Wellford's Mill, towards Freeman's Ford, Trimble's brigade being left at Hazel River to protect our trains from a movement of the enemy from across the Rappahannock. At Freeman's Ford, a portion of Stuart's cavalry was found, and an artillery fight was progressing with the enemy's batteries on the opposite bank. The three remaining brigades passed to the left from Freeman's Ford, and moved by a circuitous route through the woods and fields towards the bridge at Warrenton Springs. Late in the afternoon, Lawton's brigade moved to the bridge at the Springs for the purpose of crossing, and my brigade, followed by Hays' (formerly Taylor's) under Colonel Forno of the Louisiana Infantry, was moved to the right, under the superintendence of General Ewell, and crossed over about a mile below the Springs, on an old dilapidated dam.

Hays' brigade was to have followed, but as it was nearly dark when my brigade succeeded in getting over, and the crossing was very difficult, that brigade was left on the south bank until next morning. General Ewell ordered me to occupy a pine woods or thicket in front of the place at which I had crossed, and to establish communications with General Lawton, the whole of whose brigade it was expected would be crossed over at the Springs. There had been a hard rain before I was ordered to cross the river, and it was still raining slightly. As soon as General Ewell left me, I moved my brigade into the woods indicated, and established my left near a road found leading from the Springs towards the lower fords, throwing out pickets on the front and flanks. By this time it had become intensely dark, and we could see nothing except when the flashes of lightning gave faint glimpses of things around.

As soon as the brigade was established in its position, Major A. L. Pitzer, a volunteer aide, was sent to seek General Lawton for the purpose of opening communications with him. After he had been gone for some time, he came back with a sergeant and six privates of Federal cavalry as prisoners, with their horses, equipments and arms complete. This party had passed up the road a few minutes before I had taken position near it, and, on getting near the Springs and finding that place occupied by a portion of our troops, was deliberating as to what should be done when the Major rode into it. He was at once hailed and forced to surrender himself as prisoner, and his captors started with him down the road leading past my left. On getting near the point at which he knew my brigade was posted, the Major told the party having him in charge that they must reverse positions, and when he explained the condition of things and stated that General Lawton was on the right, my brigade on the left with pickets all around, he succeeded in inducing the whole of it to surrender to him and come quietly into my camp, to avoid being fired upon by the pickets. After this attempt, as it was very dark and quite late, I did not renew that night the effort to communicate with General Lawton.

During the night there was a very heavy rain, and by light on the morning of the 23rd, the Rappahannock, or Hedgeman's River, as it is here called, was so much swollen as to defy all attempts at crossing except by swimming, as the bridge at the Springs had been burned by the enemy.

A messenger sent to find General Lawton soon returned with the information that only one regiment of Lawton's brigade, the 13th Georgia under Colonel Douglas, and Brown's and Dement's batteries of four guns each, had crossed at the Springs, the morning before. As soon as this condition of things was ascertained, I sent a messenger, who was directed to swim the river, with a note for General Ewell or Jackson, whichever might be first met with, stating that if the enemy advanced upon us in force, the whole of our troops on the north of the river must be captured, and suggesting the propriety of my attempting to extricate them by moving up towards Waterloo bridge, several miles above.

Before this note could be delivered, I received a verbal message from General Jackson, which had been given across the river at the Springs and was brought to me by a sergeant of one of the batteries, directing me to move my brigade up to where Colonel Douglas' was, take command of the whole force, and prepare for defence, stating, at the same time, that there was a creek running a short distance from the Springs into the river below me, which was past fording also, and that no enemy was in the fork of the river and this creek; and also informing me that he was having the bridge repaired as rapidly as possible. Very shortly after the reception of this message, I received a note from General Jackson, in reply to mine, containing the same instructions conveyed by his message, and directing me in addition, in the event of the enemy's appearance in too heavy force for me to contend with, to move up towards Waterloo bridge, keeping close to the river; and stating that he would follow along the opposite bank with his whole force, to cover my movement.

I at once moved towards the Springs and found Colonel Douglas occupying a hill, a short distance below the buildings, which extended across from the river to Great Run (the creek alluded to by General Jackson). Colonel Douglas, on crossing the morning before, had captured a portion of a cavalry picket watching the ford, and there was still a small body on the opposite banks of Great Run with which he had had some skirmishing. Colonel Walker with the 13th and 31st Virginia Regiments had been posted across the road leading from below, about three-fourths of a mile from Colonel Douglas' position, and I now posted the remaining regiments of my brigade and the 13th Georgia along the hill occupied by the latter, so as to present the front to any force that might come from the direction of Warrenton, across Great Run above, resting my right on the Run and my left on the river. The artillery was also posted on this line, and the whole concealed as much as possible by the woods. In this position, Colonel Walker guarded my rear, and my right flank was the only one exposed, but that was safe for the present, as the creek was very high and Colonel Douglas had commenced the destruction of the bridges across it, which was soon completed.

The body of the enemy's cavalry on the opposite side of Great Run continued to hover about my right flank all the morning, and some companies were posted on that flank to watch the creek. Some time during the morning, General Jackson sent over an officer familiar with the country, to pilot one of the staff officers over the route to Waterloo bridge, which it might be necessary to pass over in case of emergency, and Major Hale was sent with him to ascertain the road.

In the meantime, the creek began to fall, and in the afternoon it was in a condition to be crossed.

It now began to be evident that the enemy was moving up from below in very heavy force, and that my command was in a critical condition, as large trains were seen moving on the road, east and north of us, towards Warrenton. Late in the afternoon a heavy column of infantry with artillery made its appearance on the hills beyond my right, but it moved with great caution, and the enemy was evidently of the impression that my force, which was concealed from his view, was much larger than it really was. I now changed my front so as to present it towards the force in sight, but this movement was so made as to be concealed from the enemy's view by the intervening woods.

About this time, General Robertson, who had accompanied Stuart on a raid to Catlett's Station and upon Pope's headquarters, arrived from the direction of Warrenton with two regiments of cavalry and two pieces of artillery. After consulting with me, General Robertson posted his two pieces on a hill north of the Springs, which commanded a view of the enemy's infantry and opened on it. This fire was soon replied to by one of the enemy's batteries, and I sent two Parrott guns from Brown's battery to the aid of Robertson's guns, which were of short range. A brisk cannonade ensued and was kept up until near sunset, with no damage, however, to my infantry or artillery, but one or two shells fell into one of Robertson's regiments which was in rear of the battery, on the low ground near the Springs, doing some slight damage.

After the cessation of the artillery fire and very near dark about a brigade of the enemy was seen approaching the bank of the creek opposite where my brigade was posted, and in a few moments it delivered a volley into the woods, which was followed by three cheers and a tiger in regular style. Two of Dement's Napoleons were immediately run out to the left of my line, and opened with canister upon the enemy, who was scarcely visible through the mist which had arisen. This fire was, however, so well directed and so rapid that the enemy was soon driven back in confusion, and his cheering was exchanged for cries and groans, which were distinctly audible to those in his front. The volley delivered by the enemy was entirely harmless, and my men reserved their fire with great coolness, until there should be greater need for it. A very short time before this affair, the 60th Georgia Regiment of Lawton's brigade, under Major Berry, had crossed over on the bridge, which was now in a condition for the passage of infantry, though not for artillery or wagons, and had been placed in position.

There was no further attack on me, but it was now very certain, from the noise of moving trains and artillery and the reports of scouts, that a very heavy force was being massed around me, with a view of cutting me off. I drew in Colonel Walker closer to my main force, as he reported that the enemy had crossed the creek on the road he was guarding and were massing in his front; and I sent a messenger to General Jackson, after dark, with information of the condition of things and the suggestion that I be reinforced sufficiently to hold my ground or be withdrawn. The remainder of Lawton's brigade was crossed over on the temporary bridge, and when General Lawton himself arrived, which was about 1 o'clock A.M. on the 24th, he informed me that he had seen written instructions to General Ewell, directing to cross over himself at daylight in the morning, and if it was evident that the enemy was in heavy force, to recross the troops, as it was not desired to have a general engagement at that junction.

On receiving this information, I immediately dispatched a messenger to General Ewell, to inform him that there could be no doubt that the enemy *was* in very heavy force, and if I was to be withdrawn, it had better be done that night without waiting for daylight, as by moving to my left the enemy could post artillery, so as to command the bridge and ford completely, and prevent my being either withdrawn or reinforced, and that I was satisfied that he was preparing for that very object. In response to this, General Ewell came over himself a little before three o'clock A.M., and, after consultation with me, gave the order for recrossing, which was begun at once, Lawton's brigade crossing first and carrying over the artillery by hand, and my brigade following, so as to complete the withdrawal a very little after dawn.

General Ewell had not been entirely satisfied that the enemy was in such strong force as I represented, and he was rather inclined to the opinion that movements I had observed indicated a retreating army. To satisfy him, we remained behind until the advancing skirmishers of the enemy made it prudent for us to retire, and we then rode across the bridge in rear of my brigade. Soon Sigel's whole corps, supported by those of Banks and Reno, moved to the position which I had occupied, and a very heavy cannonading followed.

My command was thus rescued from inevitable destruction, for it would have been impossible for General Jackson to have crossed his troops in time to arrest its fate, as his only means of crossing the river consisted of one narrow, temporary bridge, unsuitable for the passage of artillery, and which the enemy could have commanded from several positions beyond the reach of our artillery on the south bank. Pope's whole army was in easy supporting distance of the force sent against me, and I had in part confronted that army on the 23rd and the following night.

The men of my command, including Douglas' regiment, had had very little to eat since crossing the river, and were without rations, as there had been little opportunity for cooking since leaving the Rapidan; and they had lain on their arms during the night of the 22nd in a drenching rain; yet they exhibited a determined resolution to withstand the enemy's attack at all hazards, should he come against us.

After recrossing the river, Lawton's brigade and mine retired to the vicinity of Jefferson for the purpose of resting and cooking rations.

CHAPTER XI.

CAPTURE OF MANASSAS JUNCTION.

ON the same morning I had crossed the river, Stuart, with a portion of his cavalry, after crossing the river above, had made a raid to Catlett's Station and upon Pope's headquarters at Warrenton Junction, and among other things had captured Pope's dispatch book.

The captured correspondence showed that Pope was being reinforced from the Kanawha Valley and also from McClellan's army, and General Lee determined to send General Jackson to the enemy's rear, to cut the railroad, so as to destroy his communications and bring on a general engagement before the whole of the approaching reinforcements could arrive.

Jackson's wing of the army was put in motion early on the morning of the 25th, with no wagons but the ordnance and medical wagons, and with three days' rations in haversacks, for a "cavalry raid with infantry." Moving with Ewell's division in front, we crossed the river at Hinson's Mill above Waterloo bridge, and marched by a small place called Orleans to Salem, near which place we bivouacked after a very long day's march. On the morning of the 26th, we moved, with Ewell's division still in front, past White Plains, through Thoroughfare Gap in Bull Mountain to Gainesville on the Warrenton Pike, and there turned off to the right towards Bristow Station on the Orange & Alexandria Railroad. At Haymarket, before reaching Gainesville, we halted two or three hours to wait for Stuart to come up with his cavalry, which had started that morning to follow us, and did join us at Gainesville. Hays' brigade, under General Forno, was in the advance of the division on this day, and it arrived at Bristow Station a little before sunset, just as several trains were approaching from the direction of Warrenton Junction.

CAPTURE OF MANASSAS JUNCTION

There was but a small force of cavalry at Bristow, which Colonel Forno soon dispersed, and he then arrested and captured two trains of empty cars with their engines, the first train which approached having made its escape towards Manassas before the road could be sufficiently obstructed, and other trains in the rear running back, on hearing the alarm, towards Warrenton Junction. General Trimble was sent, soon after dark, with two of his regiments, to capture Manassas Junction, and in conjunction with General Stuart succeeded in taking the place and securing eight pieces of artillery, a considerable number of prisoners and horses, a long train of loaded cars, and a very large amount of stores of all kinds. As soon as the remainder of Ewell's division arrived at Bristow, it was placed in position to prevent a surprise by the enemy during the night.

Very early on the morning of the 27th, Hays' brigade and one regiment of Lawton's with a piece of artillery were moved towards Kettle Run in the direction of Warrenton Junction on a reconnaissance, and a train of cars was seen re-embarking a regiment which had been sent to drive off the "raiding party," but, on finding the strength of our force, was about retiring. A shot from one piece of artillery sent the train off in a hurry, and one regiment of Hays' brigade was left on picket and another regiment to tear up the railroad, with orders to fall back skirmishing towards the main body, on the approach of the enemy in force.

Trimble's other regiment, and the 12th Georgia, which was now transferred from my brigade to his, were sent to him at Manassas Junction this morning, and the two other divisions of Jackson's command were ordered to the same place. General Ewell had been ordered by General Jackson to remain at Bristow with his three remaining brigades to check any advance from Pope's army along the railroad, but, if the enemy appeared in heavy force, to retire upon the Junction, as he did not desire a general engagement at this time. General Ewell

115

accordingly disposed his command across the railroad and facing towards Warrenton Junction as follows: my brigade on the right, Lawton's on the left and Hays' in the centre, the main body being posted on a slight ridge covering the station. The 49th Virginia Regiment of my brigade was moved to a ridge on my right, on the road leading to and past Greenwich, and a regiment of Lawton's brigade (the 60th Georgia), with one piece of artillery, was advanced on the left of the railroad so as to support Forno's two regiments which were in front, while the batteries were posted so as to command the approaches on our front and flanks.

In the afternoon indications were seen of the approach of the enemy from the direction of Warrenton Junction, and the wagons were ordered to Manassas. In a short time the enemy advanced in force with infantry and artillery, and the 6th and 8th Louisiana Regiments which had been left in front fell back to a woods about three hundred yards in front of the remainder of the brigade. As soon as the enemy got within range, our batteries opened on him from their various positions, and the 6th and 8th Louisiana, and 60th Georgia Regiments received him with well directed volleys, by which two columns of not less than a brigade each were sent back. The 5th Louisiana was sent to reinforce the 6th and 8th, but by this time fresh columns of the enemy were seen advancing, and it was apparent that his force was larger than ours. As the position we occupied was a weak one, and the enemy could very easily have turned our flank by moving a force on the ridge to our right, which he appeared to be doing, General Ewell determined to retire in accordance with General Jackson's instructions. The order for the withdrawal across Broad Run was given, and I was directed to cover it with my brigade.

At this time the Louisiana regiments in front were actively engaged, and a heavy column of the enemy was moving against them. Lawton's brigade was first drawn back across the ford at the railroad bridge over Broad

Run, and took position on the northern bank. Hays'
brigade then followed, the regiments engaged in front
having retired in good order. My own brigade had been
withdrawn from a pine woods in which it was posted,
and covered the movements of the others by forming
successive lines of battle back to the ford, and was then
crossed over by regiments successively. All the artillery
was successfully withdrawn, a part crossing at Milford
several hundred yards above the bridge, at which point
the 49th Virginia also crossed.

In the meantime, the enemy had been advancing in
line of battle on both sides of the railroad, preceded by
skirmishers, and keeping up a constant artillery fire. The
13th Virginia had been deployed as skirmishers to keep
those of the enemy in check, and kept them from advancing beyond the station until all the rest of our force
had crossed the Run, when it also retired. Lawton's
brigade had been formed in line on the north bank of
the Run, and some batteries put in position. Hays'
brigade was ordered to proceed to Manassas Junction
as soon as it crossed, and my brigade was moved back
about three-fourths of a mile and formed in line on a
hill commanding the road to the Junction, and in full
view of the enemy, who had halted on the ridges near
Bristow Station.

In a short time afterwards, General Ewell with
Lawton's brigade passed through my line, which was
across the road, and ordered me to remain in position
until further orders should be sent me. He left a battery
with me and directed that one or two regiments should
be so moved and manœuvred as to present the appearance of the arrival of reinforcements to my assistance.
This was done, and a small party of the enemy which had
crossed the Run, and was moving along the railroad, was
driven back by a few shots from the artillery, but the
enemy's main force, which consisted of the advance
division of Pope's army under Hooker, did not come
further than the station.

LIEUTENANT GENERAL JUBAL A. EARLY

Shortly after dark, under orders from General Ewell, I retired to the Junction, where my men filled their haversacks with rations of hard bread and salt meat from the stores captured from the enemy, but this was all of the plunder obtained at that place which they could get.

Our loss in this affair was comparatively slight and was confined almost entirely to the 5th, 6th and 8th Louisiana, and the 60th Georgia Regiments, which were the only troops who drew trigger on our side, except the 13th Virginia when deployed as skirmishers to cover our withdrawal. The enemy reported his loss at 300.

The two captured trains had been burned in the early part of the day, and the railroad bridge across Broad Run had been destroyed. A brigade of the enemy which advanced towards Manassas, after having been landed from a train coming from Alexandria, had been met by a party of our troops moving out from the Junction and routed, its commanding officer being killed.

As soon as Ewell's division had rested and broiled a little meat, it moved from the Junction towards Blackburn's Ford on Bull Run, and the brigades became separated and bivouacked at different places, mine lying down in the open field.

The other divisions had previously moved, and Stuart proceeded to burn the trains, and such stores as had not been carried off.

CHAPTER XII.

The Affair at Groveton.

It having become evident that Pope had found it necessary to look after his "lines of retreat," and was moving his whole army back for the purpose of falling upon General Jackson's comparatively small force, the latter determined to move to the left so as to be in a position to unite with the right wing of General Lee's army under Longstreet. Jackson's division, under Brigadier General W. S. Taliaferro, had therefore been moved on the night of the 27th to the vicinity of the battlefield of the 21st of July, 1861, and A. P. Hill's to Centreville, with orders to Ewell to move up, by the northern bank of Bull Run, to the same locality with Taliaferro early on the morning of the 28th. At dawn on that morning, my brigade resumed the march, moving across Bull Run at Blackburn's Ford and then up the north bank to Stone Bridge, followed by Trimble's brigade. We crossed at a ford just below Stone Bridge, and moved across the Warrenton Pike and through the fields between the Carter house and the Stone Tavern, where the battle of the 21st of July had begun, to the Sudley road, near where Jackson's division was already in position.

Lawton's and Hays' brigades had by mistake taken the road to Centreville, but had now rejoined the rest of the division, and the whole of the brigades were placed under cover in the woods, north of the Warrenton Pike, through which the Sudley road ran. Hill's division came up from Centreville subsequently. In the meantime Pope's whole army had been moving by various roads upon Manassas Junction, with the expectation of finding Jackson's force there, but in the afternoon the corps of McDowell's en route for Manassas had been ordered to move to Centreville, and a portion of it marched along the Warrenton Pike. Very late in the afternoon, Jackson's division under Taliaferro was moved along parallel to the pike, under cover of the woods, across the track which had been graded for a railroad, until it passed the small village of Groveton on our left. Ewell's division followed Jackson's until the whole had crossed the railroad track, and the two divisions were then halted and formed in line facing the pike. General Ewell ordered me to take command of my own brigade and Hays' and form a double line in the edge of a piece of woods, with my left resting on the railroad, and to await orders; and he moved to the right with Lawton's and Trimble's brigades.

My line was formed as directed, with my own brigade in front and Hays' in rear of it, and as thus formed we were on the left and rear of Starke's brigade of Jackson's division, whose line was advanced farther towards the pike. About sunset a column of the enemy commenced moving past our position, and Jackson's division and the two brigades with General Ewell moved forward to attack him, when a fierce and sanguinary engagement took place. While it was raging, and just before dark, I received an order from General Jackson, through one of his staff officers, to advance to the front, which I complied with at once, my own brigade in line of battle being followed by that of Hays.

While advancing, I received an order to send two regiments to the right to General Jackson, and I detached the 44th and 49th Virginia under Colonel Smith for that purpose. On reaching the railroad cut in my forward movement, I found it so deep that it was impossible to cross it, and I had therefore to move to the right by flank until I found a place where I could cross. This proved to be a ravine with embankments on both sides for a bridge or culvert, and I had here to pass through by flank and form by file into line in front of a marsh beyond. This brought me near the left of the position to which Trimble's brigade had advanced, and I had passed a part of Starke's brigade on the railroad track. While my brigade was forming in line it was exposed to a galling fire of canister and shrapnel, and before it was ready to advance the enemy had begun to retreat and it had become so dark that it was impossible to tell whether we should encounter friend or foe. I therefore advanced no farther and Hays' brigade was halted on the railroad; and in this position the two brigades lay on their arms all night.

A short distance from me General Ewell was found very severely wounded by a ball through the knee, which he had received while leading one of the regiments on foot, and I had him carried to the hospital, after having great difficulty in persuading him to go, as he insisted upon having his leg amputated before he left the ground.

Lawton's and Trimble's brigades lay on their arms a short distance to my right, near the points where they were at the close of the action, and both had suffered heavily. The enemy had retired from our immediate front, and we could hear the rumbling of his artillery as he was moving off in the distance.

CHAPTER XIII.

Second Battle of Manassas.

Though the force of the enemy, consisting of King's division of McDowell's Corps moving on the left flank of that corps, with which the engagement took place on the afternoon of the 28th, had retreated in the direction of Manassas, other troops had moved up to the vicinity, and early next morning it was discovered that Pope was moving his whole army against us from the direction of Manassas and Centreville, to which point it had gone in search of us.

It now became necessary to change our front to meet the approaching columns, and Ewell's division, under the command of Brigadier General Lawton as senior brigadier, was formed in line facing Groveton, near where it had lain on its arms the night before, on a ridge running nearly at right angles to Warrenton Pike, with its right, my brigade, resting on the pike. The other divisions were retired behind the unfinished railroad on our left, and the whole line faced towards the enemy. At an early hour the enemy's batteries opened on us and were replied to by ours. After this artillery firing had continued for some time, the position of Ewell's division was changed, and General Jackson in person ordered me to move with Hays' brigade and my own, and Johnson's battery of artillery, to a ridge north of the Warrenton Pike and behind the railroad, so as to prevent the enemy from turning our right flank, a movement from Manassas indicating that purpose having been observed. Two of my regiments, the 13th Virginia and 31st Virginia, under Colonel Walker, were detached by General Jackson's order and placed in position south of the pike, for the purpose of watching the movements of the force that was advancing from the direction of Manassas towards our right.

Hays' brigade and my own were formed in line on the ridge indicated, in the edge of a piece of woods, and skirmishers were advanced to the line of the railroad, Johnson's battery being placed in position to command my front. In the meantime our main line had been established on the railroad a mile or more to my left, and Lawton's and Trimble's brigades had been moved so as to conform thereto. The artillery firing had continued all the morning, on my left at our main position, and there had been some infantry fighting. The two regiments under Colonel Walker, by skirmishing, kept the head of the force moving from Manassas on our right in check, until the appearance of the leading division (Hood's) of Longstreet's force on the Warrenton Pike from the direction of Gainesville, which occurred about ten or eleven o'clock A.M.

I remained in position until Longstreet's advance had moved far enough to render it unnecessary for me to remain longer, and, without awaiting orders, I recalled Colonel Walker with his two regiments about one o'clock P.M., and then moved the two brigades to the left, to rejoin the rest of the division. I found General Lawton with his own brigade in line in rear of the railroad, not far from the position I had occupied, the previous morning, before the fight, and Trimble's brigade was in line on the railroad between Jackson's division and Hill's, the former being on the right and the latter on the left. Along this railroad Jackson's line was mainly formed, facing to the southeast. The track of the road was through fields and woods, and consisted of deep cuts and heavy embankments, as the country was rolling. The two brigades with me were formed in line in the woods, in rear of Lawton's brigade, with Hays' on the right of mine.

We remained in this position until about half-past three P.M., and in the meantime the enemy was making desperate attempts to drive our troops from the line of the railroad, having advanced some heavy columns against Hill's brigades and been repulsed; and the battle was raging fiercely in our front. Just about half-past three, Colonel Forno, with Hays' brigade, was ordered to advance to the assistance of one of Hill's brigades which had been forced from his position, and he did so, driving the enemy from the railroad and taking position on it with his brigade. He was subsequently wounded very seriously, while holding this position, by a sharp-shooter, and had to be removed from the field.

Some time after Forno's advance, a messenger came from A. P. Hill, with the information that one of his brigades, whose ammunition was nearly exhausted, was being very heavily pressed, and with the request that I should advance to its support. I did so at once, without waiting for orders, and moved directly ahead, as I was informed the attack was immediately in my front; the 8th Louisiana Regiment under Major Lewis, which had been sent to the wagons the day before to replenish its ammunition and had just arrived, accompanying my brigade. As I passed Lawton's brigade I found the 13th Georgia Regiment preparing to move forward under the General's orders. I continued to advance until I came to a small field near the railroad, when I discovered that the enemy had possession of a deep cut in the rail-road with a part of his force in a strip of woods between the field and the cut. General Gregg's and Colonel Thomas' brigades, having very nearly exhausted their ammunition, had fallen back a short distance, but were presenting a determined front to the enemy.

My brigade, with the 8th Louisiana on its left, advanced at once across the field, and drove the enemy from the woods and the railroad cut, dashing across the railroad, and pursuing the retreating force some two or three hundred yards beyond, before I could arrest its progress. The messenger from General Hill had stated that it was not desired that I should go beyond the railroad, but should content myself with driving the enemy from it, as General Jackson's orders were not to advance but hold the line. I, therefore, drew my men back to the railroad cut and took position behind it. This charge was made with great dash and gallantry by my brigade and the 8th Louisiana Regiment, and very heavy loss was inflicted on the enemy with a comparatively slight one to us, though two valuable officers, Colonel William Smith of the 49th Virginia and Major John C. Higginbotham of the 25th Virginia, were severely wounded. At the time my brigade crossed the railroad, the 13th Georgia advanced further to the right and crossed over in pursuit.

This was the last of seven different assaults on General Hill's line that day, all of which had now been repulsed with great slaughter upon the enemy, and he did not renew the attack, but contented himself with furiously shelling the woods in which we were located. Jackson's division had also repulsed an attack on his front, and General Trimble was severely wounded during the course of the day by an explosive ball from a sharpshooter. General Jackson had accomplished his purpose of resisting the enemy until General Lee with Longstreet's force could effect a junction with him. The latter force was now up and a part of it had been engaged just about night with one of the enemy's columns.

Pope, in his report, claims that General Jackson was retreating through Thoroughfare Gap, when his attack arrested this retreat and compelled Jackson to take position to defend himself, and that he drove our troops several miles, but there was no thought of retreat, and the various movements of our troops had been solely for the purpose of defence against the enemy's threatened attacks as he changed their direction.

Hill's brigades, to whose relief I had gone, went to the rear to replenish their cartridge boxes and did not return to relieve me after the close of the fight on the 29th. I had therefore to remain in position all night with my men lying on their arms.

I had understood that some of Hill's brigades were

to my left, but it turned out that they had also gone to the rear to get ammunition and did not return; and very early in the morning of the 30th, the enemy's sharpshooters got on the railroad embankment on my left and opened fire on that flank, killing a very valuable young officer of the 13th Virginia Regiment, Lieutenant Leroy. I thus discovered for the first time that my flank was exposed, and the enemy's sharpshooters soon began to cross the railroad on my left and advance through a cornfield. I immediately sent word to General Hill of this state of things, and, after some delay, some brigades were sent to occupy positions on my left, who drove the sharpshooters back. During the morning there was very heavy skirmishing in my front, and the skirmishers of my brigade, under Captain Lilley of the 25th Virginia, drove back a heavy force which was advancing apparently for an attack on our position.

Subsequently our troops were arranged so as to place Ewell's division in the centre, leaving Hill's division on the left and Jackson's on the right, but when Lawton's brigade was moved up, there was left space for only three of my regiments, and leaving the 44th, 49th and 52nd Virginia Regiments on the line under General Smith of the 49th, I retired about 150 yards to the rear with the rest of the brigade. Hays' brigade, now under Colonel Strong, had been sent to the wagons to get ammunition and had not returned.

The fore part of the day was consumed by the main body of the enemy and Longstreet's wing of the army in manœuvring and cannonading, but about four o'clock P.M. the enemy brought up very heavy columns and hurled them against Jackson's line, when the fighting became very severe, but all of the attempts to force our position were successfully resisted, and a very heavy punishment was inflicted on the enemy. My three regiments under Colonel Smith, participated in the repulse of the enemy, and as he retired they dashed across the railroad cut in pursuit, very unexpectedly to me, as I had given orders to Colonel William Smith not to advance until the order to do so was given. His men, however, had been incapable of restraint, but he soon returned with them. In the meantime, I advanced the other regiments to the front of the line that had been vacated. Trimble's brigade, now under Captain Brown of the 12th Georgia, and Lawton's brigade had participated in this repulse of the enemy likewise.

The attack on the part of the line occupied by Jackson's division had been very persistent, but Longstreet now began to advance against the enemy from the right and was soon sweeping him from our front. Some of Hill's brigades also advanced and the enemy was driven from the field with great slaughter. While this was taking place, the other divisions of Jackson were ordered to advance, and my brigade was soon put in motion in the direction taken by Hill's brigades, advancing through the woods in our front to a large field about a quarter of a mile from the railroad. I halted at the edge of the woods to enable the other brigades to come up, as I was ahead of them, when General Jackson rode up and ordered me to move by my left flank to intercept a body of the enemy reported moving up Bull Run to our left. I did so, moving along with skirmishers ahead of the brigade until I came to the railroad, and then along that until I came to a field.

It was now getting dark, and as my skirmishers moved into the field they were fired upon from their left. This fire came from a very unexpected quarter, and I immediately sent to let General Jackson know the fact, as it would have been folly to have advanced in the direction I was going if it came from the enemy. A message was soon received from General Jackson, stating that the fire very probably came from some of Hill's troops, and directing me to send and see. This had been anticipated by sending a young soldier of the 44th Virginia, who volunteered for the purpose, and he soon returned with the information that the firing was from the skirmishers from Gregg's and Branch's brigades of Hill's division who mistook us for the enemy. Fortunately no damage was done, and I was moving on when I received an order to advance to the front from where I was, and in a few minutes afterwards another to move back by the right flank, as the report of the movement of the enemy around our left flank had proved untrue. I found that the other brigades of the division had bivouacked near where I had left them, and my own did the same.

The enemy had been driven beyond Bull Run, and was in retreat to Centreville, our pursuit having been arrested by the approaching darkness.

CHAPTER XIV.

Affair at Ox Hill or Chantilly.

Jackson's command, after having rested on the morning of the 31st, in the afternoon of that day was put in motion for the purpose of turning the enemy's position at Centreville. Crossing Bull Run at and near Sudley's Ford, it moved to the left over a country road, Jackson's division in front followed by Ewell's and Hill's bringing up the rear, until the Little River Turnpike was reached, when we turned towards Fairfax Court-House and bivouacked late at night. Early on the morning of September the 1st, the march was resumed, and continued until we reached the farm of Chantilly in the afternoon. The enemy was found in position, covering the retreat of his army, near Ox Hill, not far from Chantilly, and a short distance beyond which the Little River Pike, and the pike from Centreville to Fairfax Court-House, intersect.

General Jackson at once put his troops in position on the ridge on the east of the Little River Pike, with his own division on the left, Hill's on the right and Ewell's in the centre; Hays' and Trimble's brigades only of Ewell's division being on the front line, Lawton's and mine being formed in the woods in their rear. As we moved into position the enemy opened a heavy artillery fire on us, and soon the action commenced with some of Hill's brigades on the right, extending to Trimble's and Hays' brigades. During this action a severe thunder storm raged, and while it was progressing, General Starke, then in command of Jackson's division, represented to me that a heavy force was threatening his left, between which and the pike there was a considerable interval, and requested me to cover it with my brigade to protect him from the apprehended danger.

After examining the position I reluctantly consented

129

to yield to General Starke's entreaty, without awaiting orders, as Hays' brigade was in my front and he represented his situation as critical, and I proceeded to move my brigade by the left flank to the point designated by him. I had put myself on the leading flank, and while moving I heard a considerable musketry fire, but as the woods were very thick and it continued to rain I could see only a short distance, and took it for granted that the firing proceeded from the troops in front of where I had been.

On reaching the position General Starke desired me to occupy, which was but a short distance from the place I had moved from, as his left was drawn back in a circle towards the pike, I discovered that the 13th, 25th and 31st Virginia Regiments which were on my right had not followed the rest of the brigade. I immediately sent my aide, Lieutenant Early, back to see what had become of the missing regiments, and he found them engaged with a body of the enemy in their front. On ascertaining this fact, I moved back at once and found that my regiment had repulsed the force opposed to them and inflicted considerable loss on it. Hays' brigade under Colonel Strong had fallen back in considerable confusion about the time I commenced my movement, and passed through the three regiments on my right, followed by a considerable force of the enemy. The commanding officers had very properly detained those regiments, as the affair was entirely concealed from my view, and they had received the enemy's onset with great coolness, driving him back out of the woods.

Colonel Strong had attempted to change front when the enemy were advancing on him, and, being entirely inexperienced in the management of a brigade, he had got it into such confusion that it was compelled to retire. The 8th Louisiana Regiment, under Major Lewis, had been halted and formed into line immediately in rear of my regiments, and the remaining regiments were soon rallied and brought back by their respective commanders. After quite a severe action, in which the enemy lost two general officers, Kearney and Stevens, he was repulsed at all points, and continued his retreat during the night. After the close of the action, Jackson's division was withdrawn from the left to the rear, and Ewell's division covered the point previously covered by General Starke, and Hays' and Trimble's brigades, and the men lay on their arms during the night. While Trimble's brigade was engaged, the gallant old Captain Brown, of the 12th Georgia Regiment, in command of the brigade, was killed, and Colonel James A. Walker of the 13th Virginia Regiment was subsequently assigned to the command of the brigade, as it had no field officer present.

On the morning of the 2nd it was discovered that the enemy had retired from our front, and during that day Pope made good his escape into the fortifications around Washington. He had now seen the "rebels" in various aspects and found that his lines of retreat would not take care of themselves; and very soon he was shipped and sent to the northwest to look after the Indians in that quarter.

This affair at Ox Hill closed the series of engagements with the enemy under Pope, and it was again the old story of the "rebels in overwhelming numbers," opposed to a small army of "Union soldiers." According to Pope's account, his army was wearied out and broken down by the fatigues of the campaign on the Rappahannock, and the incessant marching and manœuvring to confront Lee's army, and was short of rations and ammunition. It does not seem to have occurred to him that the soldiers of the army which thus wearied his own were at all susceptible of fatigue or hunger, or that when his own rations were short, their chances of supplying themselves were slim.

Pope's army had at the time of the battles of the 27th, 28th, 29th and 30th of August, been reinforced by Burnside's corps under Reno, one brigade of Sturgis' division from Alexandria, and the following troops from McClellan's army: Heintzelman's corps, Porter's corps, and the division of Pennsylvania reserves commanded by Reynolds. At the time of the affair at Ox Hill he had been further reinforced by Franklin's and Sumner's corps of McClellan's army, leaving but one corps of that army (Keyes') which had not reached him. His consolidated report of the 31st of July showed a strength of 46,858 before he was joined by any of those reinforcements and in the letter of Halleck to McClellan, dated the 6th of August, Pope's army is stated to be about 40,000. In a telegram from Halleck to McClellan, dated the 12th of August, Burnside's force is stated to be nearly 13,000.

General Lee's army at the time of these battles near Manassas consisted of Jackson's wing of the army in which there were three divisions of infantry containing fourteen brigades, Longstreet's wing in which there were four divisions of infantry containing fifteen brigades, and two brigades of cavalry under Stuart. There was about one battery of artillery of four guns for each brigade attached to the divisions, and there was a reserve force of artillery which may have numbered some eight or ten batteries, but perhaps not so many.

Longstreet's command consisted of his own division, seven brigades; Hood's division, two brigades; Jones' division, three brigades; and Anderson's division, three brigades. The whole of those brigades, as well as the force of Jackson, had been in the battles around Richmond, except Evans' brigade—attached to Longstreet's division,—and Drayton's brigade, attached to Jones' division. Those two brigades had probably been brought from the South since those battles, or they may have been organized out of regiments attached to other brigades at that time; but I think they were brought from North and South Carolina, and if such was the fact, they were the only reinforcements which I ever heard of reaching General Lee after the battles around Richmond or before or during the campaign against Pope or the campaign in Maryland. D. H. Hill's division of five brigades; McLaw's division of four brigades, composed of his own and Magruder's consolidated; and the force of Holmes and Wise—all of which had constituted part of the army at Richmond during the battles,—had been left for the protection of that city until the whole of McClellan's force moved from James River.

When that event was fully ascertained, Hill's and McLaw's division and two of Holmes' brigades, under Walker, had been ordered to move North, but Hill and McLaws got up on the 2nd, the day after the affair at Ox Hill, and Walker later, so that Pope had only to confront the 29 brigades before mentioned. My brigade was fully an average one, and my effective force did not exceed 1,500. Some idea therefore may be formed of the force with which General Lee fought the second battle of Manassas; I don't think it could have exceeded 50,000 effective men in all, including artillery and cavalry, and it was probably considerably under that number.

The loss in Ewell's division, beginning with the artillery fighting on the Rappahannock and ending, with the affair at Ox Hill, was in killed 366, wounded 1,169, and missing 32, the loss in my own brigade being 27 killed and 181 wounded.

The main battle, which occurred on the 29th and 30th of August, has been called the second battle of Manassas, but I think the little village or hamlet of Groveton is entitled to the honor of giving its name to that great battle, as the fighting began there on the 28th, and was all around it on the 29th and 30th.

The first battle near the same spot, on ground which was again fought over, had been properly named, as Manassas Junction was then the headquarters and central position of our army, and was the objective point of the enemy during the battle. Such was not the case with either army at the last battle, and the Junction, several miles off, had no more relation to the battle than Bristow, Gainesville or Centreville.

CHAPTER XV.

MOVEMENT INTO MARYLAND.

On the 2nd of September our army rested, while the movements of the enemy were being ascertained. Provisions were now very scarce, as the supply in the wagons, with which we had started, was exhausted. The rations obtained by Jackson's command from the enemy's stores, at Manassas, which were confined to what could be brought off in haversacks, were also exhausted, and on this day boiled fresh beef, without salt or bread, was issued to my brigade, which with an ear or two of green corn roasted by a fire, constituted also my own supply of food, at this time. Longstreet's wing of the army was in a worse condition than Jackson's, as it had not participated in the supply found at Manassas.

On the morning of the 3rd, Jackson's wing commenced the march towards the Potomac, and moved to the left over some country roads, crossing the Loudoun & Hampshire Railroad at a station, above Vienna, until we reached the turnpike from Georgetown to Leesburg in Loudoun, and then along this road through Drainesville, until we passed Leesburg on the afternoon of the 4th, and bivouacked near Big Springs, two or three miles from the latter place, at night.

On the 5th we resumed the march and crossed the Potomac at White's Ford, about seven miles above Leesburg, into Maryland. This ford was an obscure one on the road through the farm of Captain Elijah White, and the banks of the river had to be dug down so that our wagons and artillery might cross. On the Maryland side of the river the Chesapeake & Ohio Canal runs along the bank, and the canal had to be bridged over a lock to enable our wagons to pass, as they could not get through the culvert where the road ran. That night we bivouacked near Three Springs in Maryland on the road leading towards Frederick City, and after my brigade had lain down I received a message from General Jackson to let my men get green corn for two days, but, I told the staff officer bringing it, that they had already drawn their rations in that article, which was all they had now to eat. I will here say that green Indian corn and boiled beef without salt are better than no food at all by a good deal, but they constitute a very weakening diet for troops on a long march, as they produce diarrhœa.

On the 6th we resumed the march and in the afternoon occupied Frederick City and the Monocacy Junction on the Baltimore & Ohio Railroad. Jackson's division took position near the city, and Hill's and Ewell's near the Junction, which is about three miles from the city in the direction of Washington. Ewell's division covered the railroad and the approaches from the direction of Baltimore, and Hill's those from the direction of Washington. We were now able to get some flour and salt, and our whole army was in a day or two concentrated near the same points.

We remained in position until the 10th, and on that day General Jackson's command moved through Frederick westward, for the purpose of capturing Harper's Ferry and Maryland Heights, where there was a considerable force of the enemy. At the same time, McLaws, with his own and Anderson's divisions, including three brigades of Longstreet's attached to Anderson's division, moved towards Maryland Heights, and Brigadier General Walker with his two brigades moved towards Loudoun Heights on the south of the Potomac, for the purpose of surrounding Harper's Ferry and co-operating with General Jackson in its capture.

On the night of the 10th, Ewell's division bivouacked between Middletown and South Mountain. On the 11th, we moved across the mountain at Boonsboro Gap, and through Boonsboro to Williamsport, where we crossed the Potomac; Hill's division moving from that place directly for Martinsburg on the pike, and Ewell's and

Jackson's divisions for North Mountain depot on the Baltimore & Ohio Railroad, some miles west of Martinsburg, near which they bivouacked. On the morning of the 12th we moved for Martinsburg, and found that a force of the enemy at that place under General White had retired in the direction of Harper's Ferry on the approach of Hill's division. We passed through the town in the direction of Harper's Ferry and Ewell's division bivouacked on the banks of the Opequon.

On the morning of the 13th we resumed the march, and reached the turnpike from Charlestown to Harper's Ferry, one mile above Halltown, and bivouacked in sight of the enemy's work on Bolivar Heights, covering the town at the ferry, to wait until McLaws and Walker should get in position on Maryland Heights and Loudon Heights respectively, both of which overlooked and commanded the enemy's position.

On the afternoon of the 14th, McLaws and Walker having previously gotten in position and opened fire with their artillery, General Jackson's force moved forward to invest the enemy's works, Hill's division moving on the right along the Shenandoah, Ewell's division along the turnpike, and one brigade of Jackson's division along the Potomac on the left, the rest of the division moving in support. Ewell's division moved along and on each side of the pike in three columns until it passed Halltown, when it was formed in treble line of battle with Trimble's and Hays' brigades on the front line, and Lawton's and my brigade in their rear, Lawton's forming the second line, and mine the third. In this order we moved forward through some fields on the right of the road until we reached a woods on a hill called School House Hill, confronting the main works on Bolivar Heights, and in easy range for artillery.

This was done without opposition, and Hays' brigade was then moved to the left of the road and mine posted in its rear, the right being occupied by Trimble's and Lawton's brigades in the same order. It was now dark and the artillery firing from Maryland and Loudon Heights, as well as that from the enemy's works, had ceased. General Hill had had some skirmishing with the enemy on our right, and had pushed some brigades close to the enemy's left flank to favorable positions for assaulting his works, and taking them on the flank and rear, but night also closed his operations.

Early on the morning of the 15th, preparations were made for the assault, and the batteries from Maryland Heights, Loudon Heights, from a position across the Shenandoah to which the guns belonging to Ewell's division had been moved during the night, from Hill's position, from each side of the pike in front of Ewell's division, and from the left on the Potomac, opened on the enemy. In front of the position occupied by Ewell's division was a deep valley between School House Hill and Bolivar Heights, the whole of which was cleared. On the opposite side the ascent to the enemy's works was steep and over thick brush that had been felled so as to make a formidable abattis. It was over this ground we would have had to move to the assault, and the prospect was by no means comforting.

Very early in the morning, Lawton's brigade had been moved to the right and then by flank to the upper part of the valley in front of us, for the purpose of supporting an attack to be made by Hill's division, and the latter was moving to the assault, when the white flag was hoisted on Bolivar Heights. This indication of the enemy's surrender was received with very hearty and sincere cheers all along the line, as we were thus saved the necessity of an assault, which if stubbornly resisted would have resulted in the loss of many lives to us.

Under the directions of General Jackson, General A. P. Hill received the surrender of the enemy, then under the command of Brigadier General White, Colonel Miles, the commander of the forces at Harper's Ferry, having been mortally wounded. About 11,000 prisoners were surrendered and paroled, and we secured about 12,000 small arms, 70 pieces of artillery, and a very large amount of stores, provisions, wagons and horses.

The victory was really a bloodless one so far as General Jackson's command was concerned, the only loss being a very few killed and wounded in Hill's division, but General McLaws had had heavy work in taking Maryland Heights, and had been engaged severely with the enemy coming up in his rear.

CHAPTER XVI.

BATTLE OF SHARPSBURG OR ANTIETAM.

LATE in the afternoon of the 15th, General Lawton received an order from General Jackson to move the division on the road to Boteler's Ford, on the Potomac below Shepherdstown, and he at once put his own and Trimble's brigade, which had gotten rations from Harper's Ferry, in motion, and ordered me to follow with my own and Hays' brigade as soon as they were supplied likewise from the stores of the enemy. I was detained until after night before the men of the two brigades could be supplied, and I then followed General Lawton, finding him just before morning bivouacked about four miles from Boteler's Ford. Brigadier General Hays, wounded at Port Republic while Colonel of the 7th Louisiana, had returned to the brigade on the 15th after the surrender of Harper's Ferry and assumed command of his brigade before we started on this march.

The division moved at dawn on the 16th, and, crossing the Potomac, arrived in the vicinity of Sharpsburg in the early part of the day, and stacked arms in a piece of woods about a mile in rear of Sharpsburg, Jackson's division having preceded it, and Hill's being left behind to dispose of the prisoners and property captured at Harper's Ferry.

After the different columns, which had been sent against the latter place, had moved from the vicinity of Frederick, the residue of General Lee's army had moved across South Mountain in the direction of Hagerstown, and the division of General D. H. Hill had been left to defend Boonsboro Gap against the Federal Army, composed of Pope's army and McClellan's army combined, and heavy reinforcements which had arrived to their assistance, now approaching under General McClellan. General Hill had been attacked on the 14th, at Boons-

139

boro Gap, by the main body of McClellan's army, and, after a very obstinate resistance for many hours to the vast forces brought against him, had, with the reinforcements sent to his assistance in the latter part of the day, retired late at night to Sharpsburg on the western side of the Antietam.

A position had been taken on the morning of the 15th by the force north of the Potomac, consisting of D. H. Hill's division, five brigades; the three remaining brigades of Longstreet's division; Hood's division, two brigades; D. R. Jones' division, three brigades; and Evans' brigade; fourteen brigades in all, covering Sharpsburg on the north and east, with the right resting on Antietam Creek, and the left extending to the Hagerstown pike; and the enemy had gradually moved his whole army up to the front of this position. This was the condition of things when Jackson's two divisions arrived on the 16th, and in the meantime there had been some skirmishing and artillery firing.

After remaining in position in the rear for some hours, General Lawton was ordered to move to the right to cover a bridge over the Antietam, but after the movement had commenced, it was countermanded and an order received to follow Jackson's division to the left through fields until we struck the turnpike from Sharpsburg to Hagerstown, and proceeding along this we reached a piece of woods on the west of the pike in which there was a Dunkard or Quaker Church, and found, some distance beyond the church, Jackson's division already posted in a double line on the west of the pike, and connecting on the right with the left of Hood's division. General Jackson in person directed me to place my brigade, which was at the head of the division, on the left of his own so as to protect its flank, and to communicate with Brigadier General J. R. Jones, then in command of that division.

It was then getting near dark, and there was heavy skirmishing between Hood's troops further to the right and the enemy, while shells were flying pretty thick. I had some difficulty in finding General Jones or his left. but after a while succeeded in doing so, and then posted my brigade on the left of Starke's brigade, constituting, as I was informed, Jones' left, which was formed on the west of the pike extending into the woods.

My brigade was posted on a small road running along the back of the woods past Starke's left, and thrown back at right angles to his line. Lawton's and Trimble's brigades had been halted near the church, but General Hays, under orders from General Jackson, reported to me with his brigade, and it was posted in rear of mine. The artillery firing and the skirmishing except occasional shots between the pickets was put to an end by the darkness, and about ten or eleven o'clock Lawton's and Trimble's brigades took the place, on the front line, of Hood's two brigades, which were withdrawn to the rear.

Very shortly after dawn on the morning of the 17th, I was ordered by General Jackson in person to move my brigade to the front and left, along a route pointed out by him, for the purpose of supporting some pieces of artillery which General Stuart had in position to operate against the enemy's right, and Hays was ordered to the support of Lawton's and Trimble's brigades.

Moving along the route designated by General Jackson, I discovered a body of the enemy's skirmishers close on my right pushing forward as if for the purpose of getting around the left flank of our line, and I sent some from my own brigade to hold them in check until I had passed. I found General Stuart about a mile from the position I had moved from, with several pieces of artillery in position on a hill between the left of Jackson's division and the Potomac which were engaging some of the enemy's batteries. At his suggestion, I formed my line in rear of this hill and remained there for about an hour, when General Stuart discovered a body of the enemy's infantry gradually making its way between us and the left of our main line, and determined to shift his position to a hill further to the right and a little in rear of the direction of our line.

This movement was executed by passing over a route to the rear of the one I had taken in the morning, the latter being in possession of the enemy, and, while I was forming my brigade in a strip of woods running back in an elbow from the northern extremity of the body of woods in which the Dunkard Church was located, General Stuart informed me that General Lawton had been wounded, and that General Jackson had sent for me to return with my brigade and take command of the division. Leaving the 13th Virginia Regiment, numbering less than 100 men, with General Stuart, I moved the rest of the brigade across the angle made by the elbow with the main body of the woods, through a field to the position I had started from early in the morning.

The enemy had by this time pushed skirmishers into the northern or further end of this woods, and was moving up a very heavy force to turn our left flank. When I got near my starting point, I found Colonel Grigsby of the 27th Virginia Regiment, and Stafford of the 9th Louisiana rallying some two or three hundred men of Jackson's division at the point at which Starke's brigade had been in position the night before. As I came up I halted my brigade and formed line in rear of Grigsby and Stafford, and they at once advanced against the enemy's skirmishers, who had penetrated some distance into the woods, driving them back.

My brigade was advanced in their rear until we came up with Grigsby and Stafford, where I formed line on the crest of a slight ridge running through the woods and directed them to form on my left. Heavy bodies of the enemy were now discovered in the field beyond the woods moving up to it. I left my brigade under the command of Colonel William Smith, of the 49th Virginia, with directions to resist the enemy at all hazards, and rode across the Hagerstown pike towards the right to find the brigades which had been engaged early in the morning, but I found that they had been very badly cut up and had gone to the rear, Hood having taken their place with his two brigades. Jackson's division had also been very badly used, and the whole of it, except the few men rallied by Grigsby and Stafford, had retired from the field.

The facts were, as I subsequently ascertained from the brigade commanders, that, at light, after skirmishing along the front of Lawton's and Trimble's brigades in a piece of woods occupied by him, the enemy had opened a very heavy enfilading fire from the batteries on the opposite side of the Antietam, and then advanced very heavy columns of infantry against them, at the same time pouring a destructive fire of canister and shells into their ranks from the front. Hays' brigade had gone to the support of the others and this terrible assault from the front with the flank fire from the batteries across the Antietam, had been withstood for some time with obstinacy, until General Lawton was severely wounded; Colonel Douglas, commanding his brigade, killed; Colonel Walker, commanding Trimble's brigade, had had his horse killed under him, and himself been disabled by a contusion from a piece of shell; all the regimental commanders in the three brigades except two had been killed or wounded; and Lawton's brigade had sustained a loss of very nearly one-half, Hays' of more than one-half, and Trimble's of more than a third. General Hood then came to their relief and the shattered remnants of these brigades, their ammunition being exhausted, retired to the rear.

Jackson's division in the meantime had been very heavily engaged, and had shared a like fate, all of it that was left being what I found Grigsby and Stafford rallying, after General Jones had retired from the field stunned by the concussion of a shell bursting near him, and General Starke, who had succeeded him, had been killed.

After having discovered that there was nothing of the division left on the field for me to command except my own brigade, and seeing that, what I supposed were Hood's troops, were very hard pressed, and would probably have to retire before overpowering numbers, I sent Major J. P. Wilson, a volunteer aide who had been serving with Generals Ewell and Lawton, to look after the brigades which had gone to the rear, and I rode to find General Jackson to inform him of the condition of things in front, as well as to let him know that a very heavy force was moving on the west of the pike against our flank and rear, confronted by my brigade and the small force under Grigsby and Stafford alone.

I found the General on a hill in rear of the Dunkard Church, where some batteries were posted, and when I informed him of the condition of things, he directed me to return to my brigade and resist the enemy until he could send me some reinforcements, which he promised to do as soon as he could obtain them. I found my brigade and Grigsby and Stafford's force at the point I had left them, and the movement of the enemy in that quarter was assuming very formidable proportions. The woods in which the Dunkard Church was located, ran along the Hagerstown pike on the west side for about a quarter of a mile until it came to a field on the same side, about 150 or 200 yards wide. Then the woods fell back to the left at right angles with the road, and then ran parallel to it on the other side of the field for about a quarter of a mile further, and then turned to the left and ran some distance to the rear, making the elbow before spoken of.

The field thus located between the pike and the woods formed a plateau higher than the adjacent woods, and the latter sloped towards a small road at the further edge, which extended through the elbow, and was the one on which I had been posted the night before, and along which I had moved to the support of Stuart in the early morning. The line formed by my brigade was entirely in the woods, with its right flank opposite the middle of the field or plateau, and its direction was a right angle with the Hagerstown pike. In the woods were limestone ledges which formed very good cover for troops, and they extended back towards the church. From my position the forces of both armies on my right, or rather in my rear, as I now faced, were entirely concealed from view, as the plateau on my right was considerably higher than the ground on which my brigade was formed.

After my return, the enemy continued to press up towards the woods in which I was, in very heavy force, and I sent Major Hale, my Assistant Adjutant General, to let General Jackson know that the danger was imminent, and he returned with the information that the promised reinforcements would be sent immediately. Just as Major Hale returned, a battery opened on the Hagerstown pike where the field, or plateau, and woods joined. This was in rear of my right flank and not more than two hundred yards from it. I had been anxiously looking to my front and left flank, not dreaming that there was any immediate danger to my right, as I had seen our troops on the eastern side of the pike, at an advanced position, engaged with the enemy, and I took it for granted that this was one of our batteries which had opened on the enemy, but Major Hale's attention was called to it by a soldier in our rear, who was standing on the edge of the plateau, and informed him that it was one of the enemy's batteries. Major Hale examined it himself and immediately informed me of the fact, but I doubted it until I rode to the edge of the woods and saw for myself that it was really one of the enemy's batteries, firing along the pike in the direction of the Dunkard Church.

While I was looking at it for a minute to satisfy myself, I saw a heavy column of infantry move up by its side. This column consisted of Green's division of Mansfield's corps. The fact was that Hood, after resisting with great obstinacy immensely superior numbers, had fallen back to the vicinity of the Dunkard Church, and the enemy had advanced to this position. My position now was very critical, as there was nothing between Hood and myself, thus leaving an interval of from a quarter to a half mile between my command and the rest of the army. Fortunately, however, my troops were concealed from this body of the enemy, or their destruction would have been inevitable, as it was nearly between them and the rest of the army, and the body, moving up on the left in my front, had now got into the woods. Hoping the promised reinforcements would arrive in time, I quietly threw back my right flank under cover of the woods to prevent being taken in the rear.

The situation was most critical and the necessity most pressing, as it was apparent that if the enemy got possession of this woods, possession of the hills in their rear would immediately follow, and then, across to our rear on the road leading back to the Potomac, would have been easy. In fact the possession of these hills would have enabled him to take our whole line in reverse, and a disastrous defeat must have followed. I determined to hold on to the last moment, and I looked anxiously to the rear to see the promised reinforcements coming up, the column on my right and rear and that coming up in front, with which my skirmishers were already engaged, being watched with the most intense interest.

While thus looking out, I saw the column on my right and rear suddenly move into the woods in the direction of the rear of the church. I could not now remain still, and I at once put my brigade in motion by the right flank on a line parallel to that of the enemy's movements, directing Grigsby and Stafford to fall back in line, skirmishing with the enemy coming up on the left. The limestone ledges enabled my troops to keep out of view of the enemy moving in the woods on my right, and they moved rapidly so as to get up with them.

BATTLE OF SHARPSBURG OR ANTIETAM

On passing from behind one of these long ledges, we discovered the enemy moving with flankers thrown out on his right flank. I directed Colonel William Smith, whose regiment, the 49th Virginia, was in the lead, to open fire on the flankers, which was promptly done, and they ran in on the main body, which was taken by surprise by the fire from the unexpected quarter from which it came.

I now saw two or three brigades moving in line to our assistance, at the further end of the woods, and my brigade was faced to the front as soon as the whole of it had passed from behind the ledge, and opened fire on the enemy, who commenced retiring towards the pike in great confusion, after delivering one or two volleys. I had not intended to move to the front in pursuit, as I saw a brigade of the troops coming to our assistance moving into the woods at its further end on my right so as to come upon the flank of mine if it advanced, and I was, therefore, afraid that both would be thrown into confusion by the collision, and that mine would be exposed to the fire of the other. Moreover the enemy's other column was advancing on my left, held in check, however, by Grigsby and Stafford with their men, aided by the 31st Virginia Regiment, which was on that flank. The brigade, however, without awaiting orders, dashed after the retreating column, driving it entirely out of the woods, and, notwithstanding my efforts to do so, I did not succeed in stopping it until its flank and rear had become exposed to the fire of the column on the left.

I then saw other troops of the enemy moving rapidly across the plateau from the pike to the column, opposed to Grigsby and Stafford, and I ordered my brigade to retire a short distance, so as to change front and advance against the enemy in that direction. Just as I was reforming my line for that purpose, Semmes' brigade, and two regiments of Barksdale's brigade, of McLaws' division, and Anderson's brigade of D. R. Jones' division came up, and the whole, including Grigsby's and Stafford's small command, advanced and swept the enemy from the woods into the fields, and the enemy retreated in great disorder to another body of woods beyond that from which he had been thus driven. As soon as the enemy had been thus repulsed, I recalled my regiments and caused them to be re-formed, when they were again posted in their former position on the small ridge before mentioned. As soon as his infantry had retired the enemy opened a tremendous fire with canister and shell upon the woods occupied by us, which was continued for some time.

The troops which had been opposed to us in this latter affair consisted of Sedgwick's division of Sumner's corps, which had not been previously engaged, supported by Mansfield's corps, under Williams, and which moved up for a fresh attack on our extreme left. During his advance, the enemy's columns had received a galling fire from the guns under General Stuart on a hill in the rear of our left which contributed very materially to the repulse, and General Stuart pursued the retreating force on its flank for some distance, with his pieces of artillery and the remnant of the 13th Virginia Regiment under Captain Winston.*

---

* McClellan says in reference to this affair on our left, his right: "Entering the woods on the west of the turnpike, and driving the enemy before them, the first line was met by a heavy fire of musketry and shell from the enemy's breastworks and the batteries on the hill, commanding the exit from the woods. Meantime a heavy column of the enemy had succeeded in crowding back the troops of General Green's division, and appeared in rear of the left of Sedgwick's division. By command of General Sumner, General Howard was forced the third time to the rear, preparatory to a change of front, to meet the column advancing on the left, but this line, now suffering from a destructive fire both in front and on its left, which it was unable to return, gave way towards the right and rear in considerable confusion, and was soon followed by the first and second lines."

There was nothing in the shape of breastworks in the woods or in its rear at that time, and the fight on our part was a stand up one altogether. The slight works, made mostly of rails, which McClellan saw after the battle, were made on the 18th when we were expecting a renewal of the attack.

BATTLE OF SHARPSBURG OR ANTIETAM

My brigade at that time numbered less than 1,000 officers and men present, and Grigsby and Stafford had between two and three hundred; yet with this small force we confronted, for a long time, Sumner's formidable column, and held it in check until reinforcements arrived to our assistance. Had we retired from the fear of being flanked or cut off, the enemy must have obtained possession of the woods, where we were, and, as a necessary consequence, of the hills in their rear, which would have resulted in a decisive defeat to us, and a probable destruction of our army.

While these operations on our extreme left were going on, all of which transpired in the forenoon, two other divisions of Sumner's corps, French's and Richardson's, had been moving against our centre occupied by General D. H. Hill, and were forcing it back after a hard struggle, just about the time I was contending with the two columns of the enemy in the woods. A portion of this force moving against Hood near the Dunkard Church, was met and repulsed by Kershaw's and Cobb's brigades of McLaws' division, the portion of Barksdale's brigade which had not come to my assistance, and Ransom's brigade of Walker's division, at the same time that the force opposed to me was repulsed.

Not long after my brigade had been re-formed and placed in its former position, Colonel Hodges, in command of Armistead's brigade of Anderson's division, came up and took the place of my brigade, which latter was then posted along the edge of the plateau on Hodges' right, facing towards the Hagerstown pike. Subsequently General McLaws posted Barksdale's brigade on my right, and Kershaw's and Cobb's brigades on the left of Hodges'. My line as established along the edge of the woods and plateau after the repulse of the enemy, extended beyond where the left of Jackson's division rested at daylight, and embraced inside of it all of our killed and wounded, and nearly the whole of that of the enemy, in this last affair on our left.

149

Major Wilson had by this time returned with the information that he had been able to find only a part of Hays' brigade, which was under General Hays, who was with General Hood, and that it was in no condition to render any service. He further stated that the remnants of the other brigades had gone to the rear for the purpose of re-forming and gathering up stragglers, but that he had been unable to find them.

The enemy continued to shell the woods in which we were for some time, doing, however, little or no damage, as we were under cover, and his shot and shells went over our heads. Some of our batteries, which had been brought up to the hills in our rear, opened fire on the woods where we were, on two occasions, under the impression that they were occupied by the enemy, and I had to send and have it stopped. Some pieces of our artillery were moved into the angle of the plateau on my right and opened on the enemy, but were soon compelled to retire by the superior metal and number of guns opposed to them.

We remained in position during the rest of the day, as did the troops on my left, and those immediately on my right. The enemy made no further attack on us on this part of the line, but there were several demonstrations as if for an attack, and from the top of a tree on the edge of the woods a lookout reported three lines of battle beyond the pike with a line of skirmishers extending nearly up to the pike. There were, however, some attempts against our line further to the right, and late in the afternoon a fierce attack was made on our extreme right by Burnside's corps, which drove some of our troops from the bridge across the Antietam on that flank, and was forcing back our right, when some of A. P. Hill's brigades, which were just arriving from Harper's Ferry, went to the assistance of the troops engaged on that flank, and the enemy was driven back in considerable confusion.

This affair, which terminated just before dark, closed the fighting on the 16th, and after a most protracted and desperate struggle, our centre had been forced back to some extent, but the positions on our flanks were maintained.

The attack on Jackson's command in the early morning had been made by Hooker's and Mansfield's corps, numbering, according to McClellan's statement, 24,982 men present and fit for duty, and this force had been resisted by Jackson's division and the three brigades of Ewell's, and subsequently by Hood's two brigades, aided by those of D. H. Hill's brigades sent to the assistance of Hood, until Sumner's corps, numbering 18,813 men, came up about nine A.M. to the assistance of Hooker's and Mansfield's. Hood was then compelled to retire to the woods near the Dunkard Church, and Sumner, in command now of the entire right wing of the enemy, prepared for another attack with his corps supported by Hooker's and Mansfield's. This attack was made on our left by Sedgwick's division supported by Mansfield's corps, and on the centre by French's and Richardson's divisions supported by Hooker's corps, and was repulsed as has been stated, Hill, however, losing ground in the centre to some extent. Franklin's corps numbering 12,300 men was then carried to the support of Sumner, arriving a little after twelve M., and a new attack on the woods in which our left rested was projected, but was arrested by General Sumner's orders.

Another attack, however, was made on Hill's position in the centre, which met with some success by reason of the removal of one of his brigades, by mistake, from its position, but the enemy's progress was arrested by Walker's brigades and a part of Anderson's division, which had arrived to his support. The enemy had then made the attack with Burnside's corps, numbering 13,819, on Longstreet's right, on the Antietam, held by D. R. Jones' division, which was repulsed on the arrival of Hill's brigades as stated. The above is a condensed account of the main features of this battle taken from the reports of both sides, and the figures in regard to the strength of McClellan's corps are taken from his own report. Porter's corps of his army, numbering 12,930, was held in reserve.*

Late in the afternoon, after it had become apparent that no further attack on our left was to be made, I rode to the rear in search of the missing brigades and found about one hundred men of Lawton's brigade which had been collected by Major Lowe, the ranking officer of the brigade left, and I had them moved up to where my own brigade was, and placed on its right. We lay on our arms all night, and about light on the morning of the 18th, General Hays brought up about ninety men of his brigade, which were posted on my left. During the morning Captain Feagins, the senior officer left of Trimble's brigade, brought up about two hundred of that brigade, and they were posted in my rear.

The enemy remained in our front during the whole day without making any show of an attack on our left, but there was some firing between the skirmish lines farther to right. The enemy in my immediate front showed a great anxiety to get possession of his dead and wounded on that part of the ground, and several flags of truce approached us, but, I believe, without authority from the proper source. However, a sort of informal truce prevailed for a time, and some of the dead and very badly wounded of the enemy and of that part of our army which had been engaged first on the morning of the 17th, were exchanged even while the skirmishers were firing at each other on the right. This was finally stopped and the enemy informed that no flag of truce could be recognized unless it came from the headquarters of his army. We remained in position on the 18th during the whole day, without any serious demonstration by the enemy on any part of our line, and after dark retired for the purpose of recrossing the

---

* Walker's division of two brigades (his own and Ransom's) had reached the vicinity of the battlefield on the 16th and McLaws' division, and Anderson's, including the three brigades of Longstreet's with him, did not get up until after the battle had begun.

Potomac. I held my position until my skirmishers in front were relieved by a portion of Fitz. Lee's cavalry and then retired in pursuance of orders previously received from General Jackson, carrying with me Armistead's brigade under Colonel Hodges, which had received no orders from its division commander, and bringing up, I believe, the rear of the infantry of our entire army. We found a large number of wagons and troops massed at Boteler's Ford, and the division now commanded by me did not cross until after sunrise. After getting over the river, the division was formed in line of battle on the Virginia side, under direction of General Longstreet, and remained in position several hours, until the enemy appeared on the other bank and opened on us with artillery.

I was subsequently ordered to leave Lawton's brigade, now increased to about four hundred men under Colonel Lamar of the 61st Georgia Regiment (who had returned after the battle of the 17th), at Boteler's Ford, under the command of Brigadier General Pendleton, who was entrusted with the defence of the crossing, and I was ordered to move with the rest of the division towards Martinsburg.

Our whole army with its trains had been safely recrossed and this terminated the operations properly connected with the battle of Sharpsburg.

In that battle, Ewell's division had lost in killed 119, in wounded 1,115, and in missing 38, being an aggregate loss of 1,352 out of less than 3,400 men and officers carried into action. The loss in my own brigade was in killed 18, and in wounded 156, and among the latter were Colonel Smith and Lieutenant Colonel Gibson of the 49th Virginia Regiment, both severely, and the former receiving three distinct wounds before the close of the fight, in which he was engaged. The loss in our whole army was heavy, but not so great as the estimate put upon it by the enemy.

There has been very great misapprehension, both on

153

the part of the enemy and many Confederates, not familiar with the facts, about the strength of General Lee's army at this battle. The whole of the troops then constituting that army had belonged to the army which opposed McClellan in the battles around Richmond, except Evans' and Drayton's brigades, and such absentees as had returned, and there had been troops then belonging to the army, which had not left Richmond, exceeding the number in the said two brigades. There had been heavy losses in the battles around Richmond; and the subsequent losses at Cedar Run, on the Rappahannock, at Manassas and in the vicinity, at Maryland Heights and in Pleasant Valley—where McLaws had been severely engaged,—and at South Mountain, had very materially weakened the strength of the army. Besides all this, since crossing the Rappahannock we had been without regular supplies of food, and had literally been living from hand to mouth. Our troops were badly shod and many of them became barefooted, and they were but indifferently clothed and without protection against the weather. Many of them had become exhausted from the fatigues of the campaign, and the long and rapid marches which they had made while living on short rations and a weakening diet—and many were foot-sore from want of shoes; so that the straggling from these causes, independent of that incident to all armies, had been frightful before we crossed the Potomac, and had continued up to the time of the battle.

Some idea of the diminution from these various causes may be found from the following facts: That Christian gentleman, and brave, accomplished soldier, General D. H. Hill, states that his division, which numbered ten thousand at the beginning of the battles around Richmond, had been reduced to less than five thousand which he had at the battle of South Mountain. Yet he had reached the army after all the fighting about Manassas, and he states that on the morning of the 17th of September he had but three thousand infantry. Ewell's division, with Lawton's brigade, which was attached to it after the battle of Cedar Run, must have numbered, at the time they reached McClellan's right, north of the Chickahominy, eight or ten thousand, as Lawton's brigade was then a very large one, which had never been in action. Yet that division numbered less than three thousand four hundred on the morning of the 17th.

General Lee says in his report: "This great battle was fought by less than forty thousand men on our side, all of whom had undergone the greatest labors and hardships in the field and on the march." This certainly covered our entire force of all descriptions, and I am satisfied that he might have safely stated it at less than thirty thousand. There were forty brigades of infantry in all in the army, one of which, Thomas' of A. P. Hill's division, did not cross the Potomac from Harper's Ferry, and the nine brigades of Ewell's and D. H. Hill's divisions, numbering in the aggregate less than 6,400 officers and men, were fully average ones.

General D. R. Jones states that his command, consisting of his division of three brigades and three of Longstreet's, in all six brigades, numbering on the morning of the 17th, 2,430; General J. R. Jones states that Jackson's division of four brigades numbered less than 1,600; General McLaws states that he carried into action in his four brigades, 2,893; General A. P. Hill states that his three brigades actually numbered less than 2,000; D. H. Hill's five brigades numbered 3,000; and Ewell's four brigades numbered less than 3,400; which gives 15,323 in these twenty-six brigades, leaving thirteen other brigades on the field whose strength is not stated, to-wit: the six brigades of his own division and Longstreet's brought up by General Anderson; A. P. Hill's other two brigades; Hood's two brigades, both very small; Walker's two brigades; and Evans' brigade. General Anderson was wounded, and there is no report from his division or any of his brigades, but General D. H. Hill says that Anderson came to his support, which was before Anderson's division became engaged, with some three or four hundred men, and that force consisted of five brigades, Armistead's having gone to the left. Averaging the thirteen brigades from which no estimate was given with the others and it would give a strength of 7,670, which would make our whole infantry force on the field, from the beginning to the end of the battle, twenty-three thousand at the outside. Our cavalry was not engaged, as it had merely watched the flanks, but six thousand would fully cover the whole of the cavalry and artillery which we had on that side of the river.

McClellan states his whole force in action at 87,164 men present and fit for duty, and he estimates General Lee's at 97,445. As this estimate is a very remarkable one and contains some very amusing features, it is given here in his own language. He says:

"An estimate of the forces under the Confederate General Lee, made up by direction of General Banks from information obtained by the examination of prisoners, deserters, spies, etc., previous to the battle of Antietam, is as follows:

General T. J. Jackson's corps.................. 24,778 men.
"   James Longstreet's corps.............. 23,342 "
"   D. H. Hill's 2nd division .... 15,525 "
"   J. E. B. Stuart's cavalry.............. 6,400 "
"   Ransom's and Jenkins' brigades....... 3,000 "
Forty-six regiments not included in above...... 18,400 "
Artillery, estimated at 400 guns............... 6,000 "
                                            _____
    Total .... 97,445 "

It is to be presumed that this estimate was made by Banks when General Jackson was figuring around Pope's rear, as he did not have a command in McClellan's army, and it is well known that Banks always saw things with very largely magnifying glasses when "Stonewall" Jackson was about.

That some of the affrighted civilians who magnified

one small company of cavalry at the first battle of Manassas, called the Black Horse Cavalry, into 20,000, might be misled by this estimate of McClellan's, or Banks', might well be believed, but that the Major General commanding the "Grand Army of the Potomac," should have so estimated the strength of General Lee's army at Sharpsburg, is perfectly amazing.

Who commanded the "forty-six regiments not included in above," or where were the 400 guns to come from?

This estimate of the relative strength of the two armies gives rise to some very curious reflections:

It must be recollected that Bragg and Kirby Smith were at this time in Kentucky, moving north, and if the newly established Government at Richmond had been able to put in the field and send into Maryland from the comparatively small population of the Confederacy an army of nearly 100,000 men with 400 pieces of artillery, it showed a wonderful energy on the part of that government; while, the fact that the powerful Government at Washington, with its immense resources and its very large population to draw from, after a call for 300,000 more men, and after taking everything in the way of troops from the Ohio to the Atlantic, had been able to bring into the field, for the defence of the National Capital and to oppose the large invading army of "rebels," only a force numbering less than 90,000 men, displayed a weakness not at all flattering to the energy of the head of the War Department at Washington, or to the wisdom of the occupant of the White House, and a want of "patriotism" by no means complimentary to the people of the North.

McClellan had stated that the troops in and about Washington and on the Maryland shore of the Potomac above and below, including those in Maryland and Delaware, amounted, on the 1st of March, 1862, to 193,142 present for duty and an aggregate present and absent of 221,987. This did not include the 13,000 brought by

Burnside from North Carolina, nor the troops brought by Cox from the Kanawha Valley, nor, is it presumed, the forces of Fremont under Sigel, a large part of which were probably brought from Missouri; and there had since been at least one call, if not more, for an additional levy of 300,000 men. Now the question very naturally arises, as to what had become of all that immense force, with the reinforcements and recruits, which had dwindled down to 87,164 men on the morning of the 17th of September, 1862.

It will be seen from the account previously given that on the 15th and in the early part of the day of the 16th, McClellan's large army was confronted by a very small force under Longstreet and D. H. Hill. Jackson with two divisions numbering less than 5,000 men, and Walker, with his two brigades arrived on the 16th, and it was upon the force consisting of these reinforcements and D. H. Hill's and Longstreet's troops, including in the latter Hood's two brigades, and Evans' brigade, that McClellan's army had been hurled on the morning of the 17th. McLaws with his own and Anderson's brigades, ten in all, did not arrive until the action had been progressing for some hours. McLaws arrived at sunrise, and A. P. Hill, with his five brigades, did not come up until late in the afternoon.

The 24,982 men under Hooker and Mansfield had attacked Jackson's division and Lawton's, Trimble's and Hays' brigades of Ewell's division, numbering in all 4,000 men. When they were compelled to retire, Hood with his two brigades supported by Ripley's, Colquit's and Garland's and D. H. Hill's division had withstood the enemy until Sumner arrived with his 18,813 men, and then Hood was also compelled to retire to the Dunkard Church. Sumner then with his corps and what was left of the other two, attacked my brigade of less than 1,000 men, a remnant of about two or three hundred of Jackson's division, and what was left of D. H. Hill's and Hood's divisions, when McLaws and Walker with their six brigades came to our assistance immediately after the arrival of McLaws upon the field. Sumner was repulsed and then Franklin with his 12,300 arrived to his support, and the attack was renewed on Hill in the centre, when Anderson with three or four hundred men and one brigade of Walker's came to his assistance. This force of 56,095 men was brought against a force which with all its reinforcements, from first to last, amounted to less than 18,000 men. How it had been served will appear from the following extract from McClellan's report. He says: "One division of Sumner's corps, and all of Hooker's corps, on the right, had, after fighting most valiantly for several hours, been overpowered by numbers, driven back in great disorder, and much scattered; so that they were for the time somewhat demoralized. In Hooker's corps, according to the return made by General Meade, commanding, there were but 6,729 men present on the 18th, whereas, on the morning of the 22nd, there were 13,093 present for duty in the same corps, showing that previous to and during the battle 6,364 men were separated from their command."

McClellan was not able to renew the attack on the 18th, and, according to his own showing, had to wait for reinforcements before doing so; yet he claims a great victory at Antietam, alleging that he had accomplished the object of the campaign, to-wit: "to preserve the National Capital and Baltimore, to protect Pennsylvania from invasion, and to drive the enemy out of Maryland." This was a singular claim on the part of the General who, scarce three months before, had boastingly stated that the advance of his army was within five miles of the Confederate Capital.

The truth is that the substantial victory was with us, and if our army had been in reach of reinforcements, it would have been a decisive one; but we were more than 200 miles from the point from which supplies of ammunition were to be obtained, and any reinforcements which could have been spared to us were much further off, while large reinforcements were marching to Mc-Clellan's aid. We had, therefore, to recross the Potomac.

The question had been mooted as to the propriety of the campaign into Maryland, and in regard thereto I will say: General Lee, on assuming command of the army at Richmond, had found that city, the seat of the Confederate Government, beleaguered by a vast army, while all Northern Virginia, including the best part of the beautiful valley of the Shenandoah, was held by the enemy. With a herculean effort, he had broken through the cordon surrounding his army, and with inferior numbers fallen upon the beleaguering enemy, and sent it cowering to the banks of the lower James. He had then moved north, and, after a series of hard fought battles, had hurled the shattered remains of the army that had been marauding through Northern Virginia, with all the reinforcements sent from the lately besieging army, into the fortifications around Washington. With the diminished columns of the army with which he accomplished all this, he had crossed the Potomac, captured an important stronghold defended by a strong force, securing a large amount of artillery, small arms, and stores of all kinds, and had fought a great battle with the newly reorganized and heavily reinforced and recruited army of the enemy, which later was so badly crippled that it was not able to resume the offensive for near two months.

He now stood defiantly on the southern banks of the Potomac, the extreme northern limit of the Confederacy, and the result of all these operations, of which the march into Maryland was an important part, had been that not only the Confederate Capital had been relieved from the presence of the besieging army, a danger to which it was not subjected again for two years; but the enemy's Capital had been threatened, his territory invaded, and the base of operations for a new movement on Richmond had been transferred to the north banks of the Potomac at Harper's Ferry, from which there was an overland route of more than two hundred miles. When that movement did take place, General Lee was in a position to interpose his army, and inflict a new defeat on the enemy, as was verified by subsequent events.

The following extracts from McClellan's report will give some idea of the results obtained. Speaking, as of the morning of the 18th, he says:

"At that moment—Virginia lost, Washington menaced, Maryland invaded—the national cause could afford no risks of defeat. Our battle lost, and almost all would have been lost." And he subsequently says:

"The movement from Washington into Maryland, which culminated in the battles of South Mountain and Antietam, was not a part of an offensive campaign, with the object of the invasion of the enemy's territory, and an attack on his capital, but was defensive in its purposes, although offensive in its character, and would be technically called a ' defensive-offensive ' campaign."

"It was undertaken at a time when our army had experienced severe defeats, and its object was to preserve the national capital and Baltimore, to protect Pennsylvania, and to drive the enemy out of Maryland. These purposes were fully and finally accomplished by the battle of Antietam, which brought the Army of the Potomac into what might be termed an accidental position on the upper Potomac."*

It was a great deal gained to force the enemy into a "defensive-offensive" campaign in his own territory and place the "Army of the Potomac" in that accidental position, though we did fail in arousing Maryland, or getting any reinforcements from that State.

---

* In a telegram to Halleck, dated September 22nd (Part II, Conduct of the War, p. 495), McClellan said: "When I was assigned to the command of this army in Washington, it was suffering under the disheartening influence of defeat. It had been greatly reduced by casualties in General Pope's campaign, and its efficiency had been much impaired. The sanguinary battles of South Mountain and Antietam Creek had resulted in a loss to us of ten general officers and many regimental and company officers, besides a large number of enlisted men. The army corps had been badly cut up and scattered by the overwhelming numbers brought against them in the battle of the 17th instant, and the entire army had been greatly exhausted by unavoidable overwork, and want of sleep and rest." (See also his testimony same volume, pages 439, 440 and 441.)

CHAPTER XVII.

Preparations about Fredericksburg.

On the afternoon of the 19th, after leaving Lawton's brigade at Boteler's Ford, I marched with the three other brigades on the road towards Martinsburg, about six miles from Shepherdstown, and bivouacked.

During the night the enemy had succeeded in crossing the Potomac and capturing four of General Pendleton's guns near Shepherdstown, and on the morning of the 20th I was ordered to move back to Boteler's Ford. On arriving near there, by order of General Jackson, my three brigades were formed in line of battle in rear of General A. P. Hill's division which had preceded me, and were moving against the force of the enemy which had crossed over to the south bank. My three brigades were posted in pieces of woods on each side of the road leading towards the ford, and remained there within range of the enemy's guns on the opposite side until late in the afternoon. In the meantime Hill's division advanced, under a heavy fire of artillery from across the river, and drove the enemy's infantry on the southern bank pell-mell into the river, inflicting upon him a very severe punishment for his rashness in undertaking to pursue us and making him pay very dearly for the guns he had taken. One officer in my command, Captain Frazier of the 15th Alabama Regiment,—the only regimental commander in Trimble's brigade who had not been killed or wounded at Sharpsburg,—was severely wounded by a shell, which was all the damage I sustained.

Late in the afternoon, I was ordered to move back, and that night we marched to the vicinity of the Opequon not far above its mouth. We remained at this position until the 24th, when we moved across the Opequon to the Williamsport pike, and on the next day to the vicinity of Martinsburg. On the 27th, General Jackson's whole command was moved to Bunker Hill on the road from Martinsburg to Winchester, and went into camp in that vicinity. By this time our baggage wagons, which had been sent from Manassas to the valley, when we moved into Maryland, had reached us.

We were now able to obtain supplies of flour, by threshing wheat, of which there was a good supply in the valley, and having it ground. While our camps were located at Bunker Hill, Jackson's command destroyed the Baltimore & Ohio Railroad from North Mountain to within five miles of Harper's Ferry, which latter place had been re-occupied by the enemy. More than twenty miles of the road was thus destroyed, and it was done effectively. The Winchester & Potomac Railroad was also destroyed to within a short distance of the Ferry. Previous to this there was a slight engagement between the Stonewall brigade of Jackson's division and a small force of the enemy on the railroad near Kearneysville, but the enemy did not make a serious effort to molest us, either while we were engaged in destroying the railroad or subsequently.

The Army of Northern Virginia was now organized into two regular corps of four divisions each, General Longstreet being assigned to the command of the first corps, and General Jackson to the command of the second corps, both with the rank of Lieutenant General. D. H Hill's division was attached to the second corps, and two divisions were formed out of Longstreet's, D. R. Jones' and Hood's divisions, under the command of Generals Pickett and Hood respectively, they having been promoted. The first corps consisted of the divisions of McLaws, Anderson, Pickett and Hood, and the second corps of the divisions of Ewell, D. H. Hill, A. P. Hill, and Jackson (Ewell's division being under my command and Jackson's under J. R. Jones).

For some time the second corps remained camped near Bunker Hill, and the first corps was camped in the vicinity of Winchester.

McClellan in the meantime had concentrated the

main body of his army on the north bank of the Potomac near Harper's Ferry, and was engaged in preparing for a new campaign into Virginia, while Maryland and Bolivar Heights were very strongly fortified by him.

A short time after the middle of October, General Stuart, with a portion of his cavalry, made a successful expedition through Maryland and Pennsylvania to the rear of and around McClellan's army.

Towards the last of October McClellan began to move across the Potomac on the east side of the Blue Ridge, with a view to another approach to Richmond. His army had been largely recruited, and superbly equipped. The army of General Lee had been considerably increased by the return of stragglers and convalescents, but it continued to be indifferently supplied with clothing and shoes, of which articles there was a great deficiency.

As soon as McClellan's movement was ascertained, Jackson's corps was moved towards the Shenandoah, occupying positions between Charlestown and Berryville, and one division of Longstreet's corps was sent across the Blue Ridge to watch the enemy. When the enemy began to move eastwardly from the mountain, the whole of Longstreet's corps moved across the ridge for the purpose of intercepting his march. D. H. Hill's division of Jackson's corps was subsequently moved across the ridge to watch the enemy's movements. A. P. Hill's division had been put in position near Berryville, covering the Shenandoah, at Snicker's or Castleman's Ferry, where it had an engagement with a body of the enemy that had crossed the ridge as McClellan was moving on. Ewell's division (under my command) was at first posted on A. P. Hill's left, near a church, while Jackson's division was on the Berryville and Charlestown pike in my rear, but as the enemy's covered our front I moved above, first to Millwood, and then to Stone Bridge, near White Post, and Jackson's division moved to the vicinity of the Occoquon between the positions of the other divisions and Winchester.

PREPARATIONS ABOUT FREDERICKSBURG

After the enemy had left the vicinity of the Blue Ridge, D. H. Hill's division recrossed the ridge and moved up on the east side of the Shenandoah to the vicinity of Front Royal. While my camp was at Stone Bridge, my division destroyed the Manassas Gap Railroad from Front Royal to Piedmont on the east side of the Blue Ridge, a distance of twenty miles, and D. H. Hill's division destroyed it from Front Royal to Strasburg.

In the meantime McClellan's army had been concentrated in the vicinity of Warrenton, and McClellan had been succeeded in the command by Burnside. Longstreet had previously taken position at or near Culpeper Court-House.

About the 15th of November Burnside began the movement of his army towards the lower Rappahannock opposite Fredericksburg. When this movement was discovered Longstreet's corps was moved towards Fredericksburg to dispute the enemy's crossing, and orders were sent to General Jackson to move his corps across the Blue Ridge. This movement of the latter corps began about the 20th of November, and we moved up the valley to New Market and then across Massanutten Mountain, the Shenandoah and the Blue Ridge to the vicinity of Madison Court-House. The weather had now become quite cool, and our daily marches were long and rapid, and very trying to the men. On this march I saw a number of our men without shoes, and with bleeding feet wrapped with rags. We remained in the vicinity of Madison Court-House for two or three days, and it was here that General Jackson wore, for the first time, a new regulation coat with the wreath, and a hat, and his appearance in them caused no little remark and amusement among the men. His dress hitherto had been a rusty grey coat, intended for a colonel, and a little dingy cloth cap which lay flat on his head, or rather forehead.

From Madison Court-House we moved past Orange

Court-House and along the plank road to the vicinity of Fredericksburg, arriving there on the 1st of December.

Longstreet's corps was found guarding the Rappahannock against Burnside's army which had concentrated on the opposite bank. My division was moved to the vicinity of Guiney's depot on the R., F. & P. Railroad, as was Jackson's. After remaining here two or three days, I was ordered to move towards Port Royal to support D. H. Hill, whose division had been ordered to the vicinity of that place, to watch some gun-boats there and prevent a crossing. Port Royal is some eighteen or twenty miles below Fredericksburg on the Rappahannock. I first took position some six or eight miles from Port Royal on the road from Guiney's depot, but subsequently moved to the vicinity of Buckner's Neck on the Rappahannock a few miles above Port Royal, for the purpose of watching the river and acting in concert with General Hill. The latter, by the use of one Whitworth gun and some other artillery, had driven the enemy's gunboats from Port Royal, and in revenge they fired into the houses in the little village of Port Royal and some others below as they passed down the river.

While I was watching the river at Buckner's Neck, which is in a bend of the river, and commanded by high ground on the opposite side, so as to afford a good position for forcing a passage, the enemy hauled some timbers to a place called the Hop Yard on the northern bank, as if for the purpose of constructing a bridge at that place, but this proved a feint. Jackson's division had been left near Guiney's depot, and A. P. Hill's had been camped in rear of Hamilton's Crossing for the purpose of supporting Longstreet's right, which rested at the latter place. The different divisions of Jackson's corps were thus posted, immediately preceding the battle of Fredericksburg.

CHAPTER XVIII.

BATTLE OF FREDERICKSBURG.

FREDERICKSBURG is located on the southern bank of the Rappahannock River at the head of tide water, and the river is navigable to that point for steamboats and small vessels. On the northern bank, opposite, above, and below Fredericksburg, are what are called the Stafford Heights, which are close to the river, and completely command the southern bank. Fredericksburg's exact location is on a narrow strip of low land between the river and a range of hills in the rear. These hills leaving the river opposite the small village of Falmouth, which is a short distance above Fredericksburg and on the northern bank, diverge from it below, and gradually declining, extend nearly to the Massaponix Creek, which empties into the river four or five miles below the town.

The river flats or bottoms immediately below Fredericksburg widen out considerably and continue to widen until they are from one and a half to two miles in width at the lower end of the range of hills, where they unite with similar but not so wide flats on the Massaponix, which extend back for some distance in rear of the range of hills mentioned. Below the mouth of the Massaponix there are other hills which approach near to the bank of the river, and extend down it for a considerable distance. Hazel Run, rising southeast of Fredericksburg, runs through the range of hills along a narrow valley, or ravine rather, and passing close on the east of the town, empties into the river. Deep Run rises below in the range of hills, and runs across the wide bottoms through a deep channel likewise into the river, something over a mile below the town. The hills just in rear of the town were, at the time of which I am speaking, nearly denuded of growing timber, but below, to the end of the range, they were for the most part covered with woods. The bottoms were entirely cleared and in cultivation, furnishing several extensive farms, and up Deep Run to its sources is a valley making a large re-entering angle in the line of hills, which valley was then also cleared and in cultivation.

From the town a road, called the Telegraph Road, runs south, crossing Hazel Run and then ascending the hills passes towards Richmond by the way of Hanover Junction. Another road called the Plank Road ascends the hills above Hazel Run and runs westward by Chancellorsville to Orange Court-House. A third road, called the River Road, runs from the lower end of the town, crossing Hazel Run and Deep Run, and, passing through the bottoms about half way from the river to the foot of the hills, in a direction very nearly parallel to the river, it crosses the Massaponix not far above its mouth, where it forks, one fork going to Port Royal below and the other by Bowling Green in the direction of Richmond. This is a wide road, and where it passes through the bottoms there were on both sides high, thick, and firm embankments thrown up for fences or enclosures to the adjacent fields.

The Richmond, Fredericksburg & Potomac Railroad, leaving the Potomac at the mouth of Aquia Creek, crosses the river into Fredericksburg and then runs through the bottoms below the town between the river road and the hills, which latter it approaches closely at their lower end, and then passes around at their foot to take the direction to Richmond. Just at the rear of the foot of the lower end of the hills, a country road leading from the Telegraph Road and passing along the east of the ridge crosses the railroad to get into the River Road, and this is called "Hamilton's Crossing," from a gentleman of that name formerly residing near the place. A canal runs from the river along the foot of the hills above the town to the rear of it, for the purpose of supplying water to several mills and factories in it, and this canal connects by a drain ditch with Hazel Run, over which ditch the Plank Road crosses.

What is called Marye's Heights or Hill lies between Hazel Run and the Plank Road, and at the foot of it is a stone wall, behind which and next to the hill, the Telegraph Road runs. Above Marye's Hill on the east of the Plank Road are what are called, respectively, Cemetery, Stansbury's and Taylor's Hills, all overlooking the canal. In rear of these hills and overlooking and commanding them are higher eminences. On the east of Hazel Run and the Telegraph Road is quite a high hill farther back than Marye's Hill and overlooking it and nearly the whole ground, to which the name of Lee's Hill has been given, because it was the position generally occupied by General Lee during the battle.

Burnside's army had taken position on and in rear of Stafford Heights, and the heights themselves, from Falmouth to a point very nearly opposite the mouth of the Massaponix, were covered with numerous batteries of heavy guns, while the nature of the ground was such as to afford easy access to the river by his troops. Longstreet's corps occupied the hills in rear of Fredericksburg to Hamilton's Crossing, and positions for some distance above, while strong pickets were established in the town and on the river bank above and below to watch the enemy and impede a crossing.

It was impossible to resist successfully a crossing, as the river is only between two and three hundred yards wide, and the banks are so deep, and the river so accessible, on the north bank by means of ravines running into it, that our artillery, posted on the hills occupied by our troops, could not play upon the bridges either during the progress of the construction or afterwards, while the enemy's batteries were able, by a concentrated fire, to drive off the small bodies watching the river, or to prevent any aid being sent to them over the wide open plains formed by the bottoms. In addition to all this, the bottoms towards the lower end of our lines were so wide that we had no guns which would do effective firing across them, while the enemy's heavy guns from the north bank of the river completely swept the whole of our front, and reached over beyond our line.

On the morning of the 11th of December the enemy commenced his movement, and by the use of his artillery drove the regiments which were guarding the river from its banks after an obstinate resistance, and succeeded in laying down their pontoon bridges, one at the mouth of Deep Creek, and the other two at Fredericksburg. The first was laid early in the afternoon, but the latter two not until near night, and during night and the next day the enemy crossed in heavy force.

On the afternoon of the 12th I received an order from General Jackson to move at once to the vicinity of Hamilton's Crossing, which I did by marching nearly all night, and a short time before day I bivouacked some two miles in rear of the crossing where the division had a little time to rest. At light on the morning of the 13th I moved up to the crossing, and found our army in position confronting the enemy. Longstreet's line had been constructed from the right, and General A. P. Hill's division, which was much the largest in Jackson's corps, now occupied the right of the line which rested near the crossing. He was in the front skirts of the woods which covered the hills, and on his left was Hood's division.

On the right of Hill's line was a small hill cleared on the side next the enemy, on which were posted some fourteen pieces of artillery under Lieutenant Colonel Walker, which were supported by Field's brigade, under Colonel Brockenborough, while Archer's brigade was on the left of the guns. On Archer's left there was an interval of several hundred yards in front of which was a low flat marshy piece of woodland extending across the railroad out into the bottom which was supposed to be impracticable, and was therefore not covered by any body of troops, but Gregg's brigade was posted in reserve in rear of this interval, without, however, being in the line of battle. On the left of the interval were the other three brigades of A. P. Hill's division, Lane's brigade being next to it, but in advance of the general line a considerable number of pieces of artillery were posted along the left of Hill's line, but they were on low and unfavorable ground, as there were no good positions for guns on that part of the line.

On my arrival, my division was posted on a second line several hundred yards in rear of A. P. Hill's, with Jackson's, now under Brigadier General Taliaferro, on my left. My right rested on the railroad at the crossing, and extended along the ridge road, which here crossed the railroad, for a short distance and then into the woods on my left. Hays' brigade was on my right, with Trimble's brigade under Colonel R. F. Hoke immediately in its rear, Lawton's brigade under Colonel N. N. Atkinson in the centre, and my own brigade under Colonel J. A. Walker on the left. In this position there was a thick woods intervening between my division and the enemy, and the consequence was that he was entirely excluded from our view as we were from his. D. H. Hill's division, which had followed mine from below, was posted in a third line in the open ground in my rear beyond the hills.

The weak point in our position was on our right, as there was the wide open plain in front of it extending to the river and perfectly covered and swept by the enemy's heavy batteries on the opposite heights, and to the right, extending around to our rear, were the open flats of the Massaponix, here quite wide and incapable of being covered by any position we could take. There was very great danger of our right being turned by the enemy's pushing a heavy column down the river across the Massaponix. The plains on that flank were watched by Stuart with two brigades of cavalry and his horse artillery.

A heavy fog had concealed the two armies from each

other during the early morning, but about nine o'clock it began to rise, and then the artillery fire opened, which was just as my division was moving into position. The enemy's fire at first was not directed towards the place where my division was posted, but after a short interval the shells began to fall in our vicinity, and the division remained exposed to a random but quite galling cannonading for two or three hours.

Shortly after noon we heard in our front a very heavy musketry fire, and soon a courier from General Archer came to the rear in search of General A. P. Hill, stating that General Archer was very heavily pressed and wanted reinforcements. Just at that moment, a staff officer rode up with an order to me from General Jackson, to hold my division in readiness to move to the right promptly, as the enemy was making a demonstration in that direction. This caused me to hesitate about sending a brigade to Archer's assistance, but to be prepared to send it if necessary, I ordered Colonel Atkinson to get his brigade ready to advance, and the order had been hardly given, before the adjutant of Walker's battalion of artillery came galloping to the rear with the information that the interval on Archer's left (an awful gulf as he designated it) had been penetrated by heavy columns of the enemy, and that Archer's brigade and all our batteries on the right would inevitably be captured unless there was instant relief. This was so serious an emergency that I determined to act upon it at once notwithstanding the previous directions from General Jackson to hold my division in readiness for another purpose, and I accordingly ordered Atkinson to advance with his brigade.

I was then entirely unacquainted with the ground in front, having been able when I first got up to take only a hasty glance at the country to our right, and I asked Lieutenant Chamberlain, Walker's adjutant, to show the brigade the direction to advance. In reply he stated that the column of the enemy which had penetrated our line was immediately in front of the brigade I had ordered forward, and that by going right ahead there could be no mistake. The brigade, with the exception of one regiment, the 13th Georgia, which did not hear the order, accordingly moved off in handsome style through the woods, but as it did so Lieutenant Chamberlain informed me that it would not be sufficient to cover the entire gap in our line, and I ordered Colonel Walker to advance immediately with my own brigade on the left of Atkinson.

The enemy's column in penetrating the interval mentioned had turned Archer's left and Lane's right, while they were attacked in front, causing Archer's left and Lane's entire brigade to give way, and one column had encountered Gregg's brigade, which, being taken somewhat by surprise, was thrown into partial confusion, resulting in the death of General Gregg, but the brigade was rallied and maintained its ground. Lawton's brigade advancing rapidly and gallantly under Colonel Atkinson, encountered that column of the enemy which had turned Archer's left, in the woods on the hill in rear of the line, and by a brilliant charge drove it back down the hill, across the railroad, and out into the open plains beyond, advancing so far as to cause a portion of one of the enemy's batteries to be abandoned. The brigade, however, on getting out into the open plain came under the fire of the enemy's heavy guns, and the approach of a fresh and heavy column on its right rendered it necessary that it should retire, which it did under orders from Colonel Evans, who had succeeded to the command by reason of Atkinson's being severely wounded.

Two of Brockenborough's regiments from the right participated in the repulse of the enemy. Colonel Walker advanced, at a double quick, further to the left, encountering one of the columns which had penetrated the interval, and by a gallant and resolute charge he drove it back out of the woods across the railroad into the open plains beyond, when, seeing another column of the enemy crossing the railroad on his left, he fell back to the line of the road, and then deployed the 13th Virginia Regiment to the left, and ordered it to advance under cover of the timbers to attack the advancing column on its flank. This attack was promptly made and Thomas' brigade, attacking in front at the same time, the enemy was driven back with heavy loss.

As soon as Atkinson and Walker had been ordered forward, Hoke was ordered to move his brigade to the left of Hays, but before he got into position, I received a message stating that Archer's brigade was giving way and I ordered Hoke to move forward at once to Archer's support, obliquing to the right as he moved. Just as Hoke started, I received an order from General Jackson, by a member of his staff, to advance to the front with the whole division, and Hays' brigade was at once ordered forward in support of Hoke. The 13th Georgia Regiment which had been left behind on the advance of Lawton's brigade was ordered to follow Hoke's brigade and unite with it.

Hoke found a body of the enemy in the woods in rear of Archer's line on the left, where the regiments on that flank, which had been attacked in rear, had given way, but Archer still held the right with great resolution, though his ammunition was exhausted. Upon a gallant charge, by the brigade under Hoke, the enemy was driven out of the woods upon his reserves posted on the railroad in front, and then by another charge, in which General Archer participated, the railroad was cleared and the enemy was pursued to a fence some distance beyond, leaving in our hands a number of prisoners, and a large number of small arms on the field.

The movements of the three brigades engaged have been described separately from the necessity of the case, but they were all engaged at the same time, though they went into action separately and in the order in which they have been mentioned, and Lawton's brigade had advanced further out into the plains than either of the others.

BATTLE OF FREDERICKSBURG

On riding to the front, I directed Lawton's brigade, which was retiring, to be re-formed in the woods—Colonel Atkinson had been left in front severely wounded and he fell into the enemy's hands. Captain E. P. Lawton, Assistant Adjutant General of the brigade, a most gallant and efficient officer, had also been left in front at the extreme point to which the brigade advanced, mortally wounded, and he likewise fell into the enemy's hands.

I discovered that Hoke had got too far to the front where he was exposed to the enemy's artillery, and also to a flank movement on his right, and I sent an order for him to retire to the original line, which he did, anticipating the order by commencing to retire before it reached him. Two of his regiments and a small battalion were left to occupy the line of the railroad where there was cover for them and his other two regiments, along with the 13th Georgia, which had not been engaged, were put in the slight trenches previously occupied by Archer's brigade. Walker continued to hold the position on the railroad which he had taken after repulsing the enemy. Lawton's brigade was sent to the rear for the purpose of resting and replenishing its ammunition. Hays' brigade, which had advanced in rear of Hoke, had not become engaged, but in advancing to the front it had been exposed to a severe shelling which the enemy began, as his attacking columns were retiring in confusion before my advancing brigades. Hays was posted in rear of Hoke for the purpose of strengthening the right in the event of another advance. When I had discovered Lawton's brigade retiring, I sent to General D. H. Hill for reinforcements for fear that the enemy might again pass through the unprotected interval, and he sent me two brigades, but before they arrived Brigadier General Paxton, who occupied the right of Taliaferro's line, had covered the interval by promptly moving his brigade into it.

The enemy was very severely punished for this attack,

which was made by Franklin's grand division, and he made no further attack on our right. During this engagement and subsequently there were demonstrations against A. P. Hill's left and Hood's right which were repulsed without difficulty. Beginning in the forenoon and continuing until nearly dark, there were repeated and desperate assaults made by the enemy from Fredericksburg against the positions at Marye's Hill and the one to our right of it, but they were repulsed with terrible slaughter, mainly by the infantry from Longstreet's corps posted behind the stone wall at the foot of Mayre's Hill, and the artillery on that, and on the neighboring heights. The loss to the enemy here was much heavier than that on our right, while our own loss at the same point was comparatively slight.

My two brigades, Trimble's under Hoke, and my own under Walker, and the 13th Georgia Regiment held their positions on the front until night, while Hays retained his position immediately in rear of Hoke, but there was no further attack made on that part of the line, or on any part of Hill's front, except the demonstrations on his left which have been mentioned and which resulted in some skirmishing and artillery firing.

When my division was first put in position on the second line as described, having no use for my artillery, I ordered Captain J. W. Latimer, my acting chief of artillery, to report to Colonel Crutchfield, Chief of Artillery for the Corps, with the six batteries attached to the division, to-wit: Carrington's, Brown's, Garber's, D'Aquin's, Dement's, and his own. Of these Brown's and Latimer's were posted on Hill's left, under the immediate charge of Captain Latimer, and did most effective service, and D'Aquin's and Garber's were sent to Major Pelham, Stuart's Chief of Artillery, on the right, where they likewise did good service, Captain D'Aquin losing his life while taking part in the artillery firing in that quarter. Just before sunset of the day of the battle, after having seen that all was quiet in my front, I rode a little to the rear and discovered General D. H. Hill's division moving to the front through the woods.

On my inquiring the meaning of the movement, General Colquitt, in command of the front brigade, informed me that orders had been given for the advance of the whole line, and that Hill's division was ordered to advance in support. General D. H. Hill himself rode up in a few minutes, and confirmed the information. This was the first intimation I had received of the order, as it had not reached me. While General Hill and myself were speaking of the matter, Lieutenant Morrison, aide-de-camp to General Jackson, rode up and stated that the General's orders were that I should hold my command in readiness to advance; and immediately afterwards one of my own staff officers came to me with the information that General Jackson wished me to take command of all the troops on the right and advance, regulating the distance to which I should go, by the effect produced on the enemy by our artillery which was to open.

I rode immediately to where Hoke's brigade was posted and found General Jackson himself, who repeated in person the orders to me, stating that I was to advance in support of some artillery which he was about to send forward. I informed him of the condition of my command, the separation of Walker from the rest, the fact of Lawton's brigade being in the rear, and that Hoke's and Hays' brigades and the 13th Georgia were the only troops immediately available. He told me to advance with the latter and that he would give me abundant support; I accordingly prepared to advance with Hoke's brigade and the 13th Georgia in front, followed by Hays' brigade. The programme was that a number of pieces of artillery should be run out in front, and open on the enemy's infantry, when I was to advance and the artillery to be again moved forward, followed by my infantry.

The movement with the artillery was commenced, and as soon as it left the woods the enemy opened with numerous batteries from the plains and from behind the embankments on the river road. This fire was terrific and many shells went crashing past us into the woods in our rear, where D. H. Hill's division was massed. Our own guns opened and continued to fire for a brief space, and a part of Hoke's brigade advanced to the railroad, but General Jackson soon became satisfied that the advance must be attended with great difficulties and perhaps disastrous results, and abandoned it. It was well that he did. The enemy had very heavy forces massed behind the embankments on the river road, the one nearest us being pierced with embrasures for numerous pieces of artillery. We would have had to advance nearly a mile, over an entirely bare plain swept by all this artillery, as well as cannonaded by the heavy guns on Stafford Heights, and if we had been able to force back the bodies of infantry and the artillery occupying positions on the plain between us and the woods, still when we reached the road itself we would have found a vastly superior force behind a double line of very strong breastworks.

Nothing could have lived while passing over that plain under such circumstances, and I feel well assured that, while we were all ready to obey the orders of our heroic commander, there was not a man in the force ordered to advance, whether in the front or in support, who did not breathe freer when he heard the orders countermanding the movement.

I have subsequently examined this ground with great care, and this examination has strengthened the position first entertained. It may perhaps be asked why our troops had not occupied the line of this road, to which I will reply that the road and the embankments on each side of it were perfectly commanded by the batteries of Stafford Heights, which rendered the position untenable for us, and the retreat from it most hazardous, while it afforded safe protection to the enemy from our guns.

Shortly after the termination of this effort to advance, I received a notification from General Jackson to move my troops to the rear for the purpose of resting and getting provisions as soon as they should be relieved by the troops of A. P. Hill's division which had at first occupied the positions now held by me, but no troops came to my relief, and I therefore, remained in position. Orders were received during the night for Taliaferro to relieve Hill's troops in the front line beginning from the left, and for me to occupy the remainder of the line on the right which Taliaferro could not fill out. In accordance with these directions, before dawn on the 14th, Paxton relieved Walker, Hays took the position which Paxton vacated, Hoke remained stationary, Lawton's brigade under Colonel Evans was posted on Hoke's right, and Walker was moved from the left and placed in reserve behind Hoke. The evening before, Carrington's battery had relieved Latimer's and Brown's on the left, and still remained in position, and on the morning of the 14th, Dement's battery relieved one of the batteries on the right which had been engaged the day before.

During the 14th the enemy remained in position on the plains and at Fredericksburg, an occasional shot being exchanged by the artillery and some firing from the skirmishers taking place on portions of the line, but none in my front.

Before light on the morning of the 15th, D. H. Hill's division relieved Taliaferro's and mine on the front line, and we moved to the rear in reserve, A. P. Hill's division occupying the second line.

There was quiet on the 15th, the enemy still retaining his position, but early on the morning of the 16th, as I was moving into position on the second line in accordance with previous orders, it was discovered that the enemy had re-crossed the river during the night, taking up his bridges, and I was ordered to move at once to the vicinity of Port Royal to guard against the possible contingency of the enemy's attempting to turn our right by crossing the river near that place; and I commenced the march immediately.

LIEUTENANT GENERAL JUBAL A. EARLY

The loss in the division under my command in this battle was in killed 89 and wounded 639, to-wit: in Hays' brigade, 5 killed and 40 wounded; Trimble's brigade (Hoke's), 8 killed and 98 wounded; Lawton's brigade, 55 killed and 369 wounded; my own brigade (Walker's), 17 killed and 114 wounded; and in the artillery of the division 3 killed and 18 wounded. Among the killed were Lieutenant Colonel Scott of the 12th Georgia Regiment, and Captain D'Aquin of the artillery, and among the wounded were Colonel Atkinson of the 26th Georgia Regiment (in the hands of the enemy), Captain E. P. Lawton, A. A. G. Lawton's brigade (Lawton mortally wounded and in the hands of the enemy) and Colonel Lamar, 61st Georgia Regiment.

General Lee's entire loss in the battle was in killed 458, and wounded, 3,743, to-wit: in Longstreet's corps, 130 killed, 1,276 wounded; in Jackson's corps, 328 killed and 2,454 wounded; and 13 wounded in Stuart's cavalry.

The enemy's loss was very much heavier, and over 900 prisoners, more than 9,000 stand of arms and a large quantity of ammunition fell into our hands.

The failure of General Lee to attempt to destroy the enemy's army after its repulse has been much criticised, and many speculations about the probable result of an attempt to drive the enemy into the river have been indulged in by a number of writers. In the first place, it must be recollected that no man was more anxious to inflict a decisive blow on the enemy than General Lee himself, and none understood better the exact condition of things, and the likelihood of success in any attempt to press the enemy after his defeat on the 13th. That defeat was a repulse with very heavy loss, it is true, but it was not a rout of the enemy's army; and candid persons ought to presume that General Lee knew what he was about and had very good and sufficient reasons for not sallying from his line of defence, upon the exposed plains below, to make the attempt to convert the repulse into a rout.

BATTLE OF FREDERICKSBURG

If attention is given to the previous description of the ground on which the two armies were operating, it must be seen that an attempt to pass over the wide plain intervening between our line and the enemy's position below the town, while exposed to the fire of 150 heavy guns on the Stafford Heights, and the numerous field pieces securely masked in the River road, would inevitably have resulted in disaster, unless the enemy's forces had become so paralyzed as to be incapable of an effort at defence. Burnside's army was composed of about 150,000 men in the grand divisions under Sumner, Franklin, and Hooker, respectively.

In none of the assaults on our lines were the whole of these grand divisions engaged, but when columns of attack were sent forward, there were always very heavy reserves for the attacking columns to fall back upon in case of repulse; Sumner's and Franklin's grand divisions had been mainly engaged and Hooker's scarcely at all. General Lee's army was not half as large as Burnside's and if he had at any time made an attempt to advance, any force that he could have massed for that purpose without abandoning his line of defence entirely would in all likelihood have still encountered a superior force of infantry behind a strong line of defence, in addition to the artillery.

As I have stated, General Jackson made the attempt to advance on the right late in the day on the 13th, but he was compelled to desist, very fortunately, before any disaster happened. Above the town, the same canal, at the foot of the range of hills, which had furnished an insurmountable obstacle to any attack by the enemy on our extreme left, likewise furnished the same obstacle to an advance on our part. The only other quarter from which the advance could have been made was from the hills immediately in rear of the town upon the enemy in the town, and there the difficulties were greater even than below. Any attacking columns from that quarter must either have moved down the rugged face of the

base hills, or by flank along the Telegraph and Plank
roads, and then they would have been so much scattered by the artillery from the north bank, which would
then have had a more effective range than even on the
plains, that it would not have required the reserves,
posted behind the houses and defences in the town, to
complete the repulse and disaster.

As to a night attack, that is a very easy thing to talk
about but a most hazardous experiment to try, especially on dark nights such as we then had. Such attacks
cannot be ventured on with safety unless with the most
thoroughly trained troops, and then not in large bodies,
for fear of confusion and firing into each other, the very
dread of which often paralyzes very brave troops.

It has been said that General Lee might have inflicted tremendous damage upon the enemy by forcing
hot shot and shell into Fredericksburg while the enemy's
troops were massed there. The heroic and patriotic
people of that town, when it was threatened with a
bombardment by Sumner, had not appealed to the commander of their country's army to cause the danger to
be removed from them by not resisting its occupation
by the enemy, but had exhibited most commendable un-
selfishness by, in most cases, abandoning their homes
without a murmur, while there were some too poor to
move elsewhere, and others who chose to remain and
share all the dangers of the approaching struggle; it
was not in the heart of the noble commander of the Army
of Northern Virginia to doom, by his own act, the remaining few of that devoted people and the homes of
the absent to destruction, for the sake of killing and
wounding a few thousand of the enemy, and causing
dismay among the remainder.

Is this forbearance one to be criticised with severity
as a grievous military blunder?

It is probable that if General Lee had known that
the enemy was evacuating the town, his artillery might
have inflicted considerable damage, but the enemy had

given no indication of such a purpose, and he took advantage of the darkness of the night and the prevalence of a storm and wind to make good his retreat, when the noise attending the movement could not be heard.

General Lee accomplished all that was possible with the means under his control, except, indeed, the useless destruction of what the enemy had left of the town of Fredericksburg.

There was a ridiculous story about General Jackson, to which currency was given by the newspapers, which represented that, at a council of war called by General Lee on the night after the battle, General Jackson fell into a doze while the very grave question of what ought to be done under the circumstances was being discussed, and after all the rest had given their opinion, General Lee turned to General Jackson and asked, "Well, General, what is your opinion?" to which the latter, waking out of his nap, replied, "Drive 'em in the river, drive 'em in the river." This story is by no means creditable to General Jackson, yet it obtained a wide circulation, and the narrators of it seemed to think it was very characteristic.

General Jackson was a most able commander and heroic soldier, and it was not at all likely that he would have acted so much like a besotted member of a council of war called by his chief. I presume after the facts that I have before stated, it is not necessary to assert that no such incident occurred.

Had Burnside moved down the river to the Massaponix, after crossing, or had thrown other bridges across at or near the mouth of that stream, and crossed one of his grand divisions there, he would inevitably have forced us to abandon our line of defence, and fight him on other ground.

CHAPTER XIX.

Operations in Winter and Spring, 1862–63.

On the 16th of December, as soon as it was discovered that the enemy had recrossed the river, in accordance with the orders received, I moved to the vicinity of Port Royal, arriving by nightfall.

The enemy was content with the experiment he had made, and did not attempt any further movement at that time. I proceeded the next day to picket the river from a place called the Stop-Cock, near the Rappahannock Academy, to the vicinity of Port Tobacco, below Port Royal, the river having been watched on this line previous to my arrival by some of Brigadier General Wm. H. F. Lee's cavalry, which I relieved.

My division was encamped in the vicinity of Port Royal, on the hills back from the river, and when it was ascertained that the enemy was not preparing for a new movement in any short time, the different brigades built permanent winter quarters at suitable places. After a careful examination of the country, I proceeded to fortify the banks of the river at points likely to afford facilities for crossing, and I established a line of defence also along the main road running parallel with the river, where high embankments with cedar hedges on them afforded good cover for troops and excellent breastworks. This line commenced at the upper end of the Hazelwood estate, the former residence of that distinguished Virginian, John Taylor of Caroline, and with the defences on the river extending to Camden, the residence of Mr. Pratt, some distance below Port Royal, passing in rear of that town, which was now nearly abandoned on account of the depredations of the enemy's gunboats and the fear of their repetition. New roads were constructed in rear of the line of defence out of reach of artillery from the opposite bank, for the purpose of facilitating communication between the different positions, and two Whitworth guns under Captain W. W. Hardwick were placed on a high hill in rear of Port Royal, for the purpose of preventing the gunboats which were below from ascending the river; and subsequently torpedoes were placed in the bed of the river some two or three miles below Port Royal under the superintendence of some one sent from headquarters.

The enemy established a line of cavalry pickets on the opposite bank of the river as far down as ours reached, and the two were in sight of each other. The river at Port Royal is between six and eight hundred yards wide, and immediately opposite Port Royal is the small village of Port Conway, which was occupied by the enemy's pickets.

We were compelled to haul our supplies in wagons from Guiney's depot on the railroad, and as the winter was a severe one with much snow and rain, the country roads, which we had to use, became almost impassable from the mud, and we were compelled to employ the men for a considerable time in corduroying them at the worst places.

In the month of January, 1863, I was promoted to the rank of Major General and was assigned to the permanent command of Ewell's division, the name of which was now changed. Colonel R. F. Hoke of the 21st North Carolina Regiment, who had commanded Trimble's brigade since the termination of the Maryland campaign, was promoted to the rank of Brigadier General and assigned to the brigade he already commanded, and the name of that also was changed. The brigade had previously consisted of the 21st North Carolina, the 12th and 21st Georgia, and the 15th Alabama Regiments, and a North Carolina battalion of two companies. The 12th and 21st Georgia were now transferred to a Georgia brigade in D. H. Hill's division, and the 15th Alabama to a brigade in Hood's division, the 6th, 54th, and 57th North Carolina Regiments from Hood's division, taking the place in Hoke's brigade of those transferred from it.

The 25th and 44th Virginia Regiments were transferred from my own brigade to that of J. R. Jones, in Jackson's division, and subsequently Colonel William Smith of the 49th Virginia, who had been so severely wounded at Sharpsburg and had not yet returned, was appointed Brigadier General and assigned to my old brigade as it remained after the transfer of the two regiments. The organization of the artillery was now changed, and in the place of the batteries which had heretofore been attached to brigades, battalions were organized, which were to be under the general control of the Chief of Artillery for the Corps, and a battalion to be assigned to a division on an active campaign, or when required for defence. In consequence of this arrangement, a number of promotions took place among the artillery officers, and Captain J. W. Latimer, a youthful but most gallant and efficient officer, was made a Major of Artillery, a promotion which he had richly earned, though he was scarcely twenty-one years old. All the batteries heretofore attached to the division, except Latimer's, were sent to the rear of Bowling Green to winter, in order to be more convenient to forage. Latimer's battery was retained to be used in case of need, and it became Tanner's by virtue of the promotion of the first lieutenant.

My assistant adjutant general, while I was a brigadier general, Captain F. Gardner, had resigned the previous summer, and my aide, Lieutenant S. H. Early,* had resigned while we were in the valley after the Maryland campaign, as he was over fifty years of age, and the condition of his family required his pres-

---

* Lieutenant Early, at General Early's request (and accompanied by his young son, John Cabell Early, aged fifteen years), rejoined the army in 1863 during its northern invasion, and was severely wounded at the battle of Gettysburg.

ence at home. I had had no regular personal staff since then. I found no assistant adjutant general with Ewell's division when I succeeded to the command at Sharpsburg, and Major Samuel Hale, who held the commission of a commissary, had been acting in that capacity for me while I commanded the brigade and continued to do so while I commanded the division. I found with the division Major J. P. Wilson and Mr. Henry Heaton, who had been acting as volunteer aides to General Ewell and then to General Lawton, and they continued with me in that capacity until after my promotion.

After I was assigned to the division as major general, Major Hale received the commission of adjutant general with the rank of major, and A. L. Pitzer and Wm. G. Callaway were commissioned as aides with the rank of first lieutenants.

My division staff as then organized consisted of the following officers, all of whom except those above designated had been with General Ewell as members of his staff:

Lieutenant Colonel J. M. JONES, *Inspector General.*
Major SAMUEL HALE, *Assistant Adjutant General.*
Lieutenant A. L. PITZER, *Aide.*
Lieutenant WM. G. CALLAWAY, *Aide.*
Major C. E. SNODGRASS, *Quartermaster.*
Major BEN H. GREEN, *Commissary.*
Captain WILLIAM THORNTON, *Assistant Commissary.*
Captain C. W. CHRISTIE, *Ordnance Officer.*
Captain HENRY RICHARDSON, *Engineer Officer.*

Subsequently, in the spring, Major John W. Daniel, who had been commissioned at my instance, was also assigned to me as an assistant adjutant general. Lieutenant Robert D. Early, who had been acting as aide in one of the brigades in D. H. Hill's division, also reported to me during the winter, as acting aide, and continued in that capacity until he was made an assistant adjutant general to a brigade in Jackson's old division.

LIEUTENANT GENERAL JUBAL A. EARLY

A company of mounted men organized as scouts, couriers and guides by General Ewell, had remained attached to the division under the command of Captain W. F. Randolph, but it was transferred in the spring to General Jackson's headquarters. My division, as it remained after the changes above mentioned, was composed of four brigades, to-wit: Hays' Louisiana brigade, Hoke's North Carolina brigade, Lawton's Georgia brigade (commanded by Colonel Evans), and Smith's Virginia brigade, organized as follows:

Hays' brigade: 5th, 6th, 7th, 8th, and 9th Louisiana Regiments.

Hoke's brigade: 6th, 21st, 54th, and 57th North Carolina Regiments and Wharton's North Carolina battalion.

Lawton's brigade: 13th, 26th, 31st, 38th, 60th, and 61st Georgia Regiments.

Smith's brigade: 13th, 31st, 49th, 52nd, and 58th Virginia Regiments.

In a few days after the battle, the other divisions of Jackson's corps were moved to positions above me, covering the river from the mouth of Massaponix to my left, Jackson's old division being on my immediate left, then A. P. Hill's division, and then D. H. Hill's. In January General Trimble, who had been severely wounded near Groveton on the 29th of August previous, was made a Major General and assigned to Jackson's division, which had always heretofore remained without a regular division commander, even while General Jackson was a Major General, as his command had included other troops.

The enemy made no demonstration whatever on my front, and we had nothing to disturb our quiet during the winter, except a little incident by which two officers were captured by the enemy in rather a singular manner. There were a considerable number of ducks on the river, and Major Wharton, commander of the battalion in Hoke's brigade, and Captain Adams, the assistant adjutant general of the brigade, took it into their heads to go shooting. There were several boats at Port Royal which I had directed to be hauled up on the bank with orders to the pickets to keep watch over them and not permit them to be launched.

On the day the Major and the Captain took for their sport, the picket at Port Royal happened to be from their brigade, and they easily induced the sentinel on duty to let them have the use of one of the boats, to row into the mouth of a creek above, on our side, where the ducks were most numerous. The day was a very windy one with the wind blowing across towards the enemy. By keeping near the bank they avoided the effect of the wind until they got opposite the mouth of the creek, when it struck their boat and forced it out into the stream. Not being expert boatmen, and moreover being excited by the danger, they lost control of the boat and were driven helplessly to the northern bank into the hands of the enemy's pickets, and of course were made prisoners. The Major having an old newspaper with him, pulled it out when he reached the shore and proposed an exchange, a practice sometimes prevailing with the pickets in spite of all orders, but the Federal on post was rather too shrewd to have that game played on him, insisting that it was not exactly a case for exchange of such civilities. This was a caution to all persons disposed to sporting and to interfere with the orders to the pickets; and we had no more duck shooting in boats.

Burnside made an abortive effort in January to advance again by flanking us on the left, but he stuck in the mud, and we were not put to any inconvenience by the movement. About the last of the month he was relieved of his command, and a new commander for the Federal Army was selected, in the person of Major General Joseph Hooker, called "Fighting Joe."

Though we passed the winter without the excitement attending an advance of the enemy, still we were not without some excitements of our own, and I may as well relate the following occurrence to show how men who had passed through the stirring scenes of the previous year, who had fought with Jackson in the valley, around Richmond, at Manassas, Sharpsburg, and Fredericksburg, could amuse themselves in winter quarters.

We had several severe snow storms during the winter, and after one of them, when the snow lay deep on the ground, Hoke's brigade challenged Lawton's for a battle with snow balls, which challenge was accepted. The two brigades were marshalled under their respective commanders—Hoke on the one side, and Colonel Evans on the other. Evans stood on the defensive in front of his camp and Hoke advanced against him. Evans' force was much the larger, but being Georgians who had been brought from Savannah in the beginning of the previous summer, his men were not accustomed to the fleecy element. Hoke's men were more experienced, and when they made a bold dash at the Georgians, pelting them most unmercifully with their well pressed balls, and giving the usual Confederate yell, there was no withstanding the shock of the onset. Evans' men gave way in utter confusion and rout, and Hoke's men got possession of their camp.

The Georgians seeing that their camp and all their effects were in possession of the enemy, who seemed to be inclined to act on the maxim that "to victors belong the spoils," took courage, rallied, and came back with such vim that Hoke's men in their turn were routed, and retreated in utter dismay. No time was given for them to rally, but they were pursued to their own camp, their leader having been captured in the pursuit. Evans' men did not deem it prudent to press their victory too far, but retired, though in good order. They acted magnanimously and released the leader of their opponents on his parole of honor, not, however, without his having been well wallowed in the snow.

There was no official report of this battle, but all the

particulars were related at division headquarters by one of the aides who happened to be present, and who was himself captured under suspicious circumstances on Hoke's retreat, but begged off on the ground that he was a neutral and a mere spectator. He was much joked by the other young men at headquarters, who charged him with skulking on the occasion, and there was some reason to suspect that he did not stand the storm of snow balls as well as he did that of shot and shell on many another occasion. Many, very many of the poor fellows who shared in this pastime poured out their life's blood on subsequent battlefields, and a small remnant were surrendered at Appomattox Court-House with arms in their hands, and tears rolling down their cheeks.

About the first of March my division was moved to Hamilton's Crossing to take place of Hood's, which had been sent with Longstreet south of James River, and a body of cavalry took the place of my division on the right. In my new position, it was my duty to picket and watch the river from the mouth of Hazel Run at the lower end of Fredericksburg to the mouth of Massaponix, which was done with three regiments at a time, posted at different positions on the bank. These pickets were in full view of and in musket range of the enemy's pickets on the opposite bank, and also under the fire of the guns on Stafford Heights, but by a tacit arrangement there was never any firing from either side on ordinary occasions, but the picketing detachments on both sides were moved into position and regularly relieved without molestation.

In the month of April the 31st Virginia Regiment of Smith's brigade, in company with the 25th Virginia of Jones' brigade, Trimble's division, was sent to the valley for the purpose of accompanying an expedition into Northwestern Virginia under General Imboden, and did not return until late in May.

The growing timber on the range of hills which had constituted our line of defence at the battle of Fredericksburg had been almost entirely cut down during the winter to construct tents, and furnish firewood for Hood's division, and there were left only a few scattering trees on the hills and a thin skirt in front. Shortly after my removal, General Jackson, whose headquarters had been below, near Moss Neck, removed also to the vicinity of Hamilton's Crossing.

Brigadier General J. B. Gordon, who had been Colonel of the 6th Alabama Regiment in Rodes' brigade, D. H. Hill's division, and very severely wounded at Sharpsburg, was assigned in April to the command of Lawton's brigade, which took his name.

There was perfect quiet along the river front until the night of the 28th of April, though Fitz. Lee's brigade of Stuart's cavalry had a fight with the enemy at Kelley's Ford in Culpeper in March, and there was another affair with the cavalry in April.

CHAPTER XX.

BATTLE OF CHANCELLORSVILLE.

BEFORE light on the morning of the 29th of April, the enemy, having moved three corps of his army up during the night, by taking advantage of a heavy fog that over-hung the river, threw a brigade across in boats, just below the mouth of Deep Run, and the 54th North Carolina Regiment on picket at that point, being unable to cope with the force brought against it, was forced to retire, which it did without loss. The movement had been conducted with so much secrecy, the boats being brought to the river by hand, that the first intimation of it, to the regiment on picket, was the landing of the force. Bridges were then rapidly laid down at the same crossing used by Burnside at this point and a division of infantry with some artillery was crossed over.

About a mile lower down below the house of Mr. Pratt, a similar crossing was attempted, but that was discov-ered, and resisted by the 13th Georgia Regiment under Colonel Smith until after sunrise, when that regiment was relieved by the 6th Louisiana under Colonel Mona-ghan going on picket in its regular time. The latter regiment continued to resist the crossing successfully until the fog had risen, when the enemy's guns were brought to bear, and by a concentrated fire that regiment was compelled to retire, not, however, without sustain-ing a considerable loss in killed and wounded as well as prisoners, the latter being captured in rifle pits at points below the crossing, which was effected by the enemy's coming up in their rear before they had received notice of his being across. The 13th Georgia had also sustained some loss in killed and wounded, and prisoners captured in the same way, who had not been relieved. The re-sistance made at this point delayed the enemy so that the bridges there were not laid until after 10 o'clock A.M.

193

A little after light, information reached me of the crossing at Deep Run, and I sent notice of it at once to General Jackson. Without, however, waiting for orders, I ordered my division to the front, and as soon as it was possible put it in line along the railroad, with my right resting near Hamilton's Crossing and my left extending to Deep Run. Three regiments were sent to the front and deployed along the River road as skirmishers. The 13th Virginia Regiment, under Lieutenant Colonel Terrill, on picket between the mouths of Hazel and Deep Runs, was drawn back to the line of the River road above Deep Run, and remained there until relieved by McLaws' division, when it was brought up.

As soon as the enemy had laid down his bridges at the lower crossing, a division of infantry and some artillery were crossed over at that point. When the fog rose, the slopes of the opposite hills were semi-covered with troops the whole distance from opposite Fredericksburg to a point nearly opposite the mouth of the Massaponix. The question was whether they were ostentatiously displayed as a feint, or whether they were massed for crossing. The troops which had crossed were seen throwing up breastworks covering the bridges and also epaulments for artillery; but it was impossible to discover the strength of the force already across, as below the deep banks of the river there was ample space for massing a large body of troops out of our sight. There appeared no attempt to make a crossing at Fredericksburg, or to move up towards the town.

Some artillery was put in position on the hill near Hamilton's Crossing on my right, and in rear of my left. D. H. Hill's division, now under command of Brigadier General Rodes, was soon brought up, and put in position on my right, extending across the Massaponix, one brigade being placed below that creek across the River road, so as to guard the ford. A Whitworth gun, of very long range, was also posted below the

Massaponix out of range of the enemy's guns across the river and in position to partially enfilade them.

The remaining divisions of Jackson's corps were brought up during the day, and A. P. Hill's was put in position in a second line in rear of mine. Trimble's division under the command of Brigadier General Colston arrived very late in the afternoon and was placed in reserve in the rear. Barksdale's brigade already occupied the town of Fredericksburg, and the remaining brigades of McLaws' division were brought up and placed in position on the left of my line, one of his brigades connecting with my left, which was now drawn back from the railroad, and a shorter line made across to Deep Run, to connect it with McLaws' right. For the greater part of the way the railroad track furnished a very good protection, and it was strengthened by throwing up embankments, the line being advanced a little in front on the left of my centre where there was a rise in the ground above the level of the road. In order to occupy the whole of the line my brigades had to be extended out, as the division was not strong enough to man it fully.

During the day the enemy made no attempt to advance against us in force with his infantry, and his skirmishers were effectually kept from the River road by mine, and on the right Rodes' skirmishers, which extended from the right of mine around to the river above the Massaponix, prevented any movement in that direction. There was some artillery firing, and one Whitworth gun from across the Massaponix played with very considerable effect on the bottoms on the enemy's left. Large bodies of the infantry on the opposite slopes occasionally moved down towards the river, where they were concealed from our view by the bank on the south side, which is the highest.

I retained my position on the front line during the night, which passed quietly. The next day there was very little change in the appearances in front. The enemy had made strong *tetes du pont* covering his bridges, and was constructing a line of entrenchments connecting the two, passing in front of the Pratt and Bernard houses, and extending below the lower bridge.

There was this day some apparent diminution of the infantry in view on the opposite slopes, but there were many heavy guns in battery on the heights and a very large force of infantry still visible. There were some demonstrations with the infantry on the north bank, some skirmish firing, and some artillery firing also, but the enemy on the south bank did not appear at all enterprising, and rather contracted his lines on his left, his skirmishers retiring before ours which were pushed forward on that flank. The indications were that it was a mere demonstration on our front, to cloak a more serious move in some other quarter, and so it turned out to be. When this was discovered, it is quite probable that we might have destroyed the comparatively small force on the south bank by a movement against it from our line, but this would not have compensated us for the loss we would, in all probability, have sustained from the enemy's heavy guns.

General Lee had ascertained that by far the largest portion of Hooker's army had crossed the Rappahannock and Rapidan Rivers above their junction, and were moving down on his left. He therefore determined to move up with the greater part of his own army to meet that force, which was watched by Anderson's division of Longstreet's corps and a portion of Stuart's cavalry. Accordingly late on the afternoon of the 30th I was instructed by General Jackson to retain my position on the line, and, with my division and some other troops to be placed at my disposal, to watch the enemy confronting me while the remainder of the army was absent. Barksdale's brigade occupying Fredericksburg and the heights in rear, was directed to retain his position, as was also a portion of General Pendleton's reserve artillery, which occupied positions on Marye's and Lee's Hills, and the whole was placed under my command. In addition, Graham's battery of artillery of four guns, two twenty pounders and two ten pounders, Parrots, posted on the hill on my right, was left with me, and Lieutenant Colonel Andrews was ordered to report to me with his battalion of four batteries with twelve pieces, to-wit: six Napoleons, four three-inch rifles, and two ten pounder Parrots. A Whitworth gun under Lieutenant Tunis was also left at my disposal and posted on the right across the Massaponix. With the rest of the army near Fredericksburg comprising the other three divisions of Jackson's corps, and three brigades of McLaws' division, General Lee moved on the night of the 30th and the morning of the 1st of May towards Chancellorsville to meet Hooker.

Before leaving, General Lee instructed me to watch the enemy and try to hold him; to conceal the weakness of my force, and if compelled to yield before overpowering numbers, to fall back towards Guiney's depot where our supplies were, protecting them and the railroad; and I was further instructed to join the main body of the army in the event that the enemy disappeared from my front, or so diminished his force as to render it prudent to do so, leaving at Fredericksburg only such force as might be necessary to protect the town against any force the enemy might leave behind.

The force which had made the demonstration on our front consisted at first of the 1st, 3rd, and 6th corps of Hooker's army, under the command of Major General Sedgwick. The 3rd corps moved to join Hooker during the 30th, but the 1st and 6th remained in my front still demonstrating. In his testimony before the Congressional Committee on the war, Hooker stated that the 6th corps, according to the returns of the 30th of April, 1863, numbered 26,233 present for duty. Sedgwick says that the 6th corps numbered only 22,000 when it crossed the river. Taking the medium between them, the effective strength may be put down at 24,000, which General A. P. Howe, commanding one of the divisions, says he was informed, at headquarters of the corps, it was. The first corps must have numbered at least 16,000 and perhaps more, so that I must have been left confronting at least 40,000 men in these two corps, besides the stationary batteries on Stafford Heights and Gibbon's division of the 2nd corps which was just above, near Falmouth, and, according to Hooker's statement, numbered over 6,000 for duty on the 30th.

My division by the last tri-monthly field return which was made on the 20th of April, and is now before me, had present for duty 548 officers and 7,331 enlisted men, making a total of 7,879. It had increased none, and I could not have carried into action 7,500 in all, officers and men, and not more than 7,000 muskets, as in camp when everything was quiet, a number of men reported for duty, who were not actually able to take the field. I had already lost about 150 men in the resistance which was made at the lower crossing. Barksdale's brigade did not probably exceed 1,500 men for duty, if it reached that number. I had, therefore, not exceeding 9,000 infantry officers and men in all, being very little over 8,000 muskets; and in addition I had Anderson's battalion with twelve guns; Graham's four guns; Tunis', Whitworths, and portions of Watson's; Cabell's and Cutt's battalions under General Pendleton, not numbering probably thirty guns. I think 45 guns must have covered all my artillery, and these were nothing to compare with the enemy's in weight of metal.

The foregoing constituted the means I had for occupying and holding a line of at least six miles in length, against the enemy's heavy force of infantry, and his far more numerous and heavier and better appointed artillery. It was impossible to occupy the whole line, and the interval between Deep Run and the foot of Lee's Hill had to be left vacant, watched by skirmishers, protected only by a cross fire of artillery. I could spare no infantry from the right, as that was much the weakest point of the line, and the force which had crossed, and which exceeded my whole strength, was below Deep Run, and confronting my own division. Andrews' artillery was placed in position on the morning of the 1st as follows: four Napoleons and two rifles were placed under Major Latimer, near the left of the line occupied by my division, behind some epaulments that had been made on that part of the line; two Parrots were placed with Graham's guns on the hill on my right, and two Napoleons and two rifles were posted to the right of Hamilton's Crossing, near a grove of pines, the Whitworth gun being posted on a height across the Massaponix so as to have a flank fire on the enemy if he advanced, and it was without support. Colonel Andrews had charge of all of the artillery on this part of the line, that on Marye's and Lee's Hills was under the immediate superintendence of General Pendleton, and some of the batteries were so posted as to have a cross fire on the upper part of the valley of Deep Run.

The enemy remained quiet on the 1st, except in demonstrating by manœuvres of his troops, and there was no firing on that day. His line of entrenchments, covering the two bridges, had been completed, and he still displayed a heavy force of infantry, consisting of the two corps under Sedgwick. The ensuing night also passed quietly, and during it a battery of four Napoleons was sent by General Pendleton to report to Colonel Andrews, and was posted with the four guns near the pines on the right of the crossing.

The morning of the 2nd opened with appearances pretty much the same as they had been the day before; if anything there was more infantry in view on the north bank than had appeared the previous day. Colonel Andrews was ordered early in the day to feel the enemy with his guns, and accordingly Latimer opened with his two rifle guns on the enemy's position near Deep Run, and Graham's and Brown's Parrots opened on the infantry and batteries below and near the Pratt house. Latimer's fire was not returned, but Graham's and Brown's was responded to by two of the batteries on the north bank and some guns on the south side. Shortly afterwards the infantry and artillery at the lower crossing disappeared behind the bank of the river, and that crossing was abandoned.

During the morning I rode to Lee's Hill for the purpose of observing the enemy's movements from that point, and I observed a considerable portion of his infantry in motion up the opposite river bank. While I was, in company with Generals Barksdale and Pendleton, observing the enemy's manœuvre and trying to ascertain what it meant, at about 11 o'clock A.M., Colonel R. H. Chilton, of General Lee's staff, came to me with a verbal order to move up immediately towards Chancellorsville with my whole force, except a brigade of infantry and Pendleton's reserve artillery, and to leave at Fredericksburg the brigade of infantry and a part of the reserve artillery to be selected by General Pendleton, with instructions to the commander of this force to watch the enemy's movements, and keep him in check if possible, but if he advanced with too heavy a force to retire on the road to Spottsylvania Court-House—General Pendleton being required to send the greater part of his reserve artillery to the rear at once.

This order took me very much by surprise, and I remarked to Colonel Chilton that I could not retire my troops without their being seen by the enemy, whose position on Stafford Heights not only overlooked ours, but who had one or two balloons which he was constantly sending up from the heights to make observations, and stated that he would inevitably move over and take possession of Fredericksburg and the surrounding Heights. The Colonel said he presumed General Lee understood all this, but that it was much more important for him to have troops where he was, than at Fredericksburg, and if he defeated the enemy there he could easily retake Fredericksburg; he called my attention to the fact, which was apparent to us all, that there was a very heavy force of infantry massed on the slopes near Falmouth which had moved up from below, and stated that he had no doubt the greater portion of the force on the other side was in motion to reinforce Hooker. He repeated his orders with great distinctness in the presence of General Pendleton, and in reply to questions from us, said that there could be no mistake in his orders.

This was very astounding to us, as we were satisfied that we were then keeping away from the army, opposed to General Lee, a much larger body of troops than my force could engage or neutralize if united to the army near Chancellorsville. It is true that there was the force massed near Falmouth and the indications were that it was moving above, but still there was a much larger force of infantry stationed below, which evinced no disposition to move. While we were conversing, information was brought me that the enemy had abandoned his lower crossing, and that our skirmishers had advanced to the Pratt house, but he still, however, maintained his position at the mouth of Deep Creek with a division of infantry and a number of guns on our side of the river.

The orders as delivered to me left me no discretion, and believing that General Lee understood his own necessities better than I possibly could, I did not feel justified in acting on my own judgment, and I therefore determined to move as directed. It subsequently turned out that Colonel Chilton had misunderstood General Lee's orders, which were that I should make the movement indicated if the enemy did not have a sufficient force in my front to detain the whole of mine, and it was to be left to me to judge of that, the orders, in fact, being similar to those given me at first. It also turned out that the troops seen massed near Falmouth were the 1st corps under Reynolds, moving up to reinforce Hooker, and that the 6th corps, Sedgwick's own, remained behind.

When Colonel Chilton arrived, General Pendleton was

making arrangements to move some artillery to the left to open on the columns massed near Falmouth, but the order brought rendered it necessary to desist from that attempt in order to make preparations for the withdrawal.

My division occupied a line which was in full view from the opposite hills except where it ran through the small strip of woods projecting beyond the railroad, and the withdrawal had to be made with the probability of its being discovered by the enemy. I determined to leave Hays' brigade to occupy the hills in rear of Fredericksburg with one regiment deployed as skirmishers on the River road confronting the force at the mouth of Deep Run, and also to leave one of Barksdale's regiments, which was already in Fredericksburg and along the bank of the river, picketing from Falmouth to the lower end of the town.

The orders were given at once and the withdrawal commenced, but it had to be made with great caution so as to attract as little attention as possible and therefore required much time. General Pendleton was to remain at Fredericksburg, according to the orders, and the withdrawal of such of his artillery as was to be sent to the rear was entrusted to him and executed under his directions. The Whitworth gun was ordered to the rear with the reserve artillery and Andrews' battalion and Graham's battery were ordered to follow my column, Richardson's battery, which was on the right, being returned to General Pendleton's control. When the withdrawal commenced, the enemy sent up a balloon and I felt sure that he had discovered the movement, but it turned out that he did not.* It was late in the afternoon before my column was in readiness to move, and Barksdale was ordered to bring up the rear with the three regiments left after detaching the one on picket, as soon

---

* Professor Lowe's balloon reconnaissances so signally failed on this occasion and in the operations at Chancellorsville, that they were abandoned for the rest of the war.

as he was relieved by Hays. As soon as the troops were in readiness the three brigades of my division moved along the Ridge road from Hamilton's Crossing to the Telegraph road, and then along a cross-road leading into the Plank road, Barksdale going out on the Telegraph road to join the column. Upon getting near the Plank road, a little before dark, I received a note from General Lee which informed me that he did not expect me to join him unless, in my judgment, the withdrawal of my troops could be made with safety, and I think he used the expression that if by remaining I could neutralize and hold in check a large force of the enemy, I could do as much or perhaps more service than by joining him.

I had proceeded so far that I determined to go on, as the probability was that if the enemy had discovered my movement, the mischief would be done before I could get back, and that I would not be able to recover the lost ground, but might deprive General Lee entirely of the use of my troops. When the head of my column had reached the Plank road and moved up it about a mile, a courier came to me from General Barksdale, stating that the enemy had advanced against Hays with a very large force, and that the latter and General Pendleton had sent word that all of the artillery would be captured unless they had immediate relief. The courier also stated that General Barksdale had started back with his own regiments.

I determined to return at once to my former position, and accordingly halted the column, faced it about and moved back, sending my Adjutant General, Major Hale, to inform General Lee of the fact. The fact turned out to be that just before dark Sedgwick had crossed the remainder of his corps and moved towards the River road below, called also the Bowling Green road, forcing from it the 7th Louisiana Regiment, under Colonel Penn, which occupied that road and fell back to the line on the railroad after skirmishing sharply with the enemy. There had been no advance against Hays at Fredericksburg, and Sedgwick had halted with his whole force and formed line on the river, occupying with his advance force the road from which Colonel Penn had been driven.

We regained our former lines without trouble about ten or eleven o'clock at night, throwing out skirmishers towards the River road. Barksdale occupied his old position and Hays' returned during the night to the right of my line. The night passed quietly on the right after my return except some picket firing on the front, but, just before daybreak on the morning of the 3rd, I was informed by General Barksdale that the enemy had thrown a bridge across at Fredericksburg and was moving into the town. The General had ridden to see me in person to request reinforcements, and I ordered Hays' brigade to return to the left as soon as possible, directing General Barksdale to post the brigade where it was needed, as he understood the ground thoroughly. In reply to a question from me, he informed me that the crossing had not been resisted by his regiment, which had retired skirmishing on the approach of the enemy, as the struggle was deemed useless, and it undoubtedly would have been. This was a mistake about the bridge being laid at that time, but it was a very natural one, as Sedgwick moved a portion of his force up the river into the town, while doubtless preparations were making for laying down the bridge early in the morning.

Barksdale's brigade was then posted as follows: the 21st Mississippi Regiment occupied the trenches on Marye's Hill between Marye's house and the Plank road; the 18th, the stone wall at the foot of the hill, where it was subsequently reinforced by three companies from the 21st; the 17th, the trenches on the front slope of Lee's Hill; and the 13th, the trenches further to the right. Squires' battery of the Washington Artillery was posted in the works on Marye's Hill, and the rest of Pendleton's guns on Lee's Hill on the front crest and at positions further to the right, so as to cover the interval between the hills and the upper part of Deep

Run. There were no troops on the left of the Plank road along the crest overlooking the canal. Very soon after daylight, the head of Sedgwick's column, which had moved up during the night from below, emerged from the town and advanced against the defences at Marye's Hill, but was repulsed by the fire of Barksdale's infantry and the artillery posted there.

When it became sufficiently light to see, it was discovered by us that the opposite bank of the river was bare of troops and it was very apparent that the enemy's whole force lately confronting us on that side was across for the purpose of a serious move, and the question was as to where it would be made. The heaviest force in view was in front of the crossing below the mouth of Deep Run, and there were at that point a number of pieces of artillery. The enemy, however, was also demonstrating against Marye's Hill with both infantry and artillery, but the mass of his infantry there was concealed from our view, and there were indications also as if he might attempt to pass up the valley of Deep Run on the left bank. The fact was that there was one division covering the bridge, one between Deep Run and Hazel Run, and one masked in Fredericksburg. The skirmishers from my division succeeded in getting to the River road on the right, but the position next Deep Run was held by too strong a force to be dislodged.

Very shortly after light the enemy commenced demonstrating at Deep Run as if to turn the left of my division held by Hoke's brigade, and threw bodies of troops up the ravine formed by the high banks of the run, while there were demonstrations also on the left bank of the run. Latimer opened with his guns on the ravine and the advancing bodies of infantry where they could be seen; but a considerable body succeeded in getting up to that part of the railroad next to the run and took position behind it, where they were protected against the fire of our artillery. The enemy opened with two or three batteries on Latimer's guns, and there ensued a brisk artillery duel. Andrews brought Graham's and Brown's guns from the right to replace Latimer's Napoleons, and also Carpenter's two rifles to take position with Latimer's two, and the firing was continued for some time, as well against the enemy's infantry as against his artillery. Finally Smith's brigade, which was on the right of Hoke's, moved out and dislodged the infantry which had taken position behind the railroad embankment, and as it retired the artillery played on it. This ended the demonstrations at Deep Run, and soon heavy bodies of infantry were seen passing up towards Fredericksburg, upon which Andrews' batteries opened.

I had remained on the right with my division, as I knew that that was the weakest part of our line, and I was very apprehensive that the enemy would attempt to cut my force in two by moving up Deep Run, which would have been the most dangerous move to us he could have made. I, however, kept a lookout upon the movements above and was in constant communication with Generals Barksdale and Pendleton, from whom I received several reports that they had repulsed all the attacks upon their position, and thought they could hold it. Shortly after sunrise, and after the repulse of the first attack on Barksdale's position, Gibbon's division, of the enemy's 2nd corps, was crossed over into Fredericksburg on the bridge which had been laid there, and it was then moved above the town for the purpose of turning the position on that flank, but this effort was balked by the canal, over which there was no bridge; it then attempted to effect the movement by repairing a bridge over the canal, the planking from which had been torn up, but Hays' brigade had arrived by that time, and four of his regiments filed into the trenches on the left of the Plank road just in time to thwart this attempt, and another made shortly afterwards to cross the canal at the upper end of the same division.

Hays' brigade had had a long distance to march in order to avoid the enemy, and when it arrived General

Barksdale placed one of the regiments, the 6th Louisiana, Colonel Monaghan, on his right in the trenches near what was known as the Howison house, and the other four were sent to man the trenches along the crest of the hills on the left of the Plank road, where they arrived just in time to thwart the attempt to cross the canal as before stated. The enemy's guns from the north side of the river, as well as from positions on the south side above and below the town, continued to fire upon the positions occupied by Barksdale's men and our artillery, but the latter generally reserved its fire for the infantry.

An attempt to turn the right of the position by the right bank of Hazel Run was repulsed by Pendleton's artillery and every effort to get possession of the heights was baffled and repulsed until after 11 A.M., when two large attacking columns of a division each were formed, one of the divisions from below being brought up for that purpose. One of these columns moved against Marye's Hill and the other against Lee's Hill, both at the same time, while Gibbon's division demonstrated against the heights above with storming parties in front. The column that moved against Marye's Hill, consisting of Newton's division, made its attack on the famous stone wall defended by a regiment and three companies, and its storming parties were twice broken and driven back in disorder by the gallant little band that held that position, but constantly returning to the attack with overwhelming numbers the enemy finally succeeded in carrying the work, after having sustained terrible slaughter.* Then passing around the foot of the hill a

---

* Sedgwick, in his testimony before the Congressional Committee on the War, says: "I lost a thousand men in less than ten minutes' time in taking the heights of Fredericksburg."

General Barksdale informed me that just before this final attack was made the enemy sent a flag of truce to Colonel Griffin, commanding the force behind the stone wall, asking permission to take care of his wounded lying in front under our fire, which permission was imprudently granted by Colonel Griffin, without his knowledge, and that the weakness of the force at that point was thus discovered, and immediately afterwards the assaulting columns advanced.

portion of the attacking column came up in the rear, capturing Squires' guns (which had been fought to the last minute), and along with them the Captain and his company.

The column sent against Lee's Hill did not succeed in carrying it by assault, but was kept at bay until Marye's Hill had fallen, when the position being untenable, the regiments defending it were withdrawn up the hill, and the enemy was thus able to take possession of that also. The artillery on both hills had done good service in aiding to repel all the previous assaults and to resist this. The companies of the 21st Mississippi in the trenches on the left of Marye's Hill were compelled to retire to prevent being surrounded and captured, as were also Hays' regiments in the trenches further to the left, the latter being compelled to cross the Plank road higher up, as their retreat on the Telegraph road was cut off. The enemy got on Hays' flank and rear before he was aware the hill on his right was taken, and the consequence was that he lost a few prisoners. He succeeded, however, in making good his retreat.

General Barksdale partially rallied his regiments and made obstinate resistance to the enemy's advance on the Telegraph road, falling back gradually before the large force opposing him. The greater portion of the guns on Lee's Hill were carried off, but some were lost because the horses belonging to them had been carried to the rear to be out of reach of the enemy's shells, and could not be got up in time to carry off the pieces. Ten guns were lost in all, including those taken at Marye's Hill, but two were subsequently recovered, making our final loss in that respect eight pieces.

Wilcox's brigade was above at Banks' Ford, but not under my command, and was about to move up to Chancellorsville, but hearing that the enemy was advancing up the river, General Wilcox hurried to the vicinity of Taylor's house at the extreme left of the line with two pieces of artillery and sixty men, and putting his guns in position, opened with effect on a portion of Gibbon's division when it was trying to effect a crossing of the canal at the upper end. He then detained his brigade, and subsequently started a regiment to Barksdale's assistance at his request, but before it arrived Marye's Hill had been taken and it therefore retired. General Wilcox subsequently did good service in resisting the enemy's advance up the Plank road.

While these events were transpiring above, I was near the left of the line occupied by my division, and in a position from which I could observe a good deal of the movements, but could not see Marye's Hill very well. After what was supposed to be the enemy's effort to move up Deep Run and thus break our lines had been thwarted, and when I saw the infantry moving up towards Fredericksburg, I sent one of my aides, Lieutenant Callaway, to Lee's Hill, to give notice to Generals Barksdale and Pendleton and to ascertain how they were getting on. After he had been gone some time, I became uneasy and determined to ride up myself.

While I was on my way some one came galloping up in my rear and stated that some person below had seen the enemy's troops and flag go up on Marye's Hill. I did not think this could be so, but rode on rapidly, hoping that the statement was untrue. I soon met a courier from General Pendleton with a note stating that they had so far repulsed any attack and could hold their position. This relieved me for an instant, but in a few minutes Lieutenant Callaway came galloping with the information that the enemy certainly had carried the heights, and that he had seen his attacking column ascending them at Marye's house, a very few minutes after parting with Generals Barksdale and Pendleton, who were on Lee's Hill and who had just stated to him that they thought they could hold the position.

I at once sent an order to General Gordon, who occupied my right, to move up as soon as possible with three of his regiments over the road I was following, which was the nearest practicable one. I then galloped to the Telegraph road, and soon met Pendleton's artillery going rapidly to the rear, and ordered it to be halted. Going on I found General Barksdale on the ridge immediately in rear of Lee's Hill rallying his men and skirmishing with the enemy who had ascended the hill, and before whom they were retiring gradually but obstinately. Barksdale's men were rather scattered, but the 6th Louisiana had retired in good order and I directed it to form a line, and Barksdale to halt and get his men in line, which he did. I also ordered a battery of artillery to be brought forward into action and soon one was by my side and unlimbered but did not fire.

There was a line of the enemy in front a few hundred yards on the crest of the hill, and I turned to the officer commanding the battery and asked him why he did not fire, to which he replied, "I have no ammunition, sir." I ordered another to be brought forward, and a battery of Howitzers, from Cabell's battalion, was brought up and opened with canister. The enemy's advance had been checked by the demonstration, but he soon brought up some artillery and opened on us at short range with shrapnel and canister, and I ordered the line to retire a short distance, which it did in good order, taking up another position. In this manner we continued to retire along the Telegraph road from point to point, taking advantage of favorable portions of the ground to make a stand until the enemy ceased to pursue. I then ordered General Barksdale to take position at Cox's house, about two miles in rear of Lee's Hill, where the first cross-road leaves the Telegraph road to get into the Plank road, and to establish Hays (to whom I had sent a message to come around to the Telegraph road) on the line, as well as Gordon's regiments, when they arrived.

By obtaining possession of Lee's Hill, the enemy had obtained a position from which he could completely enfilade my line on the right, and as soon as the foregoing arrangements were made, I rode rapidly to the

right and threw back the troops there into a second line
which had been previously prepared in the rear, and
which was not enfiladed; and Colonel Andrews was
ordered to take position with all of his guns on the
ridge at the head of the Deep Run valley, so as to protect
the left flank of my division and the right of Barksdale's
line.

All these movements were made without molestation
from the enemy. Of course I did not know what the
purposes of the enemy were, and took my measures to
provide as well as I could for any emergency that might
present itself. I had met Gordon with his three regiments immediately after leaving Barksdale, and directed
him to join the latter. After making the dispositions on
the right, I rode back to Barksdale's position and found
his line established with Hays and Gordon in position.

It had been now ascertained that the enemy was
moving up the Plank road, and I rode out to a position
across Hazel Run, from which I could see the moving
columns and discovered that it was moving very slowly,
and that it finally halted. Lieutenant Pitzer, one of
my aides, had been at Lee's Hill when the heights were
carried, and knowing the importance of the affair to
General Lee, had gone at once to give him the information, as he knew that it would be some time before I
could be informed so as to send a messenger myself, and
thus judiciously anticipated me in putting General Lee
on his guard.

While the events thus detailed were transpiring on
the line occupied by me, a great battle had been fought
between General Lee's forces and the main body of
Hooker's army. Hooker had crossed the river above and
concentrated four corps at Chancellorsville in a strong
position, and Anderson's division of Longstreet's corps,
Longstreet himself being still absent with two of his
divisions, had watched the movement of the enemy and
resisted his advance column, taking position on the Plank
road at Tabernacle Church. McLaws' division and the

three divisions of Jackson's corps had moved up during the night of the 30th of April and the morning of the 1st of May and united with Anderson. Our troops had thus moved forward on the Plank road and the stone turnpike, Anderson's and McLaws' divisions in front, and Jackson's divisions following Anderson's on the Plank road, and had driven an advanced line of the enemy back to within a mile of Chancellorsville upon his main force.

Early on the morning of the 2nd, Anderson's and McLaws' divisions, with the exception of Wilcox's brigade of Anderson's division, which had been sent back to Banks' Ford, and Barksdale's brigade of McLaws' division which was at Fredericksburg, were left to confront the enemy on the side next to Fredericksburg, and Jackson moved with his three divisions, by a circuitous route to the left, to gain the rear of the enemy's right. Late in the afternoon, General Jackson reached the rear of the enemy's right flank about three miles beyond Chancellorsville, and with Rodes in front—followed by Colston with Trimble's division, and A. P. Hill,—advanced at once with great vigor, driving the enemy before him, carrying position after position, routing entirely one corps, and capturing a number of guns and prisoners, until his advance was arrested by the abattis in front of the central position near Chancellorsville. Night had come on by this time, and General Jackson ordered A. P. Hill's division, which was following in rear of the other two, to the front to take the place of the latter. He himself went to the front to reconnoitre for the purpose of ordering another advance, and, having sent an order to Hill to press on, while returning in the darkness was shot and dangerously wounded * under an unfortunate mistake, by a part of Hill's advancing troops. General

---

* Captain R. E. WELBOURN:

Some conflicting accounts of the manner in which General Jackson was shot have been published, and as you were with him, I will be

A. P. Hill was soon after disabled and the advance was thus arrested.

When Jackson's guns opened, our troops on the right pressed the enemy's left heavily to prevent any troops being sent from that flank against Jackson, but no attack in front was made then and night put an end to the operations in that quarter. Hooker had been joined during the day by the 1st corps brought up from opposite

---

very much obliged, if you will give me all the details of the affair. With pleasant recollections of your official connection with me,

Yrs. very truly

LYNCHBURG, Feb. 12, 1873.   J. A. EARLY.

General J. A. EARLY:

I give you the facts relating to the wounding of General T. J. Jackson. As the details of the battle are familiar to you, I will begin with Jackson's movements after the battle was over, and all seemed quiet, the enemy having disappeared from our immediate front, and all firing consequently having ceased. Jackson took advantage of this lull in the storm to relieve Rodes' troops (who had been fighting and steadily advancing and making repeated charges from the time the fight began), and had ordered General Hill to the front to relieve Rodes with his fresh troops, directing the change to be made as quickly as possible. We were within a half mile of the open fields near Chancellorsville, where the enemy was supposed to be strongly entrenched. While the change was being made Jackson manifested great impatience to get Hill's troops into line and ready to move promptly, and to accomplish this he sent the members of his staff with orders to Hill and other general officers to hurry up the movement. From the orders sent to General Stuart it was evident that his intention was to storm the enemy's works at Chancellorsville as soon as the lines were formed, and before the enemy recovered from the shock and confusion of the previous fighting, and to place the left of his army between Hooker and the river. While these orders were being issued Jackson sat on his horse just in front of the line on the pike. From this point he sent me with an order to General Hill. I galloped back and met Hill, in about 50 yards, riding along the pike towards General Jackson. I turned and rode with him to his lines, he stopping within a few feet of their front. I then rode immediately on to General Jackson, who was in sight, and only a few paces in front of Hill, just in the position I had left him. As I reached him, he sent off the only staff officer present, with orders to Hill to move

213

Fredericksburg, but at the close of the fight his lines had been very much contracted, and his troops on his right greatly scattered; and early in the night he telegraphed to Sedgwick to cross the river and move up to Chancellorsville on the Plank road, which dispatch found Sedgwick already across.

General Jackson had been entirely disabled by his wound, and General A. P. Hill was so injured as to be unable to command in the field. Brigadier General Rodes

---

forward as soon as possible, and then started slowly along the pike towards the enemy. I rode at his left side, two of my signal men just behind us, followed by couriers, etc., in columns of twos. General Jackson thought, while awaiting Hill's movements, that he would ride to the front, as far as the skirmish line, or pickets, and ascertain what could be seen or heard of the enemy and his movements,—supposing there was certainly a line of skirmishers in front, as his orders were always very imperative to keep a skirmish line in front of the line of battle. When we had ridden only a few rods and reached a point nearly opposite an old dismantled house in the woods (near the road to our right) and while I was delivering to him General Hill's reply to his order—given a few moments before,—to our great surprise our little party was fired upon by about a battalion or probably less of our troops, a little to our right and to the right of the pike, the balls passing diagonally across the pike and apparently aimed at us. There seemed to be one gun discharged, followed almost instantly by this volley. The single gun may have been discharged accidentally, but seemed to have been taken as a signal by the troops, to announce the approach of the enemy. I hardly think the troops saw us, though they could hear our horses' feet on the pike and probably fired at random in the supposed direction of the enemy. However, the origin of the firing is mere conjecture, but it came as above stated, and many of the escorts and their horses were shot down. At the firing our horses wheeled suddenly to the left and General Jackson, at whose side I rode, galloped away—followed by the few who were not dismounted by the first firing,—into the woods to get out of range of the bullets, and approached our line a little obliquely, but had not gone over 20 steps beyond the edge of the pike, into the thicket, ere the brigade just to the left of the turnpike (on our right as we approached from the direction of the enemy), drawn up within 30 yards of us, fired a volley in their turn, kneeling on the right knee, as shown by the flash of their guns, as though prepared to guard against cavalry. By this fire General Jackson was wounded. These troops evidently mis-

was the officer next in rank, but having a very natural hesitation to assume the responsibility of so large and important a command, Major General Stuart of the cavalry, who was operating in connection with General Jackson, was requested to assume command, which he did. During the night the enemy strengthened his contracted line with breastworks and abattis, and strongly fortified other positions in his rear nearer the Rappahannock.

---

took us for the enemy's cavalry. We could distinctly hear General Hill calling, at the top of his voice, to his troops to make them cease firing. He knew that we had just passed in front of him, as did the troops immediately on the pike, and I don't think these latter fired. I was alongside of Jackson, and saw his arm fall at his side, loosing the rein, when the volley came from the left. His horse wheeled suddenly and ran through the bushes toward the enemy. The limb of a tree took off his cap and threw him flat on the back on his horse. I rode after him, passing under the same limb, which took off my hat also, but Jackson soon regained his seat, caught the bridle in his right hand, and turning his horse towards the pike and our men, somewhat checked his speed. As he turned to the pike, it gave me the inside track, and I caught his horse as he reached the pike, which he was approaching at an acute angle. Just as I caught the reins, Captain Wynn rode up on the opposite side of him and caught hold of the reins on that side, almost simultaneously. By this time the confusion was over and all was quiet, and looking up and down the pike in every direction, no living creature could be seen save us three.

As soon as I could check Jackson's horse, I dismounted, and seeing that he was faint, I asked him what I could do for him, or if he felt able to ride as far as into our lines. He answered, " You had best take me down," leaning, as he spoke, toward me and then falling, partially fainting from loss of blood.

I was on the side of the broken arm, while his horse had his head turned towards the enemy and about where we were when first fired upon, and would not be kept still, as he was frightened and suffering from his own wounds. As General Jackson fell over on me, I caught him in my arms, and held him until Captain Wynn could get his feet out of the stirrups, then we carried him in our arms some 10 or 15 steps north of the pike, where he was laid on the ground, resting his head in my lap, while I proceeded to dress his wounds, cutting off his coat sleeves, and binding a handkerchief tightly above and below his wound and putting his arm in a sling. Wynn went for Dr. McGuire

LIEUTENANT GENERAL JUBAL A. EARLY

Early in the morning of the 3rd, Stuart renewed the attack with Jackson's division on the left, while Anderson pressed forward with his right resting on the Plank road, and McLaws demonstrated on the right. The enemy was forced back from numerous strongholds until Anderson's left connected with Stuart's right, when the whole line attacked with irresistible force, driving the enemy from all his fortified positions around Chancellorsville with very heavy loss, and forcing him to retreat to the

---

and an ambulance, and I was left alone with him until General Hill came up. Just before Hill reached us, Jackson revived a little and asked me to have a skilful surgeon attend him. When I told him what had been done he said " Very good."

The enemy evidently thought the firing had thrown our men into confusion and resolved to take advantage of it by making a determined attack at this time, so in a few minutes, it was announced by Lieutenant Morrison, who had joined Jackson while he was lying on the ground, and now ran up in a very excited manner, crying out, " The enemy is within 50 yards and advancing. Let us take the General away." Jackson was still lying with his head in my lap, I had finished tying up his arm where it was broken, and asked him where his other wound was, and what I should do for that, when he replied, " In my right hand, but never mind that, it is a mere trifle." He said nothing about the wound in his left wrist, and did not seem aware of it, doubtless owing to the fact that the arm was broken above. Upon hearing Morrison's warning, I sprang up, and said, " Let us take the General in our arms, and carry him back," to which he replied, " No, if you will help me up, I can walk." He had only gone a few steps, when we met a litter and placed him on it. He was being borne off on foot, supported by Captain Lee and one or two others, I walking between them and the pike, and leading three horses, trying to keep the troops, then moving down the pike, from seeing who it was, but found this impossible, and we met some men with this litter before we had gone ten steps. While placing Jackson on it, the enemy opened fire on us at short range, from a battery planted on the pike and with infantry; a terrific fire of grape, shell, minie balls, etc., and advancing at a rapid rate. Everything seemed to be seized with a panic, and taken by surprise, our line was thrown into confusion. It recoiled and for awhile continued to give way, and the enemy pressed forward. Such was the disorder that I thought that General Jackson and party would certainly fall into the hands of the enemy. The horses jerked loose, and ran in every direction, and before we proceeded far one of the

new fortifications nearer the Rappahannock. By ten o'clock A.M. General Lee was in full possession of Chancellorsville and the field of battle. He then proceeded to reorganize his troops for an advance against the enemy's new position, to which the latter had been able to retreat under shelter of the dense woods, which covered all the ground, and also rendered an advance by our troops in line of battle very difficult and hazardous.

General Lee had just completed his arrangements to renew the attack, when he received the intelligence of the capture of Marye's Hill by Sedgwick's force and the

---

litter bearers was shot, having both of his arms broken, and General Jackson fell to the ground. As he lay there he grew faint from loss of blood, having fallen on his wounded side, and his arm began to bleed afresh. I rode away to try to get some whiskey for the purpose of reviving him, and at a short distance met Dr. McGuire and Colonel Pendleton, to whom I told what had happened, as we rode towards the place where I left Jackson. The ambulance came up; we hurried it to the front, and, reaching Jackson, placed him in it. As soon as the ambulance left, I was ordered by Colonel Pendleton, after consultation with General Rodes, to go to General Lee as quickly as possible and communicate the intelligence to him, explaining our position, what had been accomplished, who had taken command; and ask him to come to that place.

During the attack on our forces so many of our men had gone past us that we seemed to be left with no troops between us and the enemy, and I made up my mind to remain with the General to nurse him, as it seemed we should soon be in their hands However, the gallant Pender—in command after the wounding of General Hill—soon rallied his line and pressed forward, driving the enemy back to his works, at which quiet was restored for the night, the fight having ended as suddenly as it began.

Many people have thought it strange that Jackson should give an order to troops to fire at everything, especially cavalry approaching from the direction of the enemy, and then place himself in a situation to have himself fired upon. I heard of no such order, and feel sure that none such was given. If such had been the order it would have been given to the skirmish line, and there could have been no necessity for such an order to them, as they would do this anyway.

R. E. WELBOURN.

(Chief Signal Officer, 2nd Army Corps, 1863, Lieutenant General Jackson, commanding.)

advance of his column; and he found it necessary to look after the new opponent. Sedgwick had moved up the Plank road held by Wilcox's brigade, which gradually retired, and finally made a stand at Salem Church on the Plank road, about five miles from Fredericksburg, when, by a gallant resistance, the head of the column was held at bay until the arrival of McLaws with four brigades, and the further advance of the enemy was effectually opposed.*

It will be thus seen of what importance to General Lee's own movements were those below at Fredericksburg, and how the capture of the heights in rear of the two affected him. A force of at least 30,000 men had been detained from Hooker's army by considerably less than 10,000 on our side. It is true that Sedgwick had finally broken through the force opposed to him and commenced an advance up towards the rear of General Lee's army, but he had not done so until the latter had had time to gain a brilliant victory, and drive Hooker to a position of defence from which he could not advance except under great disadvantages.

Sedgwick's column had thus been detained by Wilcox until a force was brought down to arrest its progress entirely, and time was given to make arrangements to fall upon Sedgwick while separated from the rest of Hooker's army. Barksdale's brigade and the artillery posted with it had resisted all assaults upon their position for at least six hours, thus giving General Lee the requisite time to gain his victory, and in being finally

---

* In this condition of things, Lincoln telegraphed to General Hooker's Chief of Staff, who was on the north bank near Falmouth, as follows:

"WAR DEPARTMENT, WASHINGTON CITY, May 3, 1863.
"MAJOR GENERAL BUTTERFIELD:

"Where is General Hooker? Where is Sedgwick? Where is Stoneman? A. LINCOLN.

"Sent 4.35 P.M." (See report Committee on the War.)

compelled to succumb to overwhelming numbers that brigade had lost no honor. It was impossible for me to reinforce Barksdale with a larger force than I sent to him, and I then weakened very much the defences on the right. Had Sedgwick communicated his purposes to me and informed me that he would assault Marye's and Lee's Hills and those positions alone, then I would have moved my whole force to those points and held them against his entire force.

As it was, a division of Sedgwick's corps larger than my own immediately confronted the position occupied by the three brigades of my division left after Hays had been sent to Barksdale, and if that position had been abandoned and the brigades defending it moved to the left, the division confronting it, and which was constantly demonstrating towards it, would have moved up, taken possession of the line, and then moved upon my rear, compelling me to abandon the works on the left practically without a struggle, or submit to a much greater disaster than that which occurred. Sedgwick would hardly have been so blind as to rush his troops up against the strong positions at Marye's and Lee's Hill's while defended by a force sufficiently large to hold them, when there would have been an easy way open to him for their capture and that of the whole force defending them by simply moving a portion of troops to the rear. Marye's Hill would have fallen much sooner than it did, if it had been occupied by my whole force, or if a force sufficiently strong to prevent the position from being turned had not been retained on the right. By holding the position on the right, therefore, the fall of Marye's Hill and the consequent advance of Sedgwick's column above were both very considerably retarded, and when the catastrophe did happen there was left a considerable force to threaten and fall upon Sedgwick's rear. I think I may claim that the force entrusted to my command had accomplished all that could reasonably have been expected of it under the circumstances in which it was placed.

I will now return to my own position. Just as I was returning from observing Sedgwick's column I encountered, at Hazel Run, one of General McLaws' staff officers, Major Costin, coming down under an escort of cavalry, and he informed me that General McLaws had moved down the Plank road to meet the enemy, and that General Lee wished him and myself to attack Sedgwick in conjunction and endeavor to overwhelm him, and there was a note or message from General McLaws requesting information as to my position and that of the enemy, and asking what place I proposed, for attacking the enemy.

I think there was a note received later from General Lee communicating his wishes in regard to the proposed attack, similar to information brought by Major Costin— at any rate the information of his views and wishes was brought by Lieutenant Pitzer on his return. It was about an hour before sunset when Major Costin reached me, and that part of my division on the right was more than three miles from the position at Cox's, so that it was impossible to accomplish anything that night. I immediately sent a note to General McLaws informing him that I would concentrate all my force that night and move against the enemy very early next morning, drive him from Lee's and Marye's Hills, and extend my left while advancing so as to connect with his (McLaws') right, and continue to move against the enemy above, after his connection with Fredericksburg was severed; and I asked General McLaws' co-operation in this plan. During the night, I received a note from him assenting to my plan and containing General Lee's approval of it also.

As soon as the first communication had been received from General McLaws, my troops from the right were ordered up, but it was after night before they were all concentrated. Andrews' artillery was brought up before night, one battery being left on the ridge so as to cover my right flank on the line across the Telegraph road, and a regiment of infantry being posted so as to guard against a surprise on that flank, if the enemy should move around Lee's Hill up the left of Deep Run. Just before dark, we discovered a piece of artillery advancing along the Telegraph road in our front, followed by a few wagons. The men in charge of the piece of artillery came on so deliberately, though in full view of our line, that we took it for granted that it must be one of the pieces supposed to be captured, with a forge or two, that had been probably able to elude the vigilance of the enemy by concealment in some of the ravines.

The approaching darkness rendered objects very indistinct, and we therefore watched the approaching piece until it got within a few hundred yards of us, when the drivers suddenly discovered who we were, wheeled rapidly and dashed to the rear, and we became then aware that it was one of the enemy's pieces. Some of Andrews' guns which were ready opened fire, but the piece of artillery got off, though some of the mules to a wagon and to a forge were killed, and we found and secured the latter the next day with several fine mules.

The night passed quietly with us, and at light on the morning of the 4th I prepared to advance. My plan was to advance along the Telegraph road with Gordon's brigade in line in front, followed by Andrews' battalion of artillery and Graham's battery, with Smith's and Barksdale's brigades following in the rear, forming a second line, and to throw Hays' and Hoke's brigades across Hazel Run opposite my present position so as to move down the left bank, as the column moved along the Telegraph road against the heights, both of which I took it for granted the enemy held, as the affair just at dusk the evening before must have given him notice of my presence.

It was my purpose, as soon as the heights were taken and the enemy's connection with Fredericksburg cut, to advance with Gordon's and Smith's brigades up the Plank road and river, and for Hays and Hoke to advance across towards the Plank road extending to the left to connect with McLaws, while Barksdale's brigade and some of Pendleton's artillery should be posted to hold Marye's and Lee's Hills and protect my rear from the direction of Fredericksburg. The ravine of Hazel Run is so rugged that it was impossible to cross it except where there were roads, and therefore it was necessary to pass Hays' and Hoke's brigades over at the ford on my left.

Gordon's brigade was placed in line at light, and Andrews' artillery immediately in its rear, while Smith and Barksdale were ordered to take their positions and be in readiness to follow. I then went with General Hays and Hoke, whose brigades were put in motion, across Hazel Run to point out to them the positions they were to take and how they were to move. After doing this, I rode back and found to my surprise that Gordon had moved off under a misapprehension of my order, as he was to have waited until all was ready, and I designed accompanying him. Andrews had followed him and I immediately put Smith and Barksdale in motion, the former along the road by flank, and Barksdale in line of battle on the right.

The line of hills composed of Marye's, Cemetery, Stansbury's, and Taylor's Hills descends towards the Marye's Hill, which is the lowest, Taylor's, bordering on the river at the upper end of the canal, being much the highest. Stansbury's, Cemetery, and Marye's Hills are separated from a higher range on the southwest by a very small stream which rises between Taylor's Hill and the Plank road and runs across that road into Hazel Run, some distance above the crossing of the Telegraph road over that run. Cemetery and Marye's Hills slope back gradually to the little stream, and from the latter, on the southwest, rise steep hills terminating in a high, wide ridge, along which the Plank road runs; and the face of these hills fronting towards Cemetery and Marye's Hills is intersected by a number of deep ravines, up one of which the Plank road ascends to get on the main ridge. On the south side of the road and a little distance from it the main ridge terminates in a high hill which descends abruptly to Hazel Run, the face towards the run being wooded. At the lower front of the base of this hill is a mill called the Alum Spring Mill. Just at the upper part of the base of the hill a branch of Hazel Run comes in, uniting with the main stream. This branch rises some distance above near the Plank road, and runs nearly parallel to it, through a deep valley to its junction with the main stream.

On the south of this valley is another long wide ridge which extends for some distance parallel to that along which the Plank road runs and also terminates with an abrupt descent to Hazel Run. On the south of the Plank road, and on the same ridge with it, is situated Mr. Guest's house some two or three miles from Fredericksburg, and nearly opposite to it on the other ridge is Mr. Downman's house. On the extremities of the lesser ridges, projecting out from that on which the Plank road is located, was a line of small works and epaulments for artillery, extending from the river at Taylor's Hill to and across the Plank road, which had been previously made by our troops, and this line completely commanded the crests and rear slopes of Marye's, Cemetery and Stansbury's Hills, being much higher.

The Plank road crosses the little stream, with a high embankment extending for some distance on both sides, the stream passing through a culvert. The Telegraph road passes towards Fredericksburg from Cox's house, where I was, along a ridge to Lee's Hill and descends the hill on the side of the slope next to Hazel Run.

Gordon, when he started, advanced rapidly along the Telegraph road, and when he reached Lee's Hill, it was found unoccupied, but a body of infantry was moving along the Plank road from the town between Marye's

Hill and the ridge above, which halted and took position behind the embankment of the road. In the valley between Guest's and Downman's houses, was observed a considerable body of infantry, and at Downman's house a battery of artillery. Gordon threw out his skirmishers and made preparations to descend the hill and cross over Hazel Run above Marye's Hill. Andrews placed Graham's battery in position on the road and opened on the infantry in the valley, which moved out of the way. Two large bodies of infantry, supposed to be brigades, each then moved over the ridge just beyond the Alum Spring Mill, threatening Gordon's left, as he was advancing. Graham turned his guns on them and soon drove them off up the ridge. Gordon then made a dash across the run and after a sharp engagement drove off the infantry behind the road embankment, capturing some prisoners and securing several baggage and subsistence wagons, a battery wagon, and a forge—with their teams,—which were passing up the road with the infantry he encountered.

This gave us the possession of Marye's and Cemetery Hills again, and cut the enemy's connection with Fredericksburg. Arriving soon after with Smith's brigade I threw it across Hazel Run to the support of Gordon, the batteries from the Stafford Heights opening a heavy fire on it as it descended Lee's Hill. Barksdale's brigade, which had halted in the rear without orders, was then sent for, to occupy the stone wall at the foot of Marye's Hill, and General Barksdale was ordered to move rapidly into the town if not held by too large a force, get possession of the bridge, and secure a camp of wagons seen at the lower part of the town. When Graham's guns were operating upon the bodies of infantry in the valley between Guest's and Downman's houses and those threatening Gordon's flank, the enemy's battery—at Downman's house,—opened fire on them, but as soon as the infantry was disposed of, Graham turned his two 20 pounder Parrots on the enemy's guns, which returned across the valley and took position near Guest's house where they were out of reach.

Seeing the enemy's wagons moving off from the town and not hearing Barksdale's rifles, I sent a staff officer to repeat the orders, and received a reply that he was preparing to send forward his skirmishers; a second messenger sent to him returned with the information that his skirmishers reported a heavy force holding the town, entrenched within rifle pits. The enemy's wagon trains had thus made their escape, and I sent orders to Barksdale to desist from the attack on the town and to dispose of his brigade so as to resist any advance from that direction. It turned out that the town was held by Gibbon's division which had been left behind.

I had listened anxiously to hear the sound of McLaws' guns or some indication of his being engaged, but heard nothing. The enemy had not expected us in this direction, and he was therefore evidently taken by surprise, but Gordon's advance, which was so handsomely made, being sooner than I had intended, had given the enemy time to form his troops in line, to meet any further advance I could make after my arrival; and as the character of the ground was such that considerable bodies of troops could be concealed from my view from any point that was accessible to me, I could not tell what force I would have to encounter on ascending the hills above.

I could see that all the little works on the heights were occupied by infantry, making a line extending across from Taylor's Hill to the brow of the hill beyond and above the Alum Spring Mill. Gordon's and Smith's brigades had taken position in the trenches along the crests from the Plank road towards Taylor's Hill, facing towards the enemy above and with their backs towards Fredericksburg. The enemy did not open then with artillery, and as they were very much exposed, I thought possibly he did not have any on that flank, and I therefore determined to feel him and make him develop what he had.

Smith was ordered to advance his brigade towards the heights occupied by the enemy above; two regiments, the 13th and 58th Virginia, advanced against one of the positions which appeared to be occupied by the strongest force, and the 49th and 52nd separately against other points. The regiments advanced to the base of the hills and commenced ascending, when the enemy appeared in force on their crests, and also opened with artillery from the neighborhood of Taylor's house. The 13th and 58th Regiments became heavily engaged, and the 49th and 52nd slightly.

It was now apparent that the hills were held in strong force, and as an attempt to carry them from that direction, as my troops were then located, would have been under great disadvantage and attended with great difficulty, I ordered the regiments to be withdrawn. The 49th and 52nd were withdrawn without difficulty and with but slight loss, the 13th and 58th being on the right and more exposed to the enemy's guns were withdrawn with more difficulty and heavier loss. The 13th lost 17 prisoners and 58th 71, including the color bearer of the latter with his colors, the most of the men captured, including the color bearer of the 58th, taking refuge in a house at the foot of the hill, under the fire of the enemy's guns as well as his infantry, and declining to fall back over the plain while exposed to the fire of the artillery.

They were thus captured by their own misconduct, the enemy sending to take possession of them, which I could not prevent without bringing on a heavy engagement under disadvantageous circumstances, and thus incurring a much heavier loss of men. The brigade resumed its position after this affair, and I sent Lieutenant Pitzer to General McLaws to apprise him of what had been done and my position, with a request for him to begin his attack on the enemy and the information that I could move two brigades, Hays' and Hoke's, across towards the Plank road extending to the left as they

advanced to connect with his right, and, as soon as the
enemy was engaged so as to make it practicable, I would
move up from below with my other two brigades, Gordon's and Smith's; Hays' and Hoke's brigades had
moved down the left bank of Hazel Run and were put in
position to co-operate with McLaws' attack, when made,
by moving across the ridge on which Downman's house
was located, and orders were given them accordingly.
General McLaws did not make the attack, and Lieutenant
Pitzer returned with the information that Anderson's
division was coming down, and with instruction for me
to wait until he was in position, when at a signal given
by firing three guns rapidly in succession, a simultaneous
attack should be made by the whole force.

When Anderson's force began to arrive, I was able
to draw Hays and Hoke nearer to my right, and I therefore brought Hays' brigade across the branch of Hazel
Run, which has been mentioned, and put his brigade in
line at the foot of the hill near Alum Spring Mill, so that
it might move up the wooded face of the hill on to the
plain above, which was occupied by a part of the enemy's
force. Hoke's brigade was placed in line just in the edge
of the woods on the rear slope of the lower end of the
ridge on which Downman's house was, facing towards
the Plank road, concealed from the view of the enemy,
as was Hays'.

General Lee came down himself before the signal was
given, and sent for me to meet him towards my left. We
examined the position of the enemy together, as well as
we could, and I explained to him my plan of attacking
with my force, which was, for Hays to move up the hill
at foot of which he was and directly forward, which
would carry him to the Plank road, and up on the right
side; for Hoke to move over the ridge below Downman's
house and across the valley to the other ridge, as far as
the Plank road, where he was to change direction so as
to move up on the left of the road; and when the signal
was heard, Gordon was to move rapidly by the flank to

the ravine up which the Plank road runs, and then diagonally towards Taylor's house so as to sweep all the crests in front of him and Smith as they were then posted, and turn the enemy's left which rested near the river. Smith was to remain stationary so as to re-inforce the brigades engaged, or Barksdale as might be necessary. General Lee approved my plan and directed me to carry it out as soon as the signal should be given, and then left me.

Sedgwick's line covered the Plank road for some distance on the south side; being in the centre along the ridge or plateau on which the road is located, and bending back across it with both flanks which rested near the river, above and below. Guest's house was in his line and some artillery was posted near it, while Downman's house, and the ridge on which it was located were occupied by his skirmishers. In advance of the part of the line facing towards me, which was his left wing, there was an advanced line occupying the crests of the hills towards me, extending across from Taylor's Hill to the lower end of the valley which has been men-tioned, with artillery posted near the left of this ad-vanced line.

The plateau, on the ridge where Downman's house was located, was entirely cleared of timber below the house, as was the valley between the two ridges. The ridge along which the Plank road runs was cleared on the south side of it, and from the direction of Fredericks-burg up to within a short distance below Guest's house, from which point bodies of woodland extended up the road for some distance and across towards Taylor's house, with occasional intervals of cleared land.

We waited for the signal, but it was not given until a short time before sunset. When it was heard, Hoke moved at once across the plateau in his front between Downman's house and Hazel Run, then down the slope, across the valley, and up the steep ascent of the next ridge towards the Plank road, driving the enemy's skirmishers before him, while the guns at Guest's house played upon his advancing line without disturbing his beautiful order. Hays rapidly ascended the hill in front, immediately encountering the right of the enemy's front line, which he swept before him, and continued his advance without a halt. It was a splendid sight to see the rapid and orderly advance of these two brigades, with the enemy flying before them. The officers and men manning the artillery which had been posted on eminences along the Telegraph road and on the right bank of Hazel Run so as to protect the infantry retreat in case of disaster, debarred from an active participation in the action, could not refrain from enthusiastically cheering the infantry, as it so handsomely swept everything in front.

In the meantime Gordon, as soon as the signal was heard, moved his brigade by flank rapidly to the Plank road, formed in line up the ravine and swept on towards Taylor's house, clearing the crests of the enemy, compelling his artillery on that flank to retire rapidly and driving the enemy's extreme left from its position back towards Banks' Ford. On getting near the point of woods below Guest's house, Hays' and Hoke's brigades approached each other. The artillery at Guest's house had been compelled to fly in order to prevent capture, and the enemy was retiring in confusion on all parts of the line confronting them and Gordon, but just then Hoke fell from his horse, with his arm badly shattered by a ball near the shoulder joint.

The brigade thus losing its commander, to whom alone the instruction had been given, and without any one to direct its movement at that particular crisis, pushed on across the Plank road, encountered Hays' brigade in the woods still advancing, and the two commingling together were thrown into confusion. They crossed each other's paths in this condition, but still continued to advance, getting far into the woods. Hays' brigade pressed on in its proper direction, but Hoke's, now under the command of Colonel Avery of the 6th North Carolina, had got to its right. The regiments of both brigades had lost their organization, and in the woods it was impossible to restore it. Portions of both brigades penetrated a considerable distance into the woods, still driving the enemy before them, but when scattered they came across a portion of the retiring force which had been rallied, and the advance parties were compelled to retire themselves, leaving some prisoners in the enemy's hands, many of whom had become so exhausted by their rapid advance that they were unable to get out of the way, and were picked up after the fighting was over. Other portions of the brigades, hearing Gordon's firing on the right and not aware of his movements, thought the enemy was in their rear and retired also. The brigades were then rallied and reformed on the Plank road just below Guest's house. I had taken my position on the heights near the Telegraph road opposite the Alum Spring Mill, from which point I could see the movement of all three brigades, and when I discovered them all in motion and driving the enemy as described, I rode across Hazel Run in the direction taken by Hays' brigade.

I arrived just as the first men of that brigade were emerging from the woods, and directed the re-formation of the two brigades. Two regiments of Smith's brigade, the 49th and 52nd, were ordered up, but when they arrived and the two brigades had been reorganized it had become too dark to make any further advance, and I did not hear either of the other two divisions engaged. Gordon's progress was also arrested by the approach of night, and he halted and assumed a position above Taylor's house confronting the enemy's left, which he had driven back very considerably. Hays' and Hoke's brigades were put in line of battle across the Plank road, at the point where they had been rallied, with Smith's two regiments advanced to the front.

McLaws' division had not advanced at all. Anderson's division had advanced on Hoke's left, driving the enemy's skirmishers, fronting his centre, from Downman's house and the upper part of the ridge, but it did not cross to the Plank road until dark, when I saw Posey's brigade moving up the hill on my, then, left from the direction of Downman's house, and it took position above me on the Plank road, the enemy having retired from that road. Wright's brigade was subsequently moved across to the Plank road at eight or nine o'clock and took position on Posey's left. The main attack had been made by my three brigades.*

---

* The force which I encountered in front in this action was Howe's division. Brigadier General Howe testified before the Committee on the Conduct of the War.

After speaking of the battle of Chancellorsville as a sharp. skirmish, and claiming all the credit for capturing Marye's Hill, though his division advanced against Lee's Hill alone, and further claiming to have done all the fighting on the 4th, he says:

"The prisoners taken all agreed that it was Early's, Anderson's, and McLaws' divisions that attacked my division, and that the movement was led by General Lee, who told them that it would be a good thing to destroy the 6th corps, or capture it; that it would not get out the Chancellorsville way, and that the movements in our rear would cut us off."

It was my three brigades alone that attacked him, McLaws' division being above confronting Sedgwick's right, and Anderson's advancing against the centre. Again he says:

"Some time after this movement, after we had returned to our old camps, I met General Hooker, and spoke to him of the movements we had made and the positions we held. I stated to him that after the fight on the 4th of May, I could have gone with my division on to the heights at Fredericksburg, and held them, or, if necessary, could have recrossed that way. He was surprised that those heights could have been held the night of the 4th, and said: 'If I had known that you could have gone on those heights and held them, and would have held them, I would have reinforced you with the whole army.' That was the key of the position, and there was no difficulty in holding it. I told him that if I had not received orders to go back to Banks' Ford, but had been allowed to go to the Fredericksburg heights, I could have marched there uninterruptedly after nine o'clock that night; for after the fight we had had, the rebels abandoned the heights, and there was nothing to be seen of them. There was a bright moon that night, and

After dark General Lee sent for me to go to him at Downman's house, where he had established his headquarters for the night. After informing him of the condition of things on my front, he directed me to leave two of my brigades in line on the north of the road, at right angles with it and facing the enemy, and to rein-

---

we could see an object of the size of a man or a horse at a great distance."

Verily General Howe had accomplished wonders according to his own showing. He had with his solitary division routed the greater part of Lee's army, notwithstanding the rough handling it had been able to give Hooker's five corps above. Perhaps if he had made the attempt to march to the heights, he might have encountered the brigades of Gordon and Hoke which occupied a line extending from above Taylor's house towards the Plank road at Guest's house, and which had escaped his observation notwithstanding the light of the " bright moon that night." He might also have encountered Barksdale's, Hays', and Smith's brigades holding the heights, and disturbed my own headquarters on the left of Lee's Hill, which had been assumed at 12 at night after I had ridden along his whole front with my staff at a late hour, posting Hoke's brigade on Gordon's left and examining the position of the latter. General Howe was either mistaken or he was star gazing.

Hooker, in his examination before the Congressional Committee in regard to the battle, made the following statement:

" Our artillery had always been superior to that of the rebels, as was also our infantry, except in discipline, and that, for reasons not necessary to mention, never did equal Lee's army. With a rank and file mostly inferior to our own, *intellectually and physically*, that army has, by discipline alone, acquired a character for steadiness and efficiency unsurpassed, in my judgment, in ancient or modern times. We have not been able to rival it, nor has there been any near approximation to it in the other rebel armies."

Their artillery certainly surpassed ours far in numbers of guns, weight of metal, and the quality of the ammunition, and at long range their firing was admirable, while ours was defective from the defect in the ammunition, but when we came to close range so that our guns could tell, their gunners lost their coolness and ours surpassed them in the accuracy of the firing, always getting the advantage under such circumstances unless the odds were too great.

Hooker did not complain that he was overpowered by numbers, and he was the first of the commanders of that army who had not made that complaint.

force Barksdale at Fredericksburg with the other two. Hoke's brigade was moved to the right and placed on line with Gordon's on its left, and Hays' brigade was moved back and placed in the trenches at Lee's Hill on Barksdale's right, and Smith's two regiments rejoined the others and took position in the trenches on the left of the Plank road overlooking the canal.

During the night General Barksdale reported to me, once by his aide and once in person, that the enemy was crossing troops and artillery into the town, and asked for more reinforcements. I told him I had no doubt the enemy was recrossing and would be gone in the morning, and that I had no more reinforcements to give him. When it became light the enemy was gone from the town and his bridge was taken up. Sedgwick had also recrossed during the night his whole force on bridges laid at Banks' Ford and nothing remained on the south bank but Hooker's force above. Some of McLaws' brigades had advanced toward Banks' Ford during the night, picking up some prisoners, and some pieces of artillery had opened on the enemy's bridge as he was recrossing. Posey's and Wright's brigades had also advanced towards Banks' Ford, picking up some prisoners. Next morning a number of prisoners were gathered who had been left behind when the main force crossed, some of them being taken on the river by detachments from Gordon's brigade.

On the 5th, after it had been ascertained that all of Sedgwick's force was gone, I was ordered to move up the Plank road towards Chancellorsville, leaving Barksdale at Fredericksburg. I moved up to the vicinity of Salem Church, and was halted, remaining there some time, when I was ordered to return to my old position. In doing so my brigades were heavily shelled by the enemy's batteries from across the river, as they were crossing Hazel Run to the Telegraph road. Smith's brigade was left with Barksdale in the position it had occupied the night before, and the others moved to their former positions, which they regained in the morning, in a tremendous storm of rain.

General Lee had moved all his troops back to oppose Hooker, who had been confronted during the operations against Sedgwick by Jackson's three divisions alone, but on the morning of the 6th, he was found gone also, having recrossed under cover of the storm and darkness of the previous night. The whole army then returned to its former camps, and Hooker resumed his position opposite Fredericksburg.

My loss in the different actions around Fredericksburg at this time was, in my own division, 125 killed and 721 wounded, total 846; in Andrews' artillery 7 killed and 21 wounded, total 28; in Barksdale's brigade 45 killed and 181 wounded, total 226.

A little over 500 prisoners were lost in my division, more than half of which were lost in resisting the crossing at the enemy's lower bridge; from Hays' brigade at the time of the fall of Marye's Hill; and from Smith's brigade in forcing the enemy's position on the morning of the 4th; and the residue from Hays' and Hoke's brigades in the attack on Sedgwick above Fredericksburg. Barksdale's brigade lost a little over 300 prisoners captured from the 17th and 21st Mississippi Regiments at Marye's Hill. General Lee's entire loss in killed and wounded was 1,581 killed and 8,700 wounded. Hooker's loss far exceeded it in killed and wounded, and we secured several thousand prisoners, thirteen pieces of artillery, over twenty thousand stand of arms, besides a large amount of ammunition, accoutrements, etc.

Hooker's army was more than double General Lee's, which did not exceed, including my force, 50,000 muskets and including all arms was under 60,000; yet Hooker, on returning to his camps, issued a general order congratulating his troops on their achievements, and stating that they had added new laurels to their former renown, though on first crossing the river he had issued an address to his troops intimating that General Lee's army was then in his power and that he would proceed to destroy it.

During the operations at Chancellorsville and Fredericksburg, the enemy's cavalry in large force under Stoneman, having crossed the rivers higher up, made a raid in the direction of Richmond which accomplished nothing of consequence, but merely frightened and depredated upon the unarmed country people. Stoneman's force was glad to make its escape back to its former position.

On our part, our rejoicings over the brilliant and important victory that had been gained were soon dampened by the sad news of the death of General Jackson.

CHAPTER XXI.

INVASION OF PENNSYLVANIA.

UPON returning to our camps after Hooker had re-crossed the Rappahannock, the old positions were resumed, General A. P. Hill, as senior major general, being now in command of the corps.

Nothing of consequence occurred in our front during the month of May. On the 30th of the month, a general order was issued, organizing the army of Northern Virginia into three corps of three divisions each. General James Longstreet, who had returned from the south of James River, retained command of the 1st corps, now composed of McLaws', Hood's, and Pickett's divisions. General Richard S. Ewell was made a lieutenant general and assigned to the command of the 2nd corps, now composed of my division, and those of Rodes and Johnson—Brigadier General Robert E. Rodes having been promoted and assigned to the command of D. H. Hill's division,—and Brigadier General Edward Johnson having been promoted and assigned to the command of Trimble's division, formerly Jackson's.

A third corps was formed, composed of the division of Anderson (taken from the 1st corps), Heth's and Pender's; and General A. P. Hill was made lieutenant general and assigned to the command of it, and two divisions of four brigades each were formed out of it and two brigades, one of which was brought from North Carolina and the other formed of Mississippi regiments taken from other brigades, to the command of which division Brigadier Generals Heth and Pender were promoted, respectively.

My inspector general, Lieutenant Colonel John M. Jones, and Colonel James A. Walker of the 13th Virginia Regiment were made brigadier generals, and the former was assigned to J. R. Jones' brigade in Johnson's division, and the latter to Rodes' (the old Stonewall brigade), in the same division, both promotions well deserved.

General Lee now determined to make a campaign across the Potomac by turning the enemy's right flank, so as to transfer the war into the enemy's country and compel his army to withdraw from Virginia. Longstreet's corps was moved to Culpeper in advance of the others, the two divisions which had been south of the James having moved from Richmond by the way of Gordonsville on the railroad.

On the 4th of June, Ewell's corps took up its line of march towards Culpeper Court-House—my division moving by the way of Spottsylvania Court-House, followed by Johnson's and Rodes' by the way of Chancellorsville. A. P. Hill's corps was left to watch and amuse Hooker's army. The first day of the march I passed Spottsylvania Court-House and camped beyond it. On the second day, during the march, I received an order to halt and wait for further orders, as the enemy had crossed a force at Fredericksburg in front of Hill. I accordingly went into camp after crossing the Catharpin Creek and remained stationary until the next day (the 6th of June). In the afternoon of the 6th, I received orders to move on, and did so, continuing the march to Culpeper Court-House by the way of Verdierville, and Somerville Ford on the Rapidan, and, passing the Court-House on the 8th, camped three or four miles west of that place. We remained stationary near the Court-House for two days. On the afternoon of the 9th, my division was moved to the vicinity of Brandy Station during a fight between our cavalry and that of the enemy, but not being needed, it returned to its camps at night.

The 31st Virginia had returned just before our march from Fredericksburg. The official tri-monthly report of my division of the 10th of June, made at this place, shows present for duty 610 officers and 6,616 enlisted men, total 7,226. The brigade inspection reports of the same date show about the same number of effectives present. Lieutenant Colonel Hilary P. Jones' battalion of artillery of four batteries, numbering in all thirteen guns, had been assigned to duty with my division just before starting.

My division was fully an average one for the whole army, and perhaps more than an average one. Sixty-five thousand officers and men may therefore be set down as covering the whole of General Lee's infantry with which he commenced the campaign, perhaps sixty thousand would cover the effective strength. Ten thousand men would fully cover the artillery and cavalry and perhaps considerably overgo it—(The return for the 31st of May, just four days before the commencement of the movement, shows the infantry to have been 54,356 for duty, cavalry 9,536, and artillery 4,460, total 68,352. This return was not accessible to me when the within was written.)—150 guns would cover all of our artillery, and they consisted of field pieces, the most of which had been captured from the enemy. The largest guns we had were a very few twenty pounder Parrots. The brigade inspection reports in my division show that about one-third of the men were without bayonets, and this deficiency existed in the rest of the army, owing in a great measure to the fact that nearly all of our small arms had been taken from the enemy on the various battlefields. There was a very great deficiency in shoes for the infantry, a large number of the men being indifferently shod, and some barefooted. A like deficiency existed in regard to the equipment of the men in other respects, the supply of clothing, blankets, etc., being very limited.

On the 11th of June, Ewell's corps resumed the march, taking the road from the lower Shenandoah Valley across the Blue Ridge at Chester Gap. Johnson's division, followed by mine, moved on the road by Sperryville, and Little Washington through the gap, and Rodes' division on a road further to the right through the same gap. Late in the day of the 12th, my division reached

Front Royal, Rodes' and Johnson's having preceded it, crossing both forks of the Shenandoah near that place. Two of my brigades, Hoke's and Smith's, were crossed over both of the forks that night. Hays' and Gordon's and Jones' artillery with the division trains remained on the east side of the South Branch.

CHAPTER XXII.

CAPTURE OF WINCHESTER.

VERY early in the morning of the 13th, the remainder of my division crossed over the Shenandoah, and I received orders from General Ewell to move to the Valley pike at Newtown, and along that road against the enemy then occupying Winchester, while Johnson moved along the direct road from Front Royal to the town, Rodes being sent to the right to Berryville, where there was also a force. Milroy occupied the town of Winchester with a considerable force in strong fortifications, and my orders were to move along the pike to Kernstown, and then to the left, so as to get a position on the northwest of Winchester from which the main work of the enemy could be attacked with advantage.

This main work was on a hill a little outside of the town on the northwest, being an enclosed fort, with embrasures for artillery, and I was informed that there was a high hill on the northwest which commanded it, and of which I was directed to get possession, if I could. Six main roads centre at Winchester, to-wit: the Front Royal road on which we were, coming in from the southeast and uniting with the Millwood road a mile or two before it reaches town; the Valley pike coming in on the south and uniting with the Cedar Creek pike between Kernstown and Winchester, Kernstown being about two miles from the town; the Romney or Northwestern pike coming in on the west side; the Pughtown road coming in on the northwest; the Martinsburg pike coming in on the north, and uniting with the direct Charlestown and Harper's Ferry roads, three or four miles from town; and the Berryville road coming in on the east.

Lieutenant Barton of the 2nd Virginia Regiment, Walker's brigade, Johnson's division, who had been raised in the neighborhood, was furnished me as a guide, and Brown's battalion of reserve artillery, under Captain Dance, was ordered to accompany my division in addition to Jones'.

Having received my orders, and leaving all my wagons, except the regimental ordnance and medical wagons, at Cedarville on the Front Royal road, I diverged from that road at a little place called Ninevah and reached the Valley pike at Newtown. On moving along the latter road past Bartonsville towards Kernstown, I found Lieutenant Colonel Herbert of the Maryland line occupying a ridge between the two places with his battalion of infantry, a battery of artillery and a part of a battalion of Maryland cavalry, and engaged in occasional skirmishing with a body of the enemy's troops which had taken position in and near Kernstown.

This force of the enemy covered the road which I had to take to get to the west of Winchester, and it was therefore necessary to dislodge it to enable me to get into that road, and to drive it back upon the main body in order that my movement should be unobserved. Colonel Herbert could not inform me of the strength of the force in his immediate front, and I therefore halted my division and formed it in line across the pike, and proceeded to reconnoitre. The only force in sight when I arrived was a cavalry force, but I was informed that a strong infantry picket occupied the town, and the supposition was that a stronger force was in the neighborhood. Just beyond Kernstown and Pritchard's Hill and a ridge extending from it to our left, which was covered with trees, being the position occupied by Shields' troops when General Jackson attacked him on the 23rd of March, 1862. It was a position on which a considerable body of troops might be posted out of our view, and I soon discovered a battery of artillery on Pritchard's Hill which opened on us.

I then reconnoitred the ground carefully, and, after doing so, I moved Hays' brigade to the left, through a skirt of woods and a meadow, to a small road coming in from Bartonsville towards the Cedar Creek pike, and then along that to a suitable position for advancing against the artillery on Pritchard's Hill; and ordered it to advance and get possession of the hill. Whilst advancing General Hays sent me word that the enemy had a considerable infantry force on the ridge to his left. I immediately moved Gordon's brigade over the same route Hays' brigade had taken, and ordered him to advance and clear the ridge on Hays' left, sending an order to the latter, who had advanced to Pritchard's Hill, compelling the artillery and the force supporting it to retire, to wait until Gordon had got up and cleared the ridge on his left. Gordon advanced handsomely, as directed, encountering a considerable force of infantry, which, in conjunction with a body of skirmishers sent out by Hays, he drove from behind a stone fence, and then swept over the fields beyond the ridge, inclining, as he moved, to the Valley pike, and forcing the enemy across the Cedar Creek pike and Abraham's Creek, which here crosses the Valley pike, to Bower's Hill on the north of the creek under Burton's Mill, where there were some reserves. Hays, in the meantime, advanced to the front, thus coming up on Gordon's left after the latter had reached the Valley pike. As soon as Hays and Gordon were both in motion, Hoke's and Smith's brigades were advanced to the front on each side of the Valley pike past Kernstown.

The enemy had strong position on Bower's Hill, held by infantry and artillery, and it was difficult of access, from the nature of Abraham's Creek, a boggy stream, running at its base, and the steep ascent to the hill on the other side. Gordon formed his brigade in line across the Valley pike. Hays was posted on his left along a ridge between Cedar Creek pike and Abraham's Creek, and Hoke's and Smith's brigades were brought up and the latter placed on Hays' left, with a view to further operations against the enemy, in order to drive him from Bower's Hill; Hoke's brigade, under Colonel

Avery of the 6th North Carolina being held in reserve. During these arrangements the enemy shelled my brigades heavily from his guns on Bower's Hill; and by the time they were made it became too dark to proceed farther. Colonel Avery was then ordered back to Kernstown, with his brigade, where it was placed in position to protect the ambulances, ordnance and medical wagons, and the artillery from any movement around our left, and Colonel Herbert was ordered to take position with his battalion of infantry on Gordon's right, which extended across the Valley pike. The troops then lay down on their arms and spent the night in a drenching rain.

General Ewell had moved with Johnson's division on the Front Royal road to the vicinity of Winchester, and, after I had arranged my troops, I endeavored to reach him by riding across the country, but the storm was so violent and the night so dark that I was compelled to desist and return.

During the night, the enemy withdrew his artillery and the main body of his infantry from Bower's Hill to the town, leaving only a body of skirmishers confronting us. Very early on the morning of the 14th, I ordered Hays and Gordon to advance each a regiment across the creek to drive the enemy's skirmishers from Bower's Hill, which was done after some sharp skirmishing. At the same time Smith's skirmishers were advanced across the creek on the left, and we got possession of the works on the hill. While these operations were going on at Bower's Hill, Major Goldsborough, with the skirmishers of the Maryland battalion, advanced on the right into the outskirts of Winchester, but fearing that the enemy, whose principal force had taken position in and near the main fort, might shell the town, I ordered him to retire.

General Ewell came up immediately after my skirmishers had advanced to Bower's Hill, and together we proceeded to reconnoitre from that point, from which we had a very distinct view of the works about Winchester.

We discovered that the hill on the northwest, which I had been ordered to occupy, had been fortified with works facing in the direction from which I would have to approach it, and that they were occupied. It became necessary then to take this hill, which was the key to the position, by assault, and having discovered a ridge back of it from which it might be attacked, I was ordered to leave a brigade and some artillery, where I then was, to amuse the enemy in front, while I moved the rest of my command around by the left to the point from which I could make the assault, taking care to conduct my movement with secrecy so that the enemy would not discover it. I accordingly left Gordon to occupy Bower's Hill, and I left with him besides his own brigade the Maryland battalion and battery, and another battery (Hupp's) of Brown's battalion, and with the other three brigades and the rest of the artillery I moved to the left, following the Cedar Creek pike for a mile or two and then passing through fields and the woods, which latter was here sufficiently open to admit of the passage of the artillery, and crossing the Romney road at Lupton's house, about three miles west of Winchester, and half a mile from a point at which I was informed by Mr. Lupton that the enemy had had a picket the night before, and probably had one then.

Leaving the 54th North Carolina Regiment of Hoke's brigade at the point where I crossed the Romney road, to watch my rear, I moved on along a small obscure road to the rear of the position from which I wished to assault the enemy's works, and I found it a very favorable one for the purpose. My route had been a very circuitous one, in order to check the enemy's vigilance, and I was conducted over it by a very intelligent and patriotic citizen, Mr. James C. Baker, who had a son in the service, and who had been made to feel the tyranny of Milroy. Mr. Baker thoroughly understood the object in view, and fully appreciated the advantage of the position I was seeking to reach; and it was mainly owing to the intelligent and skilful manner in which he guided me that I was able to get there without attracting the slightest attention from the enemy.

Having conducted me to the desired point, he thought it prudent to retire, as he was of no further use as a guide, and his residence was in the immediate neighborhood of the town. On the route we had not seen a solitary man from the enemy's force, whether straggler, scout or picket. We had met two very ordinary looking men in the roads, and from prudential motives they were carried with us and left at Lupton's with injunctions to keep them.

After that the only person we saw was a young girl of about thirteen years of age whom we met on horseback with her young brother behind her. She was carrying before her a large bundle of clothes tied up in a sheet, and when she unexpectedly came upon us she was at first very much frightened, but soon discovering that we were Confederates, she pulled off her bonnet, waved it over her head and "hurrahed," and then burst into tears. She told us that the enemy had been shelling the woods all around, firing occasionally into her father's house, and that she had been sent from home by her father and mother to get out of the way. She said that they had not been able to imagine what the shelling meant, as they did not know that any of "our soldiers," as she called us, were anywhere in the neighborhood. It was not necessary to use any precaution as to her, and she was permitted to pass on, feeling much happier for the encounter.

To return from this digression:—the position which I reached proved to be a long ridge bordering, at the further end, on the Pughtown road and immediately confronting the fortified hill which I wished to carry, and within easy range of it for our pieces. Where it immediately confronted the enemy's work it was wooded, the trees having been partially cut down, and we found posted at different points notices to the following effect: "General Milroy orders all of the timber east of this point to be cleared off." Enough, however, remained to conceal our movements and enabled me to push forward a brigade under cover to within a short distance of the base of the hill on which was the enemy's work.

On the left of this woods, near the Pughtown road, was a cornfield on Mr. Brinly's land, facing towards the enemy's position and affording an excellent position for posting artillery in the edge of the woods bearing on the enemy. On the right of the woods, on the crest of the ridge, was an old orchard and the remains of an old house, called "Folk's old house," with the slope in front cleared, which furnished another good position for artillery to bear on the other flank of the enemy. I reached this position about four o'clock P.M., and as the day was exceedingly hot, and the men had marched a circuit of eight or ten miles without meeting with water to drink, and were very much exhausted, I massed them in the woods in the rear of the position and gave them time to rest.

In the meantime I proceeded to reconnoitre the enemy's position and the ground over which I would have to move. The enemy had no pickets thrown out in the direction where I was, and did not seem to be keeping any lookout that way. The main work on the hill presented a bastion front towards us, and appeared as if it might be an enclosed work. It was on the south of the Pughtown road, and there was a line of works running across that road from the flank of the main one along a ridge, a small redoubt which, about 150 yards from the main work, was occupied by two guns supported by infantry. On the other flank were rifle pits on the slope of the hill. The men constituting the force occupying the works in our front did not seem to apprehend any danger in their immediate neighborhood, but were looking intently in the direction of Gordon's position, against which a gradual advance was being made with skirmishers supported by a body of infantry and some pieces of artillery, which were firing in that direction.

Colonel Jones, who had been entrusted with the command of all the artillery, had been quietly getting it into position out of sight, so as to be pushed by hand rapidly to the front when the time arrived to open on the enemy. When the men had become sufficiently refreshed, Hays' brigade, which was selected to make the assault, was moved to the front near to the edge of the woods next the enemy's position, with directions to General Hays to keep his men under cover until the artillery opened, and then to advance to the assault across the field and up the hill to the enemy's works, as soon as he should discover that the force occupying them was demoralized by the artillery fire. The artillery under Jones had been posted, with twelve pieces on the right of the woods, near Folk's old house, and right on the left in rear of the cornfield the 57th North Carolina Regiment of Hoke's brigade was posted so as to protect the pieces on the left from an attack in the direction of the Pughtown road. The rest of Hoke's brigade, except the 54th North Carolina Regiment, still on picket on the Romney road, and the whole of Smith's, were placed in line in the woods about a quarter of a mile in rear of Hays', so as to be ready to support him.

About an hour before sunset, everything being ready, Jones caused his pieces to be run by hand to the front, and opened almost simultaneously with the whole twenty pieces upon the enemy, who thus received the first indication of our presence in that quarter. Of course he was taken by surprise and thrown into confusion. Our fire continued for about three-fourths of an hour very rapidly, being replied to, after the first consternation was over, by the enemy's guns, but in a very wild manner. Hays then advanced to the assault as directed, crossing the field in his front, ascending the hill—the slope of which was covered with abattis made by cutting the brush wood growing on it,—and carrying the main work on the crest in handsome style, capturing some prisoners and six pieces of artillery, including those in the small redoubt, two of which were immediately turned on a body of the enemy's infantry seen approaching from the main fort to the assistance of these outer works.

The greater portion of the force occupying the captured works was enabled to make its escape towards the town, as it proved that this main work was open in the rear with wings thrown back from the two flanks of the bastion front presented to us. As soon as I saw Hays' men entering the works, I ordered Smith's brigade forward to their support, and directed Colonel Jones, whose guns had ceased firing when Hays advanced, to move the pieces on the left to the captured hill, those on the right being left under the protection of three regiments of Hoke's brigade. Riding on myself in advance of the supports ordered to Hays I discovered him in secure possession of the captured works, and ascertained that the attempt to advance against him had been abandoned, the force that commenced advancing having been repulsed by the fire from the captured guns which had been turned on it.

The force which had been advancing upon Gordon in the direction of Bower's Hill had retired precipitately, and the enemy's whole force seemed to be in great commotion. He had turned all his guns from the main fort, and from a square redoubt on a ridge north of it, upon the position now occupied by us, and as soon as Jones' guns arrived they replied to the enemy's, firing into both forts, which were completely commanded by the one in our possession, and upon the masses of infantry near them. The enemy's force occupying the works, and around them, was quite large, and deep and rugged ravines interposed between us and the two occupied works, which rendered an assault upon them from that direction very difficult.

CAPTURE OF WINCHESTER

By the time Smith's brigade and the artillery arrived, it was too late to accomplish anything further before night, and the capture of the other works by assault would evidently require the co-operation of the other troops around Winchester. The artillery fire upon the enemy's position and his masses of infantry was continued until a stop was put to it by the approach of darkness. Hays' brigade was formed in line on the crest of the ridge behind the captured works, with Smith's in rear. The 57th North Carolina, Colonel Godwin, was sent for, to occupy a portion of the works on the north of the Pughtown road, Colonel Avery being left with two regiments, to protect the artillery which had not been brought forward and guard against a surprise in our rear, the 54th North Carolina Regiment being still left on picket on the Romney road, and the front and flanks of our main position being watched by pickets thrown out. The men then lay down on their arms to rest from the fatigues of the day.

During my operations on the northwest, Johnson's division had demonstrated and skirmished heavily with the enemy on the east of the town, while Gordon demonstrated and skirmished with him from the direction of Bower's Hill, his attention being thus diverted entirely from the point of real attack, which enabled us to effect a surprise with artillery in open day upon a fortified position. It was very apparent that the enemy's position was now untenable, and that he must either submit to a surrender of his whole force or attempt to escape during the night.

I was of opinion that he would attempt an evacuation during the night, and I sent a courier to General Ewell with information of what I had accomplished, stating my opinion of the probability of the attempt to escape, but also informing him that I would renew the attack at light if the enemy was not gone. I had been given to understand that Johnson's division would be so moved as to cut off the enemy's retreat in the event I succeeded in capturing the position commanding his works, and I took it for granted this would be done.

In order to prepare for any emergency that might exist, I sent my aide, Lieutenant Callaway, with orders to General Gordon, to move direct from Bower's Hill against the main force at light next morning, and I set my pioneer party at work during the night to turn the captured works for my artillery, so that it might have some protection from the enemy's guns, if it should be necessary to open fire in the morning. As soon as it was light enough to see it was discovered that the enemy had evacuated his works and the town of Winchester during the night, taking the Martinsburg road, and some artillery was heard on the road which proved to be Johnson's guns near Stephenson's depot firing on the retiring enemy, whose retreat had been cut off by his division.

The brigades with me, including the detached regiments of Hoke's, were immediately ordered forward to the Martinsburg road for the purpose of taking up the pursuit. Gordon had advanced at light, as ordered, and finding the main fort unoccupied had pulled down the large garrison flag still left floating over that work. The 13th Virginia Regiment under Colonel Terrill was immediately detailed by me as a guard for a large number of loaded wagons found standing outside of the town, and a considerable amount of stores left in the town by the enemy, and the rest of my command, as soon as Avery came up with Hoke's brigade, advanced in pursuit along the Martinsburg road, Gordon's brigade having preceded the others. On getting near Stephenson's depot, five or six miles from Winchester, I found that General Johnson's division had captured the greater part of Milroy's force, Milroy himself having made his escape with a small fraction of his command, principally mounted on the mules and horses taken from the wagons and artillery that had been left behind, and I therefore desisted from further pursuit.

CAPTURE OF WINCHESTER

An enemy flying for safety cannot be overtaken by a force on foot moving with arms in their hands, and as we had but a very small battalion of cavalry (that belonging to Herbert's command, which did capture some prisoners), nothing was accomplished by the attempts made at further pursuit of Milroy, and he succeeded in getting in safety to Harper's Ferry.

During the operations against Winchester, Rodes had moved to Berryville, but the enemy fled from that place before him; he then moved on to Martinsburg in conjunction with Jenkins' brigade of cavalry, and there captured several hundred prisoners, several pieces of artillery, and some stores. My division bivouacked near Stephenson's depot, and I was ordered by General Ewell into Winchester to make arrangements for securing the stores and sending off the prisoners.

The enemy had abandoned the whole of his artillery, wagon trains, camp equipage, baggage, and stores, and twenty-five pieces of artillery with all their equipments complete, including those captured by Hays' brigade at the storming of the outer work, a very large number of horses and mules, and a quantity of ammunition, though in a damaged state, which fell into our hands. In the hurry of the movement after Milroy was found to have evacuated, I made such arrangements as I could to secure the abandoned property by detailing a regiment to guard it, but as usual on such occasions the contents of the wagons and the stores in town were considerably plundered by stragglers and followers of our trains, before they could be secured, and even after our quartermasters and commissaries got possession of them, there was great waste, and perhaps misappropriation of much of them, as always seemed unavoidable on such occasions.

On getting into town I endeavored to rectify the abuses as well as I could, but much was lost to the army of what was of real value, because there was no means of holding such agents to a strict responsibility. I sent off to Richmond, under guard, by the way of Staunton,

108 commissioned officers and 3,250 enlisted men as prisoners, much the larger portion of which had been captured by Johnson's division. Besides these there were left in Winchester several hundred sick and wounded prisoners.

My loss in the operations around Winchester was slight, consisting of 30 killed and 144 wounded, total 174, all but one killed and six wounded being from Hays' and Gordon's brigades.

CHAPTER XXIII.

AT YORK AND WRIGHTSVILLE.

I REMAINED in Winchester until the afternoon of the 18th, General Ewell having moved in the meantime to Shepherdstown on the Potomac, to which place Johnson's division, and Gordon's brigade, Hays' brigade and three regiments of Smith's brigade of my own division had also moved. The 54th North Carolina Regiment of Hoke's brigade, and the 58th Virginia of Smith's brigade had been sent to Staunton in charge of the prisoners, and leaving the 13th Virginia Regiment in Winchester, I proceeded on the afternoon of the 18th with the residue of Hoke's brigade, and Jones' battalion of artillery, to Shepherdstown, which place I reached on the 19th.

By this time Longstreet's corps had begun to arrive in the valley, and Hill's was following. The crossing of the river at Fredericksburg by a portion of Hooker's army had been for the purpose of ascertaining whether our army had left the vicinity of that place, and when ascertained that we were concentrating near Culpeper Court-House, he withdrew his force from across the river and moved his army north to defend Washington.

I remained at Shepherdstown until the 22nd. The field return of my division at this place on the 20th showed 487 officers and 5,124 men present for duty, making a total of 5,611, and the brigade inspection reports for the same day showed the number of efficient present to be about the same number, the reduction since the last reports being caused by the absence of the three regiments before mentioned and which did not rejoin until the campaign was over, the permanent detaching of Wharton's battalion of Hoke's brigade as a provost guard for the corps, the loss sustained at Winchester, and the sick and exhausted men left behind.

It is as well to state here that we had no hired men

for teamsters, or in any other capacity, but all the duties usually assigned to such men with an army had to be performed by men detailed from the ranks, as were all our pioneer and engineer parties.

On the 22nd of June I crossed the Potomac with my division and Jones' battalion of artillery at Boteler's Ford below Shepherdstown and marched through Sharpsburg and Boonsboro, camping three miles beyond Boonsboro on the pike to Hagerstown. The 17th Virginia Regiment of cavalry, under Colonel French, from Jenkins' brigade, joined me on the march this day to accompany my division by orders of General Ewell. Rodes had moved through Hagerstown towards Chambersburg, and Johnson's division, which had crossed the Potomac ahead of me, moved in the same direction. I was ordered to proceed along the western base of the South Mountain. Maryland Heights and Harper's Ferry were both strongly fortified, and were occupied by a heavy force of the enemy, which we left behind us, without making any effort to dislodge it, as it would have been attended with a loss disproportionate to any good to be obtained. Our movements through and from Sharpsburg were in full view of the enemy from the heights.

On the 23rd, I moved through Cavetown, Smithtown, and Ringgold (or Ridgeville as it is now usually called) to Waynesboro in Pennsylvania. On the 24th I moved through Quincy and Altodale to Greenwood, at the western base of the South Mountain, on the pike from Chambersburg to Gettysburg. There were no indications of any enemy near us and the march was entirely without molestation. We were now in the enemy's country, and were getting our supplies entirely from the country people. These supplies were taken from mills, storehouses, and the farmers, under a regular system ordered by General Lee, and with a due regard to the wants of the inhabitants themselves, certificates being given in all cases. There was no marauding, or indiscriminate plundering, but all such acts were expressly forbidden and prohibited effectually. On the 25th my command remained stationary at Greenwood, and I visited General Ewell, by his request, at Chambersburg, where Rodes' and Johnson's divisions had concentrated.

In accordance with instructions received from General Lee, General Ewell ordered me to move with my command across the South Mountain, and through Gettysburg to York, for the purpose of cutting the Northern Central Railroad (running from Baltimore to Harrisburg), and destroying the bridge across the Susquehanna at Wrightsville and Columbia on the branch railroad from York to Philadelphia. Lieutenant Colonel Elijah White's battalion of cavalry was ordered to report to me for the expedition in addition to French's regiment, and I was ordered to leave the greater portion of my trains behind to accompany the reserve ordnance and subsistence trains of the camps. I was also ordered to rejoin the other divisions at Carlisle by the way of Dillstown from York, after I had accomplished the task assigned me.

I returned to Greenwood on the afternoon of the 25th, and directed all my trains—except the ambulances, one medical wagon, one ordnance wagon, and one wagon with cooking utensils, for each regiment, and fifteen empty wagons for getting supplies,—to be sent to Chambersburg. No baggage whatever was allowed for officers, except what they could carry on their backs or horses, not excepting division headquarters, and with my command and the trains thus reduced, I moved across South Mountain on the morning of the 26th, and we saw no more of our trains until we crossed the Potomac three weeks later.

As we were leaving, I caused the iron works of Mr. Thaddeus Stevens near Greenwood, consisting of a furnace, a forge, a rolling mill—with a saw mill and storehouse attached,—to be burnt by my pioneer party. The enemy had destroyed a number of similar works,

255

as well as manufacturing establishments of different
kinds, in those parts of the Southern States to which
he had been able to penetrate, upon the plea that they
furnished us the means of carrying on the war, besides
burning many private houses and destroying a vast deal
of private property which could be employed in no way
in supporting the war on our part; and finding in my
way these works of Mr. Stevens, who—as a member of
the Federal Congress—had been advocating the most
vindictive measures of confiscation and devastation, I
determined to destroy them. This I did on my own responsibility, as neither General Lee nor General Ewell
knew I would encounter these works. A quantity of
provisions found in store at the furnace was appropriated to the use of my command, but the houses and
private property of the employees were not molested.

On getting to the eastern slope of the South Mountain, where the road forks about one and a half miles
from Cashtown, I heard that there was probably a force
in Gettysburg, and the pike leading through Cashtown
was found to be slightly obstructed by trees felled across
the road. I determined, therefore, to move a portion
of my force along the pike, which was the direct road
to Gettysburg, in order to skirmish with and amuse
the enemy in front, while I moved with the rest on the
road to the left, by the way of Hilltown and Mummasburg, so as to cut off the retreat of such force as
might be at Gettysburg. Accordingly, Gordon was sent
on the pike directly towards the town with his brigade
and White's battalion of cavalry, and I moved with the
rest of the command on the other road. There had been
a heavy rain the night before, and it was now raining
slightly but constantly, in consequence of which the
dirt road, over which the left column moved, was very
muddy.

Gordon moving along the pike, with about forty men
of White's cavalry in front, as an advance guard, en-

countered a militia regiment a mile or two from Gettysburg, which fled across the fields at the first sight of White's advance party without waiting to see what was in the rear, and Gordon moved on without resistance into the town.

On reaching Mummasburg with French's cavalry in advance of the infantry, I was informed that there was but a comparatively small force at Gettysburg, and I halted to wait for the infantry, whose march was impeded by the mud, sending out one of French's companies towards the latter place to reconnoitre. In a short time this company encountered some of the fleeing militia and captured a few prisoners, and being informed of this fact and that the command to which they belonged was retreating through the fields between Mummasburg and Gettysburg, I sent the rest of French's cavalry in pursuit. Hays' brigade, arriving soon after, was ordered to move towards Gettysburg, while the rest of this column was ordered into the camp near Mummasburg.

I then rode to Gettysburg, and finding Gordon in possession of the town, Hays was halted and encamped within a mile of it, and two of his regiments were sent to help French in catching the frightened militia, but could not get up with it. French caught about two hundred, but the rest succeeded in getting off through enclosed fields and the woods. The regiment proved to be the 26th Pennsylvania Militia, eight or nine hundred strong. It was newly clad with the regular United States uniform, and was well armed and equipped. It had arrived in Gettysburg the night before and moved out that morning on the Cashtown road. This was a part of Governor Curtin's contingent for the defence of the State, and seemed to belong to that class of men who regard "discretion as the better part of valor." It was well that the regiment took to its heels so quickly, or some of its members might have been hurt, and all would have been captured. The men and officers taken were paroled next day and sent about their business, rejoicing at this termination of their campaign.

On entering Gettysburg myself I called for the town authorities in order to make a requisition on them for a sum of money and some supplies. The principal municipal officer was absent, but I saw one of the authorities, who informed me that the town could furnish no supplies, as they were not there, and the people were too poor to afford them. I caused the stores in town to be searched and succeeded in finding only a small quantity of articles suited for commissary supplies, which were taken. It was then late and I had to move early in the morning towards York, so that I did not have time to enforce my demands. Two thousand rations were found in a train of cars which had been brought with the militia, and these were taken and issued to Gordon's brigade. The cars, ten or twelve in number, and also a railroad bridge near the place were burnt, there being no railroad buildings of any consequence. I then ordered Colonel White to proceed with his battalion early the next morning along the railroad from Gettysburg to Hanover Junction on the Northern Central road, and to burn all the bridges on the former road, also the railroad buildings at the Junction and a bridge or two south of it on the Northern Central, and then move along that road to York, burning all the bridges. Gordon was ordered to move at the same time along the macadamized road to York, and during the night I sent him a company of French's cavalry and Tanner's battery of artillery to accompany him.

With the rest of the command I moved at light next day (the 27th) from Mummasburg towards York by the way of Hunterstown, New Chester, Hampton, and East Berlin, halting and bivouacking for the night after passing the latter place a few miles. I then rode across to the York pike to Gordon's camp to arrange with him the means of moving against the town next day in the event that it should be defended. The information which Gordon had received was that there were no troops in York, and I directed him, in the event the town should be unoccupied, to move on through to the Wrightsville and Columbia bridge and get possession of it at both ends and hold it until I came up.

On the next day (the 28th) both columns moved at daylight, and a deputation consisting of the Mayor and other citizens of York came out to meet Gordon and surrender the town, which he entered early in the day without opposition. Moving by the way of Weiglestown into the Harrisburg and York road with the other column, I entered the town shortly afterwards, and repeated my instructions to Gordon about the bridge over the Susquehanna, cautioning him to prevent the bridge from being burned if possible. At Weiglestown French had been sent with the greater part of his cavalry to the mouth of the Conewago to burn two railroad bridges at that point and all others between there and York. Before reaching town Hays' and Smith's brigades were ordered into camp about two miles on the north of it at some mills near the railroad. Hoke's brigade under Colonel Avery was moved into town to occupy it, and preserve order, being quartered in some extensive hospital buildings erected by the United States Government. I then levied a contribution on the town for 100,000 dollars in money, 2,000 pairs of shoes, 1,000 hats, 1,000 pairs of socks, and three days' rations of all kinds for my troops, for which a requisition was made on the authorities.

Gordon moved promptly towards Wrightsville, and on reaching the vicinity of that place found the western end of the bridge defended by a force, which proved to be twelve or fifteen hundred Pennsylvania militia, entrenched around Wrightsville. He immediately took measures to dislodge the enemy, and, finding it impracticable to turn the works so as to cut off the retreat of the enemy, opened with his artillery and advanced in front, the militia taking to its heels after a few shots from the artillery and outrunning Gordon's men, who had then marched a little over twenty miles. Gordon pursued as rapidly as possible, but, on getting half way across the bridge, he found it on fire, inflammable materials having previously been prepared for the purpose. He endeavored to extinguish the flames, but his men had nothing but their muskets, and before buckets, which were sent for, could be procured, the fire had progressed so far as to render the effort hopeless, as the superstructure of the bridge was of wood, it being a covered one of more than a mile in length with a track for the railroad, another for wagons, and a third as a tow-path for the canal which here crossed the river. He had therefore to desist, and retire to Wrightsville with his men.

The bridge was entirely consumed, and as one or two houses were adjoining it, at the Wrightsville end, they were also consumed. When these houses caught fire Gordon formed his brigade around them and by the exertions of his men, then much exhausted, arrested the flames and saved the town of Wrightsville from a conflagration, though the houses immediately adjoining the bridge could not be saved. The brigade which did this, and thus saved from a disastrous fire, kindled by their own defenders, one of the enemy's towns, was composed of Georgians, in whose State, just a short time before, the town of Darien had been fired and entirely destroyed by a regular expedition of Federal troops.

As soon as I had made the necessary arrangements for establishing order in the town of York, and preventing any molestation of the citizens, and had made the requisitions on the authorities for what I had determined to levy on the town, I rode in the direction of Wrightsville. By the time I got outside of the town I saw the smoke arising from the burning bridge, and when I reached Wrightsville I found the bridge entirely destroyed. I regretted this very much, as, notwithstanding my orders to destroy the bridge, I had found the country so defenceless, and the militia which Curtin had called into service so utterly inefficient, that I determined to cross the Susquehanna, levy a contribution on the rich town of Lancaster, cut the Central Railroad, and then move up in rear of Harrisburg while General Ewell was advancing against that city from the other side, relying upon being able, in any event that might happen, to mount my division on the horses which had been accumulated in large numbers on the east side of the river, by the farmers who had fled before us, and make my escape by moving to the west of the army, after damaging the railroads and canals on my route as much as possible.

This scheme, in which I think I could have been successful, was, however, thwarted by the destruction of the bridge, as there was no other means of crossing the river. Gordon was therefore ordered to return to York early the next day, and I rode back that night. The affair at Wrightsville had been almost bloodless; Gordon had one man wounded, and he found one dead militiaman, and captured twenty prisoners.

Colonel White succeeded in reaching Hanover Junction and destroying the depot at that place and one or two bridges in the vicinity, but he did not destroy all the bridges between there and York, as one or two of them, as reported by him, were defended by a force of infantry. Colonel French succeeded in destroying the bridges over the Conewago at its mouth, and all between there and York, and on the 29th he was sent to complete the destruction of the bridges south of the town, over the Codorus, which he succeeded in doing, as the force defending them had retired.

In compliance with my requisition some twelve or fifteen hundred pairs of shoes, all the hats, socks, and rations called for, and $28,600 in money were furnished by the town authorities. The number of shoes required could not be found in the place, and the Mayor assured me that the money paid over was all that could be raised, as the banks and moneyed men had run off their funds to Philadelphia. I believed that he had made an honest effort to raise the money, and I did not, therefore, take any stringent measures to enforce the demand, but left the town indebted to me for the remainder. The shoes, hats, and socks were issued to the men, who stood very much in need of them. A portion of the money was subsequently used in buying beef cattle, which could be found much more readily when they were to be paid for than when certificates were to be given, and the residue was paid into the hands of the quartermaster of the army, to be used for public purposes. No public stores were found.

A few prisoners taken in the hospitals and those captured at Wrightsville by Gordon were paroled. Some cars found in the town were burned. There were two large car factories, and two depots and other railroad buildings which I would have destroyed but for the fact that the burning of them would set fire to some private dwellings and perhaps consume a large part of the town, and I therefore determined not to run the risk of entailing so much mischief on non-combatants, notwithstanding the barbarous policy that had been pursued by the enemy in numerous similar cases. Neither were the hospitals burned or injured in any way. I think the people of York were very well satisfied and much surprised to get out of my hands as well as they did.* Certainly any Southern town into which the enemy went would have considered itself exceedingly fortunate to

---

* To the Citizens of York:

I have abstained from burning the railroad buildings and car shops in your town, because, after examination, I am satisfied the safety of the town would be endangered; and, acting in the spirit of humanity which has ever characterized my government and its military authorities, I do not desire to involve the innocent in the same punishment with the guilty. Had I applied the torch without regard to consequences, I would have pursued a course that would have been

have got off so well. Our forbearance, however, was not at all appreciated by the enemy generally, for not only did they not follow the example set them, but some of the presses actually charged Gordon's brigade with firing the town of Wrightsville.

During my movement to York, General Ewell had moved towards Harrisburg and reached Carlisle with Rodes' division and Jenkins' cavalry, Johnson's division going to Shippensburg;—Longstreet's and Hill's corps had also moved into Pennsylvania and reached the vicinity of Chambersburg, while the Federal Army had moved north on the East side of South Mountain, in-terposing between ours and Washington.

Late on the afternoon of the 29th, Captain Elliot Johnson, aide to General Ewell, came to me with a copy of a note from General Lee to General Ewell stating the enemy's army was moving north and directing a concentration of the corps on the west side of the South Mountain; and also verbal instructions from General Ewell to move back so as to rejoin the rest of the corps, and information of his purpose to move back to unite with Johnson.

In accordance with these instructions, I put my whole command in motion at daylight on the morning of the 30th, taking the route by the way of Weiglestown and East Berlin towards Heidlersburg, so as to be able to move from that point to Shippensburg or Greenwood by the way of Aaronsburg, as circumstances might require, Colonel White being directed to move his battalion of

---

fully vindicated as an act of just retaliation for the many authorized acts of barbarity perpetrated by your own army upon our soil. But we do not war upon women and children, and I trust the treatment you have met with at the hands of my soldiers will open your eyes to the monstrous iniquity of the war waged by your government upon the people of the Confederate States, and that you will make an effort to shake off the revolting tyranny under which it is apparent to all you are yourselves groaning.

J. A. EARLY, Major General, C. S. A.

cavalry on the pike from York towards Gettysburg, to ascertain if any force of the enemy was on that road. At East Berlin, a small squad of the enemy's cavalry was seen and pursued by my cavalry advance, and I received at that place information, by a courier from Colonel White, that a cavalry and infantry force had been at Abbotstown on the York and Gettysburg road, but had moved south towards Hanover Junction. A courier also reached me here with a dispatch from General Ewell, informing me that he was moving with Rodes' division by the way of Petersburg to Heidlersburg, and directing me to march for the same place.

I marched to within three miles of Heidlersburg and bivouacked my command, and then rode to see General Ewell at Heidlersburg, where I found him with Rodes' division. I was informed by him that the object was to concentrate the corps at or near Cashtown at the eastern base of the mountain, and I was directed to move to that point the next day by the way of Hunterstown and Mummasburg, while Rodes would take the route by Middletown and Arendtsville.

My march so far, to the bank of the Susquehanna and back, had been without resistance, the performances of the militia force at Gettysburg and Wrightsville amounting in fact to no resistance at all, but being merely a source of amusement to my troops. The country maps were so thorough and accurate that I had no necessity for a guide in any direction. There had been no depredations upon the people, except the taking of such supplies as were needed in an orderly and regular manner as allowed by the most liberal and intelligent rules of war. No houses had been burned or pillaged, no indignities offered to the inhabitants, who were themselves amazed at the forbearance of our troops; not even a rail had been taken from the fences for firewood. I had returned over a large portion of the route taken in going to York, and I was myself surprised to see so little evidence of the march of an invading army. It furnished a most striking contrast to the track of the Federal army, as I had witnessed the latter on many occasions in my own state.

What was the case with my command, was the case with all the rest of our army, and I venture to say that the invasion of Pennsylvania by General Lee's army, for the forbearance shown to the invaded country, is without a parallel in the history of war in any age. Yet this invasion was made by an army composed of men many of whose own houses had been destroyed by a most ruthless enemy, into the country of that very enemy, and many of the houses thus spared were those of the very men who had applied the torch to and ransacked the houses of the men now so forbearing: yet those who have left their mark indelibly all over the South charge the invaders of Pennsylvania and their countrymen with being barbarous, and with maltreating prisoners.

As we moved through the country, a number of people made mysterious signs to us, and on inquiring we ascertained that some enterprising Yankees had passed along a short time before, initiating the people into certain signs, for a consideration, which they were told would prevent the "rebels" from molesting them or their property, when they appeared. These things were all new to us, and the purchasers of the mysteries had been badly *sold*.*

---

* The "mysterious signs" referred to were supposed by the Confederates to be made by Knights of the Golden Circle, a secret organization said to sympathize with the South, but of which our soldiers knew nothing.

CHAPTER XXIV.

BATTLE OF GETTYSBURG.

HAVING ascertained, after I left General Ewell on the night of the 30th, that the road from my camp to Hunterstown was a very circuitous and rough one, on the morning of the 1st of July I moved to Heidlersburg, for the purpose of following the road from that point to Gettysburg until I reached the Mummasburg road. After moving a short distance for Heidlersburg on the Gettysburg road, I received a dispatch from General Ewell, informing me that Hill, who had crossed the mountain, was moving towards Gettysburg against a force of the enemy, which had arrived at that place and pushed out on the Cashtown road, and that Rodes' division had turned off from Middletown towards Gettysburg by the way of Mummasburg, and ordering me to move on the direct road from Heidlersburg to the same place. I therefore moved on until I came in sight of Gettysburg.

Hooker had been supplanted in the command of the Federal Army by Major General Meade, and the advance of that army, consisting of the 1st corps under Reynolds, the 11th corps under Howard, and Buford's division of cavalry, had reached Gettysburg; the cavalry on the 30th of June, and the infantry early on the morning of the 1st of July. The cavalry had moved, on the morning of the 1st, out on the Cashtown road and was there encountered by Hill's troops, two of his divisions only having as yet crossed the mountain. The enemy's infantry then moved out to support his cavalry, and a heavy engagement ensued between it and Hill's two divisions. While this was progressing Rodes' division came up on the left of Hill, on the Mummasburg road, and immediately engaged the enemy.

When I arrived in sight of Gettysburg I found the

engagement in progress on the Cashtown and Mummasburg roads, the enemy's troops being advanced out from
that town on both roads for about a mile. Rodes had
opposed to him a very large force which overlapped
his left, and seemed to be pressing back that flank. On
the hill in rear of Gettysburg, known as Cemetery Hill,
was posted some artillery so as to sweep all the ground
on the enemy's right flank, including the Heidlersburg
or Harrisburg road, and the York pike. I could not
discover whether there was any infantry supporting this
artillery, as the hill was much higher than the ground
on which I then was.

Moving on the Heidlersburg road and on Rodes' left,
I came up on the enemy's right flank. I immediately
ordered the artillery forward and the brigades into line.
Gordon's brigade being in front formed first in line on
the right of the road, then Hays', with Smith's in rear
of Hoke's, and thrown back so as to present a line
towards the York pike. Jones' battalion was posted in
a field immediately in front of Hoke's brigade, so as to
open on the enemy's flank, which it did at once with
effect, attracting the fire of the enemy's artillery on
Cemetery Hill and that in front of the town on the
enemy's right flank. Between us and the enemy on the
northeast of the town ran a small stream, called Rock
Creek, with abrupt and rugged banks.

On the opposite bank of this creek in front of Gordon
was a heavy force of the enemy, on a low ridge partially wooded, with a part of it in line moving against
the left of Rodes' division held by Doles' brigade, so
as to compel it to fall back, while the right flank of this
advancing line was protected and supported by another
in position along the crest of the ridge. While the
brigades of Hays and Hoke were being formed, as
Doles' brigade was getting in a critical condition, Gordon
charged rapidly to the front, passing over the fences
and Rock Creek and up the side of the hill, and engaged
the enemy's line on the crest, which, after a short but

obstinate and bloody conflict, was broken and routed. The right flank of the force advancing against Doles became thus exposed to Gordon's fire, and that force endeavored to change front, but Gordon immediately attacked it and drove it from the field with heavy slaughter, pursuing towards the town and capturing a number of prisoners, among them being General Barlow, commanding a division of the 11th corps, severely wounded.

While Gordon was engaged, Hays' and Hoke's brigades were advanced in line to Rock Creek, Smith's brigade being ordered to follow, supporting the artillery as it advanced in rear of the other brigades. By the time Hays and Avery had reached Rock Creek, Gordon had encountered a second line just outside of the town in a strong position behind some houses, and halted his brigade behind the crest of a low ridge in the open field. I then rode to Gordon's position and, finding that the line confronting him extended beyond his left across the Heidlersburg road, I ordered him to remain stationary while Hays and Avery advanced on his left. The latter were then ordered forward, and advancing while exposed to a heavy artillery fire of shell and canister, encountered the second line and drove it back in great confusion into the town, capturing two pieces of artillery and a large number of prisoners.

Hays encountered a portion of the force falling back on his right, on which he turned some of his regiments and entered the town fighting his way, along the left end of a street running through the middle of the town. Avery, after reaching the outskirts of the town, moved to the left, and crossed the railroad into the open fields, on the left of the town, while exposed to a heavy fire from the batteries on Cemetery Hill, and took a position confronting the rugged ascent to the hill, his men being placed in a depression under cover of a low ridge, so as to protect them from the fire of the enemy's artillery. A very large number of prisoners were taken in the town, where they were crowded in confusion, the number being so great as really to embarrass us and stop all further movement for the present.

While Hays and Avery were driving the enemy so handsomely, I saw a large force to the right of Gordon, falling back in comparatively good order, before Rodes' advancing brigades, around the right of the town, towards the hills in the rear, and I sent for a battery of artillery to be brought up so as to open on this force, and on the town from which a fire was being poured on Hays' and Avery's then advancing brigades, but before the battery reached me, Hays had entered the town and the enemy's retreating columns had got out of reach, their speed being very much accelerated and their order considerably disturbed by Rodes' rapid advance. At the same time I had sent for the battery, an order had been sent for the advance of Smith's brigade to the support of Hays and Avery, but, a report having been brought to General Smith that a large force of the enemy was advancing on the York road on our then rear, he thought proper to detain his brigade to watch that road.

As soon as I saw my men entering the town, I rode forward into it myself, having sent to repeat the order to Smith to advance, and when I had ascertained the condition of things, I rode to the right of it to find either General Ewell, General Rodes, or General Hill, for the purpose of urging an immediate advance upon the enemy, before he could recover from his evident dismay and confusion. Rodes' troops were then entering the town on the right and all plains on that flank had been cleared of the enemy. The enemy, however, held the houses in the edge of the town on the slope of Cemetery Hill with sharpshooters, from which they were pointing an annoying fire into Hays' left, and along the streets running towards the hill.

The ascent to the hill in front of Avery was very rugged, and was much obstructed by plank and stone fences on the side of it, while an advance through the town would have had to be made along the streets by flank or in columns so narrow as to have been subjected to a destructive fire from the batteries on the crest of the hill, which enfiladed the streets. I, therefore, could not make an advance from my front with advantage, and thought it ought to be made on the right.

General Hill's troops had not advanced to the town, but remained on or beyond Seminary ridge, more than a mile distant, and before I could find either General Ewell or General Rodes, General Smith's aide came to me with a message from the General that the enemy was advancing a large force of infantry, artillery, and cavalry on the York road, menacing our left flank and rear. Though I believed this an unfounded report, as it proved to be, yet I thought it best to send General Gordon with his brigade out on that road, to take command of both brigades, and to stop all further alarms from that direction.

Meeting with a staff officer of General Pender's I requested him to go and inform General Hill that if he would send a division forward we could take the hill to which the enemy had retreated. Finding General Ewell shortly afterwards in the town, I communicated to him my views, and he informed me that Johnson's division, which had moved from Shippensburg, by the way of Greenwood Gap, was coming up, and he determined to move it to a wooded hill on the left of Cemetery Hill, which seemed to command the latter hill and to be the key to the position on that flank. This hill was on the right or southwestern side of Rock Creek, and seemed to be occupied by the enemy.

Johnson's division was late in arriving and when it came, it was further delayed by a false report that the enemy was advancing on the York road, so that it became dark in the meantime, and the effort to get possession of the wooded hill was postponed until morning, by which time it had been occupied and fortified by the enemy. My division went into this action about three o'clock P.M. and at the close of the day a brilliant victory had been achieved, between six and seven thousand prisoners and two pieces of artillery falling into our hands, a considerable portion of which had been captured by Rodes' division.

Perhaps that victory might have been made decisive, so far as Gettysburg was concerned, by a prompt advance of all the troops that had been engaged on our side against the hill upon and behind which the enemy had taken refuge, but a common superior did not happen to be present, and the opportunity was lost. The only troops engaged on our side were Hill's two divisions and Ewell's two divisions, the rest of the army not being up.

Late in the evening, when it had become too dark to do anything further, General Lee came to General Ewell's headquarters, and after conferring with General Ewell, General Rodes and myself, we were given to understand that, if the rest of the troops could be got up, there would be an attack very early in the morning on the enemy's left flank, and also on the right, at the wooded hill before named.

During the night, Hays' brigade was moved to the left into the open ground on that side, and placed in front of the left end of the town, under cover from the artillery and in a position to advance upon Cemetery Hill when a favorable opportunity should offer, his line connecting with Avery's right. In this position the two brigades were behind a low ridge close to the base of Cemetery Hill.

Gordon was still retained on the York road with his own and Smith's brigades, as constant rumors were reaching us that the enemy was advancing on that road. Johnson's division had been moved to the left and posted in the valley of Rock Creek, confronting the wooded hill.

During the night a large portion of Meade's army

came up and the rest arrived in the course of the next day before the battle opened.

The general attack was not made in the morning of the 2nd because there was great delay in the arrival of Longstreet's corps, and on the left Rodes' and my divisions remained in position until late in the afternoon, waiting for the preparations on the right. Johnson, however, had some heavy skirmishing during the day.

During the morning General Ewell and myself rode to a ridge in rear of Johnson's position for the purpose of posting some artillery and several batteries were placed in position there to fire upon Cemetery Hill and the wooded hill.

I made an attempt to get possession of the wooded hill in the morning, but found it occupied by the enemy in force behind breastworks of felled trees.

The enemy's position consisted of a low range of hills extending off to the southwest from Cemetery Hill to what was called Round Top Mountain, and on the right of it, confronting Johnson's division and my two brigades, was an elbow almost at right angles with the other part of the line, and terminating with the wooded hill or range of hills in Johnson's front, which extended beyond his left, the town of Gettysburg being located just in front of the salient angle at the elbow.

For some distance on the right of Gettysburg the ground in front of the line was open and ascended to the crest of the ridge by a gradual slope. On the left of the town, the ascent was very steep and rough, and this was much the strongest part of the line and the most difficult of approach.

The enemy had during the previous night and the fore part of this day strengthened their position by entrenchments.

Having been informed that the attack would begin on the enemy's left at four o'clock P.M., I directed General Gordon to move his brigade to the railroad on the left of the town, and take position on it in rear of Hays and Avery, Smith's brigade being left with General Stuart's cavalry to guard the York road. At or a little after four o'clock P.M. our guns on the right opened on the enemy's left, and those on the ridge in rear of Johnson's division opened on that part of the line confronting them, and a very heavy cannonading ensued. After this cannonading had continued for some time the attack was begun by Longstreet on the right, two of whose divisions had only arrived, and during its progress I was ordered by General Ewell, a little before sunset, to advance to the assault of the hills in front of me as soon as Johnson should become engaged on my left, being informed at the same time that the attack would be general, Rodes advancing on my right and Hill's division on his right.

I ordered Hays and Avery to advance, as soon as Johnson was heard engaged, immediately up the hill in their front, and Gordon to advance to the position then occupied by them in order to support them. Before Johnson was heard fairly engaged it was after sunset, and Hays and Avery then moved forward on the low ridge in their front and across a hollow beyond to the base of the hill, while exposed to a severe fire from the enemy's batteries. They then commenced ascending the steep side of the hill in gallant style, going over fences and encountering bodies of infantry posted in front of the main line on the slope of the hill behind stone fences which they dislodged, and continuing their advance to the crest of the hill, when by a dash upon the enemy's works Hays' brigade and a portion of Hoke's succeeded in entering them and compelling the enemy to abandon his batteries.

In the meantime Johnson was heavily engaged on the left, but no fire was heard on the right, Rodes' division had not advanced nor had the left division of Hill. Colonel Avery, commanding Hoke's brigade, had fallen mortally wounded near the crest of the hill, and the portion of the force that had engaged the enemy's works found itself unsupported, and paused for a moment, it being now nearly dark.

During the attack on the left of the enemy's line, a portion of his troops had been withdrawn from this part of the line, but that attack had now ceased and in a few minutes a heavy force in several lines was concentrated on Hays' brigade, and that part of Hoke's which had entered the enemy's works, and finding themselves unsupported and about to be overwhelmed by numbers, they were compelled to retire, which they did with comparatively slight loss, considering the nature of the ground, and the difficulties by which they were surrounded. Hoke's brigade fell back to the position from which it had advanced to bring off its wounded commander, and was then re-formed by Colonel Godwin of the 57th North Carolina. Hays' brigade fell back to a position on the slope of the hill, where it remained for some time awaiting a further advance, and was then drawn back, bringing off four battle flags captured on Cemetery Hill. Gordon's brigade had advanced to the position from which the two brigades had moved, for the purpose of following up their attack when the divisions on the right moved, but finding that they did not advance, it was not ordered forward, as it would have been a useless sacrifice, but was retained as a support for the other brigades to fall back upon.

During the advance of my two brigades I had ascertained that Rodes was not advancing, and I rode to urge him forward. I found him getting his brigades into position so as to be ready to advance, but he informed me that there was no preparation to move on his right, and that General Lane, in command of Pender's division, on his immediate right, had sent him word that he had no orders to advance, which had delayed his own movement. He, however, expressed a readiness to go forward if I thought it proper, but by this time I had been informed that my two brigades were retiring, and I told him it was then too late. He did not advance, and the fighting for the day closed—Johnson's attack on the left having been ended by the darkness, leaving him possession of part of the enemy's works in the woods.

Before light next morning Hays and Godwin, who had taken position on Gordon's left and right, respectively, were withdrawn to the rear and subsequently formed in line on the street first occupied by Hays, Gordon being left to hold the position in front. During the night, by directions of General Ewell, Smith was ordered to report by daylight next day to General Johnson on the left and did so. Longstreet, supported by a part of the right of Hill's corps, had been very heavily engaged with the enemy's left, in the afternoon of the 2nd, gaining some advantages, and driving a part of the enemy's force from an advanced line, but at the close of the fight the enemy retained his main positions.

On the morning of the 3rd, the enemy made an attack on Johnson to dislodge him from that part of the works which he had gained the morning before, and very heavy fighting ensued, continuing at intervals throughout the day, in which Smith's three regiments were engaged under General Johnson's orders, the enemy finally regaining his works. The rest of my command did not become at all engaged on this day.

On the right, Pickett's division of Longstreet's corps having arrived, the attack on the enemy was renewed in the afternoon after a very heavy cannonading of all parts of his line, and a very sanguinary fight ensued during which the enemy's line was penetrated by Pickett's division, but it was finally repulsed, as were the supporting forces, with very heavy loss on both sides.

This closed the fighting at the battle of Gettysburg. Meade retained his position on the heights, and our army held the position it had assumed for the attack, while both armies had sustained very heavy losses in killed and wounded, as well as prisoners.

CHAPTER XXV.

Retreat to Virginia.

During the night of July 3rd, Ewell's corps was withdrawn from its position in and to the left of Gettysburg, and moved to the right, to the Cashtown road, where it took position on Seminary Hill, the other corps retaining their positions. My brigades were withdrawn from Gettysburg to the new position at two o'clock in the morning of the 4th and were formed in line in rear of Seminary Hill, Rodes' and Johnson's divisions occupying the front line on the crest of the hill across the road.

During the battle our line had encircled that of the enemy, thus extending our army, which was much smaller than his own, over a very long line.

We remained in position confronting the enemy during the whole of the 4th, being subjected in the afternoon to a very heavy shower of rain. The enemy showed no disposition to come out, but hugged his defences on the hills very closely.

General Lee sent a flag of truce on the morning of this day to General Meade proposing an exchange of prisoners, but he declined to accede to the proposition.

Before day on the morning of the 5th our army commenced retiring from before Gettysburg.

The loss in my division in the battle, beginning with the first and ending with the last day, was in killed 154, wounded 799, and missing 227, total 1,180, of which Hays' and Hoke's brigades lost in the assault at the close of the day of the 2nd, in killed 39, wounded 246, and missing 149, total 434. 194 of my command were left in hospitals near Gettysburg, the rest being carried off. The loss of our army was heavy, as was that of the enemy.

I have before stated the size of General Lee's army when this campaign was commenced. The army had received no accessions, but had been diminished by the march, from straggling, exhaustion, and sickness. My own division had been reduced from 7,226, its strength when it left Culpeper, to 5,611 when I crossed the Potomac, those numbers representing the strength in officers and men, and not muskets. A similar loss extended to the whole army, and I can venture to affirm that it was as small in my division as in any other. Besides this we were in the enemy's country, and our large trains had necessarily to be guarded. I think it may be assumed, therefore, that General Lee's infantry at this battle did not exceed 55,000 officers and men, and that his whole force engaged, and in support of that part engaged, was smartly under 60,000, the cavalry not being employed at all except in watching the flanks and rear. His artillery numbered less than 150 guns.

Meade, in his testimony before the Congressional Committee, states that his strength, in all arms, was a little under 100,000, about 95,000, making a greater reduction from Hooker's force than I have allowed for General Lee's for similar cause, and that he had but little under three hundred guns. The odds, therefore, were not very far from two to one. Hooker had conceded the fact that he outnumbered our army, yet Meade, who succeeded Hooker, taking up the old idea of superior numbers, thinks General Lee now outnumbered him by some 10,000 or 15,000 men. The figures which I give I think fully cover our force, and the probability is that it was less.

It will be seen, therefore, what difficulties we had to encounter in attacking the enemy in his strong position. That position fought the battle for him. It is exceedingly probable that, if we had moved promptly upon Cemetery Hill after the defeat of the enemy on the 1st, we would have gained the position, and thereby avoided the battle at that point. What might have been the result afterwards it is impossible to conjecture. The battle would have had to be fought somewhere else, and it may or may not have resulted differently.

The fight on the 1st had not been contemplated by General Lee, and he was not, therefore, on the ground until it was over, and the time had passed for accomplishing anything further when he arrived. This fight had been brought on by the movement of Buford's cavalry in the direction of Cashtown and the attack on it by Hill's two divisions, which brought up the two corps of the enemy. General Ewell had moved to the support of Hill, but there was no communication between them during the engagement, as they were on separate roads, and each force went into action under its own commander, without there being a common superior to direct the whole. This want of concert existed after the defeat of the enemy, and the consequence was that the opportunity was not improved.

This battle of Gettysburg has been much criticised, and will continue to be criticised. Errors were undoubtedly committed, but these errors were not attributable to General Lee. I know that he was exceedingly anxious to attack the enemy at a very early hour on the morning of the 2nd, for I heard him earnestly express that wish on the evening previous, but his troops did not arrive in time to make the attack. Why it was so I cannot tell. In the assaults which were made on the enemy's position, there was not concert of action, but that was not General Lee's fault.

Without commenting on the assault from right of our line, which I did not witness, for that part of the battle was entirely excluded from my view, I will say that I believe that if the attack which was made by Johnson on the extreme left, and my two brigades on his right, at the close of the second day, had been supported by an attack by the divisions to the right of us, Johnson would have gained all of the enemy's works in front of him, Cemetery Hill would have been carried, and the victory would have been ours.

RETREAT TO VIRGINIA

So far as the fighting itself was concerned, the battle of Gettysburg was a drawn battle, but under the circumstances a drawn battle was a failure on our part and a success for the enemy. We were far away from our supplies of ammunition, and he was in his own country and in easy communication with his depots of supplies of all kinds. We were then in a part of the country by no means abounding in provisions and there was a mountain at our back, which limited the area from which we could draw food for our men, a most difficult task always, under the most favorable circumstances, in a hostile country, and rendered doubly so by the immediate presence of a large army in our front, with its numerous cavalry to aid the citizens in resisting the demands of our foraging parties.

We were, therefore, under the necessity of retreating, not because our army had been demoralized by a defeat, but because our supply of ammunition had become short, and it was difficult to subsist our troops. That retreat was made deliberately and in perfect order, and the enemy did not venture to attack us, but was content to follow us with a corps of observation at a respectable distance. We carried off a very large proportion of our wounded, but many were left because their condition would not admit of their transportation. We carried off some captured guns, and a large number of prisoners, after having paroled some three or four thousand. The enemy had none of our guns and he had in his hands fewer prisoners than we had taken.

My division with the rest of Ewell's corps was moved from its position on the Cashtown road at two o'clock on the morning of the 5th, arriving at the Fairfield road after sunrise. The withdrawal of the other corps was then progressing, and Ewell's corps, being ordered to bring up the rear, was here halted for several hours, waiting for the others to clear the road, and confronting the enemy's position, which was still in our view, by a line of battle.

LIEUTENANT GENERAL JUBAL A. EARLY

The enemy seemed to be very cautious about coming out, but finally ran out a few pieces of artillery and opened at long range, without doing any damage. My division was ordered to constitute the rear guard of the army, and White's battalion of cavalry was ordered to accompany me. I waited on the Fairfield road until it had been cleared by the rest of the army, including the other two divisions of Ewell's corps, and then in the afternoon moved off slowly in rear of the army and all the trains, Gordon, followed by White's battalion, bringing up my rear.

On arriving in sight of Fairfield, which is situated near the eastern base of South Mountain on a wide low plain or valley surrounded by commanding hills, I found the wagon trains blocked up at the village. While waiting for the road to be cleared of the wagons in front, Colonel White sent me information that a force of the enemy was advancing in my rear, and being on the plain where I would be exposed to a fire of artillery from the surrounding hills, I sent to hasten forward the trains, but as they did not move off I was preparing to fire a blank cartridge or two for the purpose of quickening their speed, when the advance of the pursuing column of the enemy appeared on a hill in my rear with a battery of artillery supported by infantry, and I opened with shell on it. The enemy's battery replied to mine, and Fairfield was soon cleared of wagons, as the teamsters and wagon masters found it more convenient to comply with this inducement to travel than my orders and solicitations.

Gordon deployed his brigade and sent out the 26th Georgia Regiment as skirmishers to dislodge the enemy's advance, which it did after a sharp skirmish, and a loss of seven wounded. This regiment was then ordered to be withdrawn, and I moved the division in line gradually through Fairfield to a favorable position for making a defence, and here waited the enemy's advance, but he moved very cautiously, sending forward only a party of skirmishers, which kept at a respectful distance.

It was now night, and my division was formed in line, a little nearer the base of the mountain, so as to cover our trains that were packed on its side and at its base. In this position my men lay on their arms all night without molestation from the enemy.

At light on the morning of the 6th, the trains moved forward, and General Rodes, whose division was to constitute the rear guard that day, relieved my skirmishers in front, his division being formed in line just at the base of the mountain, and I moved past him to take the front of the corps; when, pursuing the road over South Mountain past Monterey Springs, I descended to the western base near Waynesboro, and bivouacked a little beyond the town, covering it on the north and west with my brigades. The other corps were found already on this side near the base of the mountain, and the rest of Ewell's corps reached the same vicinity with mine. The force following us proved to be the 6th corps under Sedgwick, acting as a corps of observation. It gave Rodes no trouble and did not come beyond Fairfield.

A body of the enemy's cavalry had previously come upon that part of our trains that had preceded the army in the retreat, but was repulsed by a few guards accompanying the trains without being able to accomplish any damage of consequence. Early on the morning of the 7th we moved towards Hagerstown by the way of Leitersburg, my division following Rodes' and Johnson's bringing up the rear. The corps was established on the north and northeast of Hagerstown, and my division took position on the Chambersburg pike about a mile north of Hagerstown. In this position we remained until the 10th, when the corps was moved to the south of Hagerstown, the other corps being already there.

The enemy's troops had now commenced arriving on the western side of the mountain, and we took position on the south and southeast of Hagerstown to await his attack—Longstreet's corps being on the right, Ewell's on the left and Hill in the centre, and our line covering the road to the Potomac at Williamsport and Falling

Waters, a few miles below, where a pontoon bridge was being constructed in the place of one previously destroyed by the enemy's cavalry. The advance of the enemy resulted in a sharp engagement between a portion of our cavalry and a part of his troops on the Boonsboro road.

In the position near Hagerstown, my division was posted across the Cumberland road on the southwest of the town, but on the next day it was moved further to the right so as to rest its right on the Hagerstown and Williamsport road, where it remained until just before dark on the 12th. In the meantime Meade's army, now reinforced by some twelve or fifteen thousand fresh troops, according to his own statement, had moved up and taken position in our front, but did not attack.

Two of my absent regiments, the 54th North Carolina and 58th Virginia, had returned by this time, after having been engaged in repelling an attack, made by the enemy's cavalry at Williamsport on the 6th, on an ordnance train coming up with a supply of ammunition. Besides these, General Lee received no other reinforcements, but our army was not at all demoralized, and calmly awaited the attack of the enemy. My own division was buoyant and defiant, for it felt that it had sustained no defeat, and though diminished in numbers it was as ready to fight the enemy as at Gettysburg.

As night was setting in, on the 12th, my division was taken out of the line and moved to the right, to the rear of Hill's position, for the purpose of supporting his corps, in front of which a very large force of the enemy had accumulated. In this position it remained during the 13th, but no attack was made. The Potomac had been very much swollen by the previous rains, and after subsiding a little was again threatened with another rise from a rain that commenced on the 13th, and it was therefore determined to recross that river so as not to have an impassable stream at our back, when we had but one bridge and that not yet fully completed, and which, being laid on pontoons, hastily constructed by our pioneer and engineer parties, was liable to be washed away. Accordingly our army commenced retiring after dusk on the night of the 13th, Longstreet's and Hill's corps going to Falling Waters and Ewell's to Williamsport to ford the river.

My division brought up the rear of Ewell's corps, and the river being found too high for the passage of artillery, Jones' battalion, under the escort of Hays' brigade, was moved down the river to Falling Waters, where it crossed during the morning of the 14th. The rest of the division forded the river, in rear of the other two divisions, after sunrise on the morning of the 14th to a little above Williamsport, with the water nearly up to the armpits of the men, who had to hold their guns and cartridge boxes above their heads to keep them out of the water. The regular ford was too swift to allow of a crossing there, and we had therefore to cross in the deeper water above.

The crossing at Williamsport was effected without any molestation whatever, but at Falling Waters there was considerable delay because of the greater number of troops crossing there and the passage of the artillery at that point, where there was but one bridge. The enemy's cavalry came by surprise upon a portion of Hill's corps covering the bridge, and succeeded in capturing some prisoners and in getting two pieces of artillery which were stuck in the mud, the surprise being caused by a mistaken opinion that the front was watched by some of our cavalry.

Our army remained in the neighborhood of Haynesville that night, near which place my division camped, and now for the first time since I moved from Greenwood, on the 26th of June, we had the benefit of our baggage wagons. On the next day we moved through Martinsburg, and on the 16th my division reached Darkville, where it went into camp and remained until the 20th, in which neighborhood the whole of Ewell's corps was concentrated, the other corps taking positions further up towards and covering Winchester. In the meantime, Meade made preparations for crossing the Potomac below Harper's Ferry, and threw his army into Loudoun, while General Lee prepared to intercept his march by crossing his army over the Blue Ridge into Culpeper.

It having been ascertained that a force had moved from Cumberland in Maryland to the mouth of Back Creek west of Martinsburg, on the afternoon of the 20th, my division was ordered to move across North Mountain and then down Back Creek for the purpose of intercepting that force, while another division should hold it in front. We moved that night to the foot of the mountain at Guardstown, and crossing early next morning (the 21st) through Mills' Gap, marched down Back Creek to the rear of Hedgesville, where we found that the force had made its escape by retiring the night before. The division was then moved across the mountain through Hedgesville and camped. During the night I received orders to move up the valley for the purpose of crossing the Blue Ridge, and next day (the 22nd) I marched to Bunker Hill.

On the 23rd I passed through Winchester to the Opequon on the Front Royal road, being joined that day by the 13th Virginia Regiment. General Ewell, who had preceded me with Rodes' and Johnson's divisions, had that day been engaged with a heavy force which came through Manassas Gap, which he moved out to meet, near the Gap, as he was moving past Front Royal, and he sent at night to inform me that he would retire up the Luray Valley for the purpose of crossing at Thornton's Gap, and to order me to cross to the Valley pike so as to move up by the way of New Market, and across from there to Madison Court-House, as the enemy was in very heavy force in Manassas Gap. The Shenandoah was then high and a pontoon bridge had been laid near Front Royal below the forks, which he ordered to be taken up during the night, and to be transported up the Valley pike under my protection.

Accordingly I moved by the way of Cedarville next day to get the pontoon train, and then crossed to the Valley pike, following the route taken by General Jackson's corps the fall before and arriving at Madison Court-House on the 28th, in the neighborhood of which I found the other divisions which had come through Thornton's Gap and by the way of Sperryville. I had to use the pontoon train for crossing the Shenandoah, as that river was up, and I then sent it up the Valley to Staunton.

After remaining near Madison Court-House until the 31st I moved to the vicinity of the Robinson River, near the road from Liberty Mills to Culpeper Court-House, and the next day I crossed the Robinson just above its mouth into Culpeper and then the Rapidan at the railroad station, and encamped near Pisgah Church about four miles from the station, the other divisions moving to the same neighborhood.

Longstreet's and Hill's corps had preceded Ewell's corps across the Blue Ridge through Chester Gap, and while Meade was moving his army up into Manassas Gap to attack Ewell, they moved into Culpeper and waited until Meade's army had moved to the vicinity of Warrenton and the Rappahannock and halted without indicating any purpose to advance further; when, after a body of the enemy's cavalry had been driven back, these two corps moved to the south of the Rapidan and took position near Orange Court-House, leaving Stuart's cavalry to occupy the county of Culpeper.

This was the close of all the operations resulting from the campaign into Pennsylvania.

There have been various opinions as to the utility of this campaign into Pennsylvania. Undoubtedly we did not accomplish all that we desired, but still I cannot regard the campaign in the light of a failure. If we had remained on the Rappahannock confronting Hooker's army, we would have been compelled to fight one or more battles, and perhaps a series of them, during the summer, which would probably have resulted in a much heavier loss to us than we sustained at Gettysburg, though the enemy might have been repulsed. Situated as we were, it was simply a matter of impossibility for us to have attacked the opposing army in its then position, for we did not have the means of forcing a passage of the river—the advantage in that respect being all on the other side. We should, therefore, have been compelled to await the enemy's attack, which could only have resulted in his repulse, in the most favorable aspect for us.

We were in a country entirely devoid of supplies and of forage, for Fredericksburg had been occupied the previous summer by a Federal army, and no crops of any consequence had been made in all that region. By moving into Pennsylvania, we transferred the theatre of the war for a time into the enemy's country. Our army was supplied from that country and from stores captured from the enemy for more than a month and this gave a breathing spell to our commissary department, which had been put to great straits. We had been living the previous winter on very limited rations of meat, only $\frac{1}{4}$ of a pound of bacon to the ration, with few or no vegetables, and a change of diet was actually necessary for our men.

When we came back, though we had lost many valuable lives, our army was reinvigorated in health, and the transfer of the two armies to the upper waters of the Rappahannock and the Rapidan was a decided advantage to us. The campaign into Pennsylvania certainly defeated any further attempt to move against Richmond that summer and postponed the war over into the next year. Could the most brilliant victories which it was in our power to gain in Virginia have accomplished more? I think not.

CHAPTER XXVI.

TREATMENT OF PRISONERS, WOUNDED AND DEAD.

IT was from the close of this campaign that the difficulties in regard to the exchange of prisoners, and the consequent complaints about the maltreatment of those in our hands, dated.

The fall of Vicksburg simultaneously with the battle of Gettysburg, gave to the enemy the excess of prisoners, which had hitherto been on our side, and he now began to discover that we would be more damaged by a cessation in the exchange than he would:—our men when they came back would go into our army for the war, and we had no means of supplying their places while they remained prisoners. Many of his prisoners in our hands had but limited terms to serve out, and the places of those whose terms were longer could be readily supplied by new drafts, while his high bounties, national, state and local, opened to him the whole civilized world as a recruiting ground. He had no inducement, therefore, to continue the exchange as a matter of policy affecting the strength of his army, while a failure to do so would very much cripple us, by detaining from our army the men held as prisoners, by imposing on our already overtaxed resources the support of the prisoners themselves, as well as the diminution of the strength of our army by the detail of a force to guard them.

While we were in Pennsylvania, President Lincoln had issued an order, declaring that no paroles given, unless at some of the places specified for the exchange of prisoners in the cartel which had been adopted, or in cases of stipulation to that effect by a commanding officer in surrendering his forces, would be recognized. I think the date of that order was the 1st of July, and it was evidently intended to embarrass us while in Pennsylvania, with the guarding and sustenance of such prisoners as should fall into our hands. This order found us in possession of more than 6,000 prisoners taken on the 1st at Gettysburg.

About 3,000 of them were paroled, but their paroles were not recognized and they subsequently returned to the army without being exchanged, including some officers who solemnly pledged their honor to surrender themselves as prisoners in the event their paroles were not recognized by their government. The rest declined to give paroles because of the order before mentioned, and they were carried to Virginia and held in custody. In addition to our willingness to parole these men, General Lee proposed to make an exchange of prisoners after the battle, but it was declined. Now if the prisoners brought off by us from Gettysburg subsequently suffered in prison, who was responsible for that suffering?

The order in regard to the recognition of paroles was in violation of the well recognized principles of modern warfare. In the most ancient times, a captive taken in battle was held to have forfeited his life to his captors and it was always taken. After a time this was changed, and from motives of humanity the prisoner's life was spared and he became by the laws of war, even among the most civilized nations, the slave of his captor—his enslavement being justified on the ground that it was a boon to him to spare his life at the expense of his liberty. The justice of this rule is recognized in Holy Writ itself, and the rule continued to prevail long after the commencement of the Christian era.

In the age of chivalry a modification of the rule prevailed, and a prisoner was allowed to ransom himself, when he could raise the means of doing so. In more modern times the system of paroles was adopted, and the prisoner was allowed to go at large upon pledging his honor not to take up arms against his captors until regularly exchanged, the penalty of a forfeiture of his parole being death if again captured. This is a contract between the prisoner and his captors, which his government is bound to respect in the interests of humanity, by the recognition of all civilized nations. It is not necessary for him to receive the permission of his government or his leader to give his parole. When he is a captive, he is beyond the power and protection of either and has a right to stipulate for his individual safety against the penalties of death, slavery, or imprisonment by neutralizing his services for the time being. If his contract is not respected by his government, what must be the consequence?

When two nations or parties are at war, the object of each is to destroy the physical power of the other, in order to obtain peace, or accomplish the object for which the war is undertaken. If one party is so situated that it cannot hold, or cannot support its prisoners, and the other will neither exchange nor recognize the validity of paroles, is it to be expected that the prisoners shall be turned loose to return again to augment the force of the antagonistic party, and thus perhaps insure the destruction of that party liberating them?

The very principle which justifies killing in battle, that is the universal principle of self-preservation, will justify the taking of no prisoners or the destruction of all those that may be taken, if they can be neutralized in no other way. It was on this principle that the great Napoleon, in his Egyptian campaign, killed a number of prisoners whom he did not have the means of feeding, and who would not recognize the validity of a parole. If he turned them loose they would have gone immediately into the ranks of his opponents, if he kept them he would have had to take the food from the mouths of his own soldiers to feed them, and the only way of getting rid of them was by killing them. It is true a clamor was raised by his enemies, whose interest it was to make him appear as a barbarian devoid of humanity, but now that the feelings of that day have subsided, impartial men do not doubt the conformity of the act to the principles of war.

So when Mr. Lincoln's order appeared, if the safety of General Lee's army, or the success of his campaign had been jeopardized by the necessity of feeding and guarding the prisoners in our hands, he would have been justified in putting them to death, and the responsibility for the act would have rested on the shoulders of the man who issued the inhuman order. So too the latter was responsible for all the sufferings to which those prisoners who were carried off were afterwards subjected, if they suffered.

The alleged reason for stopping the exchange was the fact that the Confederate Government would not parole or exchange negro slaves belonging to Southern citizens who were captured in the Federal ranks. But it cannot be doubted that this was the mere pretext and not the real reason. That is to be found in the belief existing on the part of the Federal authorities that the failure to exchange would cripple us. The constitution of the United States, then unchanged in any respect, recognized the right of property in slaves, and guaranteed the return of such as should flee from service.

The constitution of the Confederate States contained the same guaranty, and the institution of slavery was recognized by the laws and constitutions of all the States composing the Confederacy, from which States alone the Confederate Government derived its delegated powers. That government was bound to respect the laws of the States and the rights of the citizens under those laws, and to protect them. Granting, for the sake of the argument, that the United States may have had the right to employ as soldiers the captured or fugitive slaves, as it had to take into its armies deserters from ours, still it took them subject to all the rights of the owners and of the Confederate Government, in the event of their recapture, just as deserters taken in arms in the opposite camp were liable to all the penalties for their crime without any infraction of the rules of war.

Many of the slaves put into the ranks of the Federal

Army were put there by force, but whether their service was enforced or voluntary, the Confederate Government would have been recreant to its trust, and grossly neglectful of its rights and interests, to have allowed so large a proportion of its own population to be used by its enemy for the purpose of strengthening his armies, by recognizing the claim set up on the part of these slaves to the benefit of the rules of war. Most nations have denied the right of its citizens even to expatriate themselves, so as to be competent to serve in the ranks of its enemies. None permit that expatriation to take place after the commencement of hostilities, and it would be the blindest folly to do so. In the case of the recaptured slaves, our government did not propose to punish the slaves themselves, though those that had voluntarily entered the enemy's service had justly forfeited their lives, but merely returned them to their owners, to the great gratification of the negroes themselves in most cases.

It was a case in which the Federal Government had no rights whatever, any more than it could have had in the case of deserters. The claim therefore set up to have these slaves treated as other soldiers taken in battle was without the slightest foundation in the principles of international law, or the rules of civilized war; and the cessation of the exchange on that pretence was a most atrocious act of cruelty to its own prisoners by the Federal Government.

A great clamor was raised on this specious pretext in order to reconcile the soldiers and the people of the North to the discontinuance of the exchange, and blind their eyes as to the real reason. Not denying the right of the Federal Government to refuse to exchange prisoners, if it was its interest to do so, and the war could not be terminated favorably to itself in any other way, still it had no right to violate the faith pledged to the exchange by the cartel; and least of all did it have the right to deprive its own soldiers in our hands of the right to release themselves from prison by giving their paroles. If it thought proper not only to adopt the extreme harsh measure of non-exchange from motives of policy, but to go further and adopt a new rule upon the subject of paroles, then it had no right whatever to complain of any measures of harshness towards its prisoners which the necessities or the interests of our government and our army rendered necessary.

So much for the question of rights; and now for the facts as to the actual treatment which the prisoners in our hands received. I think I can safely deny that they were ever subjected to any maltreatment, suffering, or neglect, which it was in our power to avoid. We did not resort to the extreme measures which perhaps the laws of war and our own necessities would have justified, but the prisoners were treated with all the humanity possible under the circumstances in which we were placed. Doubtless there may have been rare individual acts of maltreatment, but until human nature is a very different thing from what it is, there can be no body of men in which there are not some who act unjustly and oppressively.

Such is the case everywhere over the world, in the church, in government, in society, and in all the relations which men bear to each other, it has been the case, and will continue to be the case until the end of all things that some will do wrong, and we of the South cannot claim an exemption from the common lot. What I maintain is that no harsh treatment to the prisoners was authorized or tolerated, and if there were individual cases of the kind they were exceedingly rare.

The condition of a prisoner is by no means a desirable one under any circumstances, and he who is captured in war must expect to suffer inconveniences. The soldiers of the Federal Army were supplied with an abundance of everything necessary for their comfort and even luxury, to which many of them, including some officers, had never been accustomed before, and to which but few of them perhaps, except those who enriched themselves by the plunder of our people, returned again after the war. No army that ever took the field was so well supplied in all that was necessary, and much that was superfluous.

The easy communication always kept up with the positions of that army by railway and steamboat supplied it abundantly not only with ample and comfortable clothing of every kind and the government ration of everything, but with most of the delicacies incident to city life. They had not only bread, meat, vegetables, coffee and sugar in abundance, but the enormous horde of sutlers following the army supplied it with wines, liquors, fruits, oysters, canned meats and in fact every-thing that could be desired; and which high pay and high bounties enabled both officers and men to purchase. When such men, therefore, fell into our hands and were subjected to the scanty fare to which Confederate soldiers were reduced, it was very natural for them to complain of their treatment.

Our ports were blockaded and we were cut off from the commerce of the world. The enemy made not only provisions, but medicines, contraband of war. He had devastated the portions of our country to which he had penetrated, destroying crops and farming utensils, and burning barns, mills, factories of cloth and stuffs of all kinds, and tanneries, and in fact committing every possible waste and devastation which could cripple our army or pinch the non-combatants who remained at home. Coffee, tea and sugar had disappeared early in 1862 as a part of the ration to our men, and if there was any at all, it was to be found in rare quantities and at the most enormous prices. The scanty supplies of provisions to which our own men were reduced can hardly be conceived of by one who was not present to know the actual state of the case.

On the night after the second victory at Manassas, thousands of our men lay down to rest without having had a mouthful to eat all day. I was then in command of a brigade, and I was very well content, after the fight at Ox Hill or Chantilly, to make my supper on two very small ears of green corn, which I roasted in the ashes. On the next day and for a day or two afterwards, all that I had to eat was a piece of cold boiled fresh beef without either salt or bread, which I carried in a haversack. This was the strait to which a Brigadier General was reduced in our army.

I have many a time on the march, while a division and corps commander, been glad to get a hard cracker and a very small piece of uncooked bacon for my dinner, and I have been often thankful on the road to a soldier for a biscuit from his haversack which he himself had baked, after mixing up the flour on an India rubber cloth, which he had secured on some battlefield. When our money became so depreciated as to be worth only from five to ten cents on the dollar, many of the company officers were compelled from necessity to eat with their men of the scanty food furnished them.

I have seen commissioned officers often, marching on foot with their pantaloons out behind, their coats out at the elbow and their toes sticking out of their shoes, with but a pretence for a sole, while they had but the shirt that was on their backs as their whole supply of linen. I have seen this the case with gentlemen of refinement, whose means before the war had enabled them to live with every desirable comfort, yet they submitted cheerfully not only to this, but to actual hunger; and I have seen them go into battle with the proud tread of heroes, encouraging their men, cheering over the victory, or bravely meeting death in defence of a country which could treat them no better.

What these men were content with, the prisoners taken by their valor, and who had been so well pampered in their own country, thought proper to regard, when furnished them, as evidence of a disposition to starve them. Not only was our army so meagrely supplied with what was necessary not only to its comfort, but to its very existence, but our people everywhere were pinched for the necessaries of life. Gentlemen, ladies, and children, who had been accustomed to every indulgence and luxury, were very often put to the utmost straits for clothes to wear and meat and bread to eat, and while this was the case with them there was a long, long list of the wives and the children of the privates in the ranks fighting for their homes and their altars, who were on the very brink of actual starvation.

Now, I ask, in the name of all that is sacred, did they expect that the men who had come down to make war upon a people so reduced by their barbarous acts to the very verge of starvation and nakedness should, when taken in battle, be fed and clothed better than the men who, sacrificing all mere personal considerations, were so bravely meeting their foes in deadly strife, while their wives, children, mothers and sisters were starving?

There is talk about the food furnished the sick and wounded as being unsuited for their condition. I will mention an incident that occurred under my own observation. While we were at Spottsylvania Court-House in May, 1864, battling with such immense odds, I was in command of a corps, and I received a message to come to General Lee's headquarters at night on one occasion for the purpose of receiving some instructions from him. General Lee was then himself suffering with a dysentery which had reduced him very much, and rendered all of us who were aware of his condition exceedingly uneasy, for we knew that if he failed all was gone.

When I arrived his dinner and supper, both in one, were just ready and I was invited in to partake of the meal, and I found it to consist of, what to me was most acceptable, a scant supply of hard crackers, fried fat bacon, and a beverage made as a substitute for coffee out of parched wheat, without sugar, and this was all. This was what the foremost commander of the age was reduced to in the then critical condition of his health.

Such fare, if furnished to a sick or wounded Federal soldier, would have been regarded as evidence of a barbarous purpose to cause his death. To inflame the minds of the Northern people and prejudice the civilized world against us, an investigation was had before a committee of the Federal Congress who made a report upon "rebel atrocities," founded on the testimony of men who swore to some things they had seen, many that they had heard, and a great many more that they had neither seen nor heard.

The press was flooded with stories of cruel treatment, illustrated by pictures, and during the war every device was resorted to, to fix upon us the stigma of barbarous treatment of the prisoners in our hands. After the close of the war a poor feeble foreigner, Captain Wirz, who had been in our service, and was then on the very verge of the grave from wounds received in battle, was selected as a victim to be sacrificed to the demands of the North for more blood, and, after a farce of a trial, was hung for alleged cruelty to prisoners. As a specimen of the evidence given on his trial, it is only necessary to mention that of Boston Corbet, the man who killed Booth, while the latter, with a fractured leg, was in a house in flames and surrounded by a large party of Federal cavalry, by slipping up to the side of the house and firing his revolver through a crack.

Boston Corbet testified on the trial of Wirz, stating that he was a prisoner at Andersonville, and among other atrocities testified to, by him, he mentioned the fact that bloodhounds were kept to pursue escaped prisoners, and he said that he himself with some others made an escape, and the bloodhounds were put on the track; that while he was concealed in the bushes, one of the bloodhounds came up and rubbed its nose against his. When asked why the hound did not do any mischief to him, he said that he served the same Lord that Daniel served when in the lions' den.

There were many other witnesses in whose stories

there was as little truth as in that of Boston Corbet, and "rebel" witnesses were denounced as unworthy of credit unless they would prove renegades and endeavor to propitiate their masters by turning against their comrades. Even poor Wirz himself was offered his life if he would testify against the high officials of the Confederate Government, but he was too true a man and Christian to attempt to save himself from his unjust sentence by perjuring his soul; and he, therefore, suffered on the gallows.

To appreciate at its proper worth the evidence of the witnesses who have tried to fix upon the Confederate authorities this iniquitous charge of maltreatment of prisoners, it is only necessary to refer to the evidence of the general officers of the Federal Army before the Congressional Committee on the War. Let any candid man read, for instance, the evidence contained in that part of the report which refers to the battle of Gettysburg and the operations of the Army of the Potomac under Meade, where there is such palpable conflict, not as to opinions merely, but as to facts; and when he has determined in his mind which of those general officers tell the truth and which do not, let him say how much credence is to be given to the stories of those men who testified as to the horrors of Andersonville, and other Confederate prisons. When the general officers of the army were so loose in their testimony as to important facts affecting each other, what was to be expected of the subordinates and the privates, when testifying against their enemies?

It is very easy to raise the cry of "rebel" when any statement is put forth on the part of the Confederate authorities; and that is conceded a sufficient answer. The same cry would invalidate the testimony of General Lee or "Stonewall" Jackson. If such atrocities were committed as those alleged, why is it that poor Wirz is the solitary victim offered up in expiation of the thousands of victims who, it is said, died from the effects of the atrocities? The popular heart at the time of his sacrifice thirsted for blood, notwithstanding the oceans that flowed during the war, but when the first frenzy was over the more cautious panderers to the tastes of their countrymen felt that there was danger of shocking the minds of the civilized world, and desisted.

If poor Wirz was guilty, he was the least guilty of all those charged with the same crime, and was but a mere instrument in the hands of others. His executioners owed it to themselves and to the cause of truth and justice to bring the others to trial in order to vindicate their action in his case, and failing in this, they must stand before the world as his murderers. Sufferings there were doubtless at Andersonville and other prisons, but how could they be avoided?

Our men in the army were suffering, and our women at home were suffering. Could the men who came down to kill and plunder us expect a better fate than that which befell our own soldiers and people? Many perhaps died from the want of proper medicines, but thousands upon thousands of our own wounded and sick died from the same cause. Who deprived us of the means of getting medicines? When we could not feed, clothe, and provide for these prisoners in such a manner as would satisfy them, whose fault was it that they were not released to be cared for by their own friends? Who issued the order forbidding their being paroled? Who put a stop to the exchange? Was it to be expected that we would turn those men loose to come back again to kill and plunder our people?

Kindred to this is another charge of plundering and disfiguring the dead. Now as to the question of plundering, I cannot but think that it is more cruel to plunder the living than the dead, especially if the living be helpless women and children. I presume it is not necessary to state the reasons why I entertain this opinion.

It is to me a little strange that the men who applauded

Butler, Banks, Milroy, Sherman, and Sheridan, for plundering and rendering utterly desolate the houses of thousands of woman and children, should complain that our barefooted soldiers took the shoes from the feet of some of the men who had been engaged in this plunder and were killed in order that they might not be able to follow and fight the rest.

I have myself but too often seen in the track of the Federal armies the evidence of how they plundered and destroyed the property of our people. Not content with taking provisions, cattle, horses, sheep and other things which they might use, they often took what was of no earthly use to them as soldiers, and destroyed what they could not carry away. I have seen where they had torn up the clothes of the women and children, hacked to pieces furniture, pianos, and other articles, destroying valuable papers and books, burned besides houses, plows, carts and a variety of such things. This I have seen in not a few instances, but I have seen whole communities rendered destitute in this way.

They also burned all our factories and tanneries which they could reach, taking the hides out of the vats in the latter and cutting them to pieces. When a man is naked and barefooted, is he to be blamed for taking such articles as he needs from the dead body of his enemy who has thus treated him or his comrades, in order that he may still continue to fight the despoilers of his home and his country? Let the man who is disposed to condemn him put the case to himself. He is plundered and robbed, and perhaps some of his family or friends killed, he pursues his plunderers and succeeds in killing one of them, but he finds himself faint and sorefooted from the want of shoes, and is therefore unable to continue the pursuit. Will he hesitate to strip the shoes from the feet of his fallen enemy to enable him to resume the task of recovering his own and chastising his other enemies?

LIEUTENANT GENERAL JUBAL A. EARLY

On one occasion, a very worthy chaplain in our army on riding over a battlefield found a soldier pulling the shoes from the feet of a dead Federal soldier, and this being new to him, his feelings were rather shocked. Speaking to the soldier he said: " My friend, if I were in your place, I would have more respect for the dead, and not do that." The soldier, looking at the comfortable pair of boots which the chaplain by good luck was able to sport, said: "Sir, I have as much respect for the dead as you or any other man, but if you had marched as long as I have without any shoes, and your feet were as sore as mine, you would not think it so wrong to take these shoes which can't do this man any good now, and will do me a great deal." The chaplain was silenced, and that was the whole question in a few words.

As to the other part of the charge, about disfiguring the bodies, I do not presume our enemies themselves believe it, though it was their policy to show that we were barbarous, and this was set forth in the report of a Congressional Committee. I was on many battlefields beginning with first Manassas, both during and after the battles, and I slept on some, with the enemy's dead lying all around me. I never in a solitary case saw any evidence of any such treatment, and I never heard of any except from the reports put in circulation.

As I have passed along over the ground when we were fighting I have had some of the wounded appeal to me, saying they were informed by their officers that we killed all the wounded, and I have ordered them to be carried off and cared for. It was the policy to circulate such reports in regard to the treatment of prisoners, the wounded, and the dead, not only to inflame the minds of the Northern people in order to induce them to give a hearty support to the war, but to make the soldiers in the army fight more obstinately; and there were not wanting witnesses to aid the authorities by their testimony.

TREATMENT OF PRISONERS

The appeal may be safely made to the world to decide these charges against the comrades of General Robert E. Lee and "Stonewall" Jackson, and now that the war is over, it would seem that we might even "appeal from Philip drunk to Philip sober," but it will seem as if such critics had not allowed those passions to subside, by which they were intoxicated during the existence of active hostilities.

CHAPTER XXVII.

On the Rapidan.

WE remained in camp during the month of August, and the forepart of September, resting our men from their late fatigues, and recruiting our strength by the return of the sick and wounded who had recovered. General Hoke having recovered from his wound, now returned to his brigade, but was soon sent off with one of his regiments to North Carolina on special duty. In the last of August, or first part of September, Longstreet's corps was detached from our army, leaving only Ewell's and Hill's.

The enemy's cavalry had been constantly increasing in amount, and he had now a much larger force of that arm than we had. He was able to keep his cavalry well mounted, while horses were becoming very scarce with us. On the 13th of September, a large force of the enemy's cavalry, supported by infantry, advanced into Culpeper, and Stuart's cavalry was compelled to retire. My division, followed by Rodes', was advanced to the Rapidan to prevent the enemy from crossing, and we had some sharp skirmishing with the enemy's cavalry which came up to Somerville and Raccoon Fords, and we had some brisk artillery firing also.

My division took position covering the two fords named, and Rodes' went to Morton's Ford on my right and took position covering that; some of Hill's troops covering the fords above. The demonstrations by the enemy's cavalry and the skirmishing continued a day or two on the river, and a portion of Meade's infantry, all of which had moved into Culpeper, came up and relieved the cavalry, when the pickets were again established in sight of each other. We then proceeded to strengthen our position by rifle pits and epaulments for artillery, and continued in position until the 8th of October, there being occasional reconnaissances to the right and left by the enemy's cavalry, and demonstrations with his infantry by manœuvring in our view, his camps being distinctly visible to us from a signal station on Clark's Mountain, at the base of which, on the north, the Rapidan runs.

Meade had now sent off two of his corps, the 11th and 12th, to reinforce Rosecrans at Chattanooga, Longstreet having reinforced Bragg with two of his divisions; and General Lee determined to move around Meade's right and attack him, this movement commencing on the night of the 8th. One of Rodes' brigades, and Fitz. Lee's brigade of cavalry, were left to hold the line of the river on the right of Rapidan Station until the enemy had disappeared from the front, and my pickets having been relieved, my division was concentrated that night in rear of my position, for the purpose of moving early next morning. The movement was to be made by the way of Madison Court-House so as to avoid the observation of the enemy, Hill taking the lead, Ewell following.

I moved early on the morning of the 9th, taking the road by Orange Court-House and crossing the Rapidan at a ford a little above the mouth of the Robinson River, camping a mile or two beyond. On the morning of the 10th I moved by the way of Madison Court-House, following the rest of the army, and crossing Robinson River, camped again three or four miles from it. Just before night there was a sharp fight in the advance with a portion of the enemy's cavalry. On the 11th we continued to move to the left and then in direction of Culpeper Court-House to Stone-House Mountain, when it was found that the enemy had fallen back across the Rappahannock with his infantry, but there was fighting with the cavalry in the direction of the Court-House.

On the 12th we turned off in the direction of Fauquier Springs, and our advance drove a body of the enemy's cavalry from the river and crossed over, a portion of the troops, including my division, remaining on the south side. On the 13th we crossed and proceeded to Warrenton, and Meade's army, which was on the Rappahannock below, commenced its retreat on both sides of the railroad towards Manassas. We took position that night around Warrenton, Hill's corps being advanced out on the road towards Centreville.

Stuart, with a part of his cavalry, had crossed the river and got in between two of the enemy's columns, where he spent the night of the 13th in imminent danger of capture. We moved before daybreak on the morning of the 14th, as well for the purpose of relieving Stuart as for attacking the enemy, Ewell's corps taking the road by Auburn towards Greenwich and Bristow Station, and Hill's, a route further to the left. About light, a considerable force of the enemy, composed of both infantry and cavalry, was found at Auburn, on Cedar Creek, occupying the opposite banks of the stream, where a mill pond rendered the advance against him very difficult. Rodes' division formed line in front, and some skirmishing and cannonading ensued, while I moved with my division and Jones' battalion of artillery to the left across the creek above the mill, and around to get in the enemy's rear.

After I had started Rodes, having been replaced by Johnson, moved to the right to cross the stream below. The enemy's infantry in the meantime had moved off, leaving only a cavalry force and some horse artillery to dispute the passage, and as I was moving up to attack this force in the rear and Rodes was coming up from the right, it rapidly made its escape towards the railroad, passing between us.

We then moved towards Greenwich, and near that place Ewell's corps turned off through some farms in the direction of the bridge over Kettle Run, while Hill's corps preceded us on the direct road to Bristow. At this latter place, the 2nd corps of Meade's army, under Warren, was found, and two of Hill's brigades which were in the advance moved against it while behind the railroad embankment, and were repulsed with some loss, a battery of artillery, which was advanced to the front at the same time, falling into the hands of the enemy. About this time my division, in the lead of Ewell's corps, came up on the right near Kettle Run Bridge, and was ordered to move forward against some troops and wagon trains said to be moving on the road across the run in the direction of Bristow. Gordon's brigade being in front was formed in line facing the run and he was directed to wait until the other brigades came up and were formed.

While I was hurrying these brigades up, Gordon seeing some cavalry on the opposite hills made a rapid advance across the run and up the hills on the other side, driving the cavalry from the road to Bristow and pursuing it towards Brentsville. When the other brigades were brought up, I found Gordon unexpectedly gone, and I moved to the run, expecting to find him there, but he was nowhere to be seen. Warren's corps constituted the rear of Meade's army, and the troops and trains seen across Kettle Run proved only a rear guard of cavalry with some ambulances, the main wagon trains moving on the east of the railroad by Brentsville. When I found there was no enemy to attack in the direction I had been ordered to move, I then formed my brigades in line across the railroad facing towards Bristow Station, and sent to find Gordon, for the purpose of moving against the force behind the railroad at the station, according to instructions I had received from General Lee.

After a time one of Gordon's staff officers came up with the information that he was facing a heavy cavalry force immediately in his front from which he could not retire easily, and that there was a very large train of wagons about Brentsville. Gordon's brigade was more than one-third of my division, and with the other brigades I was not strong enough to advance against the enemy's position, especially as there was a very dense thicket of

305

young pines intervening between my position and that of the enemy which rendered an advance in line almost impossible.

It was now getting late, it being very nearly dark, and though Johnson's division was ordered up to my assistance, before it could reach me it became entirely dark, so as to put a stop to all further operations that night. Very early next morning I advanced towards the station, but the enemy was found to have made good his retreat during the night. I then halted my division, and moved on to Manassas Junction with a regiment, in order to reconnoitre, picking up some stragglers on the way. The enemy was found to have crossed Bull Run and taken position behind it. Our cavalry advanced up to the Run and had some skirmishing with the enemy, but our army did not make any further movement forward.

We then proceeded to destroy the bridge over Broad Run and Kettle Run and to tear up the railroad, burning the cross-ties and bending the rails by heating them.

On the march from Rapidan, Brigadier General Pegram, who had been assigned to the command of Smith's brigade, joined us, General Smith, who had been elected Governor of Virginia, having resigned at the close of the Pennsylvania campaign.

CHAPTER XXVIII.

DEVASTATION OF THE COUNTRY.

WE remained near Bristow two or three days, but were unable to supply our army in this position, and as the enemy had destroyed the bridge over the Rappahannock on his retreat, we crossed the river on a pontoon bridge. Our army then occupied the line of the Rappahannock, and remained there until the 7th of November, my division after several moves finally going into camp in rear of Brandy Station, Rodes covering Kelly's Ford on the right, with Johnson between us, while Hill was on the left. We still held the crossing of the Rappahannock at the railroad bridge with a pontoon bridge across the river and a *tete du pont* covering it.

Meade in the meantime had gradually moved his army up to the vicinity of Warrenton and Warrenton Junction, and we had sent forward, on several occasions, wagons strongly guarded by infantry to bring back the rails that had been torn up from the railroad between Bealton and the river. On the last of these expeditions, which was protected by my division, a considerable force of the enemy's cavalry was encountered at Bealton and driven off.

The *tete du pont* in front of the Rappahannock was occupied by a brigade detailed alternately from my division and Johnson's with a battery of artillery detailed from the artillery of the corps.

On the morning of the 9th of November, his position was occupied by Hays' brigade under the command of Colonel Penn of the 7th Louisiana Regiment, and Green's battery of artillery of four guns, while some works on the south bank, immediately in rear of the *tete du pont,* were occupied by Graham's and Dance's batteries of artillery.

The *tete du pont* itself consisted of a line of rifle

307

trenches encircling the bridge and resting on the river above and below, near the right of which were two small redoubts embraced in the circle of works, one of which had been constructed in the spring of 1862 when our troops fell back from Manassas to face to the north, and the other had been constructed by the enemy subsequently to face to the north, both being remodelled for the use of artillery. The rifle pits were slight, affording in themselves no obstacle to the passage of a force over them unless held by an opposing force, and the redoubts were imperfectly remodelled—while there was no obstruction in front, in the way of ditches, abattis or otherwise.

The work was completely commanded by higher positions in front, on ridges behind which a cover for the advance of troops from that direction was afforded, while, on the immediate right of the point at which the rifle pits touched the river, on that flank, the railroad approached to the bank of the stream by a high embankment of earth, with a walled opening in it for the passage of a road just in front of that part of the work. In rear of the *tete du pont* the river was rendered impassable except over the bridge, which was near the right, by a mill dam which backed up the water, making a pond extending along the entire rear of the work, the bridge being across this pond.

The works in rear of the bridge occupied by Graham's and Dance's batteries consisted of a redoubt that had been constructed by the enemy on that side and which had been turned, and some sunken pits for guns on the left of it, the ground occupied by these works being lower than the *tete du pont* in front. Some sunken pits for artillery had been made on the south side of the river on the right of the railroad in low, flat ground so as to sweep the east side of the railroad embankment that was on the north, but was unoccupied; there were also rifle trenches connected with this epaulment, and lower down to cover a point at which the enemy had had a bridge. The works which were occupied on the south bank really afforded no protection to those on the north, but merely served to command the bridge itself in the event of the *tete du pont* being carried, as the fire from the guns posted in them would be over the latter, in order to reach an advancing enemy.

Early in the day of the 7th, a small force of infantry appeared in front of the *tete du pont,* beyond the range of the artillery there posted, passing down the river, and a little before noon a heavy force of infantry was developed in front of the works, forming a line of battle encircling them, but still out of range of our artillery; and still later a large force was seen passing down the river, that in front still remaining in line of battle.

The enemy confronting this position, subsequently ascertained to be two corps, the 5th and 6th, under Sedgwick, then commenced advancing by gradual steps, coming up a little nearer each time and forming a new line of battle; and Colonel Penn, who had three of his regiments advanced to the front and on the flanks, so as to cover the main position with a line of pickets while one was in reserve in the trenches, and the other was on picket on the river on the south bank, was compelled to retire his advanced regiments gradually, until they were withdrawn into the woods, leaving only a line of skirmishers in front as far as their safety would permit. On the first appearance of the enemy in force, Colonel Penn had sent me a dispatch informing me of the fact, but as my camp was fully five miles off it did not reach me until a little before 2 P.M.

I immediately signalled the information to General Lee and General Ewell, and ordered my other brigades, then engaged in constructing huts for quarters, to be moved to the front as soon as they could be got together. As this required some time, I rode in advance towards the position occupied by my brigade on picket, and at Brandy Station received another dispatch from Colonel Penn informing me that the enemy still remained in his front in line of battle with a very heavy force. For fear that the information by signal had not reached General Ewell, as I understood he was coming up towards Brandy Station, I sent my Adjutant General, Major John W. Daniel, to meet him and communicate the contents of the two dispatches to him.

Before reaching the river I encountered General Lee, who had not received my dispatch, and together we proceeded to the river, where we arrived a little after three o'clock. I immediately crossed over to Penn's position and going out in front of the skirmish line, then considerably advanced, I discovered a very heavy force which was gradually but very slowly and cautiously moving up, encircling the whole position. Penn's regiments had been drawn in, including the one on picket below, except one company still left on picket at that point, and now occupied the trenches, which they could not fully man, while the guns of Green's battery were posted in the works on the right.

After fully reconnoitring in front I rode back across the river and communicated the state of the case to General Lee. Shortly after I recrossed the river, the enemy commenced forcing back our skirmishers, who were compelled to retire towards the works, and having got possession of the hills in front he opened with a battery of artillery, his guns being replied to by Graham's and Dance's with little or no effect, as the distance was too great. The enemy's skirmishers in very heavy line continued to advance, forcing ours back to the protection of the line of works, and a portion of his getting to the river bank about half a mile below the right of the *tete du pont*. An attempt was then made to send one of Dance's guns to the pits on the right of the railroad, but the advance of the enemy's skirmishers up the opposite bank of the river caused it to be abandoned, for fear of losing the horses.

At four o'clock, General Hays, who had been detained from his brigade by his duties as a member of a court martial, arrived and assumed command of the *tete du pont.* In a short time afterwards the three regiments of Hoke's brigade, forming the advance of the rest of the division, came up, and I sent them across the river, under command of Colonel Godwin, to the support of Hays. General Lee directed me to send no more troops across the river, but retain the others on the south side, and Gordon was moved to the right to occupy a hill further down the river, while Pegram's brigade was formed in line in rear of the hill occupied by Graham's and Dance's batteries, the 31st Virginia being sent to occupy the rifle trenches at the gun pits on the right of the railroad.

The enemy now opened from a battery on our left and soon from another on our right, and the fire of these batteries, which crossed in rear of our works, and that from the front rendered the bridge very unsafe. The fire from Graham's and Dance's guns seemed to be doing no good, as they could not be used to advantage by reason of having to fire over the works in front, and it was therefore stopped by General Lee's orders. Green's battery, however, under the command of Lieutenant Moore, continued the fire in front, but was greatly overmatched.

On crossing the river, which was under the enemy's artillery fire, Godwin's three brigades were put in the trenches covering the river above the bridge—three regiments of Hays' brigade, the 6th, 9th and 8th, being on the right and the 5th and 7th on the extreme left. The portion of the trenches occupied by the 6th, 9th and 8th regiments of Hays' brigade covered the bridge and to the right of it and on this part of the works were the four guns of Green's battery.

The enemy continued his artillery fire vigorously and rapidly until dark, his skirmishers in the meantime advancing in such heavy force as to drive ours into the works, and themselves coming up to within easy rifle range of the trenches. Just at dark the enemy's force advanced in heavy columns immediately in front of the position occupied by Hays' three regiments and our artillery, one of the columns moving up to within a short distance under cover of the railroad embankment and then suddenly debouching through the opening made for the passage of the road, before mentioned.

This assault was resolutely met by Hays' men and Green's guns, who poured a destructive fire into the advancing masses of the enemy, breaking the heavy line of skirmishers preceding the columns, but these columns came on in such strong force and such rapid succession that after a brief but obstinate resistance, Hays' men were literally overpowered by numbers in the trenches, which they held to the last, without attempting to leave them. The enemy also rushed upon the guns at the same time and, meeting with little or no obstacle from the works themselves, overpowered the gunners at their posts.

When the guns were taken General Hays made an attempt to recapture them, but the enemy coming up in still further force in front rendered the attempt abortive. The part of the line now taken was within a hundred yards of the northern end of the bridge and completely commanded it, so that all the force on the left was completely cut off from retreat.

An attack made on Godwin's front simultaneously with that on Hays' right, but not in as strong force, had been repulsed by the 54th North Carolina Regiment, and when Godwin learned that Hays' line was broken, he endeavored to move to his assistance, but the enemy had now got between the trenches and the river and commenced moving up a strong force against Godwin's right, at the same time that another advanced against him in front. He was therefore compelled to abandon a part of the trenches on his right and present front, as well as he could in the darkness, to the two forces, thus assailing him in different directions, so as to try to cut his way to the bridge.

He made a resolute struggle, but the enemy threw such a force between him and the bridge that the attempt to reach it was hopeless, and the rest of his men were

312

forced to abandon the trenches on the left. His three regiments and the two Louisiana regiments on his left were now completely surrounded, the enemy encircling them in front and on the flanks, while an impassable river was in their rear. Nevertheless, Colonel Godwin continued to struggle, rallying and encouraging his men as he retired from point to point towards the river, until he himself, with only about seventy men still remaining to him, was overpowered and taken by an irresistible force, without surrendering himself or his command. A like fate befell the 5th and 7th Louisiana Regiments.

I had remained with General Lee, by his direction, on the hill in rear near Dance's guns, where he had taken his position, observing the enemy's movements as well as we could, until very nearly or about dark. When the enemy's artillery fire ceased, we had discovered some movement of his infantry, but we could see so indistinctly that we could not tell what it meant. We saw the flashes of the rifles from our trenches and from the guns on the side of the river, but a very heavy wind was blowing, so that we could hear no sounds, not even that of our guns, which were not more than three or four hundred yards from us.

After this firing had continued some minutes, perhaps twenty or thirty, it slackened, and not hearing from it, we were of the opinion that it was at the enemy's skirmishers. General Lee then, expressing the opinion that the movement of the enemy in our front at this point was probably intended merely as a reconnoissance or feint, and that it was too late for him to attempt anything serious that night, concluded to retire, leaving with me two dispatches for General Ewell.

A short time before we saw the last firing, I had sent my Inspector General, Major Hale, on foot across the bridge to direct General Hays and Colonel Godwin to send and have rations brought up for their men, and just as I was preparing to send off the two dispatches left with me for General Ewell, Major Hale returned and informed me that when he saw General Hays the enemy was advancing against him, but he and his men were all right and in good spirits and that he then went to Colonel Godwin, whom he found all right, but as he was returning across the bridge he saw one or two of Hays' men coming off, who said the enemy had just broken through the line, the Major himself expressing the opinion that the statement was entirely false. It was now very dark and objects could not be seen at a very short distance. General Lee could not have then gone more than a few hundred yards since he left me.

Though I did not think the information brought could be true, as what I had witnessed did not indicate such a result, yet I sent Major Daniel to ascertain the truth, and ordered Pegram to move his brigade to the bridge immediately and Graham and Dance to man their guns. I then started to the bridge and soon met Major Daniel, who informed me he had just seen General Hays, who had made his escape, and that the greater part of his brigade was captured, the enemy in possession of the works, and Godwin cut off from the bridge.

Pegram's brigade was then hurried up to the bridge to prevent the enemy from crossing and Gordon's was sent for, information of the disaster being sent to General Lee at once. Godwin's regiments had not yet been captured, and I had the mortification of seeing the flashes of their rifles, and hearing their capture without being able to render them the slightest assistance, as it would have been folly to attempt to cross the bridge, and I could not open with the guns on the south side, as it was so very dark that nothing was visible, and we would have been as apt to fire into our own men as into the enemy.

A number of Hays' officers and men had been able to effect their escape by slipping off in the dark, after the works were in possession of the enemy, many swimming the river and others getting over the bridge. Some of Godwin's officers and men also effected their escape by swimming the river, and others by slipping down the banks of it to the bridge, while the enemy was engaged in securing the rest. General Hays had effected his escape after he was entirely surrounded by the enemy, and was in their power, by his horse's taking fright at a musket fired near him and dashing off, when a number of shots were fired at him, and finding that he had to run the gauntlet anyhow, he made for the bridge and escaped unhurt.

A regiment from Pegram's brigade had been sent to the end of the bridge and the rest of the brigade formed in line in rear of it. To have attempted to cross the rest of my command over the bridge would have but added to the disaster, and therefore, after waiting for some time to give an opportunity to all the men to escape who could, and ascertaining definitely the capture of the regiments on the left, and that the enemy had a guard at the further end, the bridge was fired at the end next us, and so destroyed that it could not be used by the enemy.

Receiving orders from General Lee to move back to my camp, I did so at three o'clock in the morning, after having sent off Graham's and Dance's batteries.

The loss in my division in this affair was 5 killed, 35 wounded, and 1593 missing, making a total of 1630. The loss in Green's battery was 1 killed and 41 missing, total 42, making the loss altogether 1672, besides the four guns and the small arms. The killed are those who were known to be killed, and the wounded were those who got off. Doubtless there were a number killed and wounded who were put down in the missing, but the enemy came up to the works firing but very little, and therefore the loss in that respect was comparatively slight.

Nearly three hundred of Hays' officers and men, between one hundred and one hundred and fifty from the three regiments under Godwin, and twenty men of Green's battery made their escape. A considerable number of the men in both brigades were engaged in getting timber for building huts at the time and were not present with their brigades, thus escaping capture.

The total force occupying the works was a little over two thousand, and the force which attacked them consisted of two corps, numbering probably over thirty thousand men. The result of the attack was unavoidable, and I fully exempted my officers and men from all blame. If the enemy chose to make the attack his success was inevitable. The works were of too slight a character to enable a body of troops to hold them against such overwhelming numbers. When the enemy reached the works he had no trouble in walking over them, as there were no ditches or obstructions in front.

In constructing these works too great reliance had been placed in the want of enterprise on the part of the enemy, and there was but one mode of approach to or retreat from them, so that when the works were carried in front of the only bridge there was, the fate of the rest of the command was sealed. The enemy on this occasion had more enterprise than had been presumed on, and hence the disaster.

This was the first serious disaster that had befallen any of my immediate commands, either as a brigade or division commander, since the commencement of the war, and I felt that I was not responsible for it, though I bitterly regretted it.

The same afternoon three corps of the enemy had attacked Rodes at Kelly's and forced a passage there, inflicting on his division some loss in killed, wounded, and prisoners.

On the next morning, the 8th, we formed a line of battle, a mile or two in rear of Brandy Station, Ewell's corps occupying the right, with its left, my division, resting on the road to Culpeper Court-House, and Hill's corps occupying the left, with his right connecting with my left. In this position we awaited the advance of the enemy all day, but he made no attack on us, though there was some fighting on Hill's left with the enemy's cavalry. Being now in a very unfavorable position, and having no good line to occupy in Culpeper, we fell back that night to the

Rapidan, and next morning crossed over and occupied our old positions. Meade's army also occupied very much the same positions it had previously occupied, and the line of pickets on the Rapidan was re-established.

While we were in Culpeper on this occasion we discovered that Meade's army had almost entirely devastated that county. Many beautiful residences of gentlemen had been pulled down, and some within sight of Meade's own headquarters, for the purpose of making huts for the soldiers and chimneys to the officers' tents. It was a scene of desolation, and the population was almost gone. I had been on the track of this army under all the other commanders, but I think it committed more depredations under Meade than under any of the rest, not excepting Pope himself.

After resuming our positions on the Rapidan, the condition of things was pretty much as it had been before, the enemy making some demonstrations but no serious movement until the last of the month.

A little after the middle of the month, General Ewell's health had been impaired, and I succeeded temporarily to the command of the corps.

There had been some demonstrations with the enemy's cavalry force, and General Lee, apprehending that the enemy might attempt to turn our right by moving across some of the lower fords, directed me to examine all the country on our right as far as Mine Run, and ascertain if a line could be formed there, extending towards Verdierville on the Plank road, which we could occupy in the event of an advance in that quarter; and to make myself familiar with all the roads. Our right, then held by Rodes' division, covered Morton's Ford and extended around to the river above the mouth of Mountain Run—the extreme right flank being unfavorably located, and liable to be turned, not only by a movement across at Germana Ford, but also at Jacob's Ford higher up, and from our right, as well as at some other points in the neighborhood.

LIEUTENANT GENERAL JUBAL A. EARLY

After a careful examination of the country, I selected a line to be connected with Rodes' right, by throwing the latter back from the river and then running the new line in its prolongation across Mountain Run, and a road leading past Rodes' rear to Bartlett's Mill, to Locust Grove, to Black Walnut Run above Bartlett's Mill, from which point the line could be still further prolonged past Zoar Church to Verdierville, if necessary, on a dividing ridge between the waters of Black Walnut and Mine Runs, which streams united just above Bartlett's Mill. Johnson's division which had been camped in the rear was then moved up to construct and occupy the right of the line extending from Mountain Run to Black Walnut.

While we were engaged in constructing this new line, with a view to its further prolongation if necessary, so as to cover all the roads coming in from the right between the Plank road and the river, on the 26th of November, Meade's army was discovered to be in motion towards the fords below on our right, and preparations were at once made to meet it.

Fitz. Lee's cavalry was ordered to relieve our pickets, and late in the afternoon of that day Rodes' division was moved across Black Walnut to the right of Johnson on the ridge extending towards Zoar Church, and my own division under the command of General Hays was withdrawn from its position and concentrated with a view of moving next morning on the old stone pike leading from Orange Court-House to Fredericksburg by the way of Locust Grove or Robertson's Tavern, and the old Wilderness Tavern so as to get on Rodes' right in prolongation of the line.

CHAPTER XXIX.

Skirmishing at Mine Run.

General Lee had discovered that the enemy was crossing some of his troops as low down as Germana Ford, and to prevent him from getting too far to his rear, he determined to move forward, and not await the advance against this new line; and during the night I was ordered to advance at daylight next morning as far as Locust Grove on the three roads leading to that point, to wit: the stone pike, the road by Zoar Church, and the one by Bartlett's Mill.

In accordance with General Lee's instructions, the three divisions of the corps were advanced at light on the morning of the 27th, as follows: my own division under Hays on the stone pike on the right, Rodes' on the road by Zoar Church, and Johnson's on the road by Bartlett's Mill; and while the troops were moving forward I rode to meet General Lee at Verdierville, in accordance with a request from him to that effect.

Rodes' was a little in advance of the other divisions, and as the advance of his column came in view of the open ground around Locust Grove (Robertson's Tavern) a very large force of the enemy was discovered moving up and occupying the high ground at that point. General Rodes then formed his division in line across the road on which he was advancing, in a body of woods, and the point at which that road united with the one by Bartlett's Mill on which Johnson was. In a short time Hays came up from Bartlett's Mill and finding Rodes in position in possession of Locust Grove, formed his line across that road confronting him—Johnson in the meantime coming up from Bartlett's Mill and finding Rodes in positon in front of him, halted his division along the road with his advance a short distance in rear of Rodes' line, and his division extending back towards Bartlett's Mill, so as to make his position nearly at right angles with the line occupied by Rodes. The enemy opened with artillery on both Rodes and Hays, and some skirmishing ensued.

While I was in consultation with General Lee at Verdierville, the information that the enemy had been encountered at Locust Grove reached me in the afternoon, and I rode to the front to Hays' position. I found the enemy occupied commanding ground in front and around Locust Grove, while the position Hays had been compelled to assume was low and very unfavorable. The enemy's guns raked the road as far as they could reach, and each side of it the ground, ascending towards the enemy, was very rough and so obstructed with young pines and underbrush as to make an advance very difficult. Causing Hays to connect his left with Rodes' right and so post his troops as to render them as secure as possible, I rode to Rodes' position, which I found equally disadvantageous for defence or attack. General Rodes informed me that the force seen entering the plains around Locust Grove was very heavy and that it was evident other troops were moving up to that position.

After reconnoitring I was fully satisfied that I could not make an attack upon the enemy with advantage, and that he had decidedly the advantage of the ground for attacking me. An examination of the ground on Hays' right had caused me to suppose that an attack might be made on the enemy's left by a force coming up on that flank from the Plank road, and information of that fact had been sent to General Lee.

While we were endeavoring to find out all we could about the enemy's position and strength, a little before sunset, General Johnson sent me word (to the point of intersection of the Bartlett's Mill and Zoar Church roads where I then was, just in Rodes' rear) that a party of the enemy had fired on his ambulances, on the road from Bartlett's Mill. I had received information that a body of the enemy's cavalry had crossed in front of Fitz. Lee at Morton's Ford, and had been cautioned by General

320

Fitz. Lee to look out for my left flank against molestation
of the enemy's cavalry, and supposing the party firing on
Johnson's train might be a body of cavalry that had
crossed at some of the fords below Morton's, I sent word
to General Johnson that such was my opinion and
directed him to attack and drive off the cavalry. He at
once formed his division and moved forward to the attack,
soon encountering, instead of a cavalry force, a very
heavy force of infantry advancing towards the Bartlett's
Mill road.

A very heavy engagement with both artillery and infantry ensued, in which Johnson's division encountered
the enemy's 3rd corps under French, supported by the
6th corps under Sedgwick, and, after a very obstinate
fight lasting until after dark, Johnson effectually checked
the enemy's advance, driving his troops back, and maintaining full occupation of the road. His brigades behaved
with great gallantry, encountering many times their own
numbers, and by the check thus given to the enemy in this
quarter saved the whole corps from a very serious disaster, for if the enemy had got possession of this road,
he would have been able to come up in rear of the other
division, while they were confronting the large force at
Locust Grove.

During the engagement one of Rodes' brigades was
taken from his left and sent to Johnson's assistance, but
before it arrived the action had closed. Johnson's division did not then exceed 4,000 men, if it reached that number. The two corps moving against it numbered not less
than 30,000 men, though French's corps, the 3rd, was the
only one which became actually engaged.

This affair satisfied me that the enemy's whole army
was in the immediate neighborhood, and as Ewell's corps,
under my command, was then in a most unfavorable position, I determined to fall back across Mine Run about
two miles in our rear, where I had observed a good position as I passed on. Accordingly after Johnson's fight
was over, and all his wounded and dead had been collected

as far as practicable, in the darkness, the divisions were withdrawn across Mine Run, my own and Rodes' on the stone pike, and Johnson's on the road to Zoar Church. Division commanders were directed to place their divisions in position at light next morning, on the west side of the run, Hays' left and Rodes' right resting on the stone pike, and Johnson's division across the Zoar Church road so as to connect with Rodes' left. Anderson's division of Hill's corps had been sent from the Plank road to my assistance, by General Lee, arriving about dark in rear of Hays' right, and before withdrawing my own troops I communicated to General Anderson my purpose, and he also withdrew across the run, so as to take position on Hays' right next morning. A strong line of pickets having been posted in front, the troops lay down on their arms a short time before day to rest from their fatigue.

In the affair between Johnson's division and the enemy's 3rd corps, there was some loss of valuable officers and men in killed and wounded, among the former being Randolph of the Stonewall Brigade, and among the latter Brigadier General J. M. Jones; but a much heavier loss was inflicted on the enemy.

After light on the morning of the 28th I rode to see General Lee at Verdierville for the purpose of advising him fully of the condition of things and receiving his further instructions. After being there a short time, information was sent me that the enemy was advancing on the stone pike from Locust Grove, and on riding to the front I found his skirmishers on the hills beyond Mine Run. The line on the west bank was now taken and the men commenced strengthening it with rifle trenches. Previous to this time not a spade of earth had been thrown up on the whole line. In the course of the day the enemy moved up his whole force in our front; Hill's corps, which had come up, having taken position on my right extending across to the Plank road, and covering that also.

Some skirmish firing ensued between the advance line

of skirmishers, but no serious move was made by the enemy.

Our position was a very good one and it was rapidly strengthened with the ordinary rifle trenches and some epaulments for artillery. The enemy's position on the opposite banks of Mine Run was also a strong one for defence, the ground there being a little higher than that occupied by us; and he proceeded to throw up strong epaulments for his artillery in numerous favorable positions. A direct attack from either side would have been attended with great difficulties, on account of the necessity of having to descend the slopes to Mine Run and then after crossing that stream to ascend the opposite slopes under the fire of artillery as well as infantry.

As the enemy had crossed the river to attack us, we calmly awaited his assault for several days, with full confidence that we would be able to punish him severely for disturbance of us at this inclement season.

The weakest part of the line occupied by me was on the left, where Mine Run made a turn somewhat around that flank, so as to afford the enemy an opportunity of placing guns in position to partially enfilade the line. He was slow, however, to take advantage of this, and our lines at the exposed parts were protected in some measure by traverses hastily made. On the 30th, he was observed moving troops to his right beyond our left, and dispositions were made to meet him by extending Johnson's line to the rear around towards Zoar Church. There had been occasional artillery firing by the enemy, and on this day he opened quite heavily for a time, our fire being generally reserved for the attack when it should be made. Andrews' battalion of artillery, however, near Johnson's left, supported by some guns from the reserve artillery, replied to the enemy's for a time.

A force of infantry crossing Mine Run in front of my division, under cover of some woods on the bank of the stream, came up to an imperfect line of trenches in front, which had been abandoned for a better and shorter line in their rear and were then only held by a line of skirmishers, but was soon compelled to retire.

The enemy had possession of Bartlett's Mill road which ran on our left towards the fords above, and connected with a road from Bartlett's Mill to Zoar Church in our rear; and as there was great danger of our left being turned in this direction, a watch was kept by videttes and pickets on that flank, so as to advise us of any movement, and enable us to move the line in prolongation until it connected with the one on the river.

The enemy made no such movement, however, and though on the 30th there were indications as if he were going to attack our left, yet he did not do so.

At the same time there had been indications of a purpose to attack our right beyond the Plank road, and corresponding movements were made to meet an attack there.

We remained in position awaiting the enemy's movements until December, when, all purpose to attack on his part being apparently abandoned, General Lee determined to attack him on his left flank, and for that purpose drew out two of Hill's divisions on the right to make the attack early next morning, the other division being moved to occupy their positions and my divisions being extended out to the right to occupy the part of the line evacuated by Hill's left division (Anderson's). During the night, however, the enemy withdrew from our front, and next morning he was found gone.

As soon as this was discovered I moved forward with the whole corps on the stone pike and then towards Germana Ford, capturing some two or three hundred prisoners, but the enemy's main force had crossed the river early in the morning.* After going to within a short dis-

---

* Though Meade's performance on this occasion was somewhat like that of a King of France on a certain occasion, yet he had not failed to accomplish something towards the "suppression of the rebellion." There was a little tanyard near Locust Grove, in sight of his headquarters, which belonged to and was operated by a poor man

tance of Germana Ford, and finding that there was no prospect of accomplishing anything further, I returned that night across Mine Run and encamped. The next day we returned to our former positions and the old state of things was resumed.

During our absence a division of the enemy's cavalry had crossed at Morton's Ford, and after some fighting, had been compelled by Fitz. Lee's cavalry to retire.

The loss in the corps during this affair was slight, nearly the whole of it being sustained by Johnson's division in the fight of the 27th.

---

who took in hides to tan on shares for the neighbors, but who was in no wise engaged in tanning for the government or the soldiers. The community around it was very poor, and this was the sole dependence for shoes for the women and children of that neighborhood. The tannery building and the house of the owner were burned, the leather all destroyed, and the hides in the vats taken out and cut to pieces so as to be worthless. In addition to this, all the plows and farming utensils, and wheeled vehicles, including old ox-carts and dilapidated buggies, in the neighborhood and on the road to Germana Ford were burned, and the houses of a number of citizens ransacked and the furniture destroyed. In the very few cases where there were pianos or libraries, the former were hacked to pieces with axes, and the books in the latter torn up and scattered over the ground, private papers sharing the same fate. I saw the evidences of these things myself. The women and children around Locust Grove had no new shoes that winter, and the people in all that country were deprived of the means of properly cultivating their crops next season, to say nothing of those who lost what little source of amusement, recreation or mental employment there was left to them.

Can it be doubted that this was calculated to break the spirit of the "rebellion"? Meade's expedition to Mine Run accomplished this much if no more.

CHAPTER XXX.

AVERILL'S RAID AND THE WINTER CAMPAIGN.

A FEW days after our return from Mine Run, General Ewell came back to the command of the corps, and I returned to my division, all remaining quiet on the Rapidan.

About the middle of December a force of cavalry and infantry moved from New Creek on the Baltimore & Ohio Railroad up the south branch of the Potomac, under General Averill of the Federal Army, apparently threatening Staunton in the Valley, while at the same time another force under Colonel Wells moved up the Valley from Martinsburg to Strasburg. General Imboden commanding in the Valley, having only a small brigade of cavalry and a battery of artillery, applied to General Lee for reinforcements, and two brigades of Hill's corps, Thomas' and H. H. Walker's, were sent to Staunton over the railroad, Fitz. Lee's brigade of cavalry being ordered to move to the Valley also. General Lee then ordered me to proceed to the Valley and take command of all the troops there.

I started at once, leaving Orange Court-House by rail and, reaching Staunton, by reason of some delay on the railroad, after the middle of the night. I found Thomas' brigade in Staunton, it having arrived the evening before, ahead of me, and Walker's had moved out to Buffalo Gap, ten miles beyond Staunton on the road to McDowell, at or near which place the enemy under Averill was reported to be.

Very early next morning General Imboden came into town, and I rode with him to his camp across the mountain from Buffalo Gap near the Calf Pasture River. He reported that the enemy's force was about five thousand strong and still confronted him behind Bull Pasture River, on the other side of the intervening mountains, where it was watched by a detachment of his cavalry, and such was the report we found at his camp. After I had been at his camp but a very short time, a courier came to me with a telegraphic dispatch from General Lee, who was then in Richmond, stating that Averill had left the Sweet Springs on the morning of the day before on the road towards Salem. I then started back to Buffalo Gap, and on the way I received another telegraphic dispatch from General Lee, informing me that Averill had entered Salem on the Virginia & Tennessee Railroad the morning of that day, and directing me to make arrangements to capture him.

It turned out that Averill with his cavalry had left the front of General Imboden at least two days before I started from Orange, leaving the small infantry force with him, under Colonel Thoburn, to amuse Imboden's pickets, and that Thoburn had also started back to the valley of the South Branch before I arrived. Imboden was ordered to bring his brigade back to Buffalo Gap, that night, for the purpose of being sent after Averill.

The question was how to cut off Averill's retreat, as he had several ways of getting back to a safe position. He might return the way he went—go up the railroad and then by the way of Blacksburg in Montgomery—come back by the way of Fincastle to Covington—or by the way of Buchanan and Lexington through the Valley, there being numerous intervening roads between these main routes which afforded him ample facilities for escape if he had good guides. After consultation with General Imboden, who was very familiar with the country, I determined to send his brigade to Covington next day, where it would be in a position to intercept Averill's retreat on the road by that place or move to the right and intercept him at Callahan's if he returned the same way he went.

During the night it rained in perfect torrents—such a rain as I have rarely seen—and by the next morning all the streams were very high. The direct route to Covington was down the valley of the Little Calf Pasture crossing that stream many times, across Big Calf Pasture and Cow Pasture Rivers. Little Calf Pasture itself, it was evident from the condition of the very small streams at Buffalo, would be impassable where there were no bridges, and there was no bridge over the Cow Pasture, quite a large river, on this route. It was, therefore, impossible for him to go the direct road, but being informed by him that there was a bridge over the Cow Pasture not far above its junction with Jackson's River, which could be reached by going through Rockbridge, and avoiding the other streams, I ordered him to take that route, which was by the way of Brownsburg.

The infantry brigades I determined to move back to Staunton, to be used for the defence of that place in the event of Averill's moving that way, as it was useless to be sending them after cavalry over such a track of country. Colonel Wm. L. Jackson was at Jackson's River Depot at the termination of the Central Railroad, with about five hundred men of his brigade dismounted, and that covered a route by Clifton Forge from Fincastle up the river to Covington. Railroad communication with him was cut by the previous destruction of the bridge over Cow Pasture, but there was telegraphic communication with him, and he was ordered to keep a lookout and make disposition to stop Averill if he came that way. I expected to find Fitz. Lee in the valley by this time, either at Staunton or farther down, and I rode to that place to order him to such point as might be advisable after I heard what route Averill had taken.

On arriving at Staunton, I found General Fitz. Lee himself, who had come in advance of his brigade, which had crossed the mountain at Swift Run Gap. I was now in telegraphic communication with General Nichols at Lynchburg, and from him I received information that Averill had started back on the same route he came, but was stopped by high water at Craig's Creek some twelve or fifteen miles from Salem. I, therefore, determined to order Fitz. Lee to Covington by the way of Lexington and Colliertown, at which latter place Imboden was ordered to unite with him. His brigade passed through Staunton late that afternoon, and General Lee followed very early next morning, with instructions to make all necessary arrangements to capture the raiding force, and with directions to move to any point that might be necessary according to the information which he might receive either at Lexington or elsewhere.

About the middle of the day I received a telegraphic dispatch from General Nichols covering one from an operator, stating that he had gone on the railroad that morning to within a mile of Salem, and that Averill was returning to that place, having been unable to cross Craig's Creek. If this was true, Averill must then attempt to make his escape by the way of the western route by Blacksburg, or the northern route by the way of Buchanan, and taking it for granted that it was true, I at once sent a copy by a courier to General Lee for his information, stating to him at the same time that as he was much nearer to Averill than I was, he might have other information on which to act, and leaving it to his discretion to move to Buchanan or to Covington as his information might justify.

When my dispatch reached General Lee he had united with Imboden at Colliertown, and after consultation with the latter he determined to move to Buchanan, as he had no information which warranted him in supposing that the dispatch from Lynchburg was not true.

During the night after I had received the dispatch informing me of Averill's return to Salem, I received another from General Nichols informing me that the information sent was not true and that Averill had succeeded after some delay in crossing Craig's Creek and moving on. It was now too late to reach Fitz. Lee by courier and I hoped that he might have had some accurate information.

I now determined to try to reach Jackson's position with one of the brigades of infantry, and Thomas' was sent next morning on the railroad, to endeavor to get across Cow Pasture in boats and so reach Jackson. The running stock of the railroad was in such bad condition, and the grades beyond Millboro were so heavy, having a temporary track with inclined planes at an unfinished part of the road beyond that point, that Thomas' brigade could not get any further. I ran down on the road myself to see if the brigade could not be thrown to some point to intercept the enemy. Arriving just at night I found General Thomas in telegraphic communication with Jackson, and the information was soon received that Averill's advance had made its appearance on an obscure road across the mountains into the Jackson's River Valley, and that a small part of Jackson's men were skirmishing with the enemy. This road came in above Jackson's main position, and the party watching it was soon forced back, and Averill's force got into the road between Jackson and the bridge above him, which bridge was guarded by a party of some eight or ten reserves, who abandoned their post.

The enemy thus got possession of the bridge and commenced crossing rapidly. Jackson, in the meantime, moved up and attacked the enemy's rear, which he threw into great confusion, capturing over two hundred prisoners. In his alarm the enemy set fire to the bridge, thus cutting off all of his wagons, and some two or three hundred of his men. The wagons were burned and the men left behind subsequently moved up the river and forded by swimming.

All this information was communicated to me that night and next morning by telegram, and I knew that it was useless to make any further attempt to cut the enemy off with my infantry, as he was beyond pursuit of any kind.

When Fitz. Lee reached Buchanan and found Averill was not coming that way, he moved by the way of Fincastle in pursuit, and ascertaining what route Averill had taken, he then went to Covington and from there followed to Callahan's, but the greater part of the raiding party had made its escape, so he desisted from what was then a useless effort. The facts were that on going back on the route he had come, from the Sweet Springs, Averill found his retreat cut off that way by Echol's brigade of General Sam Jones' force from Southwestern Virginia, which was posted on what is called Potts' or Middle Mountain, and he then turned across toward Covington over Rich Patch Mountain, being compelled to come into the valley of Jackson's River at the point he did to reach the bridge on the road from Clifton Forge to Covington, as there was no bridge on the direct road to that place. He thus succeeded in making his escape by the stupidity or treachery of a telegraph operator, but the amount of damage he had been able to do did not compensate for the loss of men and horses which he sustained, and the sufferings the others endured. He had been able to burn a small depot at Salem with a few supplies in it and one or two small bridges in the neighborhood, which were rebuilt in a few days. His raid really amounted to very little except the name of it.

The same night that Averill made his escape by Jackson, I received a dispatch from General Walker at Staunton informing me that the force that had been at Strasburg was moving up the valley, and had passed New Market. I telegraphed to him to move to the North River at Mount Crawford at once, which he did early next day. Thomas' brigade was moved back to Staunton, starting early in the morning, but on account of the condition of the road, did not reach there until nearly night. On arriving at Staunton myself, I rode out to Walker's position eighteen miles beyond, leaving orders for Thomas to march up during the night. On reaching Walker I found that the enemy was in Harrisonburg, and I ordered an advance early next morning.

At light next day, Thomas came up, both brigades moving forward. The enemy was found to have retired during the night, leaving a small cavalry rear guard, which retreated as we came up. I had no cavalry except a few stragglers from different cavalry commands, which I could employ only as scouts to observe the movements of the enemy, but I pushed on in pursuit. After passing Harrisonburg, a battalion of mounted men exempt from regular service by age or otherwise, called the Augusta Raid Guards, came up, and were ordered forward in pursuit, but accomplished nothing. According to the organization of the command, the men were not bound to go beyond the limits of any adjoining county, and when they reached the Shenandoah line they halted, standing upon their legal rights, though it may be doubted if they would have stood upon them if the enemy had turned back.

This force of the enemy had now got beyond reach, and Thomas' brigade was halted at Lacy's Springs after having marched thirty-six miles since after nightfall the evening before. Walker's moved on to New Market and halted there, having then marched twenty-eight miles.

The movement in this direction had been made to divert some of the troops from the pursuit of Averill, so as to aid his escape; and the force making it now retreated rapidly to Martinsburg. Thomas being moved up to New Market, I rested the men a few days, and I then received directions from General Lee to send a cavalry expedition into the counties of Hardy and Hampshire to get some cattle and meat for his men. Our army was now very much straitened for provisions, especially for meat, of which they were sometimes devoid for days at a time. As soon as Fitz. Lee had returned from the pursuit of Averill I ordered him up to the vicinity of New Market, and when his men and horses had rested a few days he was ordered to cross the Great North Mountain into Hardy, try and dislodge an infantry force at Petersburg, cut the Baltimore & Ohio Railroad at the mouth of the South Branch of the Potomac, and of Patterson's Creek, gather all the beef cattle he could, and likewise get what of value was to be had.

By the last of December he was ready to move, and

started, accompanied by McNeil's company of partisan rangers and Gilmor's Maryland battalion, crossing the mountain over a rugged road near Orkney Springs. I started McClanahan's battery of artillery of Imboden's command with him and some wagons, but it was now the 1st of January and the weather had become excessively cold, the thermometer being near zero, and when the artillery got to the top of the mountain, it was found that the roads on the other side, which were very steep, were sheeted with ice, rendering it impracticable to get the artillery down in safety. The cavalry succeeded in getting down, by the men being dismounted to lead their horses, but the artillery and wagons had to be sent back.

To attract attention from this expedition I moved at the same time down the Valley pike to Fisher's Hill with Thomas' brigade, preceded by Imboden's cavalry under Colonel Smith, and remained there until Fitz. Lee's return, Smith being sent beyond Strasburg to demonstrate towards Winchester. Walker's brigade had been left at Mount Jackson. While we were at Fisher's Hill, there were two heavy snows, and there was very hard freezing weather all the time. The men had no tents and their only shelter consisted of rude open sheds made of split wood, yet, though Thomas' was a Georgia brigade, they stood the weather remarkably well and seemed to take a pleasure in the expedition, regretting when the time came to fall back.

In the meantime Fitz. Lee had reached Hardy, attacked a guarded train moving from New Creek to Petersburg for the supply of that post, captured more than twenty wagons and some prisoners, invested the post at Petersburg, which he found strongly fortified, but having no artillery he abandoned the attempt to dislodge the enemy without making an attack. He then moved down to the Baltimore & Ohio Railroad, destroyed the bridge over Patterson's Creek and that over the South Branch partially, collected a large number of cattle, and came off with the captured wagons, and prisoners, and some eight hundred or one thousand head of beef cattle. His men had been exposed to the same severe weather to which those at Fisher's Hill had been, and the feet of a few of them had been frosted. As soon as I heard of his safe return, I moved back up the valley, and the cattle brought off were sent to the army.

Not long afterwards, Fitz. Lee's cavalry returned to the eastern side of the ridge, but its place was taken by Rosser's brigade, which had come into the valley.

About the last of January I undertook another expedition into the Hardy Valley for the same objects for which the first had been made. This I determined to make with Rosser's brigade of cavalry and one of the brigades of infantry, accompanied by McClanahan's battery, that being the only artillery there was in the valley.

Rosser with his brigade, McNeil's company, a part of Gilmor's battalion, the battery and some wagons passed through Brock's Gap into the valley of Lost River, while Thomas' brigade moved over the mountains, at the Orkney Springs pass, to the same valley. Imboden was left with Walker's brigade of infantry at Mount Jackson, and his own brigade of cavalry advanced down the Valley pike towards Winchester, to demonstrate in that direction. Passing over the mountain to Matthews' on Lost River in advance of Thomas' brigade I found Rosser at that place, where we spent the night. From this point the road to Moorefield ascends to the summit of Branch Mountain and then along that for several miles, through a wild, mountainous and desolate looking region, until it comes to the point of descent into the Moorefield Valley, which latter, a most beautiful and fertile valley surrounded by high mountains, is reached at the western base of the mountain on the South Fork of the South Branch.

Starting early in the morning we reached the South Fork with the cavalry and artillery early in the day, and leaving the main force there, behind the mountain intervening between the two forks, McNeil's company was thrown forward to Moorefield and the North Fork, to cover our front and prevent the enemy, who occupied the fortified fort at Petersburg eight or ten miles above Moorefield on the North Fork, from discovering our presence in force; McNeil's company being composed mainly of men from that section, and being in the habit of making frequent raids into the valley.

We had ascertained that a large loaded wagon train was on the point of starting from New Creek for Petersburg, and some very trusty scouts perfectly familiar with the country were watching it. During the night, we were informed by the scouts that the train of about one hundred wagons had started, guarded by a force of infantry, and that it would be on the Patterson Creek road across Patterson Mountain from Moorefield at an early hour next day. Rosser immediately made preparations to move with his brigade and the battery of artillery before light in the morning. Crossing over Patterson Mountain, he found the road obstructed with trees felled across it, extending some distance on each side, and the obstructions defended by a force of infantry. Dismounting a part of his men, he attacked and drove the enemy from the obstructions, and clearing the road, he passed through and soon encountered the train.

The infantry guard was very strong, and McClanahan's guns were brought into action, when by a vigorous charge the guard was dispersed, taking refuge in the mountains, and over ninety loaded wagons with their teams, and more than one hundred prisoners were captured. Fifty of the wagons were sent back with their teams and loads, but the rest were so badly smashed in the confusion resulting from the attack, that they could not be moved; and securing the teams and such of the contents as could be brought off, the injured wagons were burned.

Rosser had been ordered to move around and take position on the road north and west of Petersburg, so as to cut off the retreat of the enemy from that place, against which I proposed moving at light next day, as the infantry would be up at night, and he proceeded to obey the orders.

Thomas' Georgians, moving along the summit of Branch Mountain with nothing but wild inaccessible mountains and deep ravines on each side as far as the eye could reach, could not understand why they were carried over such a route at this season and inquired of each other: " What can General Early mean by bringing us into such a country as this in the midst of winter? " But when they came suddenly in view of the beautiful valley of Moorefield and saw spread out before them what Johnson might have taken as the original of his ideas of the " Happy Valley " in Rasselas, they burst into wild enthusiasm at the unexpected scene, so beautiful and inviting even in the midst of winter and with the tread of an invading enemy upon it.

They were no longer disposed to murmur, and reaching the vicinity of Moorefield late in the afternoon, their spirits were still further cheered by the sight of a large number of beautiful girls rushing out to see and welcome " our " infantry, as they fondly called it, a sight that had not met the eyes of those warm-hearted beings since a portion of the force constituting Garnett's ill-starred expedition had retreated that way early in the war. The Georgians were ready then to go anywhere. Not discontinuing their march they were thrown across the North Fork just at dark on the road to Petersburg, by felling trees from each side so as to interlap, and enable them to crawl over.

The road to Petersburg passed through a narrow defile above, just wide enough for a wagon way, with the river on one side and a very high vertical precipice of rock on the other side, so as to make it impracticable to pass through the file if held by any force at all, and it was then strongly picketed by the enemy, whose main force was in reach. The men bivouacked and kept as quiet as possible during the night so as not to alarm the enemy, and at light next morning I moved with them over the mountain, on a mere pathway lately unused and nearly grown up with underbrush, so as to avoid the defile spoken of and get in its rear, being guided by Captain McNeil with his company.

A thick fog overspread the mountains and the valley, as it was moist, mild weather, and when we reached the open ground on the other side where we were within easy artillery range of the enemy's works, nothing could be seen of them or the town of Petersburg. We heard some drums beating and an occasional cheer, and having sent a small force to get in rear of the defile while I made disposition to advance upon the point where I was told the enemy's works were, information reached me that Rosser was in possession of the enemy's works, the force of the latter consisting of two regiments and some artillery, having evacuated during the night and taken a rough obscure road to the west through the mountains of which Rosser had not known.

Some provisions and forage were found in the works which were appropriated, and Rosser was ordered to move at once down Patterson Creek, cut the railroad, and gather all the cattle and sheep he could by sending detachments through the country. After demolishing the works, which contained several bomb-proof shelters for men and magazines for ammunition and other stores, Thomas' brigade was moved back towards Moorefield, and next day posted so as to cover the approaches from the direction of Winchester.

The men now had an abundance of provisions, and the luxury of a little coffee taken from the enemy; and the kind hospitality of the good people of Moorefield and the vicinity rendered this winter campaign into the mountains a most pleasant episode in their army experiences.

Rosser succeeded in cutting the railroad at the mouths of Patterson Creek and the South Branch where it had been previously cut by Fitz. Lee, dislodging a guard from the latter place, and also in collecting a considerable number of cattle and sheep, with which he returned to Moorefield in two or three days. The enemy, however, had moved from Cumberland with a large force of infantry and cavalry, and also a brigade of cavalry from Martinsburg to intercept, but he succeeded in passing in safety between the columns sent against him. McNeil's company and part of Gilmor's battalion had been sent west to the Allegheny Mountains to collect cattle and were now returning by the way of Petersburg with a good lot of them.

The morning after Rosser's return I made preparations to retire with the prisoners, plunder, cattle, and sheep in our possession, and as we were moving out of Moorefield, the enemy's force consisting of Kelly's command from Cumberland and Averill's brigade of cavalry came in view on the opposite banks of the river, and opened with artillery. Thomas' brigade, which had moved across to the valley of the South Fork, and commenced retiring, was brought back a short distance and formed in line across the valley with the artillery in position, while Rosser's cavalry retiring through Moorefield took position below Thomas, sending out some skirmishers to encounter those of the enemy.

The object of this was to enable Captain McNeil to get in rear with his cattle, with which he was coming up on a road around our left flank, as we were then faced, and give time to the wagons and cattle and sheep to get well up the sides of the mountain, so that they might be protected against the enemy. As soon as this was done, and we could see the wagons, cattle and sheep slowly moving up the road on the side of the mountain, extending over a distance of some two or three miles, we withdrew gradually, but a small force of the enemy's cavalry followed at a most respectful distance, to the base of the mountains, where it halted.

Rosser's brigade took an obscure road to the left

338

across the mountain, so as to come into the valley of Lost River below Matthews', and Thomas followed the trains. The enemy did not attempt to molest us further, and he had the mortification of seeing all the plunder we had obtained marched off in a long winding train, visible to him for several miles, without being able to interfere with us. It was not in accordance with the object of my expedition to give him battle at this time, and I therefore contented myself with securing what I had.

Everything reached the valley in safety, Rosser taking the route through Brock's Gap with the wagons, etc., and Thomas moving across the mountain the same way we had gone. Riding ahead of the infantry the day after we left Moorefield, I understood, on the road, there was a report at Mount Jackson that the enemy was moving up from below in strong force, and quickening my force I reached Mount Jackson just after the report had been ascertained to be false, and the commotion had been allayed. The whole report had originated in the foolish fright of a small cavalry picket at Columbia Furnace, below, where a road comes in across the mountain from the valley of Lost River, which was caused by the approach on that road of a company of Rosser's men whose homes were in that immediate neighborhood, they having been allowed to go to them for a day or two.

When discharged, after crossing the mountain, without knowing that a picket was near, the men, who had been out in a rain, commenced discharging their arms, and the picket made off, not stopping to hear the calls of the men at whose appearance it had become frightened, but continuing to retreat the faster, magnifying the force, in imagination, at every step, until, when the commander of the picket reached General Imboden, with his horse panting and foaming, it had swelled to two or three thousand men.

Those things will happen sometimes to the bravest of men. We were again able to send General Lee's army about a thousand beef cattle, and some few other supplies, which served to keep up the spirits of our much enduring men.

The weather we had had for this expedition was unusually mild and favorable for that season when, in the section into which we went, the climate is usually as harsh among the mountains as it is in that part of Canada bordering on the Lakes.

Shortly after our return, the troops were moved further up the valley, the two infantry brigades going into camp near Harrisonburg, and the cavalry going to Rockbridge and the railroad west of Staunton where forage could be obtained, a small force being left to picket down the valley.

Major Gilmor subsequently made a raid down the valley, and captured a train on the Baltimore & Ohio Railroad.

After the troops had been located, in company with Captain Hotchkiss, topographical engineer for Ewell's corps, I made a reconnoissance of the country and mountain passes west of Staunton and extending across Jackson's River to the mountains beyond, and selected a line to be fortified so as to prevent raids. Captain Hotchkiss made a sketch of this line and the country, which being sent to General Lee, he ordered the necessary works to be constructed, which I believe was subsequently done.

About the last of February, my services being no longer necessary in the valley, I left for the purpose of returning to my division, after a leave of absence of two weeks granted me. In reaching Gordonsville by the railroad, I ascertained that some movement was being made by the enemy, and I therefore ran down to Orange Court-House to be present with my command if anything serious was going on.

It turned out that the enemy's movement was for the purpose of a cavalry raid against Richmond. A force being moved towards Charlottesville on our left, while the main raiding party, under Kilpatrick, went towards

Richmond for the purpose of capturing and burning the city, releasing the Federal prisoners, and bringing off or killing the Confederate authorities. This raid proved a ridiculous failure, its approach to Richmond being prevented by some home guards and local troops composed of employees in the departments, while Hampton dispersed a part of it with a few of his cavalry hastily gotten up. The force moving on Charlottesville retired from before a few pieces of artillery which had no support.

After this affair was settled I took the benefit of my short leave—the only indulgence of the kind asked for or received by me during the whole war.

I returned to my division about the middle of March, and assumed command, finding it in its old position, nothing serious having occurred during the winter.

What was left of Hoke's brigade had been detached and sent under General Hoke to North Carolina, where it participated in some movements, including the capture of the town of Plymouth, with its garrison, by Hoke. It did not return to the division until after the commencement of the subsequent campaign, though it took part in the defence of Petersburg and the attack on Butler by General Beauregard.

We remained in position in our old place until the opening of the spring campaign. In the meantime Major General U. S. Grant had been assigned to the command of all the armies of the United States, with the rank of Lieutenant General, and had come to take immediate command of the army confronting us, which army was being very greatly strengthened by recruits, drafted men, and other troops.

The Army of the Potomac under Meade had been consolidated into three corps instead of five, to-wit: the 2nd, and 6th, and 9th corps under Burnside, which had been very greatly increased, was added to the force in our front. The Army of the Potomac, and the 9th corps, with the artillery and cavalry, the latter having been largely increased, constituted Grant's immediate command, though he had a general control of all the forces.

By the last of May it was very evident that the enemy was making very formidable preparations for a campaign against us, and to meet them we had but what remained of the army with which we had fought the year before, recruited since the close of active operations, only by such men as had recovered from wounds and sickness, and a few young men who had just arrived at the age of military service. Longstreet had returned from his expedition into Tennessee with two of his divisions, McLaws' and Field's (formerly Hood's), Pickett's being absent and south of James River.

CHAPTER XXXI.

From the Rapidan to the James.

On the 3rd of May, 1864, the positions of the Confederate Army under General Lee, and the Federal Army under Lieutenant General Grant in Virginia, were as follows: General Lee held the southern bank of the Rapidan River, in Orange County, with his right resting near the mouth of Mine Run, and his left extending to Liberty Mills on the road from Gordonsville (via Madison Court-House) to the Shenandoah Valley; while the crossings of the river on the right, and the roads on the left, were watched by cavalry: Ewell's corps was on the right, Hill's on the left, and two divisions of Longstreet's corps were encamped in the rear, near Gordonsville. Grant's army (composed of the Army of the Potomac under Meade, and the 9th corps under Burnside) occupied the north banks of the Rapidan and Robinson rivers; the main body being encamped in Culpeper County and on the Rappahannock River.

I am satisfied that General Lee's army did not exceed 50,000 effective men of all arms. The report of the Federal Secretary of War, Stanton, shows that the " available force present for duty, May 1st, 1864," in Grant's army, was 141,166, to-wit: In the Army of the Potomac 120,386, and in the 9th corps 20,780. The draft in the United States was being energetically enforced, and volunteering had been greatly stimulated by high bounties. The Northwestern States had tendered large bodies of troops to serve one hundred days, in order to relieve other troops on garrison and local duty, and this enabled Grant to put in the field a large number of troops which had been employed on that kind of duty. It was known that he was receiving heavy reinforcements up to the very time of his movement on the 4th of May, and afterwards; so that the statement of his force on the 1st of May, by

Stanton, does not cover the whole force with which he commenced the campaign. Moreover, Secretary Stanton's report shows that there were in the Department of Washington and the Middle Department, 47,751 available men for duty, the chief part of which, he says, was called to the front, after the campaign began, "in order to repair the losses of the Army of the Potomac;" and Grant says that, at Spottsylvania Court-House, "the 13th, 14th, 15th, 16th, 17th and 18th (of May) were consumed in manœuvring and awaiting the arrival of reinforcements from Washington." His army, therefore, must have numbered very nearly, if not quite, 200,000 men, before a junction was effected with Butler.

On the 4th of May, it was discovered that Grant's army was moving towards Germana Ford on the Rapidan, which was ten or twelve miles from our right. This movement had begun on the night of the 3rd, and the enemy succeeded in seizing the ford and effecting a crossing, as the river was guarded at that point by only a small cavalry picket. The direct road from Germana Ford to Richmond passes by Spottsylvania Court-House and when Grant had effected his crossing, he was nearer to Richmond than General Lee was. From Orange Court-House, near which were General Lee's headquarters, there are two nearly parallel roads running eastwardly to Fredericksburg—the one which is nearest to the river being called "The old Stone Pike," and the other "The Plank Road." The road from Germana Ford to Spottsylvania Court-House crosses the old Stone Pike at the "Old Wilderness Tavern," and two or three miles farther on it crosses the Plank road.

As soon as it was ascertained that Grant's movement was a serious one, preparations were made to meet him, and the troops of General Lee's army were put in motion —Ewell's corps moving on the old Stone Pike, and Hill's corps on the Plank Road; into which latter road Longstreet's force also came, from his camp near Gordonsville.

Ewell's corps, to which my division belonged, crossed

Mine Run, and encamped at Locust Grove, four miles beyond, on the afternoon of the 4th. When the rest of the corps moved, my division and Ramseur's brigade of Rodes' division were left to watch the fords of the Rapidan, until relieved by cavalry. As soon as this was done, I moved to the position occupied by the rest of the corps, carrying Ramseur with me.

Ewell's corps contained three divisions of infantry, to wit: Johnson's, Rodes' and my own (Early's). At this time one of my brigades (Hoke's) was absent, having been with Hoke in North Carolina; and I had only three present, to wit: Hays', Pegram's and Gordon's. One of Rodes' brigades (R. D. Johnston's) was at Hanover Junction. I had about 4,000 muskets for duty; Johnson about the same number; and Rodes (including Johnston's brigade) about 6,000.

CHAPTER XXXII.

BATTLES OF THE WILDERNESS.

On the morning of the 5th, Ewell's corps was put in motion, my division bringing up the rear. A short distance from the Old Wilderness Tavern, and just in advance of the place where a road diverges to the left from the old Stone Pike to the Germana Ford road, the enemy, in heavy force, was encountered, and Jones' brigade, of Johnson's division, and Battle's brigade, of Rodes' division, were driven back in some confusion. My division was ordered up, and formed across the pike, Gordon's brigade being on the right of the road. This brigade, as soon as it was brought into line, was ordered forward, and advanced through a dense pine thicket in gallant style. In conjunction with Daniel's, Doles' and Ramseur's brigades, of Rodes' division, it drove the enemy back with heavy loss, capturing several hundred prisoners, and gaining a commanding position on the right. Johnson, at the same time, was heavily engaged in his front, his division being on the left of the pike and extending across the road to the Germana Ford road, which has been mentioned. After the enemy had been repulsed, Hays' brigade was sent to Johnson's left, in order to participate in a forward movement; and it did move forward some half a mile or so, encountering the enemy in force; but from some mistake, not meeting with the expected co-operation, except from one regiment of Jones' brigade (the 25th Virginia), the most of which was captured, it was drawn back to Johnson's line, and took position on his left.

Pegram's brigade was subsequently sent to take position on Hays' left; and, just before night, a very heavy attack was made on its front, which was repulsed with severe loss to the enemy. In this affair, General Pegram received a severe wound in the leg, which disabled him for the field for some months.

During the afternoon there was heavy skirmishing along the whole line, several attempts having been made by the enemy, without success, to regain the position from which he had been driven; and the fighting extended to General Lee's right on the Plank road. Gordon occupied the position which he had gained, on the right, until after dark, when he was withdrawn to the extreme left, and his place occupied by part of Rodes' division.

The troops encountered, in the beginning of the fight, consisted of the 5th corps, under Warren; but other troops were brought to his assistance. At the close of the day, Ewell's corps had captured over a thousand prisoners, besides inflicting on the enemy very heavy losses in killed and wounded. Two pieces of artillery had been abandoned by the enemy, just in front of the point at which Johnson's right and Rodes' left joined, and were subsequently secured by our troops.

After the withdrawal of Gordon's brigade from the right, the whole of my division was on the left of the road diverging from the pike, in extension of Johnson's line. All of my brigades had behaved handsomely; and Gordon's advance, at the time of the confusion in the beginning of the fight, was made with great energy and dispatch, and was just in time to prevent a serious disaster.

Early on the morning of the 6th, the fighting was resumed, and a very heavy attack was made on the front occupied by Pegram's brigade (now under the command of Colonel Hoffman of the 31st Virginia Regiment); but it was handsomely repulsed, as were several subsequent attacks on the same point.

These attacks were so persistent, that two regiments of Johnson's division were moved to the rear of Pegram's brigade, for the purpose of supporting it; and when an offer was made to relieve it, under the apprehension that its ammunition might be exhausted, the men of that gallant brigade begged that they might be allowed to retain their position, stating that they were getting along very well indeed and wanted no help.

During the morning, the fact was communicated to General Ewell, by our cavalry scouts, that a column of the enemy's infantry was moving between our left and the river, with the apparent purpose of turning our left flank; and information was also received that Burnside's corps had crossed the river, and was in rear of the enemy's right. I received directions to watch this column, and take steps to prevent its getting to our rear; and Johnston's brigade, of Rodes' division, which had just arrived from Hanover Junction, was sent to me for that purpose. This brigade, with some artillery, was put in position, some distance to my left, so as to command some by-roads coming in from the river. In the meantime General Gordon had sent out a scouting party on foot, which discovered what was supposed to be the enemy's right flank resting in the woods, in front of my division; and, during my absence while posting Johnston's brigade, he reported the fact to General Ewell, and suggested the propriety of attacking this flank of the enemy with his brigade, which was not engaged. On my return, the subject was mentioned to me by General Ewell, and I stated to him the danger and risk of making the attack under the circumstances, as a column was threatening our left flank and Burnside's corps was in rear of the enemy's flank, on which the attack was suggested. General Ewell concurred with me in this opinion, and the impolicy of the attempt at that time was obvious, as we had no reserves, and, if it failed, and the enemy showed any enterprise, a serious disaster would befall, not only our corps, but General Lee's whole army. In the afternoon, when the column threatening our left had been withdrawn, and it had been ascertained that Burnside had gone to Grant's left, on account of the heavy fighting on that flank, at my suggestion, General Ewell ordered the movement which Gordon had proposed. I determined to make it with Gordon's brigade supported by Johnston's and to follow it up, if successful, with the rest of my division. Gordon's brigade was accordingly formed in line near the edge of the woods in which the enemy's right rested, and Johnston's in the rear, with orders to follow Gordon and obey his orders.

I posted my adjutant general, Major John W. Daniel, with a courier, in a position to be communicated with by Gordon, so as to inform me of the success attending the movement, and enable me to put in the other brigades at the right time. As soon as Gordon started, which was a very short time before sunset, I rode to my line and threw forward Pegram's brigade in a position to move when required. In the meantime Gordon had become engaged, and, while Pegram's brigade was being formed in line, I saw some of Gordon's men coming back in confusion, and Colonel Evans, of the 31st Georgia Regiment, endeavoring to rally them. Colonel Evans informed me that his regiment which was on Gordon's right had struck the enemy's breastworks and had given way. I immediately ordered Pegram's brigade forward and directed Colonel Evans to guide it. Its advance was through a dense thicket of underbrush, but it crossed the road running through Johnson's line, and struck the enemy's works, and one of the regiments, the 13th Virginia, under Colonel Terrill, got possession of part of the line, when Colonel Hoffman ordered the brigade to retire, as it was getting dark, and there was much confusion produced by the difficulties of advance. Gordon had struck the enemy's right flank behind breastworks, and a part of his brigade was thrown into disorder. In going through the woods, Johnston had obliqued too much and passed to Gordon's left, getting in rear of the enemy.

Major Daniel, not hearing from Gordon, had endeavored to get to him, when, finding the condition of things, he attempted to lead one of Pegram's regiments to his assistance, and was shot down while behaving with great gallantry, receiving a wound in the leg which has permanently disabled him. Notwithstanding the confusion in part of his brigade, Gordon succeeded in throwing the enemy's right flank into great confusion, capturing two brigadier generals (Seymour and Shaler), and several hundred prisoners, all of the 6th corps, under Sedgwick. The advance of Pegram's brigade, and the demonstration of Johnston's brigade in the rear, where it encountered a part of the enemy's force and captured some prisoners, contributed materially to the result. It was fortunate, however, that darkness came to close this affair, as the enemy, if he had been able to discover the disorder on our side, might have brought up fresh troops and availed himself of our condition. As it was, doubtless, the lateness of the hour caused him to be surprised, and the approaching darkness increased the confusion in his ranks, as he could not see the strength of the attacking force, and probably imagined it to be much more formidable than it really was. All of the brigades engaged in the attack were drawn back, and formed on a new line in front of the old one, and obliquely to it.

At light on the morning of the 7th, an advance was made, which disclosed the fact that the enemy had given up his line of works in front of my whole line and a good portion of Johnston's. Between the lines a large number of his dead had been left, and at his breastworks, a large number of muskets and knapsacks had been abandoned, and there was every indication of great confusion. It was not till then that we ascertained the full extent of the success attending the movement of the evening before. The enemy had entirely abandoned the left side of the road, across which Johnston's line extended, and my division and a part of his were thrown forward, occupying a part of the abandoned works on the right of the road, and leaving all those on the left in our rear. This rendered our line straight, the left having been previously thrown back, making a curve.

During the day there was some skirmishing, but no serious fighting in my front. The loss in my division during the fighting in the Wilderness was comparatively light.

BATTLES OF THE WILDERNESS

On the morning of the 8th, it was discovered that the enemy was leaving our front and moving towards Spottsylvania Court-House. General Lee's army was also put in motion, Ewell's corps moving along the line occupied by our troops on the day before, until it reached the Plank road, where it struck across to Shady Grove, which is on the road from Orange Court-House to Spottsylvania Court-House.

On reaching the Plank road, I received through General A. P. Hill, who was sick and unable to remain on duty, an order from General Lee, transferring Hays' brigade from my division to Johnson's, in order that it might be consolidated with another Louisiana brigade in that division, whose brigadier general had been killed in the Wilderness, and Johnston's brigade from Rodes' division to mine; and assigning me to the temporary command of Hill's corps, which was still in position across the Plank road, and was to bring up the rear. I accordingly turned over the command of my division to Gordon, the senior brigadier left with it, and assumed command of Hill's corps.*

---

* Grant says General Lee had the advantage of position. As the latter had to move from his lines on the Rapidan and attack Grant in the Wilderness, how happened it that he was enabled to get the advantage of position, after the two days' fighting? He also says that General Lee was enabled to reach Spottsylvania Court-House first, because he had the shorter line. The fact is, that, as the two armies lay in their positions at the Wilderness, their lines were parallel to the road to Spottsylvania Court-House. Grant had the possession of the direct road to that place, and he had the start. General Lee had to move on the circuitous route by Shady Grove, and he was enabled to arrive there first with part of his infantry, because his cavalry held Grant's advance in check for nearly an entire day.

CHAPTER XXXIII.

BATTLES AROUND SPOTTSYLVANIA.

HILL'S CORPS was composed of Heth's, Wilcox's and Mahone's (formerly Anderson's) division of infantry and three battalions of artillery under Colonel Walker. When I took command of it, the infantry numbered about 13,000 muskets for duty.

General Lee's orders to me were to move by Todd's Tavern along the Brock road to Spottsylvania Court-House as soon as our front was clear of the enemy. In order to get into that road, it was necessary to reopen an old one leading from Hill's right, by which I was enabled to take a cross-road leading into the road from Shady Grove to Todd's Tavern. The wagon trains and all the artillery, except one battalion, were sent around by Shady Grove. About a mile from the road from Shady Grove to Todd's Tavern, the enemy's cavalry videttes were encountered, and Mahone's division was thrown forward to develop the enemy's force and position. Mahone encountered a force of infantry which had moved up from Todd's Tavern toward Shady Grove and had quite a brisk engagement with it, causing it to fall back rapidly towards the former place. At the same time General Hampton, who had communicated with me, after I left the Plank Road, moved with his cavalry on my right and struck the enemy on the flank and rear; but on account of want of knowledge of the country on our part, and the approach of darkness, the enemy was enabled to make his escape. This affair developed the fact that the enemy was in possession of Todd's Tavern and the Brock road, and a continuation of my march would have led through his entire army. We bivouacked for the night, at the place from which Mahone had driven the enemy, and a force was thrown out towards Todd's Tavern, which was about a mile distant.

Very early next morning (the 9th), I received an order from General Lee, through Hampton, to move on the Shady Grove road towards Spottsylvania Court-House, which I did, crossing a small river called the Po twice. After reaching the rear of the position occupied by the other two corps, I was ordered to Spottsylvania Court-House, to take position on the right, and cover the road from that place to Fredericksburg. No enemy appeared in my front on this day, except at a distance on the Fredericksburg road.

Early on the morning of the 10th I was ordered to move one of my divisions back, to cover the crossing of the Po on the Shady Grove road; and to move with another division to the rear and left, by the way of Spottsylvania Old Court-House, and drive back a column of the enemy which had crossed the Po and taken possession of the Shady Grove road, thus threatening our rear and endangering our trains which were on the road leading by the Old Court-House to Louisa Court-House.

Our line was then north of the Po, with its left, Fields' division of Longstreet's corps, resting on that stream, just above the crossing of the Shady Grove road. The whole of the enemy's force was also north of the Po, prior to this movement of his. Mahone's division was sent to occupy the banks of the Po on Fields' left, while with Heth's division and a battalion of artillery I moved to the rear, crossing the Po on the Louisa Court-House road, and then following that road until we reached one coming in from Waite's Shop on the Shady Grove road. After moving about a mile on this road, we met Hampton gradually falling back before the enemy, who had pushed out a column of infantry considerably to the rear of our line. This column was in turn forced back to the position on Shady Grove road which was occupied by what was reported to be Hancock's corps. Following up and crossing a small stream just below a mill pond, we succeeded in reaching Waite's Shop, from whence an attack was made on the enemy, and the entire force, which had crossed the Po, was driven back with a loss of one piece of artillery, which fell into our hands, and a considerable number in killed and wounded. This relieved us from a very threatening danger, as the position the enemy had attained would have enabled him to completely enfilade Fields' position and get possession of the line of our communications to the rear, within a very short distance of which he was, when met by the force which drove him back. In this affair Heth's division behaved very handsomely, all of the brigades (Cook's, Davis', Kirkland's and Walker's) being engaged in the attack. General H. H. Walker had the misfortune to receive a severe wound in the foot, which rendered amputation necessary, but otherwise our loss was slight. As soon as the road was cleared, Mahone's division crossed the Po, but it was not practicable to pursue the affair further, as the north bank of the stream at this point was covered by a heavily entrenched line, with a number of batteries, and night was approaching.

On the morning of the 11th, Heth was moved back to Spottsylvania Court-House and Mahone was left to occupy the position on the Shady Grove road from which the enemy had been driven.*

My line on the right had been connected with Ewell's right, and covered the Fredericksburg road, as also the road leading from Spottsylvania Court-House across the Ny into the road from Fredericksburg to Hanover Junction. Wilcox was on my left, uniting with Ewell, and Heth joined him. The enemy had extended his lines across the Fredericksburg road, but there was no fighting on this front on the 10th or 11th, except some artillery firing.

---

* It will be seen that after this affair I held, for a time, both of General Lee's flanks, which was rather an anomaly, but it could not be avoided, as we had no reserves and the two other corps being immediately in front of the enemy in line of battle, and almost constantly engaged, could not be moved without great risk. It was absolutely necessary to occupy the position, held on the left by Mahone, to avoid a renewal of the danger from which we had escaped.

BATTLES AROUND SPOTTSYLVANIA

On the afternoon of the 11th, the enemy was demonstrating to our left, up the Po, as if to get possession of Shady Grove and the road from thence to Louisa Court-House. General Hampton reported a column of infantry moving up the Po, and I was ordered by General Lee to take possession of Shady Grove, by light next morning, and hold it against the enemy. To aid in that purpose, two brigades of Wilcox's division (Thomas' and Scales') were moved from the right, and Mahone was ordered to move before light to Shady Grove; but during the night it was discovered that the movement to our left was a feint and that there was a real movement of the enemy towards our right.

Before daybreak on the morning of the 12th, Wilcox's brigades were returned to him, and at dawn Mahone's division was moved to the right, leaving Wright's brigade of that division to cover the crossing of the Po on Field's left. On this morning, the enemy made a very heavy attack on Ewell's front, and the line where it was occupied by Johnson's division. A portion of the attacking force swept along Johnson's line to Wilcox's left, and was checked by a prompt movement on the part of Brigadier General Lane, who was on that flank. As soon as the firing was heard, General Wilcox sent Thomas' and Scales' brigades to Lane's assistance and they arrived just as Lane's brigade had repulsed this body of the enemy, and they pursued it for a short distance. As soon as Mahone's division arrived from the left, Perrin's and Harris' brigades of that division and, subsequently, McGowan's brigade of Wilcox's division were sent to General Ewell's assistance, and were carried into action under his orders. Brigadier General Perrin was killed and Brigadier General McGowan severely wounded, while gallantly leading their respective brigades into action; and all the brigades sent to Ewell's assistance suffered severely.

Subsequently, on the same day, under orders from General Lee, Lane's brigade of Wilcox's division and

Mahone's own brigade (under Colonel Weisiger) were thrown to the front, for the purpose of moving to the left, and attacking the flank of the column of the enemy which had broken Ewell's line, to relieve the pressure on him, and, if possible, recover the part of the line which had been lost. Lane's brigade commenced the movement and had not proceeded far, when it encountered and attacked, in a piece of woods in front of my line, the 9th corps, under Burnside, moving up to attack a salient on my front. Lane captured over three hundred prisoners and three battle flags, and his attack on the enemy's flank taking him by surprise, no doubt contributed materially to his repulse. Mahone's brigade did not become seriously engaged. The attacking column which Lane encountered got up to within a very short distance of a salient defended by Walker's brigade of Heth's division, under Colonel Mayo, before it was discovered, as there was a pine thicket in front, under cover of which the advance was made.

A heavy fire of musketry from Walker's brigade and Thomas' which was on his left, and a fire of artillery from a considerable number of guns on Heth's line, were opened with tremendous effect upon the attacking column, and it was driven back with heavy loss, leaving its dead in front of our works. This affair took place under the eye of General Lee himself. In the afternoon another attempt was made to carry out the contemplated flank movement with Mahone's brigade, and Cook's brigade of Heth's division, to be followed up by the other troops under my command; but it was discovered that the enemy had one or more entrenched lines in our front, to the fire from which our flanking column would have been exposed. Moreover the ground between the lines was very rough, being full of ragged ravines and covered with thick pines and other growth; and it was thought advisable to desist from the attempt. The two brigades which were to have commenced the movement were then thrown to the front on both sides of the Fredericksburg road, and passing over two lines of breastworks, defended by a strong force of skirmishers, developed the existence of a third and much stronger line in rear, which would have afforded an almost insuperable obstacle to the proposed flank movement. This closed the operations of the corps under my command on the memorable 12th of May.

Between that day and the 19th, there was no serious attack on my front, but much manœuvring by the enemy. General Mahone made two or three reconnaissances to the front, which disclosed the fact that the enemy was gradually moving to our right. In making one of them, he encountered a body of the enemy which had got possession of Gayle's house, on the left of the road leading from our right towards the Fredericksburg and Hanover Junction road, at which a portion of our cavalry, under Brigadier General Chambliss, had been previously posted, and drove it back across the Ny.*

Another reconnaissance, handsomely made by Brigadier General Wright, who had been brought from the left, ascertained that a heavy force of the enemy was between the Ny and the Po, in front of my right, which was held by Mahone, and was along the road towards Hanover Junction. To meet this movement of the enemy Field's division was brought from the left and placed on my right.

On the 19th, General Ewell made a movement against the enemy's right, and to create a diversion in his favor, Thomas' brigade was thrown forward, and drove the enemy into his works in front of the salient, against which

---

* The Matapony River, which, by its juncture with the Pamunkey forms York River, is formed by the confluence of four streams, called respectively, the " Mat," " Ta," " Po," and " Ny." The Ny is north and east of Spottsylvania Court-House, and behind it the enemy did most of his manœuvring in my front. It unites with the Po, a few miles to the east and south of Spottsylvania Court-House, and both streams are difficult to cross except where there are bridges.

Burnside's attack had been made on the 12th, while the whole corps was held in readiness to co-operate with Ewell, should his attack prove successful; but as he was compelled to retire, Thomas was withdrawn.

Subsequently, the enemy retired from Heth's and Wilcox's fronts; and on the afternoon of the 21st Wilcox was sent out on the road leading from Mahone's front across the Ny with two of his brigades to feel the enemy, and found him still in force behind entrenched lines, and had a brisk engagement with that force. While Wilcox was absent, an order was received by me, from General Lee, to turn over to General Hill the command of his corps, as he had reported for duty. I did so at once and thus terminated my connection with this corps, which I had commanded during all the trying scenes around Spottsylvania Court-House. The officers and men of the corps had all behaved well, and contributed in no small degree to the result by which Grant was compelled to wait six days for reinforcements from Washington, before he could resume the offensive or make another of his flank movements to get between General Lee's army and Richmond.

CHAPTER XXXIV.

OPERATIONS NEAR HANOVER JUNCTION.

THE movement of the enemy to get between our army and Richmond had been discovered, and on the afternoon of the 21st Ewell's corps was put in motion towards Hanover Junction.* After turning over to General Hill the command of his corps, I rode in the direction taken by Ewell's corps, and overtook it, a short time before day on the morning of the 22nd. Hoke's brigade, under Lieutenant Colonel Lewis, this day joined us from Petersburg, and an order was issued, transferring Gordon's brigade, now under the command of Brigadier General Evans, to Johnson's division, which was placed under the command of General Gordon, who had been made a major general. This left me in command of three brigades, to wit: Pegram's, Hoke's and Johnston's, all of which were very much reduced in strength. My Adjutant General, Major Daniel, had been disabled for life by a wound received at the Wilderness, and my Inspector General, Major Samuel Hale, had been mortally wounded at Spottsylvania Court-House on the 12th while serving with the division and acting with great gallantry during the disorder which ensued after Ewell's line was broken. Both were serious losses to me.

On this day (the 22nd) we moved to Hanover Junction, and, next day, my division was posted on the extreme right, covering a ferry two or three miles below the railroad bridge across the North Anna. While at

---

* Hanover Junction is about 22 miles from Richmond and is at the intersection of the Richmond, Fredericksburg and Potomac Railroad with the Central Railroad from Richmond west, via Gordonsville and Staunton. It is on the direct road, both from Spottsylvania Court-House and Fredericksburg, to Richmond. The North Anna River is north of the Junction about two miles and the South Anna about three miles south of it. These two streams unite south of east, and a few miles from the Junction, and form the Pamunkey River.

Hanover Junction my division was not engaged. At one time it was moved towards our left, for the purpose of supporting a part of the line on which an attack was expected, and moved back again without being required. It was subsequently placed temporarily on the left of the corps, relieving Rodes' division and a part of Field's while the line was being remodelled, and then took position on the right again. During the night of the 26th, the enemy again withdrew from our front.*

---

* At Hanover Junction General Lee was joined by Pickett's division of Longstreet's corps, and Breckenridge with two small brigades of infantry, and a battalion of artillery. These, with Hoke's brigade, were the first and only reinforcements received by General Lee since the opening of the campaign. Yet Grant's immense army, notwithstanding the advantage gained by it on the 12th of May, had been so crippled, that it was compelled to wait six days at Spottsylvania Court-House for reinforcements from Washington, before it could resume the offensive. Breckenridge's infantry numbered less than 3,000 muskets. Grant puts it at 15,000 and says, " The army sent to operate against Richmond having hermetically sealed itself up at Bermuda Hundreds, the enemy was enabled to bring the most, if not all the reinforcements brought from the South by Beauregard against the Army of the Potomac." He therefore determined to try another flank movement, and to get more reinforcements from the army at Bermuda Hundreds.

CHAPTER XXXV.

BATTLES OF COLD HARBOR.

On the 27th, the enemy having withdrawn to the north bank of the North Anna, and commenced another flank movement by moving down the north bank of the Pamunkey, Ewell's corps, now under my command, by reason of General Ewell's sickness, was moved across the South Anna over the bridge of the Central Railroad, and by a place called "Merry Oaks," leaving Ashland on the Richmond, Fredericksburg and Potomac Railroad to the right, and bivouacked for the night at Hughes' cross-road, the intersection of the road from Ashland to Atlee's Station on the Central Railroad with the road from the Merry Oaks to Richmond. Next morning I moved by Atlee's Station to Hundley's Corner, at the intersection of the road from Hanover Town (the point at which Grant crossed the Pamunkey), by Pole Green Church to Richmond, with the road from Atlee's Station, by Old Church in Hanover County, to the White House on the Pamunkey. This is the point from which General Jackson commenced his famous attack on McClellan's flank and rear, in 1862, and it was very important that it should be occupied, as it intercepted Grant's direct march towards Richmond. All of these movements were made under orders from General Lee.

My troops were placed in position, covering the road by Pole Green Church, and also the road to Old Church, with my right resting near Beaver Dam Creek, a small stream running towards Mechanicsville and into the Chickahominy. Brigadier General Ramseur of Rodes' division was this day assigned to the command of my division. Ewell's corps, the 2nd of the Army of Northern Virginia, now numbered less than 9,000 muskets for duty, its loss, on the 12th of May, having been very heavy.

On the 29th, the enemy having crossed the Tottopoto-moy (a creek running just north of Pole Green Church, and eastward to the Pamunkey), appeared in my front on both roads, and there was some skirmishing but no heavy fighting.

On the afternoon of the 30th, in accordance with orders from General Lee, I moved to the right across Beaver Dam, to the road from Old Church to Mechanics-ville, and thence along that road towards Old Church, until we reached Bethesda Church. At this point the enemy was encountered, and his troops, which occupied the road, were driven by Rodes' division towards the road from Hundley's Corner, which unites with the road from Mechanicsville, east of Bethesda Church. Pegram's brigade, under the command of Colonel Edward Willis of the 12th Georgia Regiment, was sent forward with one of Rodes' brigades on its right, to feel the enemy, and ascertain his strength; but meeting with a heavy force behind breastworks, it was compelled to retire, with the loss of some valuable officers and men, and among them were Colonel Willis, mortally wounded, and Colonel Terrill of the 13th Virginia Regiment, killed. This move-ment showed that the enemy was moving to our right flank, and at night I withdrew a short distance on the Mechanicsville road, covering it with my force. When I made the movement from Hundley's Corner, my posi-tion at that place was occupied by a part of Longstreet's corps, under Anderson.

On the next morning, my troops were placed in posi-tion on the east side of Beaver Dam across the road to Mechanicsville, but Rodes was subsequently moved to the west side of the creek. Grant's movement to our right, towards Cold Harbor, was continued on the 31st, and the 1st of June, and corresponding movements were made by General Lee to meet him, my command retaining its position with a heavy force in its front.

On the 2nd, all the troops on my left, except Heth's division of Hill's corps, had moved to the right, and in the afternoon of that day, Rodes' division moved forward, along the road from Hundley's Corner towards Old Church, and drove the enemy from his entrenchments, now occupied with heavy skirmish lines, and forced back his left towards Bethesda Church, where there was a heavy force. Gordon swung round so as to keep pace with Rodes, and Heth co-operated, following Rodes and taking position on his left flank. In this movement there was some heavy fighting and several hundred prisoners were taken by us. Brigadier General Doles, a gallant officer of Rodes' division, was killed, but otherwise our loss was not severe.

On the next day (the 3rd), when Grant made an attack at Cold Harbor in which he suffered very heavily, there were repeated attacks on Rodes' and Heth's fronts, those on Cook's brigade, of Heth's division, being especially heavy, but all of them were repulsed. There was also heavy skirmishing on Gordon's front. During the day, Heth's left was threatened by the enemy's cavalry, but it was kept off by Walker's brigade under Colonel Fry, which covered that flank, and also repulsed an effort of the enemy's infantry to get to our rear. As it was necessary that Heth's division should join its corps on the right, and my flank in this position was very much exposed, I withdrew, at the close of the day, to the line previously occupied, and next morning Heth moved to the right.

My right now connected with the left of Longstreet's corps under General Anderson. The enemy subsequently evacuated his position at Bethesda Church and his lines in my front, and having no opposing force to keep my troops in their lines, I made two efforts to attack the enemy on his right flank and rear. The first was made on the 6th, when I crossed the Matadaquean (a small stream, running through wide swamps in the enemy's rear), and got in rear of his right flank, driving in his skirmishers until we came to a swamp, which could be crossed only on a narrow causeway defended by an entrenched line with artillery. General Anderson was to have co-operated with me, by moving down the other side of the Matadaquean, but the division sent for that purpose did not reach the position from which I started until near night, and I was therefore compelled to retire, as my position was too much exposed.

On the next day (the 7th), a reconnaissance made in front of Anderson's line showed that the greater part of it was uncovered, and, in accordance with instructions from General Lee, I moved in front of, and between it and the Matadaquean, until my progress was arrested by a ravine and swamp which prevented any further advance, but a number of pieces of artillery were opened upon the enemy's position in flank and reverse, so as to favor a movement from Anderson's front, which had been ordered but was not made; and at night I retired from this position to the rear of our lines.

Since the fighting at the Wilderness, Grant had made it an invariable practice to cover his front, flank, and rear with a perfect network of entrenchments, and all his movements were made under cover of such works. It was therefore very difficult to get at him.

On the 11th, my command was moved to the rear of Hill's line, near Gaines' Mill; and on the 12th, I received orders to move, with the 2nd corps, to the Shenandoah Valley to meet Hunter. This, therefore, closed my connection with the campaign from the Rapidan to James River.

When I moved on the morning of the 13th, Grant had already put his army in motion to join Butler, on James River, a position which he could have reached, from his camp on the north of the Rapidan, by railroad transports, without the loss of a man. In attempting to force his way by land, he had already lost, in killed and wounded, more men than were in General Lee's entire army; and he was compelled to give up, in despair, the attempt to reach Richmond in that way.*

---

* Grant, in describing his movement from Spottsylvania Court-House to Hanover Junction, says: "But the enemy again having the shorter line, and being in possession of the main roads, was enabled to reach the North Anna in advance of us, and took position behind it." And, when he speaks of his final determination to join Butler, he says: "After the battle of the Wilderness it was evident that the enemy deemed it of the first importance to run no risk with the army he then had. He acted purely on the defensive, behind breastworks, or, feebly, on the offensive, immediately in front of them, and where, in case of repulse, he could retire behind them. Without a greater sacrifice of life than I was willing to make all could not be accomplished that I designed north of Richmond."

He has made some observations, in his report, about the advantages of interior lines of communication, supposed to be possessed by the Confederate commanders, which are more specious than sound. The Mississippi River divided the Confederacy into two parts, and the immense naval power of the enemy enabled him to render communication across that river, after the loss of New Orleans and Memphis, always difficult. The Ohio River, in the West, and the Potomac, in the East, with the mountains of Western Virginia, rendered it impossible for an invading army to march into the enemy's country, except at one or two fords of the Potomac, just east of the Blue Ridge, and two or three fords above Harper's Ferry. The possession of the seas, and the blockade of our ports, as well as the possession of the Mississippi, the Ohio, and Potomac Rivers, with the Baltimore and Ohio Railroad, and the railroads through Pennsylvania, Ohio, Indiana, Illinois, Kentucky and Tennessee, enabled the enemy to transport troops, from the most remote points, with more ease and rapidity than they could be transported over the railroads under the control of the Confederate Government, all of which were in bad condition. The enemy, therefore, in fact, had all the advantages of interior lines; that is, rapidity of communication and concentration, with the advantage, also, of unrestricted communication with all the world, which his naval power gave him.

CHAPTER XXXVI.

Campaign in Maryland and Virginia.

The Valley of Virginia, in its largest sense, embraces all that country lying between the Blue Ridge and Alleghany Mountains, which unite at its southwestern end.

The Shenandoah Valley, which is a part of the Valley of Virginia, embraces the counties of Augusta, Rockingham, Shenandoah, Page, Warren, Clarke, Frederick, Jefferson and Berkeley. This valley is bounded on the north by the Potomac, on the south by the county of Rockbridge, on the east by the Blue Ridge and on the west by the Great North Mountain and its ranges.

The Shenandoah River is composed of two branches, called, respectively, the " North Fork " and the " South Fork," which unite near Front Royal in Warren County. The North Fork rises in the Great North Mountain, and runs eastwardly to within a short distance of New Market in Shenandoah County, and thence northeast by Mount Jackson and Strasburg, where it turns east to Front Royal. The South Fork is formed by the union of North, Middle and South Rivers. North River and Middle River, running from the west, unite near Mount Meridian in Augusta County. South River rises in the southeastern part of Augusta, and runs by Waynesboro, along the western base of the Blue Ridge, to Port Republic in Rockingham, where it unites with the stream formed by the junction of the North and Middle Rivers, a few miles above. From Port Republic, the South Fork of the Shenandoah runs northeast, through the eastern border of Rockingham and the county of Page, to Front Royal in Warren County.

The North Fork and South Fork are separated by the Massanutten Mountain, which is connected with no other mountain but terminates abruptly at both ends. Its northern end is washed at its base, just below Strasburg, by the North Fork. Its southern end terminates near the road between Harrisonburg and Conrad's Store on the South Fork, at which latter place the road through Swift Run Gap in the Blue Ridge crosses that stream. Two valleys are thus formed, the one on the North Fork being called "The Main Valley," and the other on the South Fork, and embracing the county of Page and part of the county of Warren, being usually known by the name of "The Luray Valley." The Luray Valley unites with the Main Valley at both ends of the mountain. There is a good road across Massanutten Mountain from one valley to the other through a gap near New Market. South of this gap, there is no road across the mountain, and north of it the roads are very rugged and not practicable for the march of a large army with its trains. At the northern or lower end of Massanutten Mountain, and between two branches of it, is a valley called " Powell's Fort Valley," or more commonly "The Fort." This valley is accessible only by the very rugged roads over the mountain which have been mentioned, and through a ravine at its lower end. From its isolated position, it was not the theatre of military operations of any consequence, but merely furnished a refuge for deserters, stragglers and fugitives from the battlefields.

From Front Royal, the Shenandoah River runs along the western base of the Blue Ridge to Harper's Ferry, where it unites with the Potomac, which here bursts through the mountains. The mountain, in extension of the Blue Ridge from this point through Maryland and Pennsylvania, is called "South Mountain."

Strictly speaking, the county of Berkeley and the greater part of Frederick are not in the Valley of the Shenandoah. The Opequon, rising southwest of Winchester, and crossing the Valley Pike four or five miles south of that place, turns to the north and empties into the Potomac some distance above its junction with the Shenandoah; the greater part of Frederick and nearly the whole of Berkeley being on the western side of the Opequon.

Little North Mountain, called in the lower valley "North Mountain," runs northeast, through the western portion of Shenandoah, Frederick and Berkeley Counties, to the Potomac. At its northern end, where it is called North Mountain, it separates the waters of the Opequon from those of Back Creek.

Cedar Creek rises in Shenandoah County, west of Little North Mountain, and running northeast along its western base, passes through that mountain, four or five miles from Strasburg, and, then making a circuit, empties into the North Fork of the Shenandoah, about two miles below Strasburg.

The Baltimore & Ohio Railroad crosses the Potomac at Harper's Ferry, and passing through Martinsburg in Berkeley County, crosses Back Creek near its mouth, runs up the Potomac, crossing the South Branch of that river near its mouth, and then the North Branch to Cumberland in Maryland. From this place it runs into Virginia again and, passing through Northwestern Virginia, strikes the Ohio River by two stems, terminating at Wheeling and Parkersburg respectively.

There is a railroad from Harper's Ferry to Winchester, called "Winchester & Potomac Railroad," and also one from Manassas Junction on the Orange & Alexandria Railroad, through Manassas Gap in the Blue Ridge, by Front Royal and Strasburg to Mount Jackson, called "The Manassas Gap Railroad," but both of these roads were torn up and rendered unserviceable in the year 1862, under the orders of General Jackson.

From Staunton, in Augusta County, there is a fine macadamized road called "The Valley Pike," running through Mount Sidney, Mount Crawford, Harrisonburg, New Market, Mount Jackson, Edinburg, Woodstock, Strasburg, Middletown, Newtown, Bartonsville and Kernstown to Winchester in Frederick County, and crossing Middle River seven miles from Staunton; North River at Mount

Crawford, eighteen miles from Staunton; the North Fork of the Shenandoah at Mount Jackson; Cedar Creek between Strasburg and Middletown; and the Opequon at Bartonsville, four or five miles from Winchester. There is also another road west of the Valley Pike connecting these several villages called the ''Back Road,'' and in some places, another road between the Valley Pike and the Back Road, which is called the ''Middle Road.''

From Winchester there is a macadamized road via Martinsburg, to Williamsport on the Potomac in Maryland, and another via Berryville in Clarke County, and Charlestown in Jefferson County, to Harper's Ferry. There is also a good pike from Winchester to Front Royal, which crosses both forks of the Shenandoah just above their junction; and from Front Royal there are good roads up the Luray Valley, and by the way of Conrad's Store and Port Republic, to Harrisonburg and Staunton.

From Staunton, south, there are good roads passing through Lexington, in Rockbridge County, and Buchanan, in Botetourt County, to several points on the Virginia & Tennessee Railroad; and others direct from Staunton and Lexington to Lynchburg.

The Central Railroad, from Richmond, passes through the Blue Ridge, with a tunnel at Rockfish Gap, and runs through Waynesboro and Staunton, westwardly, to Jackson's River, which is one of the head streams of James River.

This description of the country is given in order to render the following narrative intelligible, without too much repetition. In the spring of 1864, before the opening of the campaign, the lower Shenandoah Valley was held by the Federal troops, under Major General Sigel, with his headquarters at Winchester, while the upper Valley was held by Brigadier General Imboden, of the Confederate Army, with one brigade of cavalry, or mounted infantry, and a battery of artillery. When the campaign opened, Sigel moved up the Valley and Major

General Breckenridge moved from Southwestern Virginia, with two brigades of infantry and a battalion of artillery, to meet him. Breckenridge, having united his forces with Imboden's, met and defeated Sigel at New Market on May 15th, driving him back toward Winchester. Breckenridge then crossed the Blue Ridge and joined General Lee at Hanover Junction, with his two brigades of infantry and the battalion of artillery. Subsequently, the Federal General Hunter organized another and larger force than Sigel's, and moved up the Valley, and on the 5th day of June defeated Brigadier General William E. Jones, at Piedmont, between Port Republic and Staunton—Jones' force being composed of a very small body of infantry, and a cavalry force which had been brought from Southwestern Virginia, after Breckenridge's departure from the Valley. Jones was killed, and the remnant of his force, under Brigadier General Vaughan, fell back to Waynesboro. Hunter's force then united with another column which had moved from Lewisburg, in Western Virginia, under the Federal General Crook. As soon as information was received of Jones' defeat and death, Breckenridge was sent back to the Valley, with the force he had brought with him.

CHAPTER XXXVII.

Pursuit of Hunter.

On the 12th of June, while the 2nd corps (Ewell's) of the Army of Northern Virginia was lying near Gaines' Mill, in rear of Hill's line at Cold Harbor, I received verbal orders from General Lee to hold the corps, with two of the battalions of artillery attached to it, in readiness to move to the Shenandoah Valley. Nelson's and Braxton's battalions were selected, and Brigadier General Long was ordered to accompany me as Chief of Artillery. After dark, on the same day, written instructions were given me by General Lee, by which I was directed to move, with the force designated, at 3 o'clock next morning, for the Valley, by the way of Louisa Court-House and Charlottesville, and through Brown's or Swift Run Gap in the Blue Ridge, as I might find most advisable; to strike Hunter's force in the rear, and, if possible, destroy it; then to move down the Valley, cross the Potomac near Leesburg in Loudoun County, or at or above Harper's Ferry, as I might find most practicable, and threaten Washington City. I was further directed to communicate with General Breckenridge, who would co-operate with me in the attack on Hunter and the expedition into Maryland.

At this time the railroad and telegraph lines between Charlottesville and Lynchburg had been cut by a cavalry force from Hunter's army; and those between Richmond and Charlottesville had been cut by Sheridan's cavalry, from Grant's army; so that there was no communication with Breckenridge. Hunter was supposed to be at Staunton with his whole force, and Breckenridge was supposed to be at Waynesboro or Rock-fish Gap. If such had been the case, the route designated by General Lee would have carried me into the Valley in Hunter's rear.

The 2nd corps now numbered a little over 8,000

muskets for duty. It had been on active and arduous service in the field for forty days, and had been engaged in all the great battles from the Wilderness to Cold Harbor, sustaining very heavy losses at Spottsylvania Court-House, where it lost nearly an entire division, including its commander, Major General Johnson, who was made prisoner. Of the brigadier generals with it at the commencement of the campaign, only one remained in command of his brigade. Two (Gordon and Ramseur) had been made Major Generals; one (G. H. Stewart) had been captured; four (Pegram, Hays, J. A. Walker and R. D. Johnston) had been severely wounded; and four (Stafford, J. M. Jones, Daniel, and Doles) had been killed in action. Constant exposure to the weather, a limited supply of provisions, and two weeks' service in the swamps north of the Chickahominy had told on the health of the men. Divisions were not stronger than brigades ought to have been, nor brigades than regiments.

On the morning of the 13th, at two o'clock, we commenced the march; and on the 16th, arrived at Rivanna River near Charlottesville, having marched over eighty miles in four days.*

From Louisa Court-House I had sent a dispatch to Gordonsville, to be forwarded, by telegraph, to Breckenridge; and, on my arrival at Charlottesville, on the 16th,

---

* On the 15th we passed over the ground, near Trevillian's depot, on which Hampton and Sheridan had fought on the 11th and 12th. Hampton had defeated Sheridan and was then in pursuit of him. Grant, in his report, says that on the 11th Sheridan drove our cavalry "from the field, in complete rout," and, when he advanced towards Gordonsville, on the 12th, "he found the enemy reinforced by infantry, behind well-constructed rifle-pits, about five miles from the latter place, and too strong to successfully assault." There was not an infantry soldier in arms nearer the scene of action than with General Lee's army, near Cold Harbor; and the "well-constructed rifle-pits" were nothing more than rails put up in the manner in which cavalry were accustomed to arrange them to prevent a charge. Sheridan mistook some of Hampton's cavalry, dismounted and fighting on foot, for infantry.

to which place I rode in advance of my troops, I received a telegram from him, dated at Lynchburg, informing me that Hunter was then in Bedford County, about twenty miles from that place, and moving on it.

The railroad and telegraph between Charlottesville and Lynchburg had been, fortunately, but slightly injured by the enemy's cavalry, and had been repaired. The distance between the two places was sixty miles, and there were no trains at Charlottesville except one which belonged to the Central road, and was about starting for Waynesboro. I ordered this to be detained, and immediately directed, by telegram, all the trains of the two roads to be sent to me with all dispatch, for the purpose of transporting my troops to Lynchburg. The trains were not in readiness to take the troops on board until sunrise on the morning of the 17th, and then only enough were furnished to transport about half of my infantry. Ramseur's division, one brigade of Gordon's division and part of another were put on the trains, as soon as they were ready, and started for Lynchburg. Rodes' division, and the residue of Gordon's, were ordered to move along the railroad, to meet the trains on their return. The artillery and wagon-trains had been started on the ordinary roads at daylight.

I accompanied Ramseur's division, going on the front train, but the road and rolling stock were in such bad condition that I did not reach Lynchburg until about one o'clock in the afternoon, and the other trains were much later. I found General Breckenridge in bed, suffering from an injury received by the fall of a horse killed under him in action near Cold Harbor. He had moved from Rock-fish Gap to Lynchburg by a forced march, as soon as Hunter's movement towards that place was discovered. When I showed him my instructions, he very readily and cordially offered to co-operate with me, and serve under my command.

Hunter's advance from Staunton had been impeded by a brigade of cavalry, under Brigadier General Mc-

Causland, which had been managed with great skill, and kept in his front all the way, and he was reported to be then advancing on the old stone turnpike from Liberty in Bedford County by New London, and watched by Imboden with a small force of cavalry.

As General Breckenridge was unable to go out, at his request, General D. H. Hill, who happened to be in town, had made arrangements for the defence of the city, with such troops as were at hand. Brigadier General Hays, who was an invalid from a wound received at Spottsylvania Court-House, had tendered his services and also aided in making arrangements for the defence. I rode out with General Hill to examine the line selected by him, and make a reconnaissance of the country in front. Slight works had been hastily thrown up on College Hill, covering the turnpike and Forest roads from Liberty, which were manned by Breckenridge's infantry and the dismounted cavalry of the command which had been with Jones at Piedmont. The reserves, invalids from the hospitals, and the cadets from the Military Institute at Lexington, occupied other parts of the line. An inspection satisfied me that, while this arrangement was the best which could be made under the circumstances in which General Hill found himself, yet it would leave the town exposed to the fire of the enemy's artillery, should he advance to the attack, and I therefore determined to meet the enemy with my troops in front.

We found Imboden about four miles out on the turnpike, near an old Quaker church, to which position he had been gradually forced back by the enemy's infantry. My troops, as they arrived, had been ordered in front of the works to bivouac, and I immediately sent orders for them to move out on this road, at a redoubt about two miles from the city, as Imboden's command was driven back by vastly superior numbers. These brigades, with two pieces of artillery in the redoubt, arrested the progress of the enemy, and Ramseur's other brigade, and the part of Gordon's division which had arrived, took position on the same line. The enemy opened a heavy fire of artillery on us, but, as night soon came on, he went into camp in our front.*

Upon my arrival at Lynchburg, orders had been given for the immediate return of the train for the rest of my infantry, and I expected it to arrive by the morning of the 18th, but it did not get to Lynchburg until late in the afternoon of that day. Hunter's force was considerably larger than mine would have been, had it all been up, and as it was of the utmost consequence to the army at Richmond that he should not get into Lynchburg, I did not feel justified in attacking him until I could do so with a fair prospect of success. I contented myself therefore with acting on the defensive on the 18th, throwing Breckenridge's infantry and a part of his artillery on the front line, while that adopted by General Hill was occupied by the dismounted cavalry and the irregular troops. During the day, there was artillery firing and skirmishing along the line, and, in the afternoon, an attack was made on our line, to the right of the turnpike, which was handsomely repulsed with considerable loss to the enemy. A demonstration of the enemy's cavalry on the Forest road was checked by part of Breckenridge's infantry under Wharton and McCausland's cavalry.

On the arrival of the cars from Richmond this day, Major Generals Elzey and Ransom reported for duty, the

---

* Hunter's delay in advancing from Staunton had been most remarkable. He had defeated Jones' small force at Piedmont, about ten miles from Staunton, on the 5th, and united with Crook on the 8th, yet he did not arrive in front of Lynchburg until near night on the 17th. The route from Staunton to Lynchburg by which he moved, which was by Lexington, Buchanan, the Peaks of Otter and Liberty, is about one hundred miles in distance. It is true that McCausland had delayed his progress by keeping constantly in his front, but an energetic advance would have brushed away McCausland's small force, and Lynchburg, with all its manufacturing establishments and stores, would have fallen before assistance arrived. A subsequent passage over the greater part of the same route showed how Hunter had been employed.

former to command the infantry and dismounted cavalry of Breckenridge's command, and the latter to command the cavalry. The mounted cavalry consisted of the remnants of several brigades divided into two commands, one under Imboden, and the other under McCausland. It was badly mounted and armed, and its efficiency much impaired by the defeat at Piedmont, and the arduous service it had recently gone through.

As soon as the remainder of my infantry arrived by the railroad, though none of my artillery had gotten up, arrangements were made for attacking Hunter at daylight on the 19th, but some time after midnight it was discovered that he was moving, though it was not known whether he was retreating or moving so as to attack Lynchburg on the south where it was vulnerable, or to attempt to join Grant on the south side of James River. Pursuit could not, therefore, be made at once, as a mistake, if either of the last two objects had been contemplated, would have been fatal. At light, however, the pursuit commenced, the 2nd corps moving along the turnpike, over which it was discovered Hunter was retreating, and Elzey's command on the right, along the Forest road, while Ransom was ordered to move on the right of Elzey, with McCausland's cavalry, and endeavor to strike the enemy at Liberty or Peaks of Otter. Imboden, who was on the road from Lynchburg to Campbell Court-House to watch a body of the enemy's cavalry, which had moved in that direction the day before, was to have moved on the left towards Liberty, but orders did not reach him in time. The enemy's rear was overtaken at Liberty, twenty-five miles from Lynchburg, just before night, and driven through that place, after a brisk skirmish, by Ramseur's division. The day's march on the old turnpike, which was very rough, had been terrible. McCausland had taken the wrong road and did not reach Liberty until after the enemy had been driven through the town.

It was here ascertained that Hunter had not retreated

on the route by the Peaks of Otter, over which he had advanced, but had taken the road to Buford's depot, at the foot of the Blue Ridge, which would enable him to go either by Salem, Fincastle or Buchanan. Ransom was, therefore, ordered to take the route, next day, by the Peaks of Otter, and endeavor to intercept the enemy should he move by Buchanan or Fincastle. The pursuit was resumed early on the morning of the 20th, and upon our arrival in sight of Buford's, the enemy's rear guard was seen going into the mountain on the road towards Salem. As this left the road to Buchanan open, my aide, Lieutenant Pitzer, was sent across the mountain to that place, with orders for Ransom to move for Salem. Lieutenant Pitzer was also instructed to ride all night and send instructions, by courier from Fincastle, and telegraph from Salem, to have the road through the mountains to Lewisburg and Southwestern Virginia blockaded. The enemy was pursued into the mountains at Buford's Gap, but he had taken possession of the crest of the Blue Ridge, and put batteries in position command-ing a gorge, through which the road passes, where it was impossible for a regiment to move in line. I had endeavored to ascertain if there was another way across the mountain by which I could get around the enemy, but all men, except the old ones, had gotten out of the way, and the latter, as well as the women and children, were in such a state of distress and alarm, that no reliable infor-mation could be obtained from them. We tried to throw forces up the sides of the mountains to get at the enemy, but they were so rugged that night came on before any-thing could be accomplished, and we had to desist, though not until a very late hour in the night.

By a mistake of the messenger, who was sent with orders to General Rodes, who was to be in the lead next morning, there was some delay in his movement on the 21st, but the pursuit was resumed very shortly after sun-rise. At the Big Lick, it was ascertained that the enemy had turned off from Salem towards Lewisburg, on a road which passes through the mountains at a narrow pass called the "Hanging Rock," and my column was immediately turned towards that point, but on arriving there it was ascertained that the enemy's rear guard had passed through the gorge. McCausland had struck his column at this point and captured ten pieces of artillery, some wagons and a number of prisoners; but, the enemy having brought up a heavy force, McCausland was compelled to fall back, carrying off, however, the prisoners and a part of the artillery, and disabling the rest so that it could not be removed. As the enemy had got into the mountains, where nothing useful could be accomplished by pursuit, I did not deem it proper to continue it farther.

A great part of my command had had nothing to eat for the last few days, except a little bacon which was obtained at Liberty.* The cooking utensils were in the trains, and the effort to have bread baked at Lynchburg had failed. Neither the wagon trains, nor the artillery of the 2nd corps, were up and I knew that the country, through which Hunter's route led for forty or fifty miles, was, for the most part, a desolate mountain region; and that his troops were taking everything in the way of provisions and forage which they could lay their hands on. My field officers, except those of Breckenridge's command, were on foot, as their horses could not be transported on the trains from Charlottesville. I had seen our soldiers endure a great deal, but there was a limit to the endurance even of Confederate soldiers. A stern chase with infantry is a very difficult one, and Hunter's men were marching for their lives, his disabled being carried in his provision train, which was now empty. My cavalry was not strong enough to accomplish anything of importance, and a further pursuit could only have resulted in disaster to my command from want of provisions and forage.

I was glad to see Hunter take the route to Lewisburg,

---

* Now Bedford City.

as I knew he could not stop short of the Kanawha River and he was, therefore, disposed of for some time. Had he moved to Southwestern Virginia, he would have done us incalculable mischief, as there were no troops of any consequence in that quarter, but plenty of supplies at that time. I should, therefore, have been compelled to follow him.*

My command had marched sixty miles, in the three days' pursuit, over very rough roads, and that part of it from the Army of Northern Virginia had had no rest since leaving Gaines' Mill. I determined therefore to rest on the 22nd, so as to enable the wagons and artillery to get up, and to prepare the men for the long march before them. Imboden had come up, following on the road through Salem after the enemy, and the cavalry was sent through Fincastle, to watch the enemy and to annoy him as he passed through the mountains towards Lewisburg, and also ascertain whether he would endeavor to get into the valley towards Lexington or Staunton.

---

* In his report Grant says: " General Hunter, owing to a want of ammunition to give battle, retired from before the place " (Lynchburg). Now it appears that this expedition had been long contemplated and was one of the prominent features of the campaign of 1864. Sheridan, with his cavalry, was to have united with Hunter at Lynchburg and the two together were to have destroyed General Lee's communications and depots of supplies and then have joined Grant. Can it be believed that Hunter set out on so important an expedition with an insufficient supply of ammunition? He had only fought the battle of Piedmont with a part of his force, and not a very severe one, as Jones' force was a small one and composed mostly of cavalry. Crook's column, not being there, was not engaged. Had Sheridan defeated Hampton at Trevillian's, he would have reached Lynchburg after destroying the railroad on the way, and I could not have reached there in time to do any good. But Hampton defeated Sheridan and the latter saw " infantry too strong to successfully assault." Had Hunter moved on Lynchburg with energy, that place would have fallen before it was possible for me to get there. But he tarried on the way, and when he reached there, there was discovered " a want of ammunition to give battle."

CHAPTER XXXVIII.

OPERATIONS IN LOWER VALLEY AND MARYLAND.

AT Lynchburg I had received a telegram from General Lee directing me, after disposing of Hunter, either to return to his army or to carry out the original plan, as I might deem most expedient under the circumstances in which I found myself. After the pursuit had ceased, I received another dispatch from him, submitting it to my judgment whether the condition of my troops would permit the expedition across the Potomac to be carried out, and I determined to take the responsibility of continuing it. On the 23rd, the march was resumed and we reached Buchanan that night, where we struck again the route over which Hunter had advanced.* Ransom's cavalry moved by Clifton Forge, through the western part of

---

* The scenes on Hunter's route from Lynchburg had been truly heart-rending. Houses had been burned, and women and children left without shelter. The country had been stripped of provisions and many families left without a morsel to eat. Furniture and bedding had been cut to pieces, and old men and women and children robbed of all clothing except what they were wearing. Ladies' trunks had been rifled and their dresses torn to pieces in mere wantonness. Even negro girls had lost their little finery. We now had renewed evidences of outrages committed by the commanding general's orders in burning and plundering private houses. We saw the ruins of a number of houses so destroyed. At Lexington Hunter had burned the Military Institute, with all its contents, including its library and scientific apparatus; and Washington College had been plundered and the statue of Washington taken. The residence of Ex-Governor Letcher, at that place, had been burned, and but a few minutes given Mrs. Letcher and her family, to leave the house. In the same county a Christian gentleman, Mr. Creigh, had been hung because he had killed a straggling and marauding Federal soldier while in the act of insulting and outraging the ladies of his family. The time consumed in the perpetration of those deeds was the salvation of Lynchburg, with its stores, foundries and factories, which were so necessary to our army at Richmond.

Rockbridge, to keep a lookout for Hunter and ascertain if he should attempt to get into the Valley again.

On the 26th, I reached Staunton in advance of my troops, and the latter came up next day, which was spent in reducing transportation and getting provisions from Waynesboro, to which point they had been sent over the railroad. Some of the guns and a number of the horses belonging to the artillery were now unfit for service, and the best of each were selected, and about a battalion taken from Breckenridge's artillery, under Lieutenant Colonel King, to accompany us, in addition to the two battalions brought with the 2nd corps. The rest were left behind with a portion of the officers and men in charge of them. The dismounted cavalry had been permitted to send for their horses which had been recruiting, and Col. Bradley T. Johnson, who had joined me at this place with a battalion of Maryland cavalry, was assigned to the command of Jones' brigade, with the temporary rank of brigadier general, that brigade having been reorganized and the two Maryland battalions attached to it. General Breckenridge had accompanied us from Lynchburg, and, to give him a command commensurate with his proper one, and at the same time enable me to control the cavalry more readily, Gordon's division of infantry was assigned to his command in addition to the one under Elzey, and Ransom, in charge of the cavalry, was ordered to report to me directly. Major General Elzey was relieved from duty, at his own request, and the division under him was left under the temporary command of Brigadier General Vaughan.

The official reports at this place showed about two thousand mounted men for duty in the cavalry, which was composed of four small brigades, to wit: Imboden's, McCausland's, Jackson's and Jones' (now Johnson's). Vaughan's had not been mounted, but the horses had been sent for from Southwestern Virginia. The official reports of the infantry showed 10,000 muskets for duty, including Vaughan's dismounted cavalry. Nearly, if not quite, half of the company's officers and men were bare-footed or nearly so, and a dispatch had been sent from Salem by courier, and Lynchburg by telegraph, to Richmond, requesting shoes to be sent to Staunton, but they had not arrived.

Another telegram was received here from General Lee stating that the circumstances under which my original orders were given had changed, and again submitting it to my judgment, in the altered state of things, whether the movement down the Valley and across the Potomac should be made. The accession to my command from Breckenridge's forces had not been as great as General Lee supposed it would be, on account of the disorganization consequent on Jones' defeat at Piedmont, and the subsequent rapid movement to Lynchburg from Rock-fish Gap, but I determined to carry out the original design at all hazards, and telegraphed General Lee my purpose to continue the movement.

The march was resumed on the 28th with five days' rations in the wagons and two days' in haversacks, empty wagons being left to bring the shoes when they arrived. Imboden was sent through Brock's Gap in the Great North Mountain to the Valley of the south branch of the Potomac, with his brigade of cavalry and a battery of horse artillery, to destroy the railroad bridge over that stream and all the bridges on the Baltimore & Ohio Railroad from that point to Martinsburg. The telegraph line was repaired to New Market as we marched down the Valley, and communications kept up with that point by signal stations. On the 2nd of July we reached Winchester * and I here received a dispatch from General

---

* On this day we passed through Newtown, where several houses, including that of a Methodist minister, had been burned by Hunter's orders, because a part of Mosby's command had attacked a train of supplies for Sigel's force, at this place. The original order was to burn the whole town, but the officer sent to execute it had revolted at the cruel mandate and another was sent who but partially executed it, after forcing the people to take an oath of allegiance to the United

Lee, directing me to remain in the lower Valley until everything was in readiness to cross the Potomac and to destroy the Baltimore & Ohio Railroad and the Chesapeake & Ohio Canal as far as possible. This was in accordance with my previous determination, and its policy was obvious. My provisions were nearly exhausted, and if I had moved through Loudoun, it would have been necessary for me to halt and thresh wheat and have it ground, as neither bread nor flour could otherwise be obtained, which would have caused much greater delay than was required on the other route, where we could take provisions from the enemy. Moreover, unless the Baltimore & Ohio Railroad was torn up, the enemy would have been able to move troops from the West over that road to Washington.

On the night of the 2nd, McCausland was sent across North Mountain, to move down Back Creek, and burn the railroad bridge at its mouth, and then to move by North Mountain depot to Haynesville on the road from Martinsburg to Williamsport; and, early on the morning of the 3rd, Bradley Johnson was sent by Smithfield and Leetown, to cross the railroad at Kearneysville east of Martinsburg, and unite with McCausland at Haynesville, so as to cut off the retreat of Sigel, who was at Martinsburg with a considerable force. Breckenridge moved, on the same morning, direct from Martinsburg, with his command preceded by Gilmor's battalion of cavalry, while I moved with Rodes' and Ramseur's divisions, over the route taken by Johnson, to Leetown. On the approach of Breckenridge, Sigel, after very slight skirmishing, evacuated Martinsburg, leaving behind considerable stores, which fell into our hands. McCausland burned the bridge

---

States to save their houses. Mosby's battalion, though called "guerillas" by the enemy, was a regular organization in the Confederate Army, and was merely serving on detached duty under General Lee's orders. The attack on the train was an act of legitimate warfare, and the order to burn Newtown and the burning of houses mentioned were unjustifiable.

over Back Creek, captured the guard at North Mountain depot, and succeeded in reaching Haynesville; but Johnson encountered a force at Leetown, under Mulligan, which, after hard fighting, he drove across the railroad, when, Sigel having united with Mulligan, Johnson's command was forced back, just before night, on Rodes' and Ramseur's divisions, which had arrived at Leetown, after a march of twenty-four miles. It was too late, and these divisions were too much exhausted, to go after the enemy; and during the night, Sigel retreated across the Potomac at Shepherdstown, to Maryland Heights.

On the 4th, Shepherdstown was occupied by a part of Ransom's cavalry. Rodes' and Ramseur's divisions moved to Harper's Ferry and the enemy was driven from Bolivar Heights and the village of Bolivar, to an inner line of works under the cover of the guns from Maryland Heights. Breckenridge after burning the railroad bridges at Martinsburg, and across the Opequon, moved to Duffield's depot, five miles from Harper's Ferry, destroying the road as he moved. During the night of the 4th, the enemy evacuated Harper's Ferry, burning the railroad and pontoon bridges across the Potomac.

It was not possible to occupy the town of Harper's Ferry, except with skirmishers, as it was thoroughly commanded by the heavy guns on Maryland Heights; and the 5th was spent by Rodes' and Ramseur's divisions in demonstrating at that place. In the afternoon Breckenridge's command crossed the river at Shepherdstown, and Gordon's division was advanced over the Antietam towards Maryland Heights. At night, considerable stores, which had been abandoned at Harper's Ferry, were secured; and before day, Rodes' and Ramseur's divisions moved to Shepherdstown, and crossed the Potomac early on the 6th, Lewis' brigade, of Ramseur's division, being left to occupy Harper's Ferry with skirmishers.

On this day (the 6th) Gordon's division advanced towards Maryland Heights, and drove the enemy into his works. Working parties were employed in destroying the aqueduct of the canal over the Antietam, and the locks and canal-boats.

On the 7th Rodes moved through Rohrersville, on the road to Crampton's Gap in South Mountain, and skirmished with a small force of the enemy, while Breckenridge demonstrated against Maryland Heights, with Gordon's division, supported by his other division, now under Brigadier General Echols, who had reported for duty.

While these operations were going on, McCausland had occupied Hagerstown, and levied a contribution of $20,000, and Boonsboro had been occupied by Johnson's cavalry. On the 6th I received a letter from General Lee, by special courier, informing me that, on the 12th, an effort would be made to release the prisoners at Point Lookout, and directing me to take steps to unite them with my command, if the attempt was successful; but I was not informed of the manner in which the attempt would be made—General Lee stating that he was not, himself, advised of the particulars.

My desire had been to manœuvre the enemy out of Maryland Heights, so as to enable me to move directly from Harper's Ferry for Washington; but he had taken refuge in his strongly fortified works, and as they could not be approached without great difficulty, and an attempt to carry them by assault would have resulted in greater loss than the advantage to be gained would justify, I determined to move through the gaps of South Mountain to the north of the Heights. On the 7th, the greater portion of the cavalry was sent across the mountain, in the direction of Frederick; and that night, the expected shoes having arrived and been distributed, orders were given for a general move next morning; and an officer (Lieutenant Colonel Goodwin of a Louisiana regiment) was ordered back to Winchester, with a small guard, to collect the stragglers at that place, and prevent them from following.

Imboden had reached the railroad, at the South Branch of the Potomac, and partially destroyed the bridge, but had not succeeded in dislodging the guard from the block-house at that place. He had been taken sick and very little had been accomplished by the expedition; and his brigade, now under the command of Col. George H. Smith, had returned.

Early on the morning of the 8th the whole force moved; Rodes, through Crampton's Gap, to Jefferson; Breckenridge, through Fox's Gap; and Ramseur, with the trains, through Boonsboro Gap, followed by Lewis' brigade, which had started from Harper's Ferry the night before, after burning the trestle-work on the railroad, and the stores which had not been brought off. Breckenridge and Ramseur encamped near Middletown, and Rodes near Jefferson. Ransom had occupied Catoctan Mountain, between Middletown and Frederick, with his cavalry, and had skirmished heavily with a body of the enemy at the latter place. McCausland was ordered to move to the right, in the afternoon, and the next day cut the telegraph and railroad between Maryland Heights and Washington and Baltimore—cross the Monocacy, and, if possible, occupy the railroad bridge over that stream, at the junction near Frederick.

Early on the 9th, Johnson, with his brigade of cavalry, and a battery of horse artillery, moved to the north of Frederick, with orders to strike the railroads from Baltimore to Harrisburg and Philadelphia, burn the bridges over the Gunpowder, also to cut the railroad between Washington and Baltimore and threaten the latter place; and then to move towards Point Lookout, for the purpose of releasing the prisoners, if we should succeed in getting into Washington. The other troops also moved forward towards Monocacy Junction, and Ramseur's division passed through Frederick, driving a force of skirmishers before it.

CHAPTER XXXIX.

Battle of Monocacy.

The enemy, in considerable force under General Lew Wallace, was found strongly posted on the eastern bank of the Monocacy near the Junction, with an earthwork and two block-houses commanding both the railroad bridge and the bridge on the Georgetown pike. Ramseur's division was deployed in front of the enemy, after driving his skirmishers across the river, and several batteries were put in position, when a sharp artillery fire opened from both sides. Rodes' division had come up from Jefferson and was placed on Ramseur's left, covering the roads from Baltimore and the crossings of the Monocacy above the Junction. Breckenridge's command, with the trains, was in the rear between Frederick and the Junction, while the residue of the cavalry was watching a force of the enemy's cavalry which had followed from Maryland Heights. The enemy's position was too strong, and the difficulties of crossing the Monocacy under fire too great, to attack in front without greater loss than I was willing to incur. I therefore made an examination in person to find a point at which the river could be crossed, so as to take the enemy in flank.

While I was engaged in making this examination to my right, I discovered McCausland in the act of crossing the river with his brigade. As soon as he crossed, he dismounted his men, and advanced rapidly against the enemy's left flank, which he threw into confusion, and he came very near capturing a battery of artillery, but the enemy concentrated on him, and he was gradually forced back obstinately contesting the ground. McCausland's movement, which was very brilliantly executed, solved the problem for me, and, as soon as I discovered it, orders were sent to Breckenridge to move up rapidly with Gordon's division to McCausland's assistance, and to follow up his attack. This division crossed at the same place, and Gordon was ordered to move forward and strike the enemy on his left flank, and drive him from the position commanding the crossings in Ramseur's front, so as to enable the latter to cross. This movement was executed under the personal superintendence of General Breckenridge, and, while Ramseur skirmished with the enemy in front, the attack was made by Gordon in gallant style, and, with the aid of several pieces of King's artillery which had been crossed over, and Nelson's artillery from the opposite side, he threw the enemy into great confusion and forced him from his position. Ramseur immediately crossed on the railroad bridge and pursued the enemy's flying forces and Rodes crossed on the left and joined in the pursuit.

Echols' division, which had been left to guard the trains, was ordered up during the engagement, but was not needed. The pursuit was soon discontinued, as Wallace's entire force had taken the road towards Baltimore, and I did not desire prisoners. Wallace's force I estimated at 8,000 or 10,000 men, and it was ascertained that one division of the 6th corps (Rickett's), from Grant's army, was in the fight. Between 600 and 700 unwounded prisoners fell into our hands, and the enemy's loss in killed and wounded was very heavy. Our loss in killed and wounded was about 700, and among them were Brigadier General Evans wounded, and Colonel Lamar of the 61st Georgia Regiment, Lieutenant Colonel Tavener of the 17th Virginia Cavalry and Lieutenant Hobson of Nelson's artillery, killed. The action closed about sunset, and we had marched fourteen miles before it commenced. All the troops and trains were crossed over the Monocacy that night, so as to resume the march early next day. Such of our wounded as could not be moved in ambulances or otherwise were sent to the hospitals at Frederick under charge of competent medical officers, and our dead were buried. During the operations at Monocacy, a contribution of $200,000 in money was levied on the city of Frederick, and some needed supplies were obtained.

CHAPTER XL.

In Front of Washington.

On the 10th, the march was resumed at daylight, and we bivouacked four miles from Rockville, on the Georgetown pike, having marched twenty miles. Ramseur's division, which had remained behind for a short time to protect a working party engaged in destroying the railroad bridge, was detained for a time in driving off a party of cavalry which had been following from Maryland Heights, and did not get up until one o'clock at night. McCausland, moving in front on this day, drove a body of the enemy's cavalry before them and had quite a brisk engagement at Rockville, where he encamped after defeating and driving off the enemy.

We moved at daylight on the 11th; McCausland moving on the Georgetown pike, while the infantry, preceded by Imboden's cavalry under Colonel Smith, turned to the left at Rockville, so as to reach the 7th Street pike which runs by Silver Spring into Washington. Jackson's cavalry moved on the left flank. The previous day had been very warm, and the roads were exceedingly dusty, as there had been no rain for several weeks. The heat during the night had been very oppressive, and but little rest had been obtained. This day was an exceedingly hot one, and there was no air stirring. While marching, the men were enveloped in a suffocating cloud of dust, and many of them fell by the way from exhaustion. Our progress was therefore very much impeded, but I pushed on as rapidly as possible, hoping to get into the fortifications around Washington before they could be manned. Smith drove a small body of cavalry before him into the woods on the 7th Street pike, and dismounted his men and deployed them as skirmishers. I rode ahead of the infantry, and arrived in sight of Fort Stevens on the road a short time after noon, when I discovered that the works were but feebly manned.

389

Rodes, whose division was in front, was immediately ordered to bring it into line as rapidly as possible, throw out skirmishers, and move into the works if he could. My whole column was then moving by flank, which was the only practicable mode of marching upon the road we were on, and before Rodes' division could be brought up, we saw a cloud of dust in the rear of the works towards Washington, and soon a column of the enemy filed into them on the right and left and skirmishers were thrown out in front, while an artillery fire was opened on us from a number of batteries. This defeated our hopes of getting possession of the works by surprise, and it became necessary to reconnoitre.

Rodes' skirmishers were thrown to the front, driving those of the enemy to the cover of the works, and we proceeded to examine the fortifications in order to ascertain if it was practicable to carry them by assault. They were found to be exceedingly strong, and consisted of what appeared to be enclosed forts of heavy artillery, with a tier of lower works in front of each pierced for an immense number of guns, the whole being connected by curtains with ditches in front, and strengthened by palisades and abattis. The timber had been felled within cannon range all around and left on the ground, making a formidable obstacle, and every possible approach was raked by artillery. On the right was Rock Creek running through a deep ravine which had been rendered impassable by the felling of the timber on each side, and beyond were the works on the Georgetown pike which had been reported to be the strongest of all. On the left, as far as the eye could reach, the works appeared to be of the same impregnable character. The position was naturally strong for defence, and the examination showed, what might have been expected, that every appliance of science and unlimited means had been used to render the fortifications around Washington as strong as possible. This reconnaissance consumed the balance of the day.

The rapid marching which had broken down a number

of the men who were barefooted or weakened by previous exposure, and had been left in the Valley and directed to be collected at Winchester, and the losses in killed and wounded at Harper's Ferry, Maryland Heights and Monocacy, had reduced my infantry to about 8,000 muskets. Of those remaining, a very large number were greatly exhausted by the last two days' marching, some having fallen by sunstroke, and I was satisfied, when we arrived in front of the fortifications, that not more than one-third of my force could have been carried into action. I had about forty pieces of field artillery, of which the largest were 12 pounder Napoleons, besides a few pieces of horse artillery with the cavalry. McCausland reported the works on the Georgetown pike too strongly manned for him to assault. We could not move to the right or left without its being discovered from a signal station on the top of the "Soldiers' Home," which overlooked the country, and the enemy would have been enabled to move in his works to meet us. Under the circumstances, to have rushed my men blindly against the fortifications, without understanding the state of things, would have been worse than folly. If we had any friends in Washington, none of them came out to give us information, and this satisfied me that the place was not undefended. I knew that troops had arrived from Grant's army, for prisoners had been captured from Rickett's division of the 6th corps at Monocacy.

From Sharpsburg I had sent a message to Mosby, by one of his men, requesting him to cross the Potomac below Harper's Ferry, cut the railroad and telegraph, and endeavor to find out the condition of things in Washington, but he had not crossed the river, and I had received no information from him. A Northern paper, which was obtained, gave the information that Hunter, after moving up the Ohio River in steamboats, was passing over the Baltimore & Ohio Railroad, and I knew that he would be at Harper's Ferry soon, as Imboden had done very little damage to the road west of Martinsburg. After dark on the 11th I held a consultation with Major Generals Breckenridge, Rodes, Gordon and Ramseur, in which I stated to them the danger of remaining where we were, and the necessity of doing something immediately, as the probability was that the passes of the South Mountain and the fords of the upper Potomac would soon be closed against us. After interchanging views with them, being very reluctant to abandon the project of capturing Washington I determined to make an assault on the enemy's works at daylight next morning, unless some information should be received before that time showing its impracticability, and so informed those officers. During the night a dispatch was received from Gen. Bradley Johnson from near Baltimore informing me that he had received information, from a reliable source, that two corps had arrived from General Grant's army, and that his whole army was probably in motion. This caused me to delay the attack until I could examine the works again, and as soon as it was light enough to see, I rode to the front and found the parapets lined with troops. I had, therefore, reluctantly to give up all hopes of capturing Washington, after I had arrived in sight of the dome of the Capitol, and given the Federal authorities a terrible fright.

In his report, Grant says, in regard to the condition of things when I moved towards Washington, "The garrisons of Baltimore and Washington were at this time made up of heavy artillery regiments, hundred days' men, and detachments from the invalid corps." And, in regard to the force of Wallace at Monocacy, he says: "His force was not sufficient to ensure success, but he fought the enemy nevertheless, and although it resulted in a defeat to our arms, yet it detained the enemy and thereby served to enable General Wright to reach Washington with two divisions of the 6th corps, and the advance of the 19th corps before him." Stanton says in his report: "Here (at Washington) they (we) were met by troops from the Army of the Potomac, consisting of the

6th corps under General Wright, a part of the 8th corps under General Gilmore and a part of the 19th corps, just arrived from New Orleans under General Emory.''

Taking Grant's statement of the troops which had arrived from his army, they were sufficient to hold the works against my troops, at least until others could arrive. But in addition to those which had already arrived, there were the detachments from the invalid corps, called, I believe, the ''Veteran Reserves'' (of which I was informed there were 5,000), the heavy artillery regiments, the hundred days' men, and, I suppose, the part of the 8th corps mentioned by Stanton. To all of these may be added the local troops, or militia, and the Government employees. Some of the Northern papers stated that, between Saturday and Monday, I could have entered the city: but on Saturday I was fighting at Monocacy, 35 miles from Washington, a force which I could not leave in my rear; and after disposing of that force and moving as rapidly as it was possible for me to move, I did not arrive in front of the fortifications until after noon on Monday, and then my troops were exhausted and it required time to bring them up into line. I had then made a march, over the circuitous route by Charlottesville, Lynchburg and Salem, down the Valley and through the passes of the South Mountain, which, notwithstanding the delays in dealing with Hunter's, Sigel's, and Wallace's forces, is, for its length and rapidity, I believe, without a parallel in this or any other modern war—the unopposed excursion of Sherman through Georgia not excepted. My small force had been thrown up to the very walls of the Federal Capital, north of a river which could not be forded at any point within 40 miles, and with a heavy force and the South Mountain in my rear,—the passes through which mountain could be held by a small number of troops. A glance at the map, when it is recollected that the Potomac is a wide river, and navigable to Washington with the largest vessels, will cause the intelligent reader to wonder, not why I failed to take

Washington, but why I had the audacity to approach it as I did, with the small force under my command.

It was supposed by some, who were not informed of the facts, that I delayed in the lower Valley longer than was necessary; but an examination of the foregoing narrative will show that not one moment was spent in idleness, but that every one was employed in making some arrangement, or removing some difficulty in my way, which it was necessary to make or remove; so as to enable me to advance with a prospect of success. I could not move across the Potomac and through the passes of the South Mountain, with any safety, until Sigel was driven from, or safely housed in, the fortifications at Maryland Heights.

After abandoning the idea of capturing Washington, I determined to remain in front of the fortifications during the 12th, and retire at night, as I was satisfied that to remain longer would cause the loss of my entire force.

Johnson had burned the bridges over the Gunpowder, on the Harrisburg and Philadelphia roads, threatened Baltimore, and started for Point Lookout, but I sent an order for him to return. The attempt to release the prisoners, of which I was informed by General Lee, was not made, as the enemy had received notice of it in some way. Major Harry Gilmor, who burned the bridge over the Gunpowder on the Philadelphia road, captured Major General Franklin on a train at that point, but he was permitted to escape, either by the carelessness or exhaustion of the guard placed over him, before I was informed of the capture.

On the afternoon of the 12th, a heavy reconnoitring force was sent out by the enemy, which, after severe skirmishing, was driven back by Rodes' division with but slight loss to us. About dark we commenced retiring and did so without molestation.

Passing through Rockville and Poolsville, we crossed the Potomac at White's Ford, above Leesburg in Loudoun County, on the morning of the 14th, bringing off the prisoners captured at Monocacy and everything else in safety. There was some skirmishing in the rear, between our cavalry and that of the enemy which was following, and on the afternoon of the 14th, there was some artillery firing by the enemy, across the river, at our cavalry which was watching the fords. Besides the money levied in Hagerstown and Frederick, which was subsequently very useful in obtaining supplies, we brought off quite a large number of beef cattle, and the cavalry obtained a number of horses, some being also procured for the artillery.*

---

* On the night of the 13th the house of Postmaster General Blair near Silver Spring was burned, and it was assumed by the enemy that it was burned by my orders. I had nothing to do with it and do not yet know how the burning occurred. Though I believed that retaliation was justified by previous acts of the enemy, yet I did not wish to incur the risk of any license on the part of my troops and it was obviously impolitic to set the house on fire when we were retiring, as it amounted to notice of our movement.

CHAPTER XLI.

RETURN TO VIRGINIA.

WE rested on the 14th and 15th, near Leesburg; and on the morning of the 16th, resumed the march to the Valley, through Sincker's Gap in the Blue Ridge. Hunter had arived at Harper's Ferry, and united with Sigel, and the whole force had moved from that place, under Crook, to Hillsboro, in Loudoun, and a body of cavalry from it made a dash on our train, as we were moving towards the Valley, and succeeded in setting fire to a few wagons, but was soon driven off by troops from Rodes' and Ramseur's divisions, and one piece of artillery was captured from the enemy.

On the morning of the 17th, we crossed the Shenandoah, at Snicker's or Castleman's Ferry, and took possession near Berryville—Breckenridge covering the ford at the ferry and the river above and below, and Rodes' and Ramseur's division the roads from Harper's Ferry.

On the 18th the enemy, having moved through Snicker's Gap, appeared on the banks of the Shenandoah, and there was some skirmishing. In the afternoon, a heavy column of his infantry made a dash at Parker's Ford, one mile below the ferry, and crossed over, after driving back the picket of 100 men at that point. Breckenridge moved Gordon's and Echols' divisions to the front, and held the enemy in check, while Rodes' division was brought up from the left, and attacked and drove him across the river, with heavy loss, and in great confusion.

The enemy's main body still occupied the eastern bank of the Shenandoah on the 19th, and smaller columns moved up and down the river, to effect a crossing. Imboden, with his own and McCausland's cavalry, resisted and repulsed one of these columns, which attempted to cross at Berry's Ferry, with considerable loss to the enemy. The horses of Vaughan's cavalry having been brought from Southwestern Virginia, his small force had been now mounted. On this day I received information that a column under Averill was moving from Martinsburg towards Winchester, and as the position I held near Berryville left my trains exposed to expeditions in the rear from Martinsburg and Harper's Ferry, I determined to concentrate my force near Strasburg, so as to enable me to put the trains in safety and then move out and attack the enemy. This movement was commenced on the night of the 19th; Ramseur's division, with a battery of artillery, being sent to Winchester, to cover that place against Averill, while the stores, and the sick and wounded were being removed, and the other divisions moving through Millwood and White Post to the Valley Pike at Newtown and Middletown.

Vaughan's and Jackson's cavalry had been watching Averill, and, on the afternoon of the 20th, it was reported to General Ramseur, by General Vaughan, that Averill was at Stephenson's depot, with an inferior force, which could be captured, and Ramseur moved out from Winchester to attack him; but relying on the accuracy of the information he had received, General Ramseur did not take the proper precautions in advancing, and his division, while moving by the flank, was suddenly met by a larger force, under Averill, advancing in line of battle, and the result was that Ramseur's force was thrown into confusion, and compelled to retire, with the loss of four pieces of artillery, and a number in killed and wounded— Brigadier Generals Lewis and Lilly being among the wounded, and Colonel Board of the 58th Virginia Regiment among the killed. Colonel Jackson made a vigorous charge with his cavalry, which enabled Ramseur to rally his men, restore order, and arrest the progress of Averill before he reached Winchester. The error committed, on this occasion, by this most gallant officer, was nobly retrieved in the subsequent part of the campaign. I received at New Market the news of Ramseur's misfortune, and immediately moved to his assistance with

Rodes' division; but on arriving at Winchester, I found that the enemy, after being checked, had fallen back a short distance; and, as another and much larger column was moving through Berryville, I did not go after Averill, but moved the whole command to Newtown—the stores, and such of the wounded and sick as could be transported, having been gotten off.

On the 21st my whole infantry force was concentrated near Middletown; and, on the 22nd, it was moved across Cedar Creek, towards Strasburg, and so posted as to cover all the roads from the direction of Winchester.

A report having been sent to me, from Mount Jackson, that a force of the enemy was moving from the Valley of the South Branch of the Potomac to that place, Imboden was sent to ascertain its truth, and it proved to be false. We rested on the 23rd, while waiting to ascertain the movements of the enemy, and during the day a report was received from the cavalry in front that a large portion of the force sent after us from Washington was returning, and that Crook and Averill had united and were at Kernstown, near Winchester.

CHAPTER XLII.

BATTLE OF KERNSTOWN.

On the reception of the foregoing information, I determined to attack the enemy at once; and, early on the morning of the 24th, my whole force was put in motion for Winchester. The enemy, under Crook, consisting of the "Army of West Virginia," and including Hunter's and Sigel's forces, and Averill's cavalry, was found in position at Kernstown, on the same ground occupied by Shields, at the time of General Jackson's fight with him, on March 22nd, 1862. Ramseur's division was sent to the left, at Bartonsville, to get around the enemy's right flank, while the other divisions moved along the Valley Pike, and formed on each side of it. Ransom's cavalry was ordered to move in two columns: one, on the right, along the road from Front Royal to Winchester, and the other on the left, and west of Winchester, so as to unite in rear of the latter place, and cut off the enemy's retreat. After the enemy's skirmishers were driven in, it was discovered that his left flank, extending through Kernstown, was exposed, and General Breckenridge was ordered to move Echols' division, now under Brigadier General Wharton, under cover of some ravines on our right and attack that flank. This movement, which was made under General Breckenridge's personal superintendence, was handsomely executed, and the attacking division struck the enemy's left flank in open ground, doubling it up and throwing his whole line into great confusion. The other divisions then advanced, and the rout of the enemy became complete. He was pursued, by the infantry and artillery, through and beyond Winchester; and the pursuit was continued by Rodes' division to Stephenson's depot, six miles from Winchester—this division then having marched twenty-seven miles from its position west of Strasburg. The cavalry had not been moved according to my orders; and the enemy, having the advantage of an open country and a wide macadamized road, was enabled to make his escape with his artillery and most of his wagons. General Ransom had been in very bad health since he reported to me in Lynchburg, and unable to take the active command in the field; and all of my operations had been impeded for the want of an efficient and energetic cavalry commander. I think, if I had had one on this occasion, the greater part of the enemy's force would have been captured or destroyed, for the rout was thorough. Our loss, in this action, was very light. The enemy's loss in killed and wounded was severe, and two or three hundred prisoners fell into our hands; and among them, Colonel Mulligan, in command of a division, mortally wounded. The infantry was too much exhausted to continue the pursuit on the 25th, and only moved to Bunker Hill, twelve miles from Winchester. The pursuit was continued by our cavalry, and the enemy's rear guard of cavalry was encountered at Martinsburg; but after slight skirmishing, it evacuated the place. The whole defeated force crossed the Potomac, and took refuge at Maryland Heights and Harper's Ferry. The road from Winchester, via Martinsburg, to Williamsport was strewed with débris of the rapid retreat—twelve caissons and seventy-two wagons having been abandoned, and most of them burned.

CHAPTER XLIII.

The Burning of Chambersburg.

On the 26th we moved to Martinsburg, the cavalry going to the Potomac. The 27th and 28th were employed in destroying the railroad, it having been repaired since we passed over it at the beginning of the month. While at Martinsburg, it was ascertained that while we were near Washington, after Hunter's return to the Valley, by his orders, a number of private residences had been burned,—among them the homes of Mr. Alex. R. Boteler, an ex-member of the Confederate Congress, of Mr. Andrew Hunter, a member of the Virginia Senate, and of Mr. Edmund I. Lee, a distant relative of General Lee,—all in Jefferson County, with their contents, only time enough being given for the ladies to get out of their houses. A number of towns in the South, as well as private country houses, had been burned by the Federal troops. I came to the conclusion it was time to open the eyes of the people of the North to this enormity, by an example in the way of retaliation. I did not select the cases mentioned, as having more merit or greater claims for retaliation than others, but because they had occurred within the limits of the country covered by my command and were brought more immediately to my attention.

The town of Chambersburg in Pennsylvania was selected as the one on which retaliation should be made, and McCausland was ordered to proceed, with his brigade and that of Johnson and a battery of artillery, to that place, and demand of the municipal authorities the sum of $100,000 in gold or $500,000 in U. S. currency, as a compensation for the destruction of the houses named and their contents; and in default of payment, to lay the town in ashes. A written demand to that effect was sent to the authorities, and they were informed what would be the result of a failure or refusal to comply with it: for I desired to give the people of Chambersburg an opportunity of saving their town, by making compensation for part of the injury done, and hoped the payment of such a sum would have the effect of causing the adoption of a different policy. McCausland was also directed to proceed from Chambersburg towards Cumberland, Maryland, and levy contributions in money upon that and other towns able to bear them, and if possible destroy the machinery of the coal pits near Cumberland and the machine shops, depots and bridges on the Baltimore & Ohio Railroad as far as practicable.

On the 29th, McCausland crossed the Potomac near Clear Spring above Williamsport, and I moved with Rodes' and Ramseur's divisions and Vaughan's cavalry to the latter place, while Imboden demonstrated with his and Jackson's cavalry towards Harper's Ferry, in order to draw attention from McCausland. Breckenridge remained at Martinsburg and continued the destruction of the railroad. Vaughan drove a force of cavalry from Williamsport, and went into Hagerstown, where he captured and destroyed a train of cars loaded with supplies. One of Rodes' brigades was crossed over at Williamsport and subsequently withdrawn. On the 30th, McCausland being well under way I moved back to Martinsburg, and on the 31st, the whole infantry force was moved to Bunker Hill, where we remained on the 1st, 2nd, and 3rd of August.

On the 4th, in order to enable McCausland to retire from Pennsylvania and Maryland, and to keep Hunter, who had been reinforced by the 6th and 19th corps, and had been oscillating between Harper's Ferry and Monocacy Junction, in a state of uncertainty, I again moved to the Potomac with the infantry and Vaughan's and Jackson's cavalry, while Imboden demonstrated towards Harper's Ferry. On the 5th, Rodes' and Ramseur's divisions crossed at Williamsport and took position near St. James' College and Vaughan's cavalry went into Hagerstown. Breckenridge, with his command, and

THE BURNING OF CHAMBERSBURG

Jackson's cavalry, crossed at Shepherdstown, and took position at Sharpsburg. This position is in full view from Maryland Heights, and a cavalry force was sent out by the enemy to reconnoitre, which, after skirmishing with Jackson's cavalry, was driven off by the sharp-shooters of Gordon's division. On the 6th, the whole force recrossed the Potomac at Williamsport, and moved towards Martinsburg, and on the 7th we returned to Bunker Hill.*

---

* While at Sharpsburg on this occasion, I rode over the ground on which the battle of Sharpsburg or Antietam, as it is called by the enemy, was fought, and I was surprised to see how few traces of that great battle remained. In the woods at the famous Dunkard or Tunker Church, where, from personal observation at the battle, I expected to find the trees terribly broken and battered, a stranger would find diffi-culty in identifying the marks of the bullets and shells.

I will take occasion here to say that the public, North or South, has never known how small was the force with which General Lee fought that battle. From personal observation and conversation with other officers engaged, including General Lee himself, I am satisfied that the latter was not able to carry 30,000 men into action. The exhaustion of our men, in the battles around Richmond, the subsequent battles near Manassas, and on the march to Maryland, when they were for days without anything to eat except green corn, was so great, that the straggling was frightful before we crossed the Potomac. As an instance of our weakness, and a reminiscence worthy of being recorded, which was brought forcibly to my mind while riding over the ground, I state the following facts; in the early part of the day, all of General Jackson's troops on the field except my brigade (A. P. Hill had not then arrived from Harper's Ferry) were driven from the field in great disorder, and Hood had taken their place with his division.

My brigade, which was on the extreme left, supporting some artillery with which Stuart was operating, and had not been en-gaged, was sent for by General Jackson and posted in the left of the woods at the Dunkard Church. Hood was also forced back, and then the enemy advanced to this woods—Sumner's corps, which was fresh, advancing on our left flank. My brigade, then numbering about 1000 men for duty, with two or three hundred men of Jackson's own division, who had been rallied by Colonels Grigsby and Stafford, and with an interval of at least one-half a mile between us and any other part of our line, held Sumner's corps in check for some time,

On the 30th of July McCausland reached Chambersburg and made the demand as directed, reading to such of the authorities as presented themselves the paper sent by me. The demand was not complied with, the people stating that they were not afraid of having their town burned, and that a Federal force was approaching. The policy pursued by our army on former occasions had been so lenient that they did not suppose the threat was in earnest this time, and they hoped for speedy relief. McCausland, however, proceeded to carry out his orders, and the greater part of the town was laid in ashes.*

He then moved in the direction of Cumberland, but on approaching that town, he found it defended by a force under Kelly too strong for him to attack, and he withdrew towards Hampshire County in Virginia, and crossed the Potomac near the mouth of the South Branch, capturing the garrison at that place and partially destroying

---

until Green's division, of Mansfield's corps, penetrated into the interval in the woods between us and the rest of our line, and I was compelled to move by the flank and attack it. That division was driven out of the woods by my brigade, while Grigsby and Stafford skirmished with Sumner's advancing force, when we turned on it, and with the aid of three brigades—to wit: Anderson's, Semmes' and Barksdale's—which had just arrived to our assistance, drove it from the woods in great confusion and with heavy loss. So great was the disparity in the forces at this point that the wounded officers who were captured were greatly mortified, and commenced making excuses by stating that the troops in their front were raw troops who stampeded and produced confusion in their ranks. McClellan, in his report, states that Sumner's corps and Green's division encountered in this woods " overwhelming numbers behind breastworks," and he assigns the heavy losses and consequent demoralization in Sumner's corps as one of the reasons for not renewing the fight on the 18th. We had no breastworks or anything like them in that woods on the 17th, and, on our part, it was a stand up fight there altogether. The slight breastworks subsequently seen by McClellan were made on the 18th, when we were expecting a renewal of the battle.

* For this act I, alone, am responsible, as the officers engaged in it were simply executing my orders, and had no discretion left them. Notwithstanding the lapse of time which has occurred and the result of the war, I see no reason to regret my conduct on this occasion.

the railroad bridge. He then invested the post on the railroad at New Creek, but finding it too strongly fortified to take by assault, he moved to Moorefield in Hardy County, near which he halted to rest and recruit his men and horses, as the command was now considered safe from pursuit. Averill, however, had been pursuing from Chambersburg with a body of cavalry, and Johnson's brigade was surprised in camp, before day, on the morning of the 7th of August, and routed by Averill's force. This resulted also in the rout of McCausland's brigade, and the loss of the artillery (4 pieces), and about 300 prisoners from the whole command. The balance of the command made its way to Mount Jackson in great disorder, and much weakened. This affair had a very damaging effect upon my cavalry for the rest of the campaign.

CHAPTER XLIV.

ON the 9th, Imboden reported that a large force had been concentrated at Harper's Ferry, consisting of the 6th, 19th, and Crook's corps, under a new commander, and that it was moving to our right. The new commander proved to be Major General Sheridan, from Grant's army. On the 10th, we moved from Bunker Hill to the east of Winchester, to cover the roads from Charlestown and Berryville to that place; and Ramseur's division was moved to Winchester, to cover that place against a force reported to be advancing from the west; but, this report proving untrue, it was subsequently moved to the junction of the Millwood and Front Royal roads.

On the morning of the 11th, it was discovered that the enemy was moving to our right on the east of the Opequon, and my troops, which had been formed in line of battle covering Winchester, were moved to the right, towards Newtown, keeping between the enemy and the Valley Pike. Ramseur had a brisk skirmish with a body of the enemy's cavalry on the Millwood road, and drove it back. Imboden's and Vaughan's brigades had a severe fight with another body of cavalry at the double toll-gate, at the intersection of the Front Royal road with the road from White Post to Newtown; and it was discovered that there had been a considerable accession to that arm from Grant's army.

Just before night, Gordon had very heavy skirmishing near Newtown, with a large force of cavalry, which advanced on the road from the double toll-gate, and drove it off. We encamped near Newtown; and on the morning of the 12th, moved to Hupp's Hill, between Strasburg and Cedar Creek. Finding that the enemy was advancing in much heavier force than I had yet encountered, I determined to take position at Fisher's Hill, above Strasburg, and await his attack there. Imboden with his brigade was sent to the Luray Valley, to watch that route; and, in the afternoon, we moved to Fisher's Hill. I had received information, a few days before, from General Lee, that General Anderson had moved with Kershaw's division of infantry and Fitz. Lee's division of cavalry to Culpeper Court-House; and I sent a dispatch to Anderson informing him of the state of things, and requesting him to move to Front Royal, so as to guard the Luray Valley.

Sheridan's advance appeared on the banks of Cedar Creek, on the 12th, and there was some skirmishing with it. My troops were posted at Fisher's Hill, with the right resting on the North Fork of the Shenandoah, and the left extending towards Little North Mountain; and we awaited the advance of the enemy. General Anderson moved to Front Royal, in compliance with my request, and took position to prevent an advance of the enemy on that route. Shortly after I took position at Fisher's Hill, Major General Lomax reported to me to relieve Ransom in command of the cavalry, and McCausland and Johnson joined us with the remnants of their brigades. Sheridan demonstrated at Hupp's Hill, within our view, for several days, and some severe skirmishing ensued.

Upon taking position at Fisher's Hill, I had established a signal station on the end of Three Top Mountain, a branch of Massanutten Mountain, near Strasburg, which overlooked both camps and enabled me to communicate readily with General Anderson in the Luray Valley. A small force from Sheridan's army ascended the mountain and drove off our signal-men and possession was taken of the station by the enemy, who was in turn driven away; when several small but severe fights ensued over the station, possession of it being finally gained and held by a force of 100 men under Captain Keller of Gordon's division.

On the morning of the 17th, it was discovered that the enemy was falling back, and I immediately moved forward in pursuit, requesting General Anderson, by signal, to cross the river at Front Royal and move towards Winchester. Just before night, the enemy's cavalry and a body of infantry, reported to be a division, was encountered between Kernstown and Winchester, and driven through the latter place, after a sharp engagement, in which Wharton's division moved to the left and attacked the enemy's infantry, and drove it from a strong position on Bower's Hill, south of Winchester, while Ramseur engaged it in the front and Gordon advanced against the cavalry on the right.

On the 18th we took possession to cover Winchester, and General Anderson came up with Kershaw's division of infantry, Cutshaw's battalion of artillery and two brigades of cavalry under Fitz. Lee. General Anderson ranked me, but he declined to take command, and offered to co-operate in any movement I might suggest. We had now discovered that Torbert's and Wilson's divisions of cavalry from Grant's army had joined Sheridan's force, and that the latter was very large.

On the 19th, my main force moved to Bunker Hill and Lomax's cavalry made reconnaissances to Martinsburg and Shepherdstown, while Anderson's whole force remained near Winchester.

On the 20th, our cavalry had some skirmishing with the enemy's, on the Opequon, and on the 21st, by concert, there was a general movement towards Harper's Ferry—my command moving through Smithfield towards Charlestown, and Anderson's on the direct road by Summit Point. A body of the enemy's cavalry was driven from the Opequon, and was pursued by part of our cavalry towards Summit Point. I encountered Sheridan's main force near Cameron's depot, about three miles from Charlestown, in a position which he commenced fortifying at once. Rodes' and Ramseur's divisions were advanced to the front, and very heavy skirmishing ensued and was continued until night, but I waited for General Anderson to arrive before making a general

attack.   He encountered Wilson's division of cavalry
at Summit Point, and, after driving it off, went into camp
at that place.   At light next morning, it was discovered
that the enemy had retired during the night, and his rear
guard of cavalry was driven through Charlestown towards Halltown, where Sheridan had taken a strong
position under the protection of the heavy guns on Maryland Heights.

I demonstrated on the enemy's front on the 22nd, 23rd
and 24th, and there was some skirmishing.   General
Anderson then consented to take my position in front of
Charlestown and amuse the enemy with Kershaw's division of infantry, supported by McCausland's brigade of
cavalry on the left and a regiment of Fitz. Lee's cavalry
on the right, while I moved with my infantry and artillery
to Shepherdstown and Fitz. Lee with the rest of the
cavalry to Williamsport, as if to cross into Maryland, in
order to keep up the fear of an invasion of Maryland
and Pennsylvania.

On the 25th Fitz. Lee started by way of Leetown and
Martinsburg to Williamsport, and I moved through Leetown and crossed the railroad at Kearneysville to Shepherdstown.   After Fitz. Lee had passed on, I encountered
a very large force of the enemy's cavalry between Leetown and Kearneysville, which was moving out with
several days' forage and rations for a raid in our rear.
After a sharp engagement with small arms and artillery,
this force was driven back through Shepherdstown, where
we came near surrounding and capturing a considerable
portion of it, but it succeeded in making its escape across
the Potomac.   Gordon's division, which was moved
around to intercept the enemy, became heavily engaged,
and cut off the retreat of part of his force by one road,
but it made its way down the river to the ford by another
and thus escaped.   In this affair, a valuable officer,
Colonel Monaghan, of the 6th Louisiana Regiment, was
killed.   Fitz. Lee reached Williamsport, and had some

skirmishing across the river at that place, and then moved to Shepherdstown.

On the 26th I moved to Leetown, on the 27th moved back to Bunker Hill; while Anderson, who had confronted Sheridan, during the two days of my absence, with but a division of infantry, and a brigade and a regiment of cavalry, moved to Stephenson's depot. On the 28th our cavalry, which had been left holding a line from Charlestown to Shepherdstown, was compelled to retire across the Opequon, after having had a brisk engagement with the enemy's cavalry at Smithfield. On the 29th, the enemy's cavalry crossed the Opequon near Smithfield, driving in our cavalry pickets, when I advanced to the front with a part of my infantry, and drove the enemy across the stream again, and after a very sharp artillery duel, a portion of my command was crossed over and pursued the enemy through Smithfield towards Charlestown.

Quiet prevailed on the 30th, but on the 31st there were some demonstrations of cavalry by the enemy on the Opequon, which were met by ours. On this day Anderson moved to Winchester, and Rodes, with his division, went to Martinsburg on a reconnaissance, drove a force of the enemy's cavalry from that place, interrupted the preparations for repairing the railroad, and then returned.

There was quiet on the 1st, but on the 2nd, I broke up my camp at Bunker Hill, and moved with three divisions of infantry and part of McCausland's cavalry, under Colonel Ferguson, across the country towards Summit Point, on a reconnaissance, while the trains under the protection of Rodes' division were moved to Stephenson's depot. After I had crossed the Opequon and was moving towards Summit Point, Averill's cavalry attacked and drove back in some confusion first Vaughan's and then Johnson's cavalry, which were on the Martinsburg road and the Opequon, but Rodes returned towards Bunker Hill and drove the enemy back in turn. This affair arrested my march and I recrossed the Opequon and moved to Stephenson's depot, where I established my camp.

On the 3rd, Rodes moved to Bunker Hill in support of Lomax's cavalry, and drove the enemy's cavalry from and beyond the place.

A letter had been received from General Lee requesting that Kershaw's division should be returned to him, as he was very much in need of troops, and, after consultation with me, General Anderson determined to recross the Blue Ridge with that division and Fitz. Lee's cavalry. On the 3rd, he moved towards Berryville for the purpose of crossing the mountain at Ashby's Gap, and I was to have moved towards Charlestown next day, to occupy the enemy's attention during Anderson's movement. Sheridan, however, had started two divisions of cavalry through Berryville and White Post, on a raid to our rear, and his main force had moved towards Berryville. Anderson encountered Crook's corps at the latter place, and after a sharp engagement drove it back on the main body. Receiving information of this affair, I moved at daylight next morning, with three divisions, to Anderson's assistance, Gordon's division being left to cover Winchester.

I found Kershaw's division extended out in a strong skirmish line confronting Sheridan's main force, which had taken position in rear of Berryville, across the road from Charlestown to that place, and was busily fortifying, while the cavalry force which had started on the raid was returning and passing between Berryville and the river to Sheridan's rear. As may be supposed, Anderson's position was one of great peril, if the enemy had possessed enterprise, and it presented the appearance of the most extreme audacity for him thus to confront a force so vastly superior to his own, while, too, his trains were at the mercy of the enemy's cavalry, had the latter known it. Placing one of my divisions in line on Kershaw's left, I moved with the other two along the enemy's front towards his right, for the purpose of reconnoitring and attacking that flank, if a suitable opportunity offered. After moving in this way for two miles, I reached an elevated position from which the enemy's line was visible, and within artillery range of it. I at first thought that I had reached his right flank and was about making arrangements to attack it, when, casting my eye to my left, I discovered, as far as the eye could reach, with the aid of field glasses, a line extending toward Summit Point.

The position the enemy occupied was a strong one, and he was busily engaged fortifying it, having already made considerable progress. It was not until I had had this view that I realized the size of the enemy's force, and as I discovered that his line was too long for me to get around his flank and the position was too strong to attack in front, I returned and informed General Anderson of the condition of things. After consultation with him, we thought it not advisable to attack the enemy in his entrenched lines, and we determined to move our forces back to the west side of the Opequon, and see if he would not move out of his works.

The wagon trains were sent back early next morning (the 5th) towards Winchester, and about an hour by sun, Kershaw's division, whose place had been taken by one of my divisions, moved toward the same point. About two o'clock in the afternoon my troops were withdrawn, and moved back to Stephenson's depot. This withdrawal was made while the skirmishers were in close proximity and firing at each other; yet there was no effort on the part of the enemy to molest us. Just as my front division (Rodes') reached Stephenson's depot, it met, and drove back, and pursued for some distance, Averill's cavalry, which was forcing, towards Winchester, that part of our cavalry which had been watching the Martinsburg road.

It was quiet on the 6th, but on the 7th the enemy's cavalry made demonstrations on the Martinsburg road and the Opequon at several points and was repulsed.

On the 8th it was quiet again, but on the 9th a detachment of the enemy's cavalry came to the Opequon below Brucetown, burned some mills and retreated before a division of infantry sent out to meet it.

On the 10th, my infantry moved by Bunker Hill to Darksville and encountered a considerable force of the enemy's cavalry, which was driven off, and then pursued by Lomax through Martinsburg across the Opequon. We then returned to Bunker Hill and the next day to Stephenson's depot, and there was quiet on the 12th.

On the 13th, a large force of the enemy's cavalry, reported to be supported by infantry, advanced on the road from Summit Point, and drove in our pickets from the Opequon, when two divisions of infantry were advanced to the front, driving the enemy across the Opequon again. A very sharp artillery duel across the creek then took place and some of my infantry crossed over, when the enemy retired.

On the 14th, General Anderson again started, with Kershaw's division and Cutshaw's battalion of artillery, to cross the Blue Ridge by the way of Front Royal, and was not molested. Fitz. Lee's cavalry was left with me, and Ramseur's division was moved to Winchester to occupy Kershaw's position.

There was an affair between one of Kershaw's brigades and a division of the enemy's cavalry, while I was at Fisher's Hill and Anderson at Front Royal, in which some prisoners were lost; and two affairs in which the outposts from Kershaw's command were attacked and captured by the enemy's cavalry, one in front of Winchester and the other in front of Charlestown; which I have not undertaken to detail, as they occurred when General Anderson was controlling the operations of that division, but it is proper to refer to them here as part of the operations in the Valley. On the 15th and 16th my troops remained in camp undisturbed.

The positions of the opposing forces were now as follows: Ramseur's division and Nelson's battalion of artillery were on the road from Berryville to Winchester, one mile from the latter place. Rodes', Gordon's and Wharton's divisions (the last two being under Breckenridge), and Braxton's and King's battalions of artillery were at Stephenson's depot on the Winchester & Potomac Railroad, which is six miles from Winchester. Lomax's cavalry picketed in my front on the Opequon, and on my left from that stream to North Mountain, while Fitz. Lee's cavalry watched the right, having small pickets across to the Shenandoah. Four principal roads, from positions, centred at Stephenson's depot, to wit: the Martinsburg road, the road from Charlestown via Smithfield, the road from the same place via Summit Point, and the road from Berryville via Jordan's Springs. Sheridan's main force was near Berryville, at the entrenched position which has been mentioned, while Averill was at Martinsburg with a division of cavalry. Berryville is ten miles from Winchester, nearly east, and Martinsburg twenty-two miles nearly north. The crossing of the Opequon on the Berryville road is four or five miles from Winchester. From Berryville there are two good roads via White Post to the Valley Pike at Newtown and Middletown, the last two roads running east of the Opequon. The whole country is very open, being a limestone country which is thickly settled and well cleared, and affords great facilities for the movement of troops and the operations of cavalry. From the enemy's fortifications on Maryland Heights, the country north and east of Winchester, and the main roads through it are exposed to view.

The relative positions which we occupied rendered my communications to the rear very much exposed, but I could not avoid it without giving up the lower Valley. The object of my presence there was to keep up a threatening attitude towards Maryland and Pennsylvania, and prevent the use of the Baltimore & Ohio Railroad, and the Chesapeake and Ohio Canal, as well as to keep as large a force as possible from Grant's army to defend the

Federal Capital. Had Sheridan, by a prompt movement, thrown his whole force on the line of my communications, I would have been compelled to attempt to cut my way through, as there was no escape for me to the right or left, and my force was too weak to cross the Potomac while he was in my rear. I knew my danger, but I could occupy no other position that would have enabled me to accomplish the desired object.

If I had moved up the Valley at all, I could not have stopped short of New Market, for between that place and the country, in which I was, there was no forage for my horses; and this would have enabled the enemy to resume the use of the railroad and canal, and return all the troops from Grant's army to him. Being compelled to occupy the position where I was, and being aware of its danger as well as apprised of the fact that very great odds were opposed to me, my only resource was to use my forces so as to display them at different points with great rapidity, and thereby keep up the impression that they were much larger than they really were. The events of the last month had satisfied me that the commander opposed to me was without enterprise, and possessed an excessive caution which amounted to timidity. If it was his policy to produce the impression that his force was too weak to fight me, he did not succeed, but if it was to convince me that he was not an energetic commander, his strategy was a complete success, and subsequent events have not changed my opinion.

My infantry force at this time consisted of the three divisions of the 2nd Corps of the Army of Northern Virginia, and Wharton's division of Breckenridge's command. The 2nd corps numbered a little over 8,000 muskets when it was detached in pursuit of Hunter, and it had now been reduced to about 7,000 muskets, by long and rapid marches, and the various encampments and skirmishes in which it had participated. Wharton's division had been reduced to about 1,700 muskets by the same causes. Making a small allowance for details and those unfit for duty, I had about 8,500 muskets for duty.

When I returned from Maryland, my cavalry consisted of the remnants of five small brigades, to wit: Imboden's, McCausland's, Johnson's, Jackson's and Vaughan's. Vaughan's had now been ordered to Southwestern Virginia, most of the men having left without permission. The surprise and rout of McCausland's and Johnson's brigades by Averill at Moorefield had resulted in the loss of a considerable number of horses and men, and such had been the loss in all the brigades, in the various fights and skirmishes in which they had been engaged, that the whole of this cavalry, now under Lomax, numbered only about 1,700 mounted men. Fitz. Lee had brought with him two brigades, to wit: Wickham's and Lomax's old brigade (now under Colonel Payne), numbering about 1,200 mounted men. I had three battalions of artillery which had been with me near Washington, and Fitz. Lee had brought a few pieces of horse artillery. When I speak of divisions and brigades of my troops, it must be understood that they were mere skeletons of those organizations.

Since my return from Maryland, my supplies had been obtained principally from the lower Valley and the counties west of it, and the money which was obtained by contributions in Maryland was used for that purpose. Nearly the whole of our bread was obtained by threshing the wheat and then having it ground, by details from my command, and it sometimes happened that while my troops were fighting, the very flour which was to furnish them with bread for their next meal was being ground under the protection of their guns. Latterly our flour had been obtained from the upper Valley, but also by details sent for that purpose. The horses and mules, including the cavalry horses, were sustained almost entirely by grazing.

I have no means of stating with accuracy Sheridan's force, and can only form an estimate from such data as I have been able to procure. Citizens who had seen his force stated that it was the largest which they had ever seen in the Valley on either side, and some estimated it as high as 60,000 or 70,000, but of course I made allowance for the usual exaggeration of inexperienced men. My estimate is from the following data: in Grant's letter to Hunter, dated at Monocacy, August 5th, 1864, and contained in the report of the former, is the following statement: "In detailing such a force, the brigade of cavalry now *en route* from Washington via Rockville may be taken into account. There are now on their way to join you three other brigades of the best cavalry, numbering at least 5,000 men and horses." Sheridan relieved Hunter on the 6th, and Grant says in his report, "On the 7th of August, the Middle Department and the Departments of West Virginia, Washington and the Susquehanna were constituted into the Middle Military division, and Major General Sheridan was assigned to the temporary command of the same. Two divisions of cavalry, commanded by Generals Torbert and Wilson, were sent to Sheridan from the Army of the Potomac. The first reached him at Harper's Ferry on the 11th of August."

Before this cavalry was sent to the Valley, there was already a division there commanded by Averill, besides some detachments which belonged to the Department of West Virginia. A book containing the official reports of the chief surgeon of the cavalry corps of Sheridan's army which was subsequently captured at Cedar Creek on the 19th of October, showed that there were present for duty in that corps, during the first week in September, 10,000 men. The extracts from Grant's report go to confirm this statement, as, if three brigades numbered at least 5,000 men and horses, the two divisions, when the whole of them arrived with Averill's cavalry, must have numbered over 10,000.

I think, therefore, that I can safely estimate Sheridan's cavalry at the battle of Winchester, on the 19th of September, at 10,000. His infantry consisted of the 6th, 19th, and Crook's corps, the latter being composed of the

"Army of West Virginia," and one division of the 8th corps. The report of Secretary Stanton shows that there was in the department of which the "Middle Military division" was composed the following "available force present for duty May 1st, 1864," to wit:

Department of Washington	42,124
Department of West Virginia	30,782
Department of the Susquehanna	2,970
Middle Department	5,627

making an aggregate of 81,503; but, as the Federal Secretary of War in the same report says, "In order to repair the losses of the Army of the Potomac, the chief part of the force designed to guard the Middle Department and the Department of Washington was called forward to the front," we may assume that 40,000 men were used for that purpose, which would leave 41,503, minus the losses in battle before Sheridan relieved Hunter in the Middle Military division, exclusive of the 6th and 19th corps, and the cavalry from Grant's army. The infantry of the Army of the Potomac was composed of the 2nd, 5th, and 6th corps, on the 1st of May, 1864, and Stanton says the "available force present for duty" in that army, on that day, was 120,386 men. Allowing 30,000 for the artillery and cavalry of that army, which would be a very liberal allowance, and there would be still left 90,385 infantry; and it is fair to assume that the 6th corps numbered one-third of the infantry, that is 30,000 men on the 1st of May, 1864.

If the losses of the Army of the Potomac had been such as to reduce the 6th corps to less than 10,000 men, notwithstanding the reinforcements and recruits received, the carnage in Grant's army must have been frightful indeed. The 19th corps was just from the Department of the Gulf and had not gone through a bloody campaign. A communication which was among the papers captured at Cedar Creek, in noticing some statement of a newspaper correspondent in regard to the conduct of that corps at Winchester, designated it as "a vile slander on 12,000 of the best soldiers in the Union army."

In view of the foregoing data without counting the troops in the Middle Department and the Departments of Washington and the Susquehanna, and making liberal allowances for losses in battle, and for troops detained on post and garrison duty in the Department of West Virginia, I think that I may assume that Sheridan had at least 35,000 infantry against me. The troops of the 6th corps and of the Department of West Virginia, alone, without counting the 19th corps, numbered on the 1st of May, 1864, 60,784. If with the 19th corps Sheridan did not have 35,000 infantry remaining from this force, what had become of the balance? Sheridan's artillery very greatly outnumbered mine, both in men and guns.

Having been informed that a force was at work on the railroad at Martinsburg, I moved on the afternoon of the 17th of September, with Rodes' and Gordon's divisions, and Braxton's artillery, to Bunker Hill, and on the morning of the 18th with Gordon's division and a part of the artillery to Martinsburg, preceded by a part of Lomax's cavalry. Averill's division of cavalry was driven from the town across the Opequon in the direction of Charlestown, and we then returned to Bunker Hill. Gordon was left at Bunker Hill, with orders to move to Stephenson's depot by sunrise next morning, and Rodes' division moved to the latter place that night, to which I also returned. At Martinsburg, where the enemy had a telegraph office, I learned that Grant was with Sheridan that day, and I expected an early move.

CHAPTER XLV.

Battle of Winchester.

At light on the morning of the 19th, our cavalry pickets, at the crossing of the Opequon on the Berryville road, were driven in, and information having been sent me of that fact, I immediately ordered all the troops at Stephenson's depot to be in readiness to move, directions being given for Gordon, who had arrived from Bunker Hill, to move at once, but by some mistake on the part of my staff officer, the latter order was not delivered to General Breckenridge or Gordon. I rode at once to Ramseur's position, and found his troops in line across the Berryville road skirmishing with the enemy. Before reaching this point, I had ascertained that Gordon was not moving and sent back for him, and now discovering that the enemy's advance was a real one and in heavy force, I sent orders for Breckenridge and Rodes to move up as rapidly as possible. The position occupied by Ramseur was about one mile and a half out from Winchester, on an elevated plateau between Abraham's Creek and Red Bud Run. Abraham's Creek crosses the Valley Pike one mile south of Winchester, and then crosses the Front Royal road about the same distance southeast of the town, and running eastwardly, on the southern side of the Berryville road, crosses that road a short distance before it empties into the Opequon.

Red Bud Run crosses the Martinsburg road about a mile and a half north of Winchester and runs eastwardly, on the northern side of the Berryville road, to the Opequon. Ramseur was therefore in the obtuse angle formed by the Martinsburg and Front Royal roads. In front of and to the right of him, for some distance, the country was open. Abraham's Creek runs through a deep valley, and beyond it, on the right, is high open ground, at the intersection of the Front Royal and Millwood roads. To

Ramseur's left the country sloped off to the Red Bud, and there were some patches of woods which afforded cover for troops. To the north of the Red Bud, the country is very open, affording facilities for any kind of troops. Towards the Opequon, on the front, the Berryville road runs through a ravine with hills and woods on each side, which enabled the enemy to move his troops under cover, and mask them out of range of artillery.

Nelson's artillery was posted on Ramseur's line, covering the approaches as far as practicable, and Lomax with Jackson's cavalry and part of Johnson's was on the right, watching the valley of Abraham's Creek, and the Front Royal road beyond, while Fitz. Lee was on the left, across the Red Bud, with his cavalry and a battery of horse artillery; and a detachment of Johnson's cavalry watched the interval between Ramseur's left and the Red Bud. These troops held the enemy's main force in check until Gordon's and Rodes' divisions arrived from Stephenson's depot.

Gordon's division arrived first, a little after ten o'clock A.M., and was placed under cover in a rear of a piece of woods behind the interval between Ramseur's line and the Red Bud, the detachment of Johnson's cavalry having been removed to the right. Knowing that it would not do for us to await the shock of the enemy's attack, Gordon was directed to examine the ground on the left, with a view to attacking a force of the enemy which had taken position in a piece of wood in front of him, and while he was so engaged, Rodes arrived with three of his brigades, and was directed to form on Gordon's right in rear of another piece of woods. While this movement was executed, we discovered very heavy columns of the enemy, which had been massed under cover between the Red Bud and the Berryville road, moving to attack Ramseur on his left flank, while another force pressed him in front. It was a moment of imminent and thrilling danger, as it was impossible for Ramseur's division, which numbered only about 1,700 muskets, to withstand the immense force advancing against it.

The only chance for us was to hurl Rodes and Gordon upon the flank of the advancing columns, and they were ordered forward at once to the attack. They advanced in most gallant style through the woods into the open ground, and attacked with great vigor, while Nelson's battery on the right, and Braxton's on the left, opened a destructive fire. But Evans' brigade of Gordon's division, which was on the extreme left of our infantry, received a check from a column of the enemy, and was forced back through the woods from behind which it had advanced, the enemy following to the very rear of the woods, and to within musket range of seven pieces of Braxton's artillery which were without support.

This caused a pause in our advance and the position was most critical, for it was apparent that unless this force was driven back the day was lost. Braxton's guns, in which now was our only hope, resolutely stood their ground, and under the personal superintendence of Lieutenant Colonel Braxton and Colonel T. H. Carter, my then Chief of Artillery, opened with canister on the enemy. This fire was so rapid and well directed that the enemy staggered, halted, and commenced falling back, leaving a battle flag on the ground, whose bearer was cut down by a canister shot. Just then, Battle's brigade of Rodes' division, which had arrived and been formed in line for the purpose of advancing to the support of the rest of the division, moved forward and swept through the woods, driving the enemy before it, while Evans' brigade was rallied and brought back to the charge.

Our advance, which had been suspended for a moment, was resumed, and the enemy's attacking columns were thrown into great confusion and driven from the field. This attacking force of the enemy proved to be the 6th and 19th corps, and it was a grand sight to see this immense body hurled back in utter disorder before my two divisions, numbering a very little over 5,000 muskets.

Ramseur's division had received the shock of the enemy's attack, and been forced back a little, but soon recovered itself. Lomax, on the right, had held the enemy's cavalry in check, and, with a part of his force, had made a gallant charge against a body of infantry, when Ramseur's line was being forced back, thus aiding the latter in recovering from the momentary disorder. Fitz. Lee on the left, from across the Red Bud, had poured a galling fire into the enemy's columns with his sharpshooters and horse artillery, while Nelson's and Braxton's battalions had performed wonders.

This affair occurred about 11 A.M., and a splendid victory had been gained. The ground in front was strewn with the enemy's dead and wounded, and some prisoners had been taken. But on our side, Major General Rodes had been killed, in the very moment of triumph, while conducting the attack of his division with great gallantry and skill, and this was a heavy blow to me. Brigadier General Godwin of Ramseur's division had been killed, and Brigadier General York of Gordon's division had lost an arm. Other brave men and officers had fallen, and we could illy bear the loss of any of them.

Had I then had a fresh body of troops to push our victory, the day would have been ours, but in this action, in the early part of the day, I had present only about 7,000 muskets, about 2,000 cavalry and two battalions of artillery with about 30 guns; and they had all been engaged. Wharton's division and King's artillery had not arrived, and Imboden's cavalry under Colonel Smith, and McCausland's under Colonel Ferguson, were watching the enemy's cavalry on the right, on the Martinsburg road and the Opequon. The enemy had a fresh corps which had not been engaged, and there remained his heavy force of cavalry. Our lines were now formed across from Abraham's Creek to Red Bud and were very attenuated. The enemy was still to be seen in front in formidable force, and away to our right, across Abraham's Creek, at the junction of the Front Royal and Millwood roads, he had massed a division of cavalry with some artillery, overlapping us at least a mile, while the country was open between this force and the Valley Pike and Cedar Creek Pike back of the latter; which roads furnished my only means of retreat in the event of disaster. My line did not reach the Front Royal road on the right or the Martinsburg road on the left.

When the order was sent for the troops to move from Stephenson's depot, General Breckenridge had moved to the front, with Wharton's division and King's artillery, to meet a cavalry force, which had driven our pickets from the Opequon on the Charlestown road, and that division had become heavily engaged with the enemy, and sustained and repulsed several determined charges of his cavalry, while his own flanks were in great danger from the enemy's main force on the right, and a column of his cavalry moving up the Martinsburg road on the left. After much difficulty, and some hard fighting, General Breckenridge succeeded in extricating his force, and moving up the Martinsburg road to join me, but he did not reach the field until about two o'clock in the afternoon.

In the meantime there had been heavy skirmishing along the line, and the reports from the front were that the enemy was massing for another attack, but it was impossible to tell where it would fall. As the danger from the enemy's cavalry on the right was very great and Lomax's force very weak, Wickham's brigade of Fitz. Lee's cavalry had been sent from the left to Lomax's assistance. When Wharton's division arrived, Patton's brigade of that division was left to aid Fitz. Lee in guarding the Martinsburg road, against the force of cavalry which was advancing on that road watched by Lomax's two small brigades; and the rest of the division in the centre, in order to be moved to any point that might be attacked. Late in the afternoon two divisions of the enemy's cavalry drove in the small force which had been watching it on the Martinsburg road, and Crook's corps, which had not been engaged, advanced at the same time on that flank, on the north side of Red Bud, and, before this overwhelming force, Patton's brigade of infantry and Payne's brigade of cavalry under Fitz. Lee were forced back.

A considerable force of the enemy's cavalry then swept along the Martinsburg road to the very skirts of Winchester, thus getting in the rear of our left flank. Wharton's two other brigades were moved in double quick time to the left and rear, and making a gallant charge on the enemy's cavalry, with the aid of King's artillery, and some of Braxton's guns which were turned to the rear, succeeded in driving it back. The division was then thrown into line by General Breckenridge, in rear of our left and at right angles with the Martinsburg road, and another charge of the enemy's cavalry was handsomely repulsed. But many of the men on our front line, hearing the fire in the rear, and thinking they were flanked and about to be cut off, commenced falling back, thus producing great confusion. At the same time Crook advanced against our left, and Gordon threw Evans' brigade into line to meet him, but the disorder in the front line became so great that, after an obstinate resistance, that brigade was compelled to retire also.

The whole front line had now given way, but a large portion of the men were rallied and formed behind an indifferent line of breastworks, which had been made just outside of Winchester during the first year of the war, and, with the aid of the artillery which was brought back to this position, the progress of the enemy's infantry was arrested. Wharton's division maintained its organization on the left, and Ramseur fell back in good order on the right. Wickham's brigade of cavalry had been brought from the right, and was in position on Fort Hill just outside of Winchester on the west. Just after the advance of the enemy's infantry was checked by our artillery, it was reported to me that the enemy had got around our right flank, and as I knew this was practicable and was expecting such a movement from the cavalry on the Front Royal road, I gave the order to retire, but instantly discovering that the supposed force of the enemy was Ramseur's division, which had merely moved back to keep in line with the other troops, I gave the order for the latter to return to the works before they had moved twenty paces.

This order was obeyed by Wharton's division, but not so well by the others. The enemy's cavalry force, however, was too large for us, and having the advantage of open ground, it again succeeded in getting around our left, producing great confusion, for which there was no remedy. Nothing now was left for us but to retire through Winchester, and Ramseur's division, which maintained its organization, was moved on the east of the town to the south side of it, and put in position, forming a basis for a new line, while the other troops moved back through the town. Wickham's brigade, with some pieces of horse artillery on Fort Hill, covered this movement and checked the pursuit of the enemy's cavalry. When the new line was formed, the enemy's advance was checked until nightfall, and we then retired to Newtown without serious molestation. Lomax had held the enemy's cavalry on the Front Royal road in check, and a feeble attempt at pursuit was repulsed by Ramseur near Kernstown.

As soon as our reverse began, orders had been sent for the removal of the trains, stores and sick and wounded in the hospitals to Fisher's Hill over the Cedar Creek Pike and the Back Road. This was done with safety, and all the wounded, except such as were not in a condition to be moved, and those which had not been brought from the field, were carried to the rear.

This battle, beginning with the skirmishing in Ramseur's front, had lasted from daylight till dark, and, at the close of it, we had been forced back two miles, after having repulsed the enemy's first attack with great slaughter to him and subsequently contested every inch of ground with unsurpassed obstinacy. We deserved the victory, and would have had it, but for the enemy's immense superiority in cavalry, which alone gave it to him.

Three pieces of King's artillery, from which the horses were shot, and which, therefore, could not be brought off, were lost, but the enemy claimed five, and if he captured that number, two were lost by the cavalry and not reported to me. My loss in killed, wounded and prisoners was severe for the size of my force, but it was only a fraction of that claimed by the enemy. Owing to its obedience to orders in returning to the works, the heaviest loss of prisoners was in Wharton's division. Colonel G. W. Patton, commanding a brigade, was mortally wounded and fell into the hands of the enemy; Major General Fitz. Lee was also severely wounded. In the death of Major General Rodes, I had to regret the loss, not only of a most accomplished, skilful and gallant officer, upon whom I placed great reliance, but also of a personal friend, whose counsels had been of great service to me in the trying circumstances with which I had found myself surrounded. He fell at his post, doing a soldier's and patriot's duty to his country, and his memory will long be cherished by his comrades. General Godwin and Colonel Patton were both most gallant and efficient officers, and their loss was deeply felt, as was that of all the brave officers and men who fell in this battle. The enemy's loss in killed and wounded was very heavy, and some prisoners fell into our hands.

A skilful and energetic commander of the enemy's forces would have crushed Ramseur before any assistance could have reached him, and thus ensured the destruction of my whole force; and later in the day, when the battle had turned against us, with the immense superiority in cavalry which Sheridan had, and the advantage of the open country, would have destroyed my whole force and captured everything I had. As it was, considering the immense disparity in numbers and equipment, the enemy had very little to boast of. I had lost a few pieces of artillery and some very valuable officers and men, but the main part of my force and all my trains had been saved, and the enemy's loss in killed and wounded was far greater than mine. When I look back to this battle, I can but attribute my escape from utter annihilation to the incapacity of my opponent.*

---

* The enemy has called this battle " The Battle of the Opequon," but I know of no claim it has to that title, unless it be in the fact that, after his repulse in the forepart of the day, some of his troops ran back across that stream.

CHAPTER XLVI.

Affair at Fisher's Hill.

At light on the morning of the 20th, my troops moved to Fisher's Hill without molestation from the enemy, and again took position at that point on the old line— Wharton's division being on the right, then Gordon's, Ramseur's and Rodes', in the order in which they are mentioned. Fitz. Lee's cavalry, now under Brigadier General Wickham, was sent up the Luray Valley to a narrow pass at Millwood, to try to hold that valley against the enemy's cavalry. General Ramseur was transferred to the command of Rodes' division, and Brigadier General Pegram, who had reported for duty about the 1st of August, and been in command of his brigade since that time, was left in command of the division previously commanded by Ramseur. My infantry was not able to occupy the whole line at Fisher's Hill, notwithstanding it was extended out in an attenuated line, with considerable intervals. The greater part of Lomax's cavalry was therefore dismounted, and placed on Ramseur's left, near Little North Mountain, but the line could not then be fully occupied.

This was the only position in the whole Valley where a defensive line could be taken against an enemy moving up the Valley, and it had several weak points. To have retired beyond this point would have rendered it necessary for me to fall back to some of the gaps of the Blue Ridge, at the upper part of the Valley, and I determined therefore to make a show of a stand here, with the hopes that the enemy would be deterred from attacking me in this position, as had been the case in August.

On the second day after our arrival at this place, General Breckenridge received orders from Richmond, by telegraph, to return to Southwestern Virginia, and I lost the benefit of his services. He had ably co-operated with me, and our personal relations had been of the most pleasant character.

In the afternoon of the 20th, Sheridan's forces appeared on the banks of Cedar Creek, about four miles from Fisher's Hill, and the 21st, and the greater part of the 22nd, were consumed by him in reconnoitring and gradually moving his forces to my front under cover of breastworks. After some sharp skirmishing, he attained a strong position immediately in my front and fortified it, and I began to think he was satisfied with the advantage he had gained and would not probably press it further; but on the afternoon of the 22nd, I discovered that another attack was contemplated, and orders were given for my troops to retire, after dark, as I knew my force was not strong enough to resist a determined assault. Just before sunset, however, Crook's corps, which had moved to our left on the side of Little North Mountain, and under cover of the woods, forced back Lomax's dismounted cavalry and advanced against Ramseur's left.

Ramseur made an attempt to meet this movement by throwing his brigades successively into line to the left, and Wharton's division was sent for from the right, but it did not arrive. Pegram's brigades were also thrown into line in the same manner as Ramseur's, but the movement produced some disorder in both divisions, and as soon as it was observed by the enemy, he advanced along his whole line and the mischief could not be remedied. After a very brief contest, my whole force retired in considerable confusion, but the men and officers of the artillery behaved with great coolness, fighting to the very last, and I had to ride to some of the officers and order them to withdraw their guns, before they would move. In some cases, they had held out so long, and the roads leading from their positions into the Pike were so rugged, that eleven guns fell into the hands of the enemy. Vigorous pursuit was not made, and my force fell back through Woodstock to a place called the Narrow Passage, all the trains being carried off safely.

AFFAIR AT FISHER'S HILL

Our loss in killed and wounded in this affair was slight, but some prisoners were taken by the enemy, the most of whom were captured while attempting to make their way across the North Fork to Massanutten Mountain, under the impression that the enemy had possession of the Valley Pike in our rear. I had the misfortune to lose my Adjutant General, Lieutenant Colonel A. S. Pendleton, a gallant and efficient young officer, who had served on General Jackson's staff during his Valley campaign, and subsequently to the time of the latter's death. Colonel Pendleton fell mortally wounded about dark, while posting a force across the Pike, a little in rear of Fisher's Hill, to check the enemy. He was acting with his accustomed gallantry, and his loss was deeply felt and regretted.

CHAPTER XLVII.

The March up the Valley.

On the morning of the 23rd, I moved back to Mount Jackson, where I halted to enable the sick and wounded, and the hospital stores at that place to be carried off. In the afternoon Averill's division of cavalry came up in pursuit, and after some heavy skirmishing was driven back. I then moved to Rude's Hill between Mount Jackson and New Market.

On the morning of the 24th, a body of the enemy's cavalry crossed the North Fork below Mount Jackson, and attempted to get around my right flank, but was held in check. The enemy's infantry soon appeared at Mount Jackson, and commenced moving around my left flank, on the opposite side of the river from that on which my left rested. As the country was entirely open, and Rude's Hill an elevated position, I could see the whole movement of the enemy, and as soon as it was fully developed, I commenced retiring in line of battle, and in that manner retired through New Market to a point at which the road to Port Republic leaves the Valley Pike, nine miles from Rude's Hill.

This movement was made through an entirely open country, and at every mile or two a halt was made, and artillery opened on the enemy, who was pursuing, which compelled him to commence deploying into line, when the retreat would be resumed. In this retreat, under fire in line, which is so trying to a retiring force, and tests the best qualities of the soldier, the conduct of my troops was most admirable, and they preserved perfect order and their line intact, notwithstanding their diminished numbers, and the fact that the enemy was pursuing in full force, and every now and then dashing up with horse artillery under the support of cavalry, and opening on the retiring lines. At the last halt, which was at a place

432

called "Tenth Legion," near where the Port Republic road leaves the Pike, and was a little before sunset, I determined to resist any further advance so as to enable my trains to get on the Port Republic road; and skirmishers were sent out and artillery opened on the advancing enemy, but after some skirmishing, he went into camp in our view, and beyond the reach of our guns. At this point a gallant officer of artillery, Captain Massie, was killed by a shell. As soon as it was dark, we retired five miles on the Port Republic road and bivouacked.

In the morning Lomax's cavalry had been posted to our left, on the Middle and Back Roads from Mount Jackson to Harrisonburg, but it was forced back by a superior force of the enemy's cavalry, and retired to the latter place in considerable disorder. Wickham's brigade had been sent for from the Luray Valley to join me through the New Market Gap, but it arrived at that gap just as we were retiring through New Market, and orders were sent for it to return to the Luray Valley, and join me at Port Republic. In the meantime, Payne's small brigade had been driven from Millford by two divisions of cavalry under Torbert, which had moved up the Luray Valley, and subsequently joined Sheridan through the New Market Gap. This cavalry had been detained by Wickham with his and Payne's brigades, at Millford, a sufficient time to enable us to pass New Market in safety. If, however, it had moved up the Luray Valley by Conrad's store, we would have been in a critical condition.

On the morning of the 25th, we moved towards Port Republic,—which is in the fork of the South Fork and South River, and where the road through Brown's Gap in the Blue Ridge crosses those rivers,—in order to unite with Kershaw's division which had been ordered to join me from Culpeper Court-House. We crossed the river below the junction, and took position between Port Republic and Brown's Gap. Fitz. Lee's and Lomax's cavalry joined us here, and on the 26th, Kershaw's division with Cutshaw's battalion of artillery came up, after having crossed through Swift Run Gap, and encountered and repulsed, below Port Republic, a body of the enemy's cavalry. There was likewise heavy skirmishing on my front on the 26th with the enemy's cavalry, which made two efforts to advance towards Brown's Gap, both of which were repulsed after brisk fighting in which artillery was used.

Having ascertained that the enemy's infantry had halted at Harrisonburg, on the morning of the 27th, I moved out and drove a division of his cavalry from Port Republic, and then encamped in the fork of the rivers. I here learned that two divisions of cavalry under Torbert had been sent through Staunton to Waynesboro, and were engaged in destroying the railroad bridge in the latter place, and the tunnel through the Blue Ridge at Rock-fish Gap, and on the 28th I moved for those points. In making this movement I had the whole of the enemy's infantry on my right, while one division of cavalry was in my rear and two in my front, and on the left was the Blue Ridge. I had therefore to move with great circumspection.

Wickham's brigade of cavalry was sent up South River, near the mountain, to get between the enemy and Rock-fish Gap, while the infantry moved in two columns, one up South River, with the trains guarded in front by Pegram's and Wharton's divisions, and in rear by Ramseur's division, and the other, composed of Kershaw's and Gordon's divisions with the artillery, on the right through Mount Meridian, Piedmont and New Hope. McCausland's cavalry, under Colonel Ferguson, was left to blockade and hold Brown's Gap, while Lomax, with the rest of his cavalry and Payne's brigade, watched the right flank and rear. Wickham's brigade, having got between Rock-fish Gap and Waynesboro, drove the enemy's working parties from the latter place, and took position on a ridge in front of it, when a sharp artillery fight ensued. Pegram's division, driving a small body of cavalry before it, arrived just at night and advanced upon the enemy, when he retired in great haste, taking the roads through Staunton and west of the Valley Pike, back to the main body. A company of reserves, composed of boys under 18 years of age, which had been employed on special duty at Staunton, had gone to Rockfish Gap, and another company of reserves from Charlottesville, with two pieces of artillery, had moved to the same point, and when the enemy advanced towards the tunnel and before he got in range of the guns, they were opened and he retired to Waynesboro.

On the 29th and 30th, we rested at Waynesboro, and an engineer party was put to work repairing the bridge, which had been but partially destroyed.

On the 1st of October, I moved my whole force across the country to Mount Sidney on the Valley Pike, and took position between that place and North River, the enemy's forces having been concentrated around Harrisonburg, and on the north bank of the river. In this position we remained until the 6th, awaiting the arrival of Rosser's brigade of cavalry, which was on its way from General Lee's army. In the meantime there was some skirmishing with the enemy's cavalry on the North River, at the bridge near Mount Crawford and at Bridgewater above.

On the 5th, Rosser's brigade arrived and was temporarily attached to Fitz. Lee's division, of which Rosser was given the command, as Brigadier General Wickham had resigned. The horses of Rosser's brigade had been so much reduced by previous hard service and the long march from Richmond, that the brigade did not exceed six hundred mounted men for duty, when it joined me. Kershaw's division numbered 2,700 muskets for duty and he had brought with him Cutshaw's battalion of artillery. These reinforcements about made up my losses at Winchester and Fisher's Hill, and I determined to attack the enemy in his position at Harrisonburg, and for that purpose made a reconnaissance on the 5th, but on the morning of the 6th it was discovered that he had retired during the night down the Valley.

When it was discovered that the enemy was retiring, I moved forward at once and arrived at New Market with my infantry on the 7th. Rosser pushed forward on the Back and Middle roads in pursuit of the enemy's cavalry, which was engaged in burning houses, mills, barns, and stacks of wheat and hay, and had several skirmishes with it, while Lomax also moved down the Valley in pursuit, and skirmished successfully with the enemy's cavalry on the 8th; but on the 9th they encountered his whole cavalry force at Tom's Brook, in rear of Fisher's Hill, and both of their commands were driven back in considerable confusion, with a loss of some pieces of artillery,—nine were reported to me as the number lost, but Grant claims eleven. Rosser rallied his command on the Back Road, at Columbia furnace opposite Edinburg, but a part of the enemy's cavalry swept along the Pike to Mount Jackson, and then retired on the approach of a part of my infantry. On the 10th, Rosser established his line of pickets across the Valley from Columbia Furnace to Edinburg, and on the 11th Lomax was sent to the Luray Valley to take position at Millford.

CHAPTER XLVIII.

Battle of Cedar Creek, or Belle Grove.

Having heard that Sheridan was preparing to send part of his troops to Grant, I moved down the Valley again on the 12th. On the morning of the 13th we reached Fisher's Hill, and I moved with part of my command to Hupp's Hill, between Strasburg and Cedar Creek, for the purpose of reconnoitring. The enemy was found posted on the north bank of Cedar Creek in strong force, and while we were observing him, without displaying any of my force except a small body of cavalry, a division of his infantry was moved out to his left and stacked arms in an open field, when a battery of artillery was run out suddenly and opened on this division, scattering it in great confusion.

The enemy then displayed a large force, and sent a division across the creek to capture guns which had been opened on him, but when it had advanced near enough, Conner's brigade of Kershaw's division was sent forward to meet this division, and after a sharp contest drove it back in considerable confusion and with severe loss. Conner's brigade behaved very handsomely indeed, but unfortunately, after the enemy had been entirely repulsed, Brigadier General Conner, a most accomplished and gallant officer, lost his leg by a shell from the opposite side of the creek. Some prisoners were taken from the enemy in this affair, and Colonel Wells, the division commander, fell into our hands mortally wounded. The object of the reconnaissance having been accomplished, I moved back to Fisher's Hill, and I subsequently learned that the 6th corps had started for Grant's army but was brought back after this affair.

I remained at Fisher's Hill until the 16th observing the enemy, with the hope that he would move back from his very strong position on the north of Cedar Creek, and that we would be able to get at him in a different position, but he did not give any indications of an intention to move, nor did he evince any purpose of attacking us, though the two positions were in sight of each other. In the meantime there was some skirmishing at Hupp's Hill, and some with the cavalry at Cedar Creek on the Back Road. On the 16th Rosser's scouts reported a brigade of the enemy's cavalry encamped on the Back Road, and detached from the rest of his force, and Rosser was permitted to go that night, with a brigade of infantry mounted behind the same number of cavalry, to attempt the surprise and capture of the camp. He succeeded in surrounding and surprising the camp, but it proved to be that of only a strong picket, the whole of which was captured—the brigade having moved its location.

At light on the morning of the 7th, the whole of my troops were moved out in front of our lines, for the purpose of covering Rosser's return in case of difficulty, and, after he had returned, General Gordon was sent with a brigade of his division to Hupp's Hill, for the purpose of ascertaining, by close inspection, whether the enemy's position was fortified, and he returned with the information that it was. I was now compelled to move back for want of provisions and forage, or attack the enemy in his position with the hope of driving him from it, and I determined to attack. As I was not strong enough to attack the fortified position in front, I determined to get around one of the enemy's flanks and attack him by surprise if I could.

After General Gordon's return from Hupp's Hill, he and Captain Hotchkiss, my topographical engineer, were sent to the signal station on the end of Massanutten Mountain, which had been re-established, for the purpose of examining the enemy's position from that point, and General Pegram was ordered to go as near as he could to Cedar Creek on the enemy's right flank, and see whether it was practicable to surprise him on that flank.

BATTLE OF CEDAR CREEK, OR BELLE GROVE

Captain Hotchkiss returned to my headquarters after dark, and reported the result of his and General Gordon's examination, and he gave me a sketch of the enemy's position and camps. He informed me that the enemy's left flank, which rested near Cedar Creek, a short distance above its mouth, was lightly picketed, and that there was but a small cavalry picket on the North Fork of the Shenandoah, below the mouth of the creek, and he stated that, from information he had received, he thought it was practicable to move a column of infantry between the base of the mountain and the river, to a ford below the mouth of the creek. He also informed me that the main body of the enemy's cavalry was on his right flank on the Back Road to Winchester.

The sketch made by Captain Hotchkiss, which proved to be correct, designated the roads in the enemy's rear, and the house of a Mr. Cooley at a favorable point for forming an attacking column, after it crossed the river, in order to move against the enemy and strike him on the Valley Pike in rear of his works. Upon this information, I determined to attack the enemy by moving over the ground designated by Captain Hotchkiss, if it should prove practicable to move a column between the base of the mountain and the river. Next morning, General Gordon confirmed the report of Captain Hotchkiss, expressing confidence that the attack could be sucessfully made on the enemy's left and rear, and General Pegram reported that a movement on the enemy's right flank would be attended with great difficulty, as the banks of Cedar Creek on that flank were high and precipitous and were well guarded. General Gordon and Captain Hotchkiss were then sent to examine and ascertain the practicability of the route at the base of the mountain, and General Pegram, at his request, was permitted to go to the signal station on the mountain to examine the enemy's position himself from that point. Directions were given, in the meantime, for everything to be in readiness to move that night (the 18th) and the division commanders were requested to be at my quarters at two o'clock in the afternoon, to receive their final instructions.

The river makes a circuit to the left in front of the right of the position at Fisher's Hill and around by Strasburg, leaving a considerable body of land between it and the mountain, on which are several farms. Whenever Fisher's Hill had been occupied by us, this bend of the river had been occupied by a portion of our cavalry, to prevent the enemy from turning the right of the position, and it was now occupied by Colonel Payne with his cavalry, numbering about 300. In order to make the contemplated movement, it was necessary to cross the river into this bend, and then pass between the foot of the mountain and the river below Strasburg, where the passage was very narrow, and across the river again below the mouth of Cedar Creek. The enemy's camps and position were visible from a signal station on Round Hill in rear of Fisher's Hill, and had been examined by me from that point, but the distance was too great to see with distinctness. From the station on the mountain, which immediately overlooked the enemy's left, the view was very distinct, but I could not go to that point myself, as the ascent was very rugged, and it required several hours to go and come, and I could not leave my command for that time. I had, therefore, necessarily, to rely on the reports of my officers.

General Gordon and Captain Hotchkiss, on their return, reported the route between the mountain and river, which was a blind path, to be impracticable for infantry, but not for artillery, and a temporary bridge was constructed under Captain Hotchkiss' superintendence, at the first crossing of the river on our right.

The plan of attack on which I determined was to send the three divisions of the 2nd corps, to wit: Gordon's, Ramseur's and Pegram's, under General Gordon, over the route which has been specified to the enemy's rear, to make the attack at five o'clock in the morning, which would be a little before daybreak—to move myself, with

Kershaw's and Wharton's divisions, and all the artillery, along the Pike through Strasburg, and attack the enemy on the front and left flank as soon as Gordon should become engaged, and for Rosser to move with his own and Wickham's brigade, on the Back Road across Cedar Creek, and attack the enemy's cavalry simultaneously with Gordon's attack, while Lomax should move by Front Royal, across the river, and come to the Valley Pike, so as to strike the enemy wherever he might be, of which he was to judge by the sound of the firing.

At two o'clock P.M. all the division commanders, except Pegram, who had not returned from the mountain, came to my headquarters, and I gave them their instructions. Gordon was directed to cross over the bend of the river immediately after dark; and move to the foot of the mountain, where he would rest his troops, and move from there in time to cross the river again and get in position at Cooley's house in the enemy's rear, so as to make the attack at the designated hour, and he was instructed, in advancing to the attack, to move for a house on the west side of the Valley Pike called the "Belle Grove House," at which it was known that Sheridan's headquarters were located.

A guide, who knew the country and the roads, was ordered to be sent to General Gordon, and Colonel Payne was ordered to accompany him with his force of cavalry, and endeavor to capture Sheridan himself. Rosser was ordered to move before day, in time to attack at five o'clock next morning, and to endeavor to surprise the enemy's cavalry in camp. Kershaw and Wharton were ordered to move, at one o'clock in the morning, towards Strasburg under my personal superintendence, and the artillery was ordered to concentrate where the Pike passed through the lines at Fisher's Hill, and, at the hour appointed for the attack, to move at a gallop to Hupp's Hill—the movement of the artillery being thus delayed for fear of attracting the attention of the enemy by the rumbling of the wheels over the macadamized road

Swords and canteens were directed to be left in camp, so as to make as little noise as possible.

The division commanders were particularly admonished as to the necessity for promptness and energy in all their movements, and they were instructed to press the enemy with vigor after he was encountered, and to allow him no time to form, but to continue the pursuit until his forces should be completely routed. They were also admonished of the danger to be apprehended from a disposition to plunder the enemy's camps by their men, and they were enjoined to take every possible precaution against it.

Gordon moved at the appointed time, and, after he had started, General Pegram reported to me that he had discovered, from the signal station on the mountain, what he supposed to be an intrenchment thrown up since Gordon and Hotchkiss made their examination; and he suggested the propriety of attacking the enemy's left flank' at the same time Gordon made his attack, as he would probably have more difficulty than had been anticipated. I adopted this suggestion and determined to cross Kershaw's division over Cedar Creek, at Bowman's Mill, a little above its mouth, and strike the enemy's left flank simultaneously with the other attacks, of which purpose notice was sent to General Gordon by General Pegram.

At one o'clock on the morning of the 19th, Kershaw and Wharton moved, and I accompanied them. At Strasburg Kershaw moved to the right on the road to Bowman's Mill, and Wharton moved along the Pike to Hupp's Hill, with instructions not to display his forces but avoid the enemy's notice until the attack began, when he was to move forward, support the artillery when it came up, and send a force to get possession of the bridge on the Pike over the creek. I accompanied Kershaw's division, and we got in sight of the enemy's fires at half-past three o'clock. The moon was now shining and we could see the camps. The division was halted under cover to await the arrival of the proper time, and I pointed out to Kershaw, and the commander of his leading brigade, the enemy's position and described the nature of the ground, and directed them how the attack was to be made and followed up. Kershaw was directed to cross his division over the creek as quietly as possible, and to form it into column of brigades, as he did so, and advance in that manner against the enemy's left breastwork, extending to the right or left as might be necessary.

At half-past four he was ordered forward, and, a very short time after he started, the firing from Rosser, on our left, and the picket firing at the ford at which Gordon was crossing were heard. Kershaw crossed the creek without molestation and formed his division as directed, and precisely at five o'clock his leading brigade, with little opposition, swept over the enemy's left work, capturing seven guns, which were at once turned on the enemy. As soon as this attack was made, I rode as rapidly as possible to the position on Hupp's Hill to which Wharton and the artillery had been ordered. I found the artillery just arriving, and a very heavy fire of musketry was now heard in the enemy's rear from Gordon's column. Wharton had advanced his skirmishers to the creek, capturing some prisoners, but the enemy still held the works on our left of the Pike, commanding that road and the bridge, and opened with his artillery on us. Our artillery was immediately brought into action and opened on the enemy, but he soon evacuated his works, and our men from the other columns rushed into them.

Just then the sun rose, and Wharton's division, and the artillery were ordered immediately forward. I rode in advance of them across the creek, and met General Gordon on the opposite hill. Kershaw's division had swept along the enemy's works on the right of the Pike, which were occupied by Crook's corps, and he and Gordon had united at the Pike, and their divisions had pushed across it in pursuit of the enemy. The rear division of Gordon's column (Pegram's) was crossing the river at the time Kershaw's attack was made, and General Gordon moved rapidly to Cooley's house, formed his troops and advanced against the enemy with his own division on the left, under Brigadier General Evans, and Ramseur's on the right, with Pegram in the right supporting them.

There had been a delay of an hour at the river before crossing it, either from a miscalculation of time in the dark, or because the cavalry which was to precede his column had not gotten up, and the delay thus caused, for which no blame is to be attached to General Gordon, enabled the enemy partially to form his lines after the alarm produced by Kershaw's attack, and Gordon's attack, which was after light, was therefore met with greater obstinacy by the enemy than it would otherwise have encountered, and the fighting had been severe.

Gordon, however, pushed his attack with great energy, and the 19th and Crook's corps were in complete rout, and their camps, with a number of pieces of artillery and a considerable quantity of small arms, abandoned. The 6th corps, which was on the enemy's right, and some distance from the point attacked, had had time to get under arms and take position so as to arrest our progress. General Gordon briefly informed me of the condition of things and stated that Pegram's division, which had not been previously engaged, had been ordered in. He then rode to take command of his division, and I rode forward on the Pike to ascertain the position of the enemy, in order to continue the attack.

There was now a heavy fog, and that, with the smoke from the artillery and small arms, so obscured objects that the enemy's position could not be seen; but I soon came to Generals Ramseur and Pegram, who informed me that Pegram's division had encountered a division of the 6th corps on the left of the Valley Pike, and, after a sharp engagement, had driven it back on the main body of that corps, which was in their front in a strong position. They further informed me that their divisions were in line confronting the 6th corps, but that there was a vacancy in the line on their right which ought to be filled.

BATTLE OF CEDAR CREEK, OR BELLE GROVE

I ordered Wharton's division forward at once, and directed Generals Ramseur and Pegram to put it where it was required. In a very short time, and while I was endeavoring to discover the enemy's line through the obscurity, Wharton's division came back in some confusion, and General Wharton informed me that, in advancing to the position pointed out to him by Generals Ramseur and Pegram, his division had been driven back by the 6th corps, which, he said, was advancing. He pointed out the direction from which he said the enemy was advancing, and some pieces of artillery, which had come up, were brought into action. The fog soon rose sufficiently for us to see the enemy's position on a ridge to the west of Middletown, and it was discovered to be a strong one. After driving back Wharton's division he had not advanced, but opened on us with artillery, and orders were given for concentrating all our guns on him.

In the meantime, a force of cavalry was advancing along the Pike, and through the fields to the right of Middletown, thus placing our right and rear in great danger, and Wharton was ordered to form his division at once, and take position to hold the enemy's cavalry in check. Wofford's brigade of Kershaw's division, which had become separated from the other brigades, was ordered up for the same purpose. Discovering that the 6th corps could not be attacked with advantage on its left flank, because the approach in that direction was through an open flat and across a boggy stream with deep banks, I directed Captain Powell, serving on General Gordon's staff, who rode up to me while the artillery was being placed in position, to tell the General to advance against the enemy's right flank and attack it in conjunction with Kershaw, while a heavy fire of artillery was opened from our right; but as Captain Powell said he did not know where General Gordon was and expressed some doubt about finding him, immediately after he started, I sent Lieutenant Page of my own staff, with orders for both Generals Gordon and Kershaw to make the attack.

In a short time Colonel Carter concentrated 18 or 20 guns on the enemy, and he was soon in retreat. Ramseur and Pegram advanced at once to the position from which the enemy was driven, and just then his cavalry commenced pressing heavily on the right, and Pegram's division was ordered to move to the north of Middletown, and take position across the Pike against the cavalry. Lieutenant Page had returned and informed me that he delivered my order to General Kershaw, but the latter informed him that his division was not in a condition to make the attack, as it was very much scattered, and that he had not delivered the order to General Gordon, because he saw that neither his division nor Kershaw's was in a condition to execute it. As soon as Pegram moved, Kershaw was ordered from the left to supply his place.

I then rode to Middletown to make provision against the enemy's cavalry, and discovered a large body of it seriously threatening that flank, which was very much exposed. Wharton's division and Wofford's brigade were put in position on Pegram's right, and several charges of the enemy's cavalry were repulsed. I had no cavalry on that flank except Payne's very small brigade, which had accompanied Gordon, and made some captures of prisoners and wagons. Lomax had not arrived, but I received a message from him, informing me that he had crossed the river after some delay from a cavalry force guarding it, and I sent a message to him requiring him to move to Middletown as quickly as possible, but, as I subsequently ascertained, he did not receive that message. Rosser had attacked the enemy promptly at the appointed time, but he had not been able to surprise him, as he was found on the alert on that flank, doubtless owing to the attempt at a surprise on the night of the 16th.

There was now one division of cavalry threatening my right flank and two were on the left, near the Back Road, held in check by Rosser. The force of the latter was too weak to make any impression on the enemy's cavalry, and all he could do was to watch it. As I passed across Cedar Creek after the enemy was driven from it, I had discovered a number of men in the enemy's camps plundering, and one of Wharton's battalions was ordered to clear the camps, and drive the men to their commands.

It was reported to me, subsequently, that a great number were at the same work, and I sent all my staff officers who could be spared, to stop it if possible, and orders were sent to the division commanders to send for their men.

After he was driven from his second position, the enemy had taken a new position about two miles north of Middletown, and, as soon as I had regulated matters on the right so as to prevent his cavalry from getting in rear of that flank, I rode to the left, for the purpose of ordering an advance.

I found Ramseur and Kershaw in line with Pegram, but Gordon had not come up. In a short time, however, I found him coming up from the rear, and I ordered him to take position on Kershaw's left, and advance for the purpose of driving the enemy from his new position—Kershaw and Ramseur being ordered to advance at the same time. As the enemy's cavalry on our left was very strong, and had the benefit of an open country to the rear of that flank, a repulse at this time would have been disastrous, and I therefore directed General Gordon, if he found the enemy's line too strong to attack with success, not to make the assault. The advance was made for some distance, when Gordon's skirmishers came back, reporting a line of battle in front behind breastworks, and Gordon did not make the attack.

It was now apparent that it would not do to press my troops further. They had been up all night and were much jaded. In passing over rough ground to attack the enemy in the early morning, their own ranks had been much disordered, and the men scattered, and it had required time to re-form them. Their ranks, moreover, were much thinned by the advance of the men engaged in plundering the enemy's camps. The delay which had unavoidably occurred had enabled the enemy to rally a portion of his routed troops, and his immense force of cavalry, which remained intact, was threatening both of our flanks in an open country, which of itself rendered an advance extremely hazardous.

I determined, therefore, to try and hold what had been gained, and orders were given for carrying off the captured and abandoned artillery, small arms and wagons. A number of bold attempts were made during the subsequent part of the day, by the enemy's cavalry, to break our line on the right, but they were invariably repulsed.

Late in the afternoon, the enemy's infantry advanced against Ramseur's, Kershaw's and Gordon's lines, and the attack on Ramseur's and Kershaw's fronts was handsomely repulsed in my view, and I hoped that the day was finally ours, but a portion of the enemy had penetrated an interval which was between Evans' brigade, on the extreme left, and the rest of the line, when that brigade gave way, and Gordon's other brigades soon followed. General Gordon made every possible effort to rally his men, and lead them back against the enemy, but without avail. The information of this affair, with exaggerations, passed rapidly along Kershaw's and Ramseur's lines, and their men, under the apprehension of being flanked, commenced falling back in disorder, though no enemy was pressing them, and this gave me the first intimation of Gordon's condition.

At the same time the enemy's cavalry, observing the disorder in our ranks, made another charge on our right, but was repulsed. Every effort was made to stop and rally Kershaw's and Ramseur's men, but the mass of them resisted all appeals, and continued to go to the rear without waiting for any effort to retrieve the partial disorder. Ramseur, however, succeeded in retaining with him two or three hundred men of his division, and Major Goggin of Kershaw's staff, who was in command of Conner's brigade, about the same number from that brigade; and these men, with six pieces of artillery of Cutshaw's battalion, held the enemy's whole force on our left in check for one hour and a half, until Ramseur was shot down mortally wounded, and the ammunition of those pieces of artillery was exhausted. While the latter were being replaced by other guns, the force that had remained with Ramseur and Goggin gave way also. Pegram's and Wharton's divisions, and Wofford's brigade had remained steadfast on the right and resisted all efforts of the enemy's cavalry, but no portion of this force could be moved to the left without leaving the Pike open to the cavalry, which would have destroyed all hope at once.

Every effort to rally the men in the rear having failed, I now had nothing left for me but to order these troops to retire also. When they commenced to move, the disorder soon extended to them, but General Pegram succeeded in bringing back a portion of his command across Cedar Creek in an organized condition, holding the enemy in check, but this small force soon dissolved. A part of Evans' brigade had been rallied in the rear, and held a ford above the bridge for a short time, but it followed the example of the rest. I tried to rally the men immediately after crossing Cedar Creek, and at Hupp's Hill, but without success.

Could 500 men have been rallied, at either of these places, who would have stood by me, I am satisfied that all my artillery and wagons, and the greater part of the captured artillery could have been saved, as the enemy's pursuit was very feeble. As it was, a bridge broke down on a very narrow part of the road between Strasburg and Fisher's Hill, just above Strasburg, where there was no other passway, thereby blocking up all the artillery, ordnance and medical wagons and ambulances which had not passed that point; and, as there was no force to defend them, they were lost, a very small body of the enemy's cavalry capturing them.

The greater part of the infantry was halted at Fisher's Hill, and Rosser, whose command had retired in good order on the Back Road, was ordered to that point with his cavalry. The infantry moved back towards New Market at three o'clock next morning, and Rosser was left at Fisher's Hill to cover the retreat of the troops, and hold that position until they were beyond pursuit. He remained at Fisher's Hill until after ten o'clock on the 20th, and the enemy did not advance to that place while he was there. He then fell back without molestation to his former position, and established his line on Stony Creek, across from Columbia Furnace to Edinburg, seven miles below Mount Jackson. My other troops were halted at New Market, about seven miles from Mount Jackson, and there was an entirely open country between the two places, they being very nearly in sight of each other.

Lomax had moved, on the day of the battle, on the Front Royal road towards Winchester, under the impression that the enemy was being forced back towards that place, and he did not reach me. When he ascertained the reverse which had taken place in the latter part of the day, he retired up the Luray Valley to his former place at Millford, without molestation.

My loss in the battle of Cedar Creek was twenty-three pieces of artillery, some ordnance and medical wagons and ambulances, which had been carried to the front for the use of the troops on the field, about 1860 in killed and wounded, and something over 1,000 prisoners. Major General Ramseur fell into the hands of the enemy mortally wounded, and in him not only my command, but the country sustained a heavy loss. He was a most gallant and energetic officer, whom no disaster appalled, but his courage and energy seemed to gain new strength in the midst of confusion and disorder. He fell at his post fighting like a lion at bay, and his native State has reason to be proud of his memory. Brigadier General Battle was wounded at the beginning of the fight, and other valuable officers were lost. Fifteen hundred prisoners were captured from the enemy and brought off, and his loss in killed and wounded in this action was very heavy.

This was a case of a glorious victory given up by my own troops after they had won it, and it is to be accounted for on the ground of the partial demoralization caused by the plunder of the enemy's camps, and from the fact that the men undertook to judge for themselves when it was proper to retire. Had they but waited, the mischief on the left would have been remedied. I have never been able to satisfy myself that the enemy's attack in the afternoon was not a demonstration to cover his retreat during the night. It certainly was not a vigorous one, as is shown by the fact that the very small force with Ramseur and Goggin held him in check so long; and the loss in killed and wounded in the division which first gave way was not heavy, and was the least in numbers of all but one, though it was the third in strength, and its relative loss was the least of all the divisions.

I read a sharp lecture to my troops, in an address published to them a few days after the battle, but I have never attributed the result to a want of courage on their part, for I had seen them perform too many prodigies of valor to doubt that. There was an individuality about the Confederate soldier which caused him to act often in battle according to his own opinions, and thereby impair his own efficiency; and the tempting bait offered by the rich plunder of the camps of the enemy's well-fed and well-clothed troops was frequently too great for our destitute soldiers, and caused them to pause in the career of victory.

Had my cavalry been sufficient to contend with that of the enemy, the rout in the morning would have been complete; as it was, I had only about 1,200 cavalry on the field under Rosser, and Lomax's force, which numbered less than 1,700, did not get up. My infantry and artillery was about the same strength as at Winchester. The reports of the Ordnance officers showed in the hands of my troops about 8,800 muskets in round numbers, as follows: in Kershaw's division 2,700, Ramseur's 2,100, Gordon's 1,700, Pegram's 1,200 and Wharton's 1,100. Making a moderate allowance for the men left to guard the camps and the signal station on the mountain, as well as for a few sick and wounded, I went into this battle with about 8,500 muskets and a little over forty pieces of artillery.

The book containing the reports of the chief surgeon of Sheridan's cavalry corps, which has been mentioned as captured at this battle, showed that Sheridan's cavalry numbered about 8,700 men for duty a few days previous, and from information which I had received of reinforcements sent him, in the way of recruits and returned convalescents, I am satisfied that his infantry force was fully as large as at Winchester. Sheridan was absent in the morning at the beginning of the fight, and had returned in the afternoon before the change in the fortunes of the day.*

It may be asked why with so small a force I made the attack. I can only say we had been fighting large odds during the whole war, and I knew there was no chance of lessening them. It was of the utmost consequence that Sheridan should be prevented from sending troops to Grant, and General Lee, in a letter received a day or two before, had expressed an earnest desire that a victory should be gained in the Valley if possible, and it could not be gained without fighting for it. I did hope to gain one by surprising the enemy in his camp, and then thought and still think I would have had it, if my directions had been complied with, and my troops had awaited my orders to retire.

---

* The retreat of the main body of his army had been arrested, and a new line formed behind breastworks of rails, before Sheridan arrived on the field; and he still had immense odds against me when he made the attack in the afternoon.

CHAPTER XLIX.

Close of the Valley Campaign.

After the return from Cedar Creek, the main body of my troops remained in their camp for the rest of the month without disturbance, but on the 26th of October the enemy's cavalry attacked Lomax at Millford and after sharp fighting was repulsed. Having heard that Sheridan was preparing to send troops to Grant, and that the Manassas Gap Railroad was being repaired, I moved down the Valley again on the 10th of November. I had received no reinforcements except about 250 cavalry under General Cosby from Breckenridge's department in Southwestern Virginia, some returned convalescents and several hundred conscripts who had been on details which had been revoked.

On the 11th, on our approach to Cedar Creek, it was found that the enemy had fallen back towards Winchester, after having fortified and occupied a position on Hupp's Hill subsequently to the battle of Cedar Creek. Colonel Payne drove a small body of cavalry through Middletown to Newtown and I followed him and took position south of the latter place and in view of it. Sheridan's main force was found posted north of Newtown in a position which he was engaged in fortifying.

I remained in front of him during the 11th and 12th, Rosser being on my left flank on the Back Road, and Lomax on my right between the Valley Pike and the Front Royal road, with one brigade (McCausland's) at Cedarville on the latter road. Rosser had some skirmishing with the enemy's cavalry on the 11th, and on the 12th two divisions advanced against him, and after a heavy fight the enemy was repulsed and some prisoners captured. Colonel Payne, who was operating immediately in my front, likewise had a sharp engagement with a portion of the enemy's cavalry and defended it. When

Rosser was heavily engaged, Lomax was ordered to his assistance, with a part of his command, and during his absence, late in the afternoon, Powell's division of the enemy's cavalry attacked McCausland at Cedarville, and after a severe fight drove him back across the river with the loss of two pieces of artillery.

At the time of this affair, a blustering wind was blowing and the firing could not be heard; and nothing was known of McCausland's misfortune until after we commenced retiring that night. In these cavalry fights, three valuable officers were killed, namely: Lieutenant Colonel Marshall of Rosser's brigade, Colonel Radford of McCausland's brigade, and Captain Harvie of McCausland's staff.

Discovering that the enemy continued to fortify his position, and showed no disposition to come out of his lines with his infantry, and not being willing to attack him in his entrenchments, after the reverses I had met with, I determined to retire, as we were beyond the reach of supplies. After dark on the 12th, we moved to Fisher's Hill, and next day returned in the direction of New Market, where we arrived on the 14th, no effort at pursuit being made. I discovered by this movement that no troops had been sent to Grant, and that the project of repairing the Manassas Gap Railroad had been abandoned.

Shortly after our return to New Market, Kershaw's division was returned to General Lee, and Cosby's cavalry to Breckenridge. On the 22nd of November two divisions of the enemy's cavalry advanced to Mount Jackson, after having driven in our cavalry pickets. A part of it crossed over the river into Meem's Bottom at the foot of Rude's Hill, but was driven back by a portion of my infantry, and the whole retreated, being pursued by Wickham's brigade, under Colonel Munford, to Woodstock.

On the 27th, Rosser crossed Great North Mountain into Hardy County, with his own and Payne's brigade, and, about the 29th, surprised and captured the fortified post at New Creek, on the Baltimore & Ohio Railroad. At this place, two regiments of cavalry with their arms and colors were captured and eight pieces of artillery and a very large amount of ordnance, quartermaster and commissary stores fell into our hands. The prisoners, numbering 800, four pieces of artillery, and some wagons and horses, were brought off, the other guns, which were heavy siege pieces, being spiked, and their carriages and a greater part of the stores destroyed. Rosser also brought off several hundred cattle and a large number of sheep from Hampshire and Hardy counties.

This expedition closed the material operations of the campaign of 1864 in the Shenandoah Valley, and, at that time, the enemy held precisely the same portion of that valley which he held before the opening of the campaign in the spring, and no more, and the headquarters of his troops were at the same place, to wit: Winchester. There was this difference, however: at the beginning of the campaign, he held it with comparatively a small force, and, at the close, he was compelled to employ three corps of infantry, and one of cavalry, for that purpose, and to guard the approaches to Washington, Maryland and Pennsylvania. When I was detached from General Lee's army, Hunter was advancing on Lynchburg, 170 miles south of Winchester, with a very considerable force, and threatening all of General Lee's communications with a very serious danger.

By a rapid movement, my force had been thrown to Lynchburg, just in time to arrest Hunter's march into that place, and he had been driven back and forced to escape into the mountains of Western Virginia, with a loss of ten pieces of artillery and subsequent terrible suffering to his troops. Maryland and Pennsylvania had been invaded, Washington threatened and thrown into a state of frantic alarm, and Grant had been compelled to detach two corps of infantry and two divisions of cavalry from his army. Five or six thousand prisoners had been captured from the enemy and sent to Richmond, and according to a published statement by Sheridan, his army had lost 13,831, in killed and wounded, after he took command of it. Heavy losses had been inflicted on that army by my command, before Sheridan went to the Valley, and the whole loss could not have been far from double my entire force. The enemy moreover had been deprived of the use of the Baltimore & Ohio Railroad, and the Chesapeake and Ohio Canal, for three months.

It is true that I had lost many valuable officers and men, and about 60 pieces of artillery, counting those lost by Ramseur and McCausland, and not deducting the 19 pieces captured from the enemy; but I think I may safely state that the fall of Lynchburg with its foundries and factories, and the consequent destruction of General Lee's communications, would have rendered necessary the evacuation of Richmond, and that, therefore, the fall of the latter place had been prevented; and by my subsequent operations, Grant's operations against General Lee's army had been materially impeded, and for some time substantially suspended.

My loss in killed, wounded and prisoners, at Winchester and Fisher's Hill, had been less than 4,000, and at Cedar Creek, about 3,000, but the enemy has claimed as prisoners several thousand more than my entire loss. I know that a number of prisoners fell into the enemy's hands who did not belong to my command: such as cavalrymen on details to get fresh horses, soldiers on leave of absence, conscripts on special details, citizens not in the service, men employed in getting supplies for the departments, and stragglers and deserters from other commands. My army during the entire campaign had been self-sustaining so far as provisions and forage were concerned, and a considerable number of beef cattle had been sent to General Lee's army; and when the difficulties under which I labored are considered, I think I may confidently assert that I had done as well as it was possible for me to do.

CLOSE OF THE VALLEY CAMPAIGN

Shortly after Rosser's return from the New Creek expedition, Colonel Munford was sent with Wickham's brigade to the counties of Hardy and Pendleton, to procure forage for his horses, and, cold weather having now set in so as to prevent material operations in the field, the three divisions of the 2nd corps were sent, in succession, to General Lee,—Wharton's division, the cavalry, and most of the artillery being retained with me.

On the 16th of December, I broke up the camp at New Market, and moved back towards Staunton, for the purpose of establishing my troops on or near Central Railroad—Lomax's cavalry, except one brigade left to watch the Luray Valley, having previously moved across the Blue Ridge so as to be able to procure forage. Cavalry pickets were left in front of New Market, and telegraphic communications kept up with that place, from which there was communication with the lower Valley, by means of signal stations on the northern end of Massanutten Mountain, and at Ashby's Gap in the Blue Ridge, which overlooked the enemy's camps and the surrounding country.

The troops had barely arrived at their new camps when information was received that the enemy's cavalry was in motion. On the 19th, Custer's division moved from Winchester towards Staunton, and, at the same time, two other divisions of cavalry, under Torbert or Merrit, moved across by Front Royal and Chester Gap towards Gordonsville. This information having been sent me by signal and telegraph, Wharton's division was moved on the 20th, through a hailstorm, towards Harrisonburg, and Rosser ordered to the front with all the cavalry he could collect. Custer's division reached Lacy's Spring, nine miles north of Harrisonburg, on the evening of the 20th, and next morning before day, Rosser, with about 600 men of his own and Payne's brigades, attacked it in camp, and drove it back down the Valley in some confusion.

Lomax had been advised of the movement towards

Gordonsville, and as soon as Custer was disposed of, Wharton's division was moved back, and on the 23rd a portion of it was run on the railroad to Charlottesville, Munford, who had now returned from across the great North Mountain, being ordered to the same place.

On my arrival at Charlottesville on the 23rd, I found that the enemy's two divisions of cavalry, which had crossed the Blue Ridge, had been held in check near Gordonsville by Lomax, until the arrival of a brigade of infantry from Richmond, when they retired precipitately. I returned to the Valley and established my headquarters at Staunton—Wharton's division and the artillery being encamped east of that place, and Rosser's cavalry west of it; and thus closed the operations of 1864 with me.

CHAPTER L.

OPERATIONS IN 1865.

ON the 2nd of January, 1865, I had a consultation with General Lee at Richmond, about the difficulties of my position in the Valley, and he told me that he had left me there with the small command which still remained in order to produce the impression that the force was much larger than it really was, and he instructed me to do the best I could. Before I returned from Richmond, Rosser started with between 300 and 400 picked cavalry, for the post of Beverly in West Virginia, and, on the 11th, surprised and captured the place, securing over 500 prisoners and some stores. This expedition was made over a very mountainous country, amid the snows of an unusually severe winter. Rosser's loss was very light, but Lieutenant Colonel Cook, of the 8th Virginia Cavalry, a most gallant and efficient officer, lost his leg in the attack, and had to be left behind.

The great drought during the summer of 1864 had made the corn crop in the Valley a very short one, and, as Sheridan had destroyed a considerable quantity of small grain and hay, I found it impossible to sustain the horses of my cavalry and artillery where they were, and forage could not be obtained from elsewhere. I was therefore compelled to send Fitz. Lee's two brigades to General Lee, and Lomax's cavalry was brought from across the Blue Ridge, where the country was exhausted of forage, and sent west into the counties of Pendleton, Highland, Bath, Alleghany and Greenbrier, where hay could be obtained. Rosser's brigade had to be temporarily disbanded, and the men allowed to go to their homes with their horses, to sustain them, with orders to report when called on,—one or two companies, whose homes were down the Valley, being required to picket and scout in front of New Market.

LIEUTENANT GENERAL JUBAL A. EARLY

The men and horses of Lieutenant Colonel King's artillery were sent to Southwestern Virginia to be wintered, and most of the horses of the other battalions were sent off under care of some of the men, who undertook to forage them until spring. Nelson's battalion, with some pieces of artillery with their horses, was retained with me and the remaining officers and men of the other battalions were sent, under the charge of Colonel Carter, to General Lee, to man stationary batteries on his lines. Brigadier General Long, who had been absent on sick leave for some time and had returned, remained with me, and most of the guns which were without horses were sent to Lynchburg by railroad. This was a deplorable state of things, but it could not be avoided, as the horses of the cavalry and artillery would have perished had they been kept in the Valley.

Echols' brigade of Wharton's division was subsequently sent to Southwestern Virginia to report to General Echols for special duty, and McNeil's company of partisan rangers, and Woodson's company of unattached Missouri cavalry, were sent to the county of Hardy, Major Harry Gilmor being likewise ordered to that county, with the remnant of his battalion, to take charge of the whole, and operate against the Baltimore & Ohio Railroad; but he was surprised and captured there, at a private house, soon after his arrival. Two very small brigades of Wharton's division, and Nelson's battalion with the few pieces of artillery which had been retained, were left, as my whole available force, and these were in winter quarters near Fishersville, on the Central railroad between Staunton and Waynesboro. The telegraph to New Market and the signal stations from there to the lower Valley were kept up, and a few scouts sent to the rear of the enemy, and in this way was my front principally picketed, and I kept advised of the enemy's movements. Henceforth my efficient and energetic signal officer, Captain Welbourn, was the commander of my advance picket line.

The winter was a severe one, and all material operations were suspended until its close. Late in February.
Lieutenant Jesse McNeil, who was in command of his
father's old company, with forty or fifty men of that
company and Woodson's, made a dash into Cumberland,
Maryland, at night and captured and brought off Major
Generals Crook and Kelly, with a staff officer of the latter, though there were at the time several thousand troops
in and around Cumberland. The father of this gallant
young officer had performed many daring exploits during
the war, and had accompanied me into Maryland, doing
good service. When Sheridan was at Harrisonburg in
October, 1864, Captain McNeil had burned the bridge at
Edinburg in his rear, and had attacked and captured the
guard at the bridge at Mount Jackson, but in this affair
he received a very severe wound from which he subsequently died. Lieutenant Baylor of Rosser's brigade,
who was in Jefferson County with his company, made one
or two dashes on the enemy's outposts during the winter,
and, on one occasion, captured a train loaded with supplies, on the Baltimore & Ohio Railroad.

On the 20th of February, an order was issued by
General Lee, extending my command over the Department of Southwestern Virginia and East Tennessee, previously commanded by General Breckenridge, the latter
having been made Secretary of War.

On the 27th, Sheridan started from Winchester up the
Valley with a heavy force, consisting, according to the
statement of Grant, in his report, of "two divisions of
cavalry, numbering about 5,000 each." I had been informed of the preparations for a movement of some kind,
some days previous, and the information had been telegraphed to General Lee. As soon as Sheridan started, I
was informed of the fact by signal and telegraph, and
orders were immediately sent by telegraph to Lomax,
whose headquarters were at Millboro, on the Central
Railroad, forty miles west of Staunton, to get together
all of his cavalry as soon as possible. Rosser was also

directed to collect all of his men that he could, and an order was sent by telegraph to General Echols, in South-western Virginia, to send his brigade by rail to Lynch-burg. My own headquarters were at Staunton, but there were no troops at that place except a local provost guard, and a company of reserves, composed of boys under 18 years of age, which was acting under the orders of the Conscript Bureau. Orders were therefore given for the immediate removal of all stores from that place.

Rosser succeeded in collecting a little over 100 men, and with these he attempted to check the enemy at North River, near Mount Crawford, on the first of March, but was unable to do so. On the afternoon of that day, the enemy approached to within three or four miles of Staun-ton, and I then telegraphed to Lomax to concentrate his cavalry at Pound Gap in Rockbridge County, and to fol-low and annoy the enemy should he move towards Lynch-burg, and rode out of town towards Waynesboro, after all the stores had been removed.

Wharton and Nelson were ordered to move to Waynesboro by light next morning, and on that morning (the 2nd) their commands were put in position on a ridge covering Waynesboro on the west and just outside of the town. My object in taking this position was to secure the removal of five pieces of artillery for which there were no horses, and some stores still in Waynes-boro, as well as to present a bold front to the enemy, and ascertain the object of his movement, which I could not do very well if I took refuge at once in the mountain. The last report for Wharton's command showed 1,200 men for duty; but as it was exceedingly inclement, and raining and freezing, there were not more than 1,000 muskets on the line, and Nelson had six pieces of artillery. I did not intend making my final stand on this ground, yet I was satisfied that if my men would fight, which I had no reason to doubt, I could hold the enemy in check until night, and then cross the river and take position in Rock-fish Gap; for I had done more difficult things than that during the war.

About twelve o'clock in the day, it was reported to me that the enemy was advancing, and I rode out at once on the line, and soon discovered about a brigade of cavalry coming up on the road from Staunton, on which the artillery opened, when it retired out of range. The enemy manœuvred for some time in our front, keeping out of reach of our guns until late in the afternoon, when I discovered a force moving to the left. I immediately sent a messenger with notice of this fact to General Wharton, who was on that flank, and with orders for him to look out and provide for the enemy's advance; and another messenger, with notice to the guns on the left, and directions for them to fire towards the advancing force, which could not be seen from where they were.

The enemy soon made an attack on our left flank, and I discovered the men on that flank giving back. Just then, General Wharton, who had not received my message, rode up to me and I pointed out to him the disorder in his line, and ordered him to ride immediately to that point and rectify it. Before he got back, the troops gave way on the left, after making very slight resistance, and soon everything was in a state of confusion and the men commenced crossing the river. I rode across it myself to try and stop them at the bridge and check the enemy; but they could not be rallied, and the enemy forded the river above and got in our rear. I now saw that everything was lost, and after the enemy had got between the mountain and the position where I was, and retreat was thus cut off, I rode aside into the woods, and in that way escaped capture. I went to the top of a hill to reconnoitre, and had the mortification of seeing the greater pa-' of my command being carried off as prisoners, and , force of the enemy moving rapidly towards Rock-fish Gap.

I then rode with the greater part of my staff and 15 or 20 others, including General Long, across the mountain, north of the Gap, with the hope of arriving at Greenwood depot, to which the stores had been removed, before the enemy reached that place; but on getting near it, about dark, we discovered the enemy in possession. We then rode to Jarman's Gap, about three miles from the depot, and remained there all night, as the night was exceedingly dark, and the ice rendered it impossible for us to travel over the rugged roads.

The only solution of this affair which I can give is that my men did not fight as I had expected them to do. Had they done so, I am satisfied that the enemy could have been repulsed; and I was and am still of opinion that the attack at Waynesboro was a mere demonstration, to cover a movement to the south towards Lynchburg. Yet some excuse is to be made for my men, as they knew that they were weak and the enemy very strong.

The greater part of my command was captured, as was also the artillery, which, with five guns on the cars at Greenwood, made eleven pieces. Very few were killed or wounded on either side. The only person killed on our side, as far as I have ever heard, was Colonel Wm. H. Harman, who had formerly been in the army but then held a civil appointment; and he was shot in the streets of Waynesboro, either after he had been made prisoner, as some said, or while he was attempting to make his escape, after everything was over. My aide, Lieutenant Wm. G. Callaway, who had been sent to the left with one of the messages, and my medical director, Surgeon H. McGuire, had the misfortune to fall into the hands of the enemy. All the wagons of Wharton's command were absent getting supplies; but those we had with us, including the ordnance and medical wagons and my own baggage wagon, fell into their hands.

On the 3rd, I rode, with the party that was with me, towards Charlottesville; but on getting near to that place, we found the enemy entering it. We had then to turn back and go by a circuitous route under the mountains to Gordonsville, as the Rivanna River and other streams were very much swollen. On arriving at Gordonsville, I found General Wharton, who had made his escape to Charlottesville on the night of the affair at Waynesboro, and he was ordered to Lynchburg, by the way of the Central and Southside Railroads, to take command of Echols' brigade, and aid in the defence of the city. General Long was ordered to report to General Lee at Petersburg.

The affair at Waynesboro diverted Sheridan from Lynchburg, which he could have captured without difficulty, had he followed Hunter's route and not jumped at the bait unwillingly offered him, by the capture of my force at the former place. His deflection from the direct route to the one by Charlottesville was without adequate object, and resulted in the abandonment to capture Lynchburg, or to cross the James River to the south side. He halted at Charlottesville for two or three days, and then moved towards James River below Lynchburg, when, being unable to cross that river, he crossed over the Rivanna, at its mouth, and then moved by the way of Frederick's Hall on the Central Railroad, and Ashland on the R., F. & P. Railroad, across the South and North Anna, and down the Pamunkey to the White House.

At Gordonsville, about 200 cavalry were collected under Colonel Morgan of the 1st Virginia Cavalry, and, with this force, I watched the enemy for several days while he was at Charlottesville, and when he was endeavoring to cross the James River. When Sheridan had abandoned this effort, and on the day he reached the vicinity of Ashland, while I was riding on the Louisa Court-House and Richmond Road, towards the bridge over the South Anna, with about 20 cavalry, I came very near being captured, by a body of 300 cavalry sent after me, but I succeeded in eluding the enemy with most of those who were with me, and reached Richmond at two o'clock next morning, after passing twice between the enemy's camps and his pickets. My Adjutant General, Captain Moore, however, was captured, but made his escape.

Lomax had succeeded in collecting a portion of his cavalry and reaching Lynchburg, where he took position on the north bank of the river, but the enemy avoided that place. Rosser had collected a part of his brigade and made an attack, near New Market, on the guard which was carrying back the prisoners captured at Waynesboro, with the view of releasing them, but he did not succeed in that object, though the guard was compelled to retire in great haste. He then moved towards Richmond on Sheridan's track.

After consultation with General Lee, at his headquarters near Petersburg, Rosser's and McCausland's brigades were ordered to report to him under the command of General Rosser, and I started for the Valley, by the way of Lynchburg, to reorganize what was left of my command. At Lynchburg, a despatch was received from General Echols, stating that Thomas was moving in East Tennessee, and threatening Southwestern Virginia with a heavy force, and I immediately went, by train, to Wytheville. From that place I went with General Echols to Bristol, on the state line between Virginia and Tennessee, and it was ascertained, beyond doubt, that some important movement by the enemy was on foot. We then returned to Abingdon, and while I was engaged in endeavoring to organize the small force in that section, so as to meet the enemy in the best way we could, I received, on the 30th of March, a telegraphic despatch from General Lee, directing me to turn over the command in Southwestern Virginia to General Echols, and in the Valley to General Lomax, and informing me that he would address a letter to me at my home. I complied at once with this order and thus terminated my military career.

Conclusion.

In the afternoon of the 30th of March, after having turned over the command to General Echols, I rode to Marion in Smythe County and was taken that night with a cold and cough so violent as to produce hemorrhage from the lungs, and prostrate me for several days in a very dangerous condition. While I was in this situation, a heavy cavalry force under Stoneman, from Thomas' army in Tennessee, moved through North Carolina to the east, and a part of it came into Virginia from the main column, and struck the Virginia & Tennessee Railroad at New River east of Wytheville; whence, after destroying the bridge, it moved east, cutting off all communication with Richmond, and then crossed over into North Carolina. As soon as I was in a condition to be moved, I was carried on the railroad to Wytheville, and was proceeding thence to my home, in an ambulance under charge of a surgeon, when I received, most unexpectedly, the news of the surrender of General Lee. Under the disheartening influence of the sad tidings I had received, I proceeded to my journey's end, and I subsequently received a letter from General Lee, dated on the 30th of March, explaining the reasons for relieving me from command. This letter, written on the very day of the commencement of the attack on General Lee's lines, which resulted in the evacuation of Richmond, and just ten days before the surrender of the Army of Northern Virginia, has a historical interest; for it shows that Lee, even at that late day, was anxiously and earnestly contemplating the continuation of the struggle with unabated vigor, and a full determination to make available every element of success.

Immediately after the battle of Cedar Creek, I had written a letter to General Lee, stating my willingness to be relieved from command, if he deemed it necessary for the public interests, and I should have been content with the course pursued towards me, had his letter not contained the expressions of personal confidence in me that it does; for I knew that in everything he did as commander of our armies, General Lee was actuated solely by an earnest and ardent desire for the success of the cause of his country. As to those among my countrymen who judged me harshly, I have not a word of reproach.

467

LIEUTENANT GENERAL JUBAL A. EARLY

When there was so much at stake, it was not unnatural that persons entirely ignorant of the facts, and forming their opinions from the many false reports set afloat in a time of terrible war and public suffering, should pass erroneous and severe judgments on those commanders who met with reverses.

I was not embraced in the terms of General Lee's surrender or that of General Johnston, and, as the order relieving me from command had also relieved me from all embarrassment as to the troops which had been under me, as soon as I was in a condition to travel, I started on horseback for the Trans-Mississippi Department to join the army of General Kirby Smith, should it hold out; with the hope of at least meeting an honorable death while fighting under the flag of my country. Before I reached that Department, Smith's army had also been surrendered, and, without giving a parole, after a long, weary and dangerous ride from Virginia, through the states of North Carolina, South Carolina, Georgia, Alabama, Mississippi, Arkansas, and Texas, I finally succeeded in leaving the country.

LETTER FROM GENERAL LEE.

"HD. QRS., C. S. ARMIES,
30th March, 1865.

"LT.-GENERAL J. A. EARLY, FRANKLIN CO., VA.

"General,—My telegram will have informed you that I deem a change of commanders in your Department necessary; but it is due to your zealous and patriotic services that I should explain the reasons that prompted my action. The situation of affairs is such that we can neglect no means calculated to develop the resources we possess to the greatest extent, and make them as efficient as possible. To this end, it is essential that we should have the cheerful and hearty support of the people, and the full confidence of the soldiers, without which our efforts would be embarrassed and our means of resistance weakened. I have reluctantly arrived at the conclusion that you cannot command the united and willing co-operation which is so essential to success. Your reverses in the Valley, of which the public and the army judge chiefly by the results, have, I fear, impaired your influence both with the people and the soldiers, and would add greatly

CONCLUSION

to the difficulties which will, under any circumstances, attend our military operations in S. W. Virginia. While my own confidence in your ability, zeal, and devotion to the cause is unimpaired, I have nevertheless felt that I could not oppose what seems to be the current of opinion, without injustice to your reputation and injury to the service. I therefore felt constrained to endeavor to find a commander who would be more likely to develop the strength and resources of the country, and inspire the soldiers with confidence; and to accomplish this purpose, I thought it proper to yield my own opinion, and to defer to that of those to whom alone we can look for support.

"I am sure that you will understand and appreciate my motives, and no one will be more ready than yourself to acquiesce in any measures which the interests of the country may seem to require, regardless of all personal considerations.

"Thanking you for the fidelity and energy with which you have always supported my efforts, and for the courage and devotion you have ever manifested in the service of the country,

"I am, very respectfully and truly

"Your ob't servant,

"R. E. LEE,

"Gen'l."

APPENDIX.

The Testimony of Letters.

I FEEL reluctant to add a word to what General Early has written of himself and yet his letters, bearing (as many of them do) upon his manuscript, show that there are some things he has left untold which would interest the reader of his life.

My feeling in this matter proceeds from the remembrance of his sentiments on the subject of biography, which he forcibly expressed in a letter written in 1866 to a correspondent who proposed writing an account of his life, saying:

> I trust that you will not suspect me of rudeness or a desire to offend when I respectfully request that you omit mine from the list of biographies you propose writing. If I were to furnish you the materials desired, you would become the biographer of my choice, and I would be bound by what you might write. I hope you will understand what I mean, and will not interpret what I say as intended in an offensive sense. I cannot, of course, prevent your writing on any subject you may choose.

> If my biography was of sufficient importance to require its being placed before the world, and my wishes were consulted, I would not trust its compilation to any but one who had known me personally and well: you and I are, personally, entire strangers. During my life I have often associated with men who thought they knew me, but who in fact had very little appreciation of my true character. I would not therefore expect it to be understood by one who is a stranger.

Naturally possessing a reserved disposition, and in his bachelor life cut off from the softening influences of familiar intercourse to be found in the home, it was not entirely the fault of others that he was often misunderstood: but as he has said, those who knew him best were the ones who best appreciated him. The opportunity of intimate acquaintance enabled one to fathom the depths of his kindly nature and to discover his real feelings.

In his autobiographical sketch he writes of the mother whose death was the source of grief to her family, but he does not tell of the affection which caused him to choose her companionship preferably to that of any other, nor of the sense of deprivation he felt upon the loss of her tender counsels at the early age of sixteen. His father was a most thoughtful and affectionate parent, but from him, too, he was parted during the crucial period of his youth, though that parent's watchful care followed closely in a correspondence, preserved by the son, during a long life of many vicissitudes.

As the son's character developed, he inspired more and more confidence and respect, until the relations of father and son seemed to become reversed, and, as years wore on, the position of head of the family was insensibly accorded the son. Possessing a sense of right never swayed by impulse, his opinion and advice were never questioned by members of his family. His grandmother, observing the promise of his youth, had said of him that he was born to make a name for himself.

In his nineteenth year, while a cadet at West Point Academy, his sympathies were very much aroused for the Texans in their revolt against the tyranny of Santa Anna, and he wrote urging his father's consent to his joining in their cause. This letter portrays the disposition of the future patriot, and is in part as follows:

The Texans are bound by every principle of self-preservation and are justified by the natural law of rights, as well as by precedent, to declare their independence and to resist the attempt which is being made to annihilate them. And we of the United States are called upon by every principle of humanity, by our love of liberty and our detestation of oppression, to go to the succor of our countrymen and aid in overwhelming the tyrant. Shall we shed tears over the fate of Greece and Poland, yet see our countrymen slaughtered with indifference? The respect we entertain for our forefathers of the Revolution forbids it. The gratitude we owe another country for espousing our cause imperiously commands us to espouse that of the oppressed. The cause of the Texans is more justifiable than was ours. We resisted the usurpation of our lawful government. They are resisting the tyranny and cruelty of an usurped government. Liberty has been driven from the old world and its only asylum is in the new. It is the imperious duty of every one, who in this fair land has received it and its principles unsullied from his ancestors, to extend its dominion and to perpetuate its glorious light to posterity. How can this be done if tyranny more despotic than that which exists in Europe is allowed to exist in our very confines? In succoring the Texans we should consider that we extend the sway of the goddess we worship, that we secure to their progeny the benefits of which we are so tenacious, and secure to oppressed freemen of other countries an asylum which our own country will, ere long, not be able to afford them. . . .

The great end of all education is to expand the mind and gain a knowledge of human nature. What is more calculated to expand the mind than the espousing and working in the cause of liberty? What better book in which to study human nature than such a variety of characters as I would be constantly thrown with? All things cry out to me to go. Oh, my dear father, will you not give me permission? Do not think that my resolution has been taken unadvisedly, and do not smile at my aspirations. I do not believe that I shall become a Bonaparte or a Bolivar, but he who never aspires, never rises.

I have confined this letter to one subject because my whole soul is taken up with that subject.

General Early returned from Canada to the States in 1869; that winter was devoted to visits among his relatives and friends from whom he had been so long parted. His father died in 1870. In the autobiography he writes of his father as still living: it is therefore presumable that his manuscript was, at least, commenced while he was in Canada.

Previously he had published at Toronto (in 1866), "A Memoir of the Last Year of the War for Independence," which was written, he states, "under a solemn sense of duty to my unhappy country, and to the brave soldiers who fought under me, as well as to myself."

His correspondence was very large and in many cases continued during years. Through this runs the story of his unflagging interest and industry in endeavoring to confirm every minutest detail of the narrative he desired to complete. The letters all show the esteem in which he was held. Many of them are written to thank him for contributions, already written, in the defence of the South. Others urge that he prepare a complete history of the war giving the Southern side.

From among these letters the following are selected; not the least of the interest in which proceeds from the fact that they are voluntary offerings, generally from

APPENDIX

warm personal friends and received in the course of private correspondence.

The first is from the pen of the beloved leader and is followed by tributes from Jefferson Davis, Generals D. H. Hill and W. H. Payne, Colonels Marshall and Johnston, Senator John W. Daniel, Professors Peters and Venable, Dr. McGuire, and others,—if less known to fame,—none the less ardent in the expression of their regard.

GENERAL J. A. EARLY: LEXINGTON, VA., Nov., 1865.

I received last night your letter, which gave me the first authentic information of you I had received since the cessation of hostilities and relieved the anxiety I had felt on your account. I am very glad to hear of your health and safety, and I wish you every happiness and prosperity: you will always be present to my recollections.

I desire, if not prevented, to write a history of the campaigns in Virginia; all of my records, books, orders, etc., were destroyed in the conflagration and retreat from Richmond, only such reports as were printed are preserved. Your reports of your operations in '64 were among those destroyed. Can you not repeat them and send me copies of such letters, orders, etc., of mine and particularly give me your recollection of our effective strength at the principal battles? My only object is to transmit, if possible, the truth and do justice to our brave soldiers.   ROBERT E. LEE.

March, 1866.

I am much obliged for the copies of my letters. Send me reports of the operations of your commands in the campaign from the Wilderness to Richmond, at Lynchburg, in the Valley, Maryland, etc. . . . All statistics as regards numbers, destruction of private property by the Federal troops, etc., I should like to have, as I wish my memory strengthened on these points. It will be difficult to get the world to understand the odds against which we fought and the destruction or loss of all returns of the army embarrasses me. We shall have to be patient and suffer till a period when reason and charity may resume their sway. At present the public mind is not prepared to receive the truth. I hope in time peace will be restored to the country and that the South may enjoy some measure of prosperity. I fear, however, much suffering is still in store for her and that the people must be prepared to exercise fortitude and forbearance.

ROBERT E. LEE.

GENERAL J. A. EARLY: MONTREAL, CANADA.

I wish to thank you for your last offering to the cause you served so zealously and efficiently in the field. To vindicate the struggle of the South to preserve their political and social inheritance by truthfully stating events was alike due to those to whom its regeneration must be confided, as well as to those who suffered for that cause. Your career as a commander met my entire approval and secured my admiration. It was such estimate concurrently held by General Lee and myself that led to your selection to command the vitally important and difficult campaign which you have described in your recent publication. The means were known to be disproportionate to the task before you when you marched against General Hunter. That they proved adequate, is glory enough for you and your associates. It would be easy to show, if it were desirable now to enter upon that question, at whose door lies the responsibility of subsequent disasters. You have rendered the more grateful and useful service of showing at whose door it does not belong.   JEFFERSON DAVIS.

GENERAL J. A. EARLY: UNIVERSITY OF VIRGINIA.

I have thought much of this matter of the Army of Northern Virginia, and my earnest, honest belief is that you should write memoirs of its campaigns. I don't know any nobler labor of love, even if you do not publish it.

If you write and leave it unfinished even, I will pledge myself to edit it and have it published as a true memorial of your love and affection for that noble army of martyrs. General Lee ought to have done this thing. Now that he is gone, the duty devolves on you to give the account of all the campaigns in detail from the beginning to the end. This is the only way to defeat the deplorable effects of thousands of books of misapprehension, because nobody has written authoritatively on the subject. I do hope you will take the matter into consideration and undertake the work. I will do everything I can to collect material for you. . . . Your address at Washington and Lee is the best piece of military criticism which has been written on our war, and I beg you earnestly and solemnly as a duty to that old Army of Northern Virginia to write a history of its campaigns; it would be most appropriate and essential.

                                    CHARLES S. VENABLE.

GENERAL J. A. EARLY: UNIVERSITY OF VIRGINIA.

I write, at the lapse of twenty-five years from the close of the war, on a matter in which you are interested as well as every man who served under you. It is due to yourself and to the truth of history that you should write a minute, calm and complete history of your campaigns, from the time you were detached from the army around Petersburg, in 1864, until the affair at Waynesboro.

My honest conviction is that your campaign will lose nothing by

APPENDIX

comparison with that of our great Jackson in the same field, and for the following reasons:

(1st) With about 12,000 (perhaps fewer) men you met and defeated Hunter at Lynchburg with an army of 20,000 men. You pursued him, driving him out of Virginia into Kanawha Valley, thus diverting him from the valley of Virginia. He had (I think) two brigades of cavalry,—you did not have over 1,500 cavalry.

(2nd) You made a forced march down the valley, whipping another army of 12,000 men at Monocacy, after driving all the Federal forces out of the valley, marched to the very walls of Washington City, causing the withdrawal of a large force from the front of Lee, for the protection of the city.

(3rd) You fell back into Virginia, when your force reduced by fighting and marching could not have exceeded 9,000 men. Sheridan was sent to meet you with 35,000 or 40,000 men. Up to this period your campaign was brilliantly successful. The disproportion was vastly greater between your forces and Sheridan's than between Jackson's and Shields' at Kernstown. If it had been possible to reinforce you at Winchester to the extent of 20,000, you would have driven Sheridan into the Potomac.

(4th) Now observe. After Kernstown, Jackson fell back up the valley, was reinforced by Ewell; the latter was left to hold Banks in check. Jackson marched with his own force, 4,500 men, took command of Johnston's force of two brigades, 3,500 men, defeated Milroy, 7,000 men, returned centre with Ewell and with a force, now something over 20,000, expelled Banks (who commanded not over 7,000) from the valley. When threatened by Fremont from the west and Shields from the east—each with about 18,000 men—he retired, keeping them in check, and fought with equal numbers, the battle of Port Republic.

Again. At Chancellorsville Jackson, by order of Lee, by a forced and daring march, attacked the right flank of the Federal Army, surprised and routed it. You, by a similar march, surprised and routed the advance forces of Sheridan at Cedar Creek. His remaining force would have been routed had not the troops halted to plunder the captured camp. Who was responsible for this? Those who commanded under you, whose business and duty it was to keep their troops well in hand, and pursue the routed army.

I have thought much of your campaign in the valley when our military affairs were *in extremis* and think you did all that could have been done. I urge that you will write a full, consecutive history of that campaign, not leaving out of view the service rendered by your cavalry; they acted a most important part in saving Lynchburg until your arrival.

You reached Lynchburg late in the afternoon; the day before

475

your cavalry met the Federal force at New London at 2 o'clock P.M. and held them until night; fell back during the night to the old Quaker Church and there held them till the following night. Had the cavalry not so detained Hunter, he would have captured Lynchburg during the forenoon of the day in which you reached the city. No campaign of the war was superior to this.   WILLIAM E. PETERS.

GENERAL J. A. EARLY: LEXINGTON, VIRGINIA.

I throw out a suggestion for your consideration, which would be to the country a matter of inestimable value, for the merit of truth and knowledge. I refer to a history of Virginia. You have given the subject more accurate study than anybody else. Write it out and publish it. I write after a good deal of reflection about it. Though you may not know it, your explicit, lucid pen reflects your mind more accurately always than your tongue, which must banter, willy-nilly.

WM. PRESTON JOHNSTON.

GENERAL J. A. EARLY: NEW YORK.

More than a year ago in some correspondence with the sons of General R. E. Lee, I was referred to you by General W. H. F. Lee, for information respecting the intention of the commanding general of the Army of Northern Virginia at the time of the assault on Fort Steadman and Haskell before Petersburg, March 25th, 1865. Although you may not have been actually engaged there, General Lee says you are an authority on all the operations of that army.

GEORGE L. KILMER.

TREASURY DEPARTMENT, WASHINGTON, D. C.

GENERAL J. A. EARLY:

Accept my special thanks for a copy of your narrative of the military operations in the Shenandoah Valley and east of the Blue Ridge. Knowing your strict and straightforward fidelity to the truth makes the perusal all the more interesting.   W. S. ROSECRANS.

For the benefit of history, a physician would prolong his life indefinitely.

GENERAL J. A. EARLY: RICHMOND, VIRGINIA.

I leave the city to-night on my way to England, but I cannot go without telling you how glad I am that you have been chosen to deliver the address at Lexington.

I know General Jackson admired you and believe, if he could be consulted in the matter, he would select you to make the address.

I wish you could live forever, if only to keep history straight.

HUNTER MCGUIRE, M.D.

APPENDIX

There are so many pages devoted to recalling war incidents and exploits that it becomes difficult to make the choice, from among them, of such as might serve to gain the especial interest of the reader; those which disclose critical situations and unconscious heroism, such as these sent from Charlotte, North Carolina, and Farmdale, Kentucky, will best appeal to veterans of the war:

CHARLOTTE, N. C.

GENERAL J. A. EARLY:

You remember that I was the cause of your being sent to Ross Pole just before the first Fredericksburg battle. Did you ever notice that Burnside said that Halleck had selected Ross Pole for the crossing of the Federal Army, but that he had taken the responsibility of crossing at Fredericksburg, because Halleck had selected Ross Pole before troops had been sent to guard it, and that as the circumstances had changed he felt at liberty to disobey orders? Your presence at the first place made Burnside cross at Fredericksburg. On that horrible Sunday I rode up with young Morrison from Port Royal to Ross Pole, and found that we did not have even a cavalry picket there, while the Federals were in force on the other side and were working on a batteau bridge. I wrote to General Jackson about the condition of things, and you were sent down. You never rendered more important service. . . .

You and I were long side by side, and, like you, I was only unpopular with those soldiers who did not do their duty. . . .

Your letter was full of touching interest to me, who am alive to any incident connected with the rank and file.

I have laid it away for the benefit of my children's children. You are so accurate in statistics, I would be afraid of a blunder, if I differed with you.

In comparing my statistics with yours in my address, I wished to say, " General Early knows more of Confederate history than any man now living, probably for the reason that he has never moved out of the Confederacy "—but I know you did not like some haversack anecdotes which were entirely to your credit, and which endeared you to thousands of our people. You were so fortunate, or unfortunate, as to be considered the wittiest man in the army and doubtless many clever and witty things were put upon you in consequence.

Heaven bless you always!   D. H. HILL.

477

APPENDIX

KENTUCKY MILITARY INSTITUTE,
Farmdale, Ky.

GENERAL J. A. EARLY:

Captain Sam Gaines went to the reunion at Gettysburg some years ago and while standing at the point taken by you (Hays' and Hoke's brigades on Cemetery Heights) he says a Federal officer, who was also in the battle, told him that your charge was more serious than you or our people seemed to be aware of,—that you really had passed in rear of Meade's headquarters and that Meade and his staff would certainly have been your prisoners had you been supported on your right, so that you could have held the ground you had taken. The officer pointed out the house in which Meade and his staff, virtually for the time (you held the heights) your prisoners, were at the time you made the assault, and that it was in the rear of your position; that it was indeed a crisis with the Federals.   D. F. BOYD, Supt.

In his manuscript, General Early refers to his order for the burning of Chambersburg; this I do not find, but in an article in the Richmond *State,* June 22nd, 1887, he makes this statement:

The act was done in retaliation for outrages committed by General David Hunter in the Valley of Virginia.

I thought it was time to try and stop this mode of warfare by some act of retaliation, and I accordingly sent a cavalry force to Chambersburg, Pennsylvania, to demand of the authorities of that town compensation for the houses of Messrs. Hunter, Lee and Boteler, upon pain of having their town reduced to ashes on failure to pay the compensation demanded. The three houses burned were worth fully $100,000 in gold and I demanded that, or what I regarded as equivalent in greenbacks. No attempt was made to comply with my demand and my order to burn the town was executed.

This was in strict accordance with the laws of war and was a just retaliation. I gave the order on my own responsibility, but General Lee never in any manner indicated disapproval of my act, and his many letters to me expressive of confidence and friendship forbade the idea that he disapproved of my conduct on that occasion. It afforded me no pleasure to subject non-combatants to the rigors of war, but I felt that I had a duty to perform to the people for whose homes I was fighting and I endeavored to perform it, however disagreeable it might be.

It may not be out of keeping with General Early's object in writing a history of the war to insert a letter

APPENDIX

from a former Federal soldier acknowledging kindness received while he was held as prisoner within Southern lines. The one chosen gives the address at the National Military Home in Montgomery County, Ohio:

GENERAL J. A. EARLY:

I write in memory of old times and a special act of kindness on your part, when in the midst of battle, with your self-earned brave army around, and General Sheridan's army contending at Cedar Creek, Virginia, October 19th, 1864. I was wounded, early at dawn of day, in the face and right thigh, and was unable to walk on account of my wounds. Your men came to me and asked how long since I was paid off; and then searched me, but I had no money, as I had not lately been paid. One of the men came up to me and took my canteen; just then you came riding along and spoke to me, asking if I was badly hurt. I said "Yes, sir, I am." I looked earnestly at you and said to you, "Do you allow a man to rob another of the last drop of water he possesses?" You replied, "No." "Well," I said, pointing to a man who had just robbed me, "there stands the man who took my canteen."

Straightway you rode up to him, made him give up my canteen, and filled it, yourself, with water for me.

"Now," said you, "get away to your command."

THOMAS DOUGLAS,
Late of Co. G, 12th Reg.

Volumes might be filled from the collection, which in length of time covers the period of his manhood to old age, all attesting respect for the veracity of his character. Perhaps the finest tribute to him comes from the pen of his devoted friend, General Wm. H. Payne, of Warrenton, who writes:

There is no man now living who so entirely commands my respect, or of whose good opinion I am so covetous, as yours. What I most admire in you is your passionate love of truth. I am truly pleased to know that you are to deliver the address on the Jackson statue. So many false conceptions of men and events are cultivated, that one gives up all hope of truth ever having an audience. It is a consolation to know that it will be spoken at Lexington.

The friendship between General Early and Senator Daniel dated from the time the latter became a member of Early's staff.

The acquaintance thus begun ripened into a friendship

APPENDIX

which never paled, and which afforded General Early great satisfaction. I have selected from a bundle of his letters a hurried note written in 1874 while Senator Daniel was a candidate for Congress,—in order to show the friendly relations existing between these two.

MY DEAR GENERAL:

The three tickets enclosed were elected here to-night by overwhelming majorities. I shall have 60 votes on first ballot. I ask that you will do me the honor to nominate me in convention. It will be glory enough whether I succeed or not. I beg that you will come and help me now. You said, in Richmond, you "raised me." Come then and stand by your boy.

Yours truly,

JOHN W. DANIEL.

After an interval of eight years, there is a letter telling of Daniel's desire to write the life of his friend. To accomplish this purpose he seems to have collected a vast deal of material. The answer to his request has not been found.

MY DEAR GENERAL: December 3rd, 1882.

I have wished to talk with you about a contemplated undertaking in which you are not disinterested. With your permission and good will in the plan, I desire to render such contribution to the history of the war as I may be able to do, in the shape of a volume to bear the title "The Life and Campaigns of Lieutenant General Jubal A. Early."

I have some elements of qualification in familiarity with some of your campaigns and a very good general knowledge of the conditions under, and means with which you conducted others. My mind continually recurs to the war and not a day passes that its various scenes and phases are not revolved over and over again. It would be a relief to work on the subject, and did you consent to my doing so in the manner indicated, in a year or two I could prepare the work as well as my poor abilities permit: and while, to tell the truth would be ever the uppermost thought, it would be a labor of love to me to recount it in the themes proposed. If for any reason you do not wish me to write such a book, your wishes would of course control me, but unless you object, my mind is made up to the undertaking. If you approve there are many things in which I would need your assistance. Think over this matter and let me know your views. Most truly yours,

JOHN W. DANIEL.

INDEX